POWER AND AUTHORITY IN
BRITISH UNIVERSITIES

By Graeme C. Moodie

The Universities: A Royal Commission?

Opinions, Publics and Pressure Groups
(with Gerald Studdert-Kennedy)

POWER AND AUTHORITY IN BRITISH UNIVERSITIES

by
Graeme C. Moodie
Professor of Politics at the University of York

and

Rowland Eustace
former Fellow in the Institute for Social and Economic Research at the University of York

McGill–Queen's University Press
Montreal 1974

First published in 1974

ISBN 0-7735-0223-8
Library of Congress Catalog Card Number 74-76083
Legal Deposit 2nd Quarter 1974

Printed in Great Britain
in 10 on 11 point Times Roman type
by T. & A. CONSTABLE LTD
Hopetoun Street, Edinburgh

ACKNOWLEDGEMENTS

This study of universities could not have been undertaken but for the grant awarded by the Calouste Gulbenkian Foundation in 1966. To it therefore I wish to record my first debt of gratitude. My next must go to my co-author, Rowland Eustace, whose appointment as Research Fellow in the Institute of Social and Economic Research at the University of York was the first fruit of the Gulbenkian Foundation's generosity. His status as co-author indicates the extent to which he became a partner and not a mere research assistant. Not only did he carry out most of the documentary research and the bulk of the interviews on which this study depended, but he contributed immeasurably to the gradual evolution of our perspective and to its translation into the written word. Nevertheless, the ultimate responsibility for this final version of our common labours is mine.

We have benefited immensely (but probably insufficiently) from the comments of Sir Eric Ashby, M. L. Shattock and Harry Kidd (on certain sections) and of Robert Berdahl and Andrew Dunsire, both of whom read an earlier draft in its entirety. To the latter we wish to pay particular tribute for his detailed critique of the end-product as for his share in the initial design of the whole project.[1]

For general encouragement, both initially and throughout, we wish especially to thank Sir Eric Ashby and Lord James of Rusholme; but neither bear any responsibility for more than a friendly and sustaining interest; they were never formally interviewed.

Because I am engaged in the government of the University of York we refrained, on principle, from interviewing any of my colleagues there, though we have benefited from numerous informal conversations as well from participant observation. Between us, however, Rowland Eustace and I did interview something over 300 others engaged in university government at all levels and in almost every institution. We cannot name them, but wish to record the immense amount of help and co-operation we received from virtually everyone we approached. Without

---

[1] Regrettably the pressure of other commitments prevented him from continuing as a fellow researcher.

their readiness to talk to us the whole project would have foundered at a very early stage; we hope they will accept our gratitude and, if we have at any point misunderstood them, our apologies.

Finally, I wish to thank both our families for their tolerance while we were absorbed elsewhere and the publishers for their patience.

G. C. M.

CONTENTS

INTRODUCTION

'In the old days,' lamented the Chancellor of the University of Paris in 1218, 'when . . . the name of *Universities* was unknown, lectures . . . were more frequent and there was more zeal for study. But now that you are invited into a *University* lectures are rare, things are hurried and little is learned, the time taken for lectures being spent in Meetings and discussions.'[1] If this be true it is remarkable that so little has been written about university government in the subsequent 750 years—unless those interested in Meetings are too busy attending them to attend to what is happening in them.

In an attempt to make good a small part of this omission we offer here a general and methodologically old-fashioned survey of the processes of decision-making within British universities today. It is general because, no such general study having been undertaken before, it seemed impossible at the outset to make any sensible choice of particular institutions or processes on which to concentrate.[2] (We hope, however, that our work will make it easier for others to probe more deeply into special aspects of university government—and especially into the grass-roots level of the department and subject.) The lack of previous work also made it difficult to identify in advance those areas which would have repaid the use of sophisticated research tools like the attitude survey.

We have therefore relied for our evidence upon a series of open-ended interviews and an intensive study of documents prepared for internal consumption by a large number of universities, of formal constitutions, and of other published material. Wherever possible we have quoted from or referred to published sources, but our primary source has in fact been the material gleaned from over 300 formal interviews, the vast majority of which were carried out in the period 1966–9, and innumerable discussions of a more informal nature.[3]

---

[1] Quoted in HASTINGS RASHDALL: *The Universities of Europe in the Middle Ages*, eds. A. B. EMDEN and F. M. POWICKE (Oxford, 1936) Vol. I, p. 298.

[2] Some of the other problems and objections we faced initially are discussed in GRAEME C. MOODIE: 'University Government', in H. J. BUTCHER and ERNEST RUDD, eds.: *Contemporary Problems in Higher Education* (McGraw-Hill, 1972) pp. 261–70.

[3] We have talked with every category of participant in university government and with members of almost every institution covered by our account. Some institutions have been investigated more intensively than others; most have been

This source has the disadvantage that much of our information cannot be published in an attributable form, but it might not otherwise have been obtainable. One reason for our dependence on the confidential discussion is suggested by Lord Percy of Newcastle, a politician turned vice-chancellor. In his memoirs he says: 'Is it significant, I wonder, that I should feel so much more diffidence in writing of university administration . . . than of political experiences in Cabinets and the House of Commons? . . . Probably the reason is that a university has a continuing life of its own . . . more real than the shifting scenes of a party or a Cabinet . . . Just because one is intimately committed . . . one may well be as reluctant to write about [a university] as about one's living friends or one's family.'[4] Fortunately for us, most people nevertheless enjoy talking to others about common friends, and we felt (rightly or wrongly) that our informants talked both freely and honestly, on the understanding that we would respect their confidence.

Much of our evidence thus remains undisclosed. This is so not only because the reader might tire of too many assertions supported merely by anonymous quotations. It is also because much of what we learned related to specific local incidents. As we soon discovered, however, the details peculiar to particular institutions are much less important than the elements common to the governmental processes throughout the university system. We have therefore concentrated upon the latter, using specific detail primarily for purposes of illustration.

Frequently, of course, we have had to exercise our own judgement about events described to us by a variety of informants. The problem of interpretation is inescapable. Mr David Caute once entertained the readers of *Encounter* (March, 1966) with his account of an incident in the internal government of All Souls College, Oxford. One of us discussed this with two of the fellows. One commented: 'Well, David got all the actual facts right enough, but he's never understood how the thing *works*'; the other that 'of course, David got completely the wrong end of the stick about what was actually

---

visited by one of the present authors; but on all we managed to obtain some personal 'line' to supplement the documents. We deliberately refrained, however, from close studies of the important universities of Edinburgh and Manchester, since they are already the objects of detailed investigation by others (Professors Tom Burns and Peter Worsley), the results of which we eagerly await.

[4] *Some Memories* (London, 1958) p. 206. Lord Percy was Rector of King's College, Newcastle, 1937–52, and as such was several times Vice-Chancellor of the federal University of Durham. (King's College is now the University of Newcastle.)

Chapter I

UNIVERSITIES AS POLITICAL SYSTEMS

The first question to be answered is this: in what way, if any, is it legitimate to regard universities as having a system of government and other political characteristics? To some people, for example Professor D. D. Raphael[1], it is 'absurd' to talk of politics outside the activities of the State except in a purely metaphorical sense. To others, of whom David Easton[2] may be cited as an example, the internal affairs of a university would constitute, at best, a 'para-political system'. Partly for these reasons perhaps, in the United States (where alone there is much literature on the subject) it is customary to talk not so much about university government, as of university 'governance'[3]. We do not wish to labour this point, but some explanation of our terminology is probably called for if only to explain the scope and purpose of the present discussion.

Any human group, in our view, must be able to take common action on those matters which, at any particular time, constitute its common or public affairs. For a group to survive, this is to say, it is necessary that its members concert their behaviour in appropriate ways. On what those ways are, and possibly even on whether concerted behaviour is necessary, members are likely to disagree. To secure the agreement indispensable for action is not always easy since it may involve the exercise of various kinds of persuasion, argument, or pressure, including, even, the threat of force. This process of agreement-seeking, of trying to induce others to act together in a particular fashion, is what we regard as the activity of politics. Survival also demands that the process be successful, in the sense

---

[1] *Problems of Political Philosophy* (Macmillan, 1970) p. 32.

[2] D. EASTON: *A Framework for Political Analysis* (Prentice-Hall, 1965) pp. 50–6.

[3] See too, the title of the Committee of Enquiry into the Governance of the University of London set up in 1970 under the chairmanship of Lord Murray of Newhaven, which reported in 1972. For a general survey of recent American studies see HENRY L. MASON: *College and University Government* (Tulane University, 1972), particularly the first ninety pages.

that it lead to a decision being taken about the nature of the common action (or policy) to be adopted and that this decision be then accepted as binding upon all members of the group. The activity of governing is the taking of this type of decision. In many groups, but not all, there will exist a specialization of function (and often a division of labour) such that the activity of governing is carried out through special procedures (and often by particular people). Those procedures constitute the governmental structure (and the men are often referred to as 'the government')[4]. These processes and activities are detectable not only in states and nations, and there seems to us no point in denying to them the common labels of 'politics' and 'government' wherever they occur.

In extreme circumstances one may conceive of a political process so chaotic and inefficient that no decisions, no government, result and, on the other hand, of a government so god-like or so tyrannical that political activity is, respectively, unnecessary or impossible. But in the normal situation government is the outcome of a group's political life and is therefore incomprehensible in abstraction from it. In this book, consequently, we shall be concerned both with the government and the politics of universities; and, to begin with, in this chapter we propose to offer some general comparisons between university and other kinds of politics.

In talking of university politics we are referring, here, only to the internal life of universities. To assert that a university is, in one of its aspects, a political entity is, moreover, different from saying that it is 'political' in the sense of being partisan or an integral part of the national political battle. Every group, institution, or association is undeniably part of society and therefore, to a greater or lesser degree, of the politically relevant scene. But, unlike trade unions or employers' associations, for example, universities never contribute to political parties, nor, unlike the Charities Commission, do they even form a semi-autonomous part of the governmental machine. On the other hand, universities are probably more political, in this everyday sense of the word, than the Lawn Tennis Association or a group of philatelists. Perhaps, in their importance to national life and in their semi-public function or duty, they may best be likened to a body such as the Bar Association, or even, in a largely secular age, the Church of England.

British universities are thus not 'political' in the same sense as are the Conservative and Labour parties, certain proselytizing pressure

---

[4] For a fuller statement of this view see G. C. MOODIE and G. STUDDERT-KENNEDY: *Opinions, Publics, and Pressure Groups* (George Allen and Unwin, 1970) pp. 11–13.

groups, or the permanent Civil Service. All we are claiming is that each of them clearly has its own internal government and politics. This being granted, one can proceed to specify some of the political attributes which they share with any system of government.

Firstly, it is clear that one can distinguish the public affairs of a university from the private affairs of its members. This is to say that there will be certain problems, disputes, attitudes and interests that relate to those aspects of the university and its life which constitute the members' shared public world of action.

Secondly, decisions have frequently to be taken about matters lying within those public affairs, decisions which constitute the policy of or for the university. Prominent examples include decisions about whether or not to expand and by how much, what balance to maintain between subjects and how to allocate scarce resources.

Thirdly, a university makes and/or is bound by rules and regulations of various kinds. Of greatest legal importance are those rules, commonly found in the university's charter or an Act of Parliament, which lay down its fundamental constitution. In the charter or statute, therefore, one will find the basic definitions of the university and its purposes and of the most important governmental bodies. Within the limits there laid down, the university will normally possess a set of statutes which contain general legislation about detailed decision-making procedures, the academic curricula, the nature and kinds of degrees, and certain aspects of the general behaviour of its members including, but not confined to, those behavioural matters that are normally thought of as being disciplinary. In addition, the university is governed by sets of detailed regulations and procedures applying to particular areas of its life: administrative procedures, departmental activities, colleges, the students' union, societies and so on. As in other political systems, one consequence of a university's rules is to establish a complex system of offices, jurisdictions, obligations, entitlements and ranks. Without knowing these and the rules from which they derive one cannot properly understand what is happening within a university, despite the fact that the rules do not provide a total description of the university's system of government. Our account of British universities therefore begins, in the next two chapters, with what is primarily a discussion of the constitutional rules and their development.

Fourthly, universities have a system of sanctions and rewards, as well as machinery for their application. The most important sanction is the right to suspend, expel or dismiss any of those people who work within it. The most important rewards are graduation, promotion, support of applications for grants and employment, and such less tangible marks of success as status and esteem. Functions not unlike those performed by the judiciary and police in a state are thus also discharged in universities, but we shall find that there is no single body that exercises all of them nor, in many instances, will any structure be concerned exclusively with any one of them.

Fifthly, universities are political in the sense that in making, changing, and applying the rules, penalties, and sanctions they activate or mobilize important and conflicting perspectives and attitudes. The consequent disputes must be resolved, in the sense that decisions must be taken on the issues in contention without undermining or disrupting the coherence of the university itself. Moreover, one finds that at least some of the differences and disagreements in perspective and attitude are related, if not necessarily closely, to certain important underlying interests. In particular, at least some of the differences in perspective and attitude will be related to an individual's status, as a member of the academic staff, as a student, or as an administrator. Finally, the distinguishing mark of political activity in the eyes of many is that it involves the exercise of power and authority by some men over the behaviour of others.[5] If we take this to mean that in any political system some men are likely to be better placed than others to take decisions which will in fact be acted upon by others, and that some are believed to be entitled to take decisions for others, then power and authority also characterize universities. In this sense too, there is a political dimension to academic life.

If these are political attributes which universities share with any system of government, there are other political attributes which combine to distinguish a university from national or even local government as well as from other important non-state organizations. They too are worth describing, if only briefly, both to highlight certain features of the internal government of British universities and to illustrate our basic perspective.

The first and most important distinction is the simple fact that universities are voluntary associations. The differences between a voluntary association, like a university, and the state may be only of degree; one strand in the history of western political theory is a recommendation that the state itself be seen as a special form of voluntary association. Nevertheless, the differences are important. In particular, because it is a voluntary association a university's membership is more selective and more transient than membership

[5] See, for example, ROBERT A. DAHL: *Modern Political Analysis* (Prentice-Hall, 1963) p. 6: 'a political system is any persistent pattern of human relationships that involves, to a significant extent, power, rule, or authority'.

of the state (citizenship). In the language of citizenship one may say that members of the university community are all immigrants and that it is much easier to emigrate than it is from most states. In some respects this makes universities easier to run, for it may thus be safer to assume that there is a significant degree of common interest amongst the members. But this system of selective and transient membership also means that the possibilities of mortality are different for universities than for a state system of government. It means, for one thing, that dissolution from either internal dissension or external coercion is easier to bring about. But, to balance their vulnerability, universities are probably easier to establish or re-establish than states or cities; nor should one forget that universities have shown a much greater power of survival than nation states. However transient university membership may be in principle, nevertheless universities normally contain at least a core of staff who intend to make a career there and a body of students who, like the staff, prefer not to have their brief sojourn prematurely terminated. This is sufficient to create, on occasion, a serious political predicament; conflict must normally be resolved without recourse to large-scale dismissals or resignations, and peace be kept between the existing contestants over policy.

A second implication of its status as a voluntary association is that a university will have more limited purposes than a system of national government. The nature of these purposes may be debated and ambiguous, they are probably not singular, and they certainly neither define nor apply themselves, but we propose to assume, without argument, 'that the prime responsibility of a university teacher is to diminish ignorance'[6] and that this is also the main purpose of a university. This statement clearly leaves ample room for further enquiry. It may, for example, at once be asked why a university attempts to diminish ignorance: is it for the greater prestige of a father- or motherland, or *ad majorem Dei gloriam*, or neither? Is it to produce gentlemen, rulers, or better trained common men? Does the university wish to diminish ignorance for its own sake, or in order to produce dissent and stimulate criticism, or simply to transmit a cultural heritage? One may also ask how it should propose to do this. Does this task involve, for example, teaching sociology, technology, hairdressing, or none of these things? Does it require universities to follow student demands or the needs of manpower planning in deciding upon which subjects to concentrate?

[6] SIR ERIC ASHBY: *The Academic Profession* (Oxford University Press, 1969) p. 10. And *cf.* Peter Marris, *The Experience of Higher Education* (Routledge and Kegan Paul, 1964), final chapter, where the stress is on 'to increase understanding'.

Who, furthermore, is capable of joining in this common enterprise of diminishing ignorance? And whose ignorance must be diminished, in what order of priority—society's, the academics' (research) or the students'? All these and many other questions may be debated at fundamental or superficial levels. Nevertheless we take it as something which does not require argument that a university's purpose has to do with scholarship and education and that a university is not, unless consequentially, responsible for the production of material goods, for the defence of the realm, for the provision of welfare services, for saving souls or for the maintenance of general law, order, security, and progress.

Most members of a university, moreover, are unlike dedicated patriots (or priests) in the sense that their loyalty to their institution is likely to be more limited and conditional.[7] In the modern world academic loyalty to the university must compete with that to the profession or discipline, and the latter may well reinforce the propensity to emigrate. These ambiguities in academic loyalties present a problem for university government to the extent that policy decisions must never damage loyalty to the point of large-scale defections.

To be a voluntary association is also to be in a position subordinate to the state in various formal ways, ways which differ from those in which every state is constrained by the international political system or in which some states are subordinated to others. In particular this subordination means that a university has no autonomous command over significant means or implements of physical force in the resolution of its conflicts. This is to say that although a university may decide whether to ask for help from the forces of law and order within the society, it cannot decide whether or how they will be used.[8] One consequence of this is that again a special premium is placed, within the university world, upon securing consent by persuasion and peaceful means. Another is the (sometimes superficial) vulnerability of a university to the threat or use of force by its own members or others.

A second form of subordination is that the legal form, status, and

[7] Admittedly, the graduate who never quite cuts the umbilical cord to his *alma mater* is a familiar figure, and, at a more elevated level, there are academics whose commitment to 'the pursuit of truth' becomes inescapably tied to one particular university, college or department. But not all are like this.

[8] One may note here the complaints of some British academics that the police are too reluctant to intervene in dealing with sit-ins, and the experience of United States academics who find themselves so incapable of controlling a police force, some of whose members no one seems able to control, that they are increasingly reluctant ever to involve the police in campus disputes.

powers of all British universities are defined by the State, both in the sense that the university, as a corporation, is subject to the general rules of society and in the specific sense that a university (nowadays, at least) obtains its charter from the Privy Council (or an Act from Parliament) and cannot amend it without the latters' consent. The Privy Council is almost certainly accessible to university influence and may on occasion do little more than ratify a constitution drafted by the university in question. But there are limits to university influence, and on other occasions the Council may insist that a university come closer to its own 'Model Charter'. To these forms of legal subordination must be added the increasing dependence of the universities on the State for money. What this amounts to is that some of the most important decisions about the public affairs of a university may on occasion be taken for it, not by it. Or, to put it differently, it is only in so far as the university and its individual members are part of the national political system that they may help shape some of the basic elements in their own nature. In these ways, of course, the universities are like other important voluntary associations and in particular like those which (to adapt and slightly misuse an American legal phrase) are 'affected with a public interest'. They are also, of course, in these respects like local government authorities to which the State grants the right to perform socially valuable functions, on the understanding that the grant may later be modified, revoked, or withheld.

Internally, although there exists a clear academic ladder, yet a university is not a simple hierarchical type of organization. What one finds on the contrary, is an untidy diffusion of responsibility and a proliferation of centres of initiative and decision-making which are related to one another in ways which are not neatly bureaucratic. There is no direct and comprehensive chain of command, and the notion of an order being issued from one person to another is generally felt to be alien to the way in which British universities should govern their affairs. (It is true that aspects of the relationship between academic staff or administration and students, and of professorial head to junior staff within some departments constitute counter-evidence, but they do not invalidate this broad generalization.[9]) Even the chief executive body in an English provincial university, namely the Council, is not normally in the position either of a board of directors or even of the executive committee of a trade union.

The limitations to hierarchy characteristic of university government are not unconnected with the difficulty, or impossibility, of

[9] These aspects will be explored below, and particularly (with regard to relations within departments) in Chapter IV.

measuring the 'end product' of a university enterprise and of 'controlling' it even from the centre of a web of government. Whether the produce be thought of as being fruitful research, good graduates, or enlightenment, the fact is that it involves qualities which are not readily amenable to judgement, let alone measurement. In practice, indeed, universities are judged by reference to the opinion of their peers, internationally as well as nationally. There is, furthermore, no evident direct relationship between academic distinction or reputation and such things as business efficiency, the ratio of administrative overheads to total expenditure, or the salaries obtained by collective bargaining.[10]

The difficulties created by the lack of measurable criteria of performance are reinforced by the conditions widely believed to be conducive to good performance. For universities (in a free society) are predicated on the view that those who actually teach and research ought (unless possibly during an initial apprenticeship period) to be free from constraint, or even detailed supervision, in their methods of working. In terms of organization charts, furthermore, this work is performed at the periphery. From these points it does not follow that efficient administration and good government in a university are irrelevant, but it does follow that the connection between them and a university's purpose may be tenuous and elusive; that there is a greater relative importance attaching to the personal qualifications of university members; and, to put it in another way, that university government is more obviously concerned with the context of life than with its substance. Partly as a consequence of these differences, whose significance is further intensified thereby, academics are traditionally peculiarly resistant to being governed at all. It is not only among student militants that one may find a natural tendency to anarchy.

In these respects universities are clearly distinguishable from the archetypal industrial enterprise for whose productive and marketing activities (at least) disciplined co-ordination seems to be necessary, and for the effectiveness of which monetary costs and returns seem to provide a relatively satisfactory measure. Academics are prone to exaggerate the disciplinary and measurable elements in actual large industrial organizations, but as a relative judgement it has validity and this tendency to exaggerate itself constitutes evidence for the point we are making. If a university were like an industrial company,

---

[10] Academic distinction seems not even to depend on such factors as library facilities and the staff/student ratio. This, at least, is the implication of an American study of university effectiveness reported by A. W. ASTIN in *Science* (August 1968).

it may be suggested, it would be like a business whose most important and powerful members were its chief designers and engineers and whose overriding purpose was the production of an elegant and durable prototype rather than a steady flow of marketable commodities.

In its internal political relations a university is perhaps more like a trade union than a business. This is so, for example, in the consistent ambition of academics to vest control of policy and administration in their own hands rather than leave it to the university's own bureaucracy or 'leaders'; and in this respect universities are becoming more rather than less like trade unions. On the other hand promotion within a university is more a matter of the judgement or good opinion of one's peers and superiors than of an electorate. The great organizational difference from trade unions, however, is in the lack of either the desire or the need for solidarity or collective discipline. From this follows, among other things, the insistence upon and the possibility of consensus politics within universities, as opposed to the emphasis upon majority decision-making found in the rule-books of most trade unions.

Many of the characteristics which, we are suggesting, distinguish universities are but illustrations of the general point that an organization's methods, style, and structure of government are largely determined by its own purpose and function. As Sir Eric Ashby has put it, 'an institution is the embodiment of an ideal'.[11] But the converse relationship is also important; the composition and powers of any important organ of government affect the ideal and the possibility of its realization. And this is one reason why academics have been anxious about their role on university governing bodies. It should also be added that both the purposes and the constitution of a university are continuously influenced, often in very subtle ways, by the social context within which the university must exist.

Together, the constitution and purposes of universities present conflicting necessities which might appear to make universities virtually ungovernable. Thus it is commonplace to assert that knowledge is a 'seamless web' but, even more commonly, its advancement is held to require increased specialization. Similarly, it may be pointed out that learning and teaching call for increasing co-operation and co-ordination and for more elaborate and expensive physical plant, but that the individual creative scholar must neverthe-

---

[11] *Universities: British, Indian, African. A Study in the Ecology of Higher Education* (Weidenfeld and Nicolson, 1966) p. 3. And in the nature of its ideal a university clearly differs very significantly from a business, a trade union or any other of the institutions with which we have compared it.

less still choose his own areas of interest while few others, if any, can appraise the value, at least of the most advanced work, let alone measure the worth of disparate projects competing for resources. Another conflict arises from the fact that although the time scale and the complexity of decision-making require an increasing resort to central and possibly impersonal long-term planning, government grants may not be predictable for much more than a year ahead, while as we have seen, the end product of a university emerges from processes which are in an important sense both intimate and personal. A third conflict arises from the contradictory pressures to which universities are currently subject. On the one hand external social, governmental, and financial pressures seem to call for a more centralized and controlled form of organization between universities as well as within them, while on the other hand universities face mounting internal demands both to enlarge the boundaries of the university community and to translate the ideal of community into a more participatory system of government answerable to students and all members of staff.

Despite these and other problems inherent in the nature of a university, British universities continue to govern themselves and, by almost any test, seem to do so reasonably well. In particular, they have undergone an immense expansion in student numbers, staff, and range of activity in the twenty-five years since the end of the Second World War, including an increase of 46 per cent in student enrolment in the 'redbrick' universities during the period 1961-6 alone, and have done so with notable economy. Moreover, there is evidence to suggest that, even in terms of mere administrative efficiency, the state may have something to learn from university governments.[12] This ability to conjure policy decisions out of conflict and the apparently irreconcilable is not, as such, exceptional; it is to be interpreted merely as a sign that universities have reasonably successful political systems. For all politics are concerned with real or apparent contradictions, just as personal life requires the constant toleration of ambiguity. Both public and private affairs thus involve the ability to strike balances between forces and principles which contradict one another; but in life, contradictions may be mutually exclusive only when extreme groups insist upon making them so. For the successful politician, academic or other, they may be merely among the more difficult, but still common parts of his ordinary work.

[12] See, for example, the evidence of Lord James of Rusholme to the House of Commons Committee of Public Accounts, printed in the latter's Special Report on *Parliament and Control of University Expenditure* (HMSO 1967) p. 92, questions 486-9.

Chapter II

THE DEVELOPMENT OF MODERN
UNIVERSITY GOVERNMENT

The Birth of the System

Until 1826, when what is now University College, London, first admitted students, there were only seven universities in the United Kingdom—Oxford, Cambridge and the five ancient Scottish universities, the latest of which had been founded in 1593.[1] In 1825 there were some 3,000 students at the English universities and 4,000 at the Scottish.[2] In 1970 there were forty-seven universities (i.e. degree-granting institutions) counting the federations of Wales and London as one each, and including the Open University, Cranfield, and the Royal College of Art; but, more realistically, ten or so of the non-medical schools at London and the six non-medical constituents of Wales should be counted individually, bringing the total to over sixty.[3] In the same year the total of full-time students had reached well over 200,000. The present university system is thus largely the creation of the last 125 years, but the system of university government is much younger; it cannot nevertheless be understood without some reference to its origins.

The university system in this country has extremely ancient origins (indeed the precise date on which it began is not known) and since the appearance in 1895 of Dean Rashdall's *The Universities of Europe in the Middle Ages* the apparently democratic (and, indeed

[1] St Andrews (founded in 1412), Glasgow (1451), Aberdeen (1494 and 1593), and Edinburgh (1583). (From 1593 until 1860 there were two independent colleges at Aberdeen; in 1860 they were joined as the University of Aberdeen.)

[2] ERIC ASHBY and MARY ANDERSON: *The Rise of the Student Estate in Britain* (Macmillan, 1970) p. 3.

[3] The usual formal test of university status is inclusion on the University Grants Committee (UGC) list of grant-receiving institutions. By it one must exclude Cranfield (the former College of Aeronautics), the Royal College of Art, and the Open University. In any case the first two lie outside the main stream of university traditions, while the Open University's dispersal, purpose, and methods join to impose special requirements upon its procedures and atypical relations between its staff.

egalitarian) organization of the early universities has greatly
preoccupied many commentators on academic government.[4] Their
beliefs must certainly be part of the reason for the considerable
degree of self government enjoyed by academic staff in this country
today. It is, however, not easy to analyse medieval university
government in terms of such a modern concept; the evidence is
extremely scanty and scholars have been little interested in the sorts
of question we discuss in this study.[5] Even more to the point, perhaps,
the circumstances and objectives of the ancient university are so
remote from those of today that the truth, whatever it may be, is not
likely to be relevant. Certainly those, whether staff or student, who
believe that precedent is important should be extremely cautious in
appealing to ancient practice.[6]

Two points in particular may, however, be made about medieval
university government. First, it is not clear that any body of persons
comparable to modern career-staff controlled the 'magisterial'
universities, or that any body resembling modern undergraduates
controlled the 'student' so-called 'universities'.[7] If it is possible to
say anything at all that is illuminating in our context, it might be
that both types of university were controlled by people roughly
resembling modern postgraduates. Second, to the extent that there
existed a situation which might be described as formal academic self-
government, the reasons were not clearly related to the needs of the
academic process.[8]

After the early medieval period universities came under external

[4] There had before that been much antiquarian interest, but there was little
accurate knowledge of government.

[5] For instance little is known of the effective, as opposed to the formal,
membership of bodies such as the Black Congregation at Oxford.

[6] For a fuller discussion see ROWLAND EUSTACE: 'The Origins of Self-Government of University Staff' (a paper presented to the British Sociological Association at its Annual Conference in 1970) of which this chapter is mainly an abstract.
We are indebted to several scholars, and in particular to Dr A. B. Emden, Mr
John Sparrow, and Professor G. Leff, for invaluable informal advice and guidance
on particular points; they bear, of course, no sort of responsibility for what
appears here.

[7] See, for example, G. LEFF: *Paris and Oxford in the Thirteenth and Fourteenth
Centuries* (Wiley, 1968) p. 7: 'the entire system was based on a continuous
succession of Masters who taught for one or two years before giving way—
usually with relief—to those newly graduated'. At Bologna, the student 'university' never gained full control over the College of Doctors which reserved
effective power over, for example, degree-granting and most academic appointments. Bologna was, in any case, a 'higher faculty' institution and its students
were normally arts graduates.

[8] The political consequences of tavern brawls must feature among the actual
reasons.

pressures both on their institutional autonomy and on the internal autonomy of their 'staffs'. In addition, the traditions of scholarship fluctuated so that, long before the mid-nineteenth century reforms, it becomes difficult to discern any sizeable group at Oxford or Cambridge which might be regarded as in any way the equivalent of the staff of a modern university.[9] Moreover, the form of government at Oxbridge placed great power in the hands of men who were often more like laymen[10] than scholars, that is, of the heads of colleges, the graduates, and non-resident (and certainly non-teaching) fellows.[11] Even after reform had begun there is evidence for the view that the rationale of staff self-government was based as much on the rights of property as on the needs of scholarship.[12]

It is not therefore surprising that, in the group of new institutions founded in the 1820s and 1830s, no provision was made for any participation by academic staff in government, and this despite the fact that three of the four institutions were explicitly traditionalist.[13] Nor was it merely participation in general government that was denied. All strictly academic authority, for instance over the curriculum and the examinations, was reserved to the lay governors who, either precisely because they were reformers or for sectarian reasons,

[9] Mark Pattison, as a young fellow of Lincoln College, Oxford, in the 1840s, was appalled at the poverty of the scholarly 'outfit of those whose names carried scholastic weight in the university' (see his *Memoirs* (1885) p. 234). Sir Eric Ashby dates the formation of an academic profession from 1870. Though this is unjust to Scotland, it is an eminently defensible proposition. ('The Academic Profession', *Minerva*, January 1970, VII: 1). See also HAROLD PERKIN: *Key Profession* (Routedge and Kegan Paul, 1969) p. 3.

[10] Up to the present century, of course, the prime meaning of 'layman' was 'non-clerical'. It was often applied to scholars in their universities who had not taken Orders. It is used here in the little less ancient (S.E.D. 1477) senses of 'non-expert' and 'outsider', though it must be remembered that laymen are, legally, 'members' of the institutions they govern. A layman, in our sense, may of course be a graduate, a scholar, or even, much less commonly, an academic from another university.

[11] Normally only the few college fellows who also held tutorships taught, and much of the teaching in the nineteenth century was done by non-collegiate coaches. See, e.g. C. R. M. WARD: *Oxford University Statistics* (1845) p. 6.

[12] 'In 1854 we disputed the right of interference and invoked our Charters and the sacredness of private property': MARK PATTISON: *Essays on the Endowment of Research* (1876) p. 3.

[13] In none of the various instruments (of the 1826 University of London (University College), of University College proper, King's College, London, Lampeter, Durham (1832 and 1837), and the 1836 University of London) is there any mention at all of staff participation. University College's internal regulations positively forbade any form of staff combination and staff were permitted to communicate with the governors (Proprietors) only in writing (H. BELLOT: *University College London* (University of London, 1929) p. 50).

took the liveliest interest in these matters. This separation of teaching from decision-making was most clearly seen in the structure of the 1836 University of London, a body in effect confined to drawing up syllabuses, appointing examiners, and awarding degrees for students whose teachers in the colleges had no say, as such, or indeed at all, in these matters.[14] With variations, this device was copied elsewhere, notably by the Victoria University of 1880 (centred on Manchester). By the end of the century, as a result, English university education outside Oxford and Cambridge was in effect organized on a university college system in which teaching was divorced from academic control.[15] In short, scholars were deprived of almost all discretion in the management of their affairs.

This limitation can be said to have become a matter of public policy, because lay control over finance (and some academic matters) was extended to Scotland by the Universities (Scotland) Act of 1858. It was increased by a further Act (1889) which also reduced the academic independence of each university by requiring it to obtain the approval of the others for every major innovation. Both Acts went so far as to provide for the introduction of the university college system to Scotland by providing 'for the foundation of a National University of Scotland [to which] the Scottish Universities . . . may . . . surrender . . . the powers of examining and granting Degrees . . . and to become Colleges . . . of the said National University'.[16]

Insistence on lay control cannot be seen merely as the rising middle class exerting its dominance. In none even of the new institutions founded in the wake of the Oxbridge extension movement was there much staff participation.[17] Nor was there much staff participation in

[14] The governing body, the Senate, was nominated by the Crown.

[15] This system was defended before the Privy Council inquiry into the granting of a charter to Liverpool in 1901 as being essentially the same as the college/university relationship at Oxbridge; and indeed one of the functions of the University of London Senate was to act in the same way as the public examiners at Cambridge. This divided system was developed concurrently in Ireland and in India and remains the system in Wales. (See, e.g., SIR ERIC ASHBY: *Universities: British, Indian, African* (Weidenfeld and Nicholson, 1966).)

[16] Universities (Scotland) Act 1858, Chapter 83, section 16. The option was never taken up.

[17] The most blatant case was at the University College of Nottingham where Oxford and Cambridge nominees sat on a governing body that was otherwise a committee of the City Council, almost until the Second World War. Mark Pattison was appealed to by a former pupil, the principal of the University College of Wales at Aberystwyth, against a decision of the lay governing body about examinations. 'The issue,' replied Pattison, 'was whether the College should be "managed by those who find the money or by those who receive it".' See E. L. ELLIS: *The University College of Wales at Aberystwyth* (University of Wales, 1972) pp. 31 and 60. Pattison had personally eliminated staff participation at

the New Foundations within Oxford itself.[18] Thus even if there could be said to be an ancient tradition of staff self-government in England it became extremely tenuous for a considerable period, while even the more robust Scottish tradition was severely buffeted in the last half of the nineteenth century.

Nevertheless, almost from the start of the new university movement there were in fact signs, erratic and slow, of attempts to re-establish (or possibly to establish) the right of active scholars to control over their affairs. This was the effect, and indeed largely the intention, of the mid-century reforms at Oxbridge—though the effect took long to be completed (the graduates at Cambridge still have certain powers). It had begun to emerge at University College, London, as early as 1832.[19] And there were other signs, notably in the charter granted to Queen's College, Birmingham, in 1843.[20] But the real landmark was the constitution drafted for Owens College, Manchester, by James Bryce in 1880. This formalized the modern system of mixed government, with lay majorities on court and council and an academic senate.[21]

In the wave of new institutions founded in the 1870s and early 1880s[22]

Bedford College, London, even though some of the staff concerned were academically eminent. (M. TUKE: *A History of Bedford College for Women*, 1939, pp. 32 and 60.) Pattison was one of the leading Oxford reformers.

[18] Outsiders remained on the governing bodies of these colleges and of the women's colleges until the early 1950s. Only one college tutor served on the governing body of Keble College from its foundation in 1868 until the new Charter of 1952 (College *Registers*).

[19] H. BELLOT: *op. cit.*, p. 213. An academic senate (with a lay chairman) was set up by internal regulation.

[20] This was predominately a medical institution (and formed a basis for the faculty of medicine in the University of Birmingham today). Medical teachers, probably because they were specialized and socially respected, generally enjoyed much more participation than other academics. Thus, at King's College, London, they gained substantial representation nearly ten years before the rest of the College teachers gained a very limited position in 1870; see F. J. C. HEARNSHAW: *The Centenary History of King's College* (Harrap, 1929) pp. 16, 139 and 233.

[21] The staff were represented on the court of forty-two members by two professors and the Principal (then a professor), and these three also sat on the council of thirteen members.

[22]
Newcastle	1871	Birmingham	1880
Leeds	1874	Dundee	1881
Bristol	1876	Liverpool	1881
Sheffield	1879	Nottingham	1881

The dates are not all comparable one with another. For instance, Bristol was founded as Bristol University College but Birmingham did not take the title of Mason University College until 1898, while Newcastle was founded 'in connection with' Durham University and remained as part of it until 1963.

various degrees of staff participation began to appear, and by the end of the century in all the institutions claiming university status the principal and a few staff members had seats on the governing council. One major step was the formation of a teaching University of London in 1900 (on the basis of an Act of 1898) for all that it affected only London staffs and did so only in limited ways. The reasons for this movement are curiously obscure for, even in all the long debate on the formation of the teaching university in London, the assumptions of the reformers about staff participation are largely tacit. Neither Lord Haldane nor Sidney Webb, for instance, despite their close involvement, seem to have been explicit on this subject.[23]

At the end of the last century, then, the government of the emerging institutions outside Oxbridge already showed the general characteristics to be seen today. This is to say, first, that the governing bodies were a large (and largely inert) court and a smaller (and executive) council, each with a heavy lay majority.[24] These bodies bore a direct financial responsibility for their colleges and therefore exercised close control over all expenditure as well as playing a major role in soliciting funds from private benefactors (some of whom were themselves lay members of court or council). In addition they had control of appointments and new developments, but had little responsibility for other academic matters because, under the university college system, such functions as examining and the prescribing of curricula remained the responsibility of the federal universities (and especially the University of London). These laymen were, for the most part, local notabilities.[25]

The power of the laymen, as we have already seen, was shared increasingly with academics, and this is the second general charac-

---

[23] It is in general curious how little interest historians and commentators have taken in government. Newman, for instance, despite painful experiences in Dublin, said almost nothing on the subject beyond that he favoured Church control of curriculum and lay control of finance (*Idea of a University* (M. J. SVAGLIC, ed., Holt, Rinehart and Winston, 1966) p. 164, and WILFRED WARD: *Life* (Longmans, Green, 1912) Vol. 1, p. 381).

[24] There was no court at Durham, but the Cathedral Chapter (of which some members of staff might be members in their clerical capacity) may be equated with a council.

[25] In the original 'London University' they consisted of the proprietors, who had bought shares (expecting if not receiving a fair return). But later, and elsewhere, the laymen were representative of 'all classes and interests'. They therefore were drawn from local magnates, local authorities, and, as at Leeds in 1903, 'coalowners, livery companies, the Yorkshire Board of Legal Studies, the principal grammar schools, and the training colleges'—see A. N. SHIMMIN: *The University of Leeds* (Cambridge, 1954) p. 77.

teristic of the modern system. The academic staff were headed by a permanent principal (as he was generally called) who sometimes also held a chair. He was a member of both court and council, where he was joined by a small (but steadily increasing) number of professors. The principal and all professors were also members of the senate, a purely advisory body concerned mainly with the academic matters which lay within the jurisdication of the colleges. The existence and status of the professors represented an important organizational principle in an area on which the charters were generally silent. Following a precedent established in the ancient Scottish universities and the even more influential practice of the reformed and research-oriented German universities, the new English foundations came to centre all teaching and research upon the subject, while the subject was entrusted to a professor who was personally responsible for the work of what rapidly emerged as the department.[26]

The final development on which the modern system is founded was instigated by events in Birmingham. In 1897 Joseph Chamberlain had been installed as Rector of the University of Glasgow. 'When I get back to Birmingham,' he declared, 'I mean to have a university of my own.'[27] He did; in 1900 Mason College was chartered as the autonomous University of Birmingham. As a result plans for a new federation of university colleges including Bristol, Birmingham, and Nottingham were dropped and the Victoria Federation broke up. From then on the modern system of autonomous unitary universities rapidly became the dominant one except in London and in Wales. This gave staff direct access to the determination of purely academic matters through their senates which, while still largely advisory, began to acquire both formal rights and, more important, extensive customary rights of decision-making.[28] The charters granted to the new universities finally established the right of staff to participate in the general government of their universities by giving staff substantial representation on the councils. The basic pattern of modern university government was thus established. We will now turn to a more detailed discussion of the ways in which the position of academic staff in university government has been extended and strengthened in this century.

[26] This principle of the professionally run subject-department had very little influence in Oxford and Cambridge (except in the natural sciences) despite the attempts of mid-century reformers to introduce it there.

[27] J. L. GARVIN: Life of Joseph Chamberlain, ed. J. Amery (Macmillan, 1951) Vol. IV, p. 212.

[28] Charters have tended to incorporate, as rules, what has already been established as practice elsewhere.

The Growth of Academic Rule—1900–70

To attempt a comprehensive history of the internal government of British universities would take us too far afield. To do so even for the twentieth century alone would be an immense task, if only because the past seventy years have witnessed a larger number of new constitutions than in all the previous centuries. There have been three groups of brand new charters. The first was the group of newly independent civic universities already mentioned, with which one may include Reading. The second consisted of the five colleges remaining from the London-centred university college system which became independent between 1948 and 1957.[29] To these may be added the new University College of North Staffordshire (1959)[30] and the University of Sussex, the constitutions of which were broadly in line. The third and largest group includes Newcastle and Durham (in 1963 they ended their long association), Keele (1962), Dundee (on its separation from St Andrews in 1967), the so-called 'new' universities (other than Sussex)[31], and the former colleges of advanced technology (CATs).[32] Throughout the whole period, moreover, other universities were revising their constitutions and in all various changes took place which neither received nor required formal amendments to charters.

There were, however, no radical new departures; there was, rather, a continuation of the trends towards greater academic self-government which had already set in and which were carried further largely within the same broad structures first created at Owens College in 1870. In this section, therefore, we propose merely to plot the course of that trend, and to do so only as it manifested itself (in university charters and only with respect to certain selected areas or criteria) of staff participation. These two restrictions, to charters and to selected areas, call for initial comment.

Charters[33] are, admittedly, unreliable guides to the actual conduct

[29] Nottingham (1948), Southampton (1952), Hull (1954), Exeter (1955), and Leicester (1957).

[30] Founded under the sponsorship of the Universities of Birmingham, Manchester, and Oxford, but empowered to grant its own degrees. It achieved full independence in 1962 as the University of Keele.

[31] East Anglia and York (1963), Essex and Lancaster (1964), Coleraine, Kent and Warwick (1965), and Stirling (1967).

[32] Strathclyde (1964), Aston, Bath, Bradford, Brunel, City, Loughborough, Surrey, and Heriot-Watt (all in 1966), and Salford (1967).

[33] By 'charters' here, and throughout, we mean the 'formal instrument or constitution'; the term is used to include Acts of Parliament or Papal Bulls, where appropriate, as well as royal charters, and to include the formal statutes or ordinance where these form effective, often the effective, associated rules. See the discussion of terminology, at the end of Chapter III, below.

of government, As we have already noted, they may do little more than enact the practices already established at the time they were drafted. The allocation of powers they prescribe are likely, in a highly consensual university society, to be descriptive only of what could happen in the last resort—a resort very seldom reached. What may seem to be a significant variation from other charters is sometimes nothing more than a draughtsman's quirk. It also happens on occasion that, in a particular university, government is carried on in substantial ignorance of the constitution—we came across important instances in the course of our interviews. In universities, as elsewhere, the formal rules nourish conventions which modify, even negate, their intended impact. A striking example is provided by two of the London colleges in whose creation the Webbs played some part. The London School of Economics, founded in 1895, has no charter, but is a limited company with the barest minimum of a structure providing for no trace at all of academic participation. The Imperial College, itself a federation within a federation, under the Charter of 1907 has an elaborate constitutional framework assuring a place to staff, including a place to junior staff, which seems rapidly to have become semi-moribund. In current practice, however, staff involvement in government at LSE is as great, and at Imperial as small, as almost anywhere in the country.

To trace the evolution of charters is nonetheless informative. Charters and statutes are the most formal, and ceremonial, expressions of society's views. It is also clear that they do in fact provide evidence of changing practice, if only at a long remove. Moreover, the charters prescribe the legal composition of the governing bodies at various levels, and though this need not always be decisive, the charters have thus set the main framework in which staff have had in fact to operate.

We restrict the discussion which follows to certain constitutional areas simply because they are the key areas affecting the governmental role of academic staff and because this is the respect in which change has been most marked. The general trends, and the areas with which we will be concerned, may be stated briefly. There has, firstly, been a growth in the importance of senates relative to councils. Second, staff representation on councils has increased. Third, a larger number of junior staff has been included on all bodies, including some 'below' the level of the senate[34] to which the most recent charters have devoted more attention than was previously the practice. In tracing these developments note will be taken principally of innovations as

[34] There are certain respects in which to talk of 'below' is to give a misleading impression; see the discussion at the end of Chapter III and in Chapter IV below.

B

they first appeared and of the main exceptions to the general rule that such innovations are followed in later charters.

Powers of Council and Senate. In the nineteenth century the internal powers of court and council were virtually unqualified.[35] In this century, however, council's powers have been steadily reduced by insistence upon the need to consult senate and by the grant of specific powers to the latter including, in particular, the vesting in senate of the initiative in important areas. But this took time. Thus, in the Birmingham Charter of 1900, despite Sonnenschein's gallant fight, there appeared a 'litany' of overriding powers which, usually but not invariably with declining severity, appear in every charter (except those of Manchester and Leeds and Durham's 1937 version) for the next sixty years and more. In addition to numerous specific powers the Birmingham council was enabled 'to review and control or disallow any act of the Senate and give directions to be obeyed by the Senate'.[36]

Manchester, perhaps reflecting its origin in Owens College, not only omitted this 'litany' but gave its senate the right to be consulted about all legislation and even senior academic appointments including that of the vice-chancellor.[37] Moreover senate obtained the right 'to discuss and declare an opinion upon' any matter affecting the university.[38] Leeds followed the Manchester pattern. So did the 1937 Durham constitution in these respects; furthermore, it declared the federal senate to be the 'supreme' academic body which had even to be consulted on any financial matter which 'directly affects the educational policy of the University'.[39] These constitutions demonstrate how long the idea of senate involvement in such areas has been publicly accepted, but even today some senates lack some or all of these formal attributes. In Reading's Charter (1926) the litany of council powers was modified and council had to consult senate on all legislation, but neither it nor the immediate post-war charters give comparable rights in the financial sphere, and senate's rights in the sphere of appointments and legislation vary almost in a random fashion. Thus the Sussex Charter of 1961 guarantees that

[35] Court's powers, other than those to appoint council (or, increasingly, representatives to it), have been so seldom used that we do not discuss them here. On court today, see Chapter V below.

[36] S. 25:5.

[37] S. IV and V.

[38] This phrase appeared earlier, e.g. as a right of convocation at Victoria in 1880; it has since become a virtually standard item in lists of powers of senates and/or general assemblies of all staff.

[39] S. 10 and S. 11 (3).

senate should be consulted on one appointment only, that of the vice-chancellor, and does not even insist upon senate concurrence in making statutes; but the new Liverpool charter of the same year gave senate the initiative in all academic appointments as well as the right of consultation in the appointment of both registrar and vice-chancellor. In neither charter does senate have anything approaching a veto on legislation; by contrast the Nottingham Charter of 1948 had provided that academic legislation had to be on the 'joint recommendation' of council and senate. On the other hand, while this whole group of charters (1948–61) contained the litany, it was invariably in modified form—Exeter (1955), for example, omitted council's powers to 'give directions' to senate or to 'disallow' its acts, retaining only the power to 'amend, review or refer back'. Despite the variations, however, the general direction of movement is clearly to give senates greater significance than was given to the Birmingham one in 1900. This is evident even in the Model Charter issued by the Privy Council in 1963 to guide the many new and old institutions then known to be seeking charters. The Model Charter retained the general litany of council powers and reserved for council the full control over financial matters; but it also gave senates extensive rights to initiate and be consulted about legislation as well as significant rights of initiative in making appointments. Subsequent charters have not, however, followed the Model Charter consistently. Even the Newcastle Charter (1963)—one of the most radical of charters in the position it accords to staff, and especially non-professorial staff[40]—permits senate to initiate appointments only of junior staff. In this respect Newcastle lags behind both the model and the majority of charters granted in the sixties.[41] Only some of the latter, on the other hand, give senates as great a role in financial decision-making. Among those that do, East Anglia, Aston, and Bradford provide for consultation on any financial matter that 'directly affects the educational policy' (as in Durham, 1937) while Essex, Bath, and Surrey omit the word 'directly' from this provision. Bradford and Warwick, in more sophisticated language, add the power of senate 'to advise the council on the allocation of resources for teaching and research'.

By 1970, therefore, the jurisdiction of senate had been extended, in

---

[40] Senate is described as the 'supreme' academic body and, as in the federal Durham constitution of 1937, its rights include consultation over finance (including the terms of service of academic and administrative staff), while there is no echo of the council litany. On the role of non-professorial staff, see below.

[41] At Aston and the Open University senate actually makes the academic appointments.

varying degree but with formal public approval, to the fields of academic and senior non-academic appointments, of general and not merely academic legislation, and of finance. Simultaneously there had been some weakening or erosion of the litany of council powers where it remained at all. If account is also taken of the extent to which all charters, and particularly the Privy Council model, embody accepted (if often formal) practice rather than serve as 'ice-breakers', then it is indisputable that the century has witnessed a substantial move towards internal academic self-government in all major areas of decision-making. The University of Aston perhaps acknowledges this shift in the clearest way: there council must consult senate even in the selection of the symbols of the university's authority, its seal and mace.

Staff Representation on Council. Merely by looking at a charter it is not always possible to tell what proportion of the membership is occupied by academic staff. This is because most charters permit council to co-opt additional lay members up to a maximum figure, but it is not mandatory to co-opt even a minimum number. On the other hand it is sometimes possible to guess the outcome expected or intended by a charter's framers and at other times (but not invariably) to obtain reliable information as to what the proportion actually was.[42]

In this area what may be called the liberal trend toward academic self-government is less clearly marked and much more uneven than it was with respect to the relative powers of council and senate. On the other hand the shift in formal power has been reinforced by the stronger, even if not strikingly more numerous, voice of the academic at council meetings.[43] Significantly, too, the 1963 Model Charter gives no guide to the proportions in which the various constituencies should be represented. Nevertheless, the general direction of such movement as may be measured was liberal.

At Birmingham the 1900 Charter set a maximum proportion of a little under 25 per cent. At Leeds and Liverpool the maximum was only 20 per cent. The other pre-1914 charters fixed no maximum. Taking the group as a whole, the actual proportions (taken from

[42] In our calculations we have omitted the chancellor and the representatives of academic advisory committees (appointed to the councils of the 'new'—1960s—universities during their 'probationary' periods). Somewhat arbitrarily we have generally not counted vice-chancellors and principals as 'academic' (for this purpose), but have counted full-time deans of medicine.

[43] See Chapter V, below.

their *Calendars*) ranged from 22 per cent at Manchester[44] to 10 per cent at Leeds. On the other hand, at Newcastle all professors could attend meetings of Armstrong College's equivalent of council as observers, and at the federal Durham 'council'[45] academics seem to have occupied a very high proportion of seats[46] (by the 1937 constitution staff were guaranteed at least 30 per cent of the membership). Reading (1926) gave staff a quarter of the seats, but Nottingham (1948) and Hull (1954) gave only about a fifth. But, with the variations characteristic of charters in this area, North Staffordshire established a council in 1949 with almost one-third of its members academics. In Exeter (1955) the figure reached a third, and in St Andrews (1955) it was over one-third. Of the early sixties a similar story can be told: Sussex (1961) had only a little over a quarter, York (1963) a little less, but Liverpool (1961) had a staff contingent on council which could vary between a minimum of one-fifth and a maximum of two-fifths.[47] On the break-up of the Durham federation the new university at Durham gave two-fifths of council seats to academics (a figure which could rise to one-half if the power to co-opt were not used) and at Newcastle the maximum of nearly two-fifths could easily be raised even higher than that at Durham.[48] More indicative of the general trend, perhaps, is a more summary statement. Whereas, in 1962, the normal proportion of academic staff on council varied between a sixth and a third, the next nineteen charters to be granted gave a quarter or less in only four cases and over a third in fourteen cases (including four cases where the proportion was at least two-fifths).

The Privy Council, in granting or approving charters and amendments thereto, thus seems to have no rigid policy, but it is rumoured that the drafters of Durham's 1963 charter were led to believe that the Privy Council would accept any academic proportion which left a lay majority. Academic control may not require an actual majority

---

[44] At Manchester an academic majority was theoretically possible, if there was co-operation of Convocation in electing staff to council (as had in fact occurred in Victoria), though 17·5 per cent was 'expected'. Oddly enough, one of the proposals for the amendment of this charter made in 1967 sought to rule out this possibility.

[45] We will refer to such equivalents as 'council' where they had a different title. See our discussion of equivalents in Chapter III below.

[46] The *Report* (p. 94) of the Board of Education, 1913, appears to give them 80 per cent of the seats; but there are certain problems of interpretation here.

[47] The limits were fixed by the charter, the actual proportion depended on how many, if any, pro-vice-chancellors (who had to be academics and were ex-officio members of council) were appointed.

[48] The possible size is left exceptionally indeterminate by the charter.

of seats, however. If one remembers that staff members usually attend council meetings with greater regularity than is possible for many lay members, that they are more knowledgeable about the university's internal affairs, and that they are more likely to share a common interest, then it becomes apparent that staff may well be in a controlling position even while in a numerical minority, and particularly if, as is usually the case, the vice-chancellor may be counted as an academic.[49] The liberal trend has thus, in some institutions, proceeded almost as far as it can without entirely reversing the older relationship with laymen. As we suggest later, however, this particular trend seems at least as likely to be reversed as to be extended.[50]

The Role of the non-professorial Staff. It has often been suggested that when senates first appeared their academic membership was drawn from the professoriate because almost all the academic staff were professors. Senates thus, so the argument goes, began life as congregations of virtually all staff. Though this line of argument requires qualification even in the earliest stages, it was fairly true of the Scottish Universities and the nineteenth-century university colleges.[51] It is less tenable of the new charters of the 1900s. Even allowing for due caution in assessing the standing of junior staff seventy or so years ago, not all of whom were graduates, it is apparent that hierarchy was both intended and achieved. At Birmingham University in 1901, for example, Senate included twenty-nine professors, but among the staff were also listed twenty-six lecturers. Elsewhere this hierarchy amongst academics was even more marked, as the following table clearly indicates.

	Professors	Lecturers	Other 'Career' Academic Staff[52]
Manchester (1904)	39	56	35
Leeds (1904)	30	18	34
Liverpool (1903)	29	46	40
Sheffield (1908)	24	45	30

[49] See the discussion of vice-chancellors in Chapter VI, below.

[50] See Chapters V and IX below.

[51] At Victoria University in 1886, when most of the staff were provided by Owen's College, there were (according to the *Calendar*) forty-four professors and twenty-six lecturers. Lecturer was a title usually given to heads of departments or sub-departments and at all events to a senior man. Eighteen of the lecturers had seats on the federal 'senate' (General Board). None had seats on the college senate.

[52] The figures, taken from the appropriate *Calendar* for the year indicated, include associate professors and readers as lecturers; clinical lecturers, some of whom will have been part-time, also come under this heading; 'other' staff does not include staff listed as honorary, nor does it include fellows, assistants, instructors, etc., or any staff obviously sub-academic.

It should also be borne in mind that, at the time, there was no compulsory retiring age so that many members even of the non-professorial staff (NPS) might be chronologically very senior. In such young institutions, moreover, growth could even then be expected to increase the proportion of NPS. Senates thus do not seem to have been designed as egalitarian bodies embracing the whole community of scholars. Nor can it be said with confidence that senates were intended specifically to be assemblies representative of all the subjects taught within the institution. For one thing there are several cases where there were two or more professors in a subject, each on senate.[53] There were, secondly, substantial numbers of readers or lecturers in charge of subjects who were nevertheless not members of senate.[54] To the extent that academics were involved in university government, therefore, it was principally through the professors.

None the less there was formal recognition that NPS did have rights and responsibilities. The Manchester Charter reserved seats on court for election by non-senators, and two others reserved seats for election by the staff as a whole.[55] At council and senate level, though the signs are very sparse, the principle seems to have been at least admitted. Birmingham and Sheffield left a possible avenue to council through election as dean; Liverpool and Leeds provided for the election of academics to council by faculties. NPS might also aspire to a seat on senate through a deanship or, sometimes, a few co-optative places.[56]

At faculty level, the rights of NPS were clearer. The existence of faculty bodies was specified in some charters, though it is difficult to be quite clear about their functions or even titles. Birmingham, like Manchester and Leeds, put no limit on non-professorial membership

---

[53] It is not easy to be clear here what constitutes a 'subject' or a department. No doubt it would be better not to instance the five professors in classical subjects at Manchester in 1901. But there were two in each of history, education, physics and law. At Leeds in 1900 there were two in classics and two in French literature, and at Bristol in 1910 there were two in maths, and also two each in medicine and surgery.

[54] Here again, definition is difficult, and probably should be avoided in the professional subjects, where there are many ancillary specialties (so spelt). At Manchester, Spanish, economics, and music provide clear cases; at Leeds (1904), philosophy and English; and at Sheffield (1907), law, music, and biology. At Bristol, the 1910 *Calendar* specifically lists nineteen 'Lecturers in charge of Departments' in (mainly) languages or medicine, but also in logic, botany, zoology, and education. None were on senate.

[55] Sheffield and Leeds.

[56] At Liverpool W. J. Anderson, a non-professor, reached both council and senate before 1906.

of the faculty body, which 'appointed' the dean.[57] In 1904 NPS held about half the seats on the boards at Manchester, though there were few at Leeds. Liverpool and Sheffield introduced a limit to NPS membership of one-third, and Bristol of one-quarter, an unmistakable admission of the right to belong.[58] On the other hand, the right to membership was of limited value since few powers were given to faculty bodies, and these wholly advisory; exceptionally, the faculties at Liverpool were entitled (as they are still, under the 1961 charter) to report on the qualifications of applicants for academic posts. None of the charters of the period mentioned departments, nor were many references made to any sub-faculty organization. In Manchester, however, all members of the faculty boards (with about half the membership drawn from the NPS) meeting together were entitled 'to report to the Senate on matters concerning teaching . . . which affect the University as a whole'. Here, with similar bodies created by the 1908 Durham Charter, may be seen the origin of the assemblies of all staff established by many charters in the 1960s. (Manchester also provided for Student Representative Councils [sic] which could 'enter into communication with the Vice-Chancellor on matters affecting the university'.[59])

The first appearance of the principle of reserved seats for the NPS were in Reading's Charter (1926); it not only specified that lecturers were eligible for election to deanships but also ear-marked three seats on senate. Durham (1937) introduced a further principle: professors were not made *ex officio* members of the federal senate, instead they merely formed one electoral constituency, the other seats being elected by the faculty boards (in which the NPS could hold a majority of seats) and the 'senates' in each of the member institutions. (In these 'senates' NPS were less well represented, but the Durham division introduced the further principle that the NPS members be elected, and by their peers only.) One further case may be cited, if only to indicate the importance even of modest liberal reform. After years of agitation for greater NPS participation at Leeds, leading eventually to the threat of NPS intervention on court

[57] This was evidently a faculty meeting, rather than an executive or board. At Manchester, however, it was an executive board.

[58] The limit was not on NPS as such, but on 'other persons' who might, and at Liverpool, did, include outsiders (e.g. local lawyers). The point becomes clear at Reading, where the position of the NPS element in the 'other persons' was safeguarded. Thus the limitation could have been a form of safeguard of the staff position against lay dilution. On the other hand, precision was characteristic of the later documents, and the limitation may merely have reflected a desire for clarity about the seat and balance of power.

[59] In 1967 the university proposed to omit all reference to student bodies.

elections to council, the university's statutes were amended in 1948. The minor reforms made drew comment from the official historian: 'This impact of democratic thought has effected a transfer of the site of what may be termed "academic power" (away from Council and towards Faculties) . . . the newest recruit to the staff today cannot know what it means to be "in the university but not of it".'[60]

The period since the Second World War has witnessed a slow extension in the rights of NPS to membership of the main university bodies and, increasingly, themselves to elect their members. In securing this advance public policy has played an important part. In 1961, for example, Liverpool sought Privy Council approval for amendments to its charter which would provide NPS with two seats on its council (out of forty-six) and six on senate. In support of the latter proposal the Liverpool petition pleaded prolonged pressure to this end from the UGC.[61] It is improbable that the Privy Council required such a plea, for its own Model Charter (1963) recommended that NPS should constitute one-third of senate, and seemed to favour the election of that third by the NPS.[62] The model also incorporated the setting up of an assembly of all academic staff. The latter, admittedly, had the right only to discuss university business and the duty (or fate) only of receiving addresses from the vice-chancellor. Nevertheless, an assembly is a tacit acceptance of the right of all academics, regardless of rank, to be informed and to comment and, in fact, the institution has been set up, though not always under this label[63], by most subsequent charters and occasionally, as at Warwick, has been given the power to elect members to senate.[64]

A potentially more important development is the occasional omission of any seats specially reserved for NPS under circumstances in which it is expected no longer to be necessary. When revising its charter in 1969 the senate at Lancaster considered that 'election by grades of staff implies a divergence of interest which does not necessarily exist, and should certainly not be encouraged'.[65] A

[60] A. N. SHIMMIN: *The University of Leeds* (Cambridge, 1954) p. 80.

[61] Liverpool Court, Petition to the Privy Council, 1961, paras. 22 and 23.

[62] Our evidence for this is the inclusion of this electoral requirement in Ordinance XIV of Keele's 1963 Charter which was based on the model.

[63] Durham (1973) calls it merely the Annual Meeting, for instance.

[64] Exceptions, among the newest universities, are Kent, Lancaster and York—possibly because the college systems adopted there were felt to make an assembly unnecessary; but the colleges perform no significant academic functions other than, at Lancaster, electing to senate.

[65] From Vice-Chancellor's memorandum of explanation, January 1969, p. 4. In its original charter a third of the seats on senate had been reserved for the NPS. Under the new charter a similar guarantee was inserted at the request of the Privy Council (see Chapter IV, below).

midway stage to a condition of complete formal equality between academics is found in many of the charters from Newcastle and York onwards: professors, on ceasing to be assured of individual *ex officio* membership of senate, become the group for whom a certain number of seats are reserved. The actual range of practice is very wide, however, even amongst the newest charters: most reserve places for NPS on council, though three of the former CATs represent the egalitarian assembly at this level; several universities, including six of the ex-CATs, give assembly seats on senate; some retain the practice of reserving seats on senate for NPS; and at York, uniquely, all staff as a single constituency elect the General Academic Board (the 'lower house' of 'senate'), including the professors who must fill at least eight of the forty-odd seats, while the professors are also *ex officio* members of the Professorial Board (the 'upper house').[66] In part these variations seem to be almost accidental, but they seem also to reflect different views about the extent to which any form of 'fancy franchise' is illiberal or about the extent to which different ranks also possess separate interests that require separate representation.

NPS have also benefited from another tendency detectable in the newest charters, that of legislating for wide representation at levels lower than senate, those of faculty (or its organizational equivalent) and its component bodies. In nine charters some reference is made to entities with labels like 'school' and 'board of study', each with guarantees of wide staff participation in decision-making and with significant powers in the realms of teaching and research.[67]

By 1970, it may be said in an attempt to summarize this brief historical survey of university charters, certain important governmental principles had been accepted by the Privy Council even if they had not all been enshrined in every charter. These principles are:

1. that general university government may be substantially in the hands of staff and that junior staff should have a significant part in it;
2. that senate should have a wide area of complete independence, a veto at least on academic and senior administrative appointments, and the right of consultation in financial matters; and

---

[66] See the further discussion in Chapter IV below. By convention, however, the 'lower house' always nominates NPS members to important committee positions and to council.

[67] The nine are Bath, Bradford, East Anglia, Essex, Heriot-Watt, Salford, Stirling, Sussex and Warwick. At least one other, York, has interpreted a charter reference (to Boards of Study) in the same spirit. The general trend away from the traditional subject-department is discussed further in Chapter IV, below.

3. that it is proper, and perhaps necessary, to specify machinery of collective government at the 'subject' level.

To these may be added the most recent development, for all that it has not yet been consolidated in many charters, namely:

4. that students should have some share in general university government.

Student participation has been recognized since 1900 by seats on the Birmingham and Liverpool courts, and many charters have provided for student unions. At Belfast even before the 1908 Charter[68] students had appeared on council. After the Second World War all the ex-university colleges and North Staffordshire had students on court. The major civics began to follow suit later, e.g. Leeds in 1961. The Model Charter gave no opinion on court membership, but recognized the union. There was then an odd reversal. Except for Essex, Keele, and Kent, none of the next 'new' universities' charters legislate for either. From the appearance of the ex-CAT charters, however, these omissions are in every case repaired. In this last group may be found the first instances of formal student power; the Bradford Charter (1965) gives council the power to co-opt a student 'after considering nominations from the students'.[69] At Salford (1967) the draughtsmen appear to have sought (or at least obtained) a similar result by forbidding it.[70] These precedents were developed by Coleraine (1967), which gave the student president an *ex officio* seat, and by the Open University (1969), which reserved two seats for students elected by students, thus formally recognizing full representative participation without qualification.[71]

As a final historical post-script, note must be made of another applicant for a formal governmental role: the non-academic staff (administrators, technicians, secretaries and domestic staff) who have traditionally been regarded as employees rather than members of the universities in which they work—all the other actors mentioned hitherto are normally listed in charters as 'members'.

[68] This was in itself a carry-over from the former Queen's College. See the Queen's University, Belfast, *Calendar* for 1965, p. 23.

[69] S. 16:(1):(ix). It may be noted that this charter was approved well before the first student disturbances in this country.

[70] S. XVI: 'nor shall the President of the Students' Union of the University become an Appointed Member of Council'. This leaves it possible to co-opt him. Surrey (1966) has a similar, even less overt device (S. 14:(2):(D), last sentence).

[71] Heriot-Watt and Stirling have a form of the Scottish rectorial system, the *honorary* president of union having a seat. We have failed to enquire why he is not called Rector. At Edinburgh student participation has been extended by electing a student as Rector in 1971 and 1972.

There were one or two hints of non-academic staff participation before the 1960s, but in 1966 Loughborough specifically mentioned 'other staff'[72] on council, and Surrey felt it necessary to limit 'non-academic staff' to one seat.[73] It is, however, impossible to offer even a confident guess as to whether these are constitutional aberrations or the start of a new development.

Throughout this chapter we have confined our analysis almost entirely to the texts of university charters, to the evolution of university constitutional law. We have also focused most of our attention upon the innovations to be found in new instruments and amendments to old ones, largely ignoring the many older charters which are still little changed from their original form.[74] From our discussion little may safely be inferred either about the general position in a particular university, or indeed, about the actual practice of university government. In some universities not even the registrar is familiar with the formal rules[75], and in any case no charter provides a fully informative guide to the way in which decisions are actually taken. On the other hand charters do, in prescribing the formal membership of the major bodies, establish a measure of the *minimum* role to which the various groups may aspire. As such they are of immediate relevance. It is in any case virtually impossible to understand the present system, to which we now turn, without some knowledge of the rules as they have developed, for it is those rules which must be worked, modified, or circumvented by the people responsible for the internal government of universities.

[72] S. XIII:I:(vi).
[73] S. 14:(1):F. In a rather special case the Royal College of Art Charter includes the 'technical Instructors' as members of the college (S. 2:1).
[74] The rate of change, even of radical reformulation, has considerably increased since the mid-1960s, however.
[75] The chairman of the council of one of the ex-university colleges recalled to us how the council at its first meeting after the grant of the charter suspended one of its provisions—with doubtful legality, he feared.

Chapter III

THE CONTEMPORARY SYSTEM
IN OUTLINE

Autonomy

The universities in the United Kingdom are autonomous institutions. They are, without exception, independent corporations, able to own property, to sue and be sued, and to regulate their own affairs within the wide powers granted to them by the instruments of their incorporation. A few of the instruments are Acts of Parliament[1] whose operative part is a set of statutes, but the characteristic instrument is a Royal Charter, granted through the Privy Council, also with a set of statutes similar to those under an Act.[2] The charter proper is largely a somewhat magniloquent preamble to the statutes; and though its provisions may sometimes be of interest, it is normally to the statutes that one must turn for any detailed rules about the allocation of powers and responsibilities within the institution.

The chief formal restraints upon complete autonomy are the obligation to keep within the powers granted by these instruments; the need to obtain the permission of the Privy Council[3] for important alterations to these instruments; and the restrictions imposed by law upon the use of their endowments. Most universities are subject to visitorial enquiry[4] and all are liable to special investigation by Royal Commissions or other similar committees[5]; they are subject to the

[1] E.g. London, Durham, Newcastle and the older Scottish universities.

[2] Oxbridge have neither an Act of Parliament nor a charter, but do have a body of statutes, changes to the more important of which require the authority of the Privy Council, and which, for our purposes, are similar to the statutes of other institutions. The incorporated colleges of London University (University and King's) have statutes made by the federal senate, but other colleges (and units of the University of Wales) have their own charters.

[3] Or, where appropriate, as in Durham and the ancient Scottish universities, of Parliament. (Parliamentary authority is in any case required for transfers of property, so that amalgamations and transformations require an Act.)

[4] See Chapter V, below.

[5] Of which the most recent example is the (Robbins) Committee on Higher Education 1961-3. See its *Report* on Higher Education (Cmnd 2154 of 1963).

ordinary law of the land and ultimately, of course, like all institutions and persons, to direct interference by Parliament. Some of the ancient universities, in addition, suffer direct interference by the Government in certain appointments, as to the Regius chairs.[6]

Some of these formal restraints are not inconsiderable; for example, the universities of Oxford and Cambridge have been quite extensively, and involuntarily, reformed by Parliament, and it is said that some universities have been reluctant to propose certain classes of alterations to statutes for fear that the Privy Council might attempt to impose a minimum degree of student participation.[7]

In general, however, the formal limitations upon institutional autonomy are minimal. There is a tradition of non-interference by the State in the affairs of universities and a widespread belief in the merits of autonomy. The limitations are, in the words of most charters, 'ever construed benevolently'; those in universities who know what the formal limitations amount to in practice do not (except for some of those to be mentioned) appear to find them irksome or important. This is in large measure because these formal limitations are indirect.[8] In any case, apart from the appointments mentioned, external control is of the legal basis—charters and statutes—rather than of the actual administration.[9] Within these instruments, in their internal government, universities have a very wide degree of autonomy, financial and academic, especially in contrast to universities in many systems abroad.[10]

This formal autonomy is affected in various ways by other restraints, some of which may today exercise so direct a control on purely academic decisions[11], or be so extensive in their appearance[12]

[6] And to certain administrative appointments, notably to principalships in some ancient Scottish universities or the mastership of Trinity College, Cambridge.

[7] See *The Times*, October 13, 1970.

[8] In Scotland, however, the Royal Commissions in the nineteenth century interfered not only by statute but also directly in curricular matters. See, e.g. G. E. DAVIE: *The Democratic Intellect* (Edinburgh, 1961), and R. S. RAIT: *The Universities Commission 1889–97. A Review* (Aberdeen, 1898).

[9] *Ad hoc* interference, as by commissions, has at times involved control of administration, e.g. by requiring statements of accounts in stated forms.

[10] For a discussion of the limitations on autonomy abroad see, e.g. *University Autonomy—its meaning today* (International Association of Universities. Paris 1965), and the *Report* of the subsequent meeting of the IAU in Tokyo in the IAU *Bulletin*, supplement to Vol. XIII, No. 4, November 1965.

[11] See our discussion of the University Grants Committee in Chapter VIII, below.

[12] E.g. notably, the activity of the Comptroller and Auditor General's office. This is not, however, supposed to issue in directives, nor is the office an arm of

as to raise reasonable questions about the reality of autonomy.[13] But this is not a study of institutional autonomy, and it will be sufficient to say here that however powerful the external pressures on universities may be, they remain for the most part pressures rather than directions. The universities are still today required to make up their own minds, individually, on a great range of their activities; even where the choice may be strictly limited, it still has to be made.[14] Moreover, because new funds have been so much more available, the range of their activities and the options open to universities are today enormously greater than before the last war; thus both the amount and the importance of their internal and autonomous decision-making has at the least kept up with diminutions due to outside pressures.[15] Even the sharp reduction in the availability of new funds for some purposes since the late 1960s has of itself presented universities with very serious decisions that they must take for themselves. It is part of the conventional wisdom to believe that he who pays the piper calls the tune. But there are limitations. To start with, it is no use calling outside the piper's repertoire, and there are things some pipers will not play.[16] But in any event universities are not only pipers: they are also composers. Thus a study of internal government in isolation would still be as possible now as it ever has been, even if the worst fears now being expressed were found to be justified. Universities are in no way to be compared, governmentally, with the state secondary schools.

---

the Government, but of Parliament. Another, new, form of external pressure comes from the local planning authorities, who are not always sympathetic and who, it is sometimes feared, can be prejudiced by, e.g., student demonstrations. We have been told by members of staff that they have been asked by their vice-chancellor to moderate their political activities for this reason.

[13] See, for example, SIR MAX BELOFF, 'British Universities and the Public Purse', *Minerva*, Summer 1967. A list of forms of interference is given by Sir Sidney Caine in *British Universities: Purpose and Prospects* (Bodley Head, 1969) pp. 186–7.

[14] 'Because external circumstances, including government action, stimulated the growth of universities generally Aberdeen expanded. . . . Nevertheless the initiative in the choice of rate and direction of expansion has rested with the university.' See W. S. ANGUS: 'Growth of the University of Aberdeen', University of Aberdeen *Record*, 1967, p. 110.

[15] Sir William Mansfield Cooper has asked: 'How far was the almost unique pre-war freedom of the British universities a function of their poverty . . . ? How far was their freedom a freedom *not* to do things because they did not have the means . . . ?' *Minerva* X:2 1972, pp. 333–4. Donors' wishes have often been more restrictive than the UGC's.

[16] 'Today no university is interested in an offer to endow a Chair unless such Chair forms an integral part of its academic development programme. . . .' University of London, Principal's *Report* 1967–8, p. 13.

Types of University

By the criterion of internal governmental structure British universities may be grouped in three categories: Oxford and Cambridge; the federal universities of London and Wales; and the rest, including the constituent university colleges in Wales and the dozen or so major non-medical schools which help make up the University of London.[17]

The first groups are governed through structures which are peculiar to themselves and unlikely to be copied elsewhere. In any discussion of university government it is impossible to avoid reference to, especially, Oxford and Cambridge, but we have not attempted to make a detailed or comprehensive study of any of them.[18] A brief indication of some of their distinctive characteristics may nevertheless be useful at this stage.

Oxford and Cambridge, apart from being the oldest of the English universities, are distinguished by the governmental role of the general body of staff and the continuing importance of their colleges. The colleges still[19] play a major role in teaching, in the appointment of staff, and the admission of students, though that of the universities has considerably increased in the first two respects during the past fifty years. They also elect representatives to the main governing bodies of the university and, in Cambridge but not Oxford, the vice-chancellor is drawn (for a limited term of office) from the college heads. The continuing importance of the colleges is buttressed by their financial independence and their legal status as independent self-governing corporations.[20] The most important governmental characteristic of these two universities, however, is that the ultimate authority still lies with the legislative assembly of all the resident masters (the vast majority of whom are members of the academic staff, the remainder consisting of senior university and college officials). And, though some distinction is drawn between professorial and other academic staff in academic decision-making (especially in the natural science departments), the tradition has tended to greater equalitarianism than is generally found in other universities. Nevertheless, much that we have to say about the

---

[17] See comments at the beginning of Chapter II, above.

[18] We could not hope, in any case, to add anything of significance to the studies of the (Franks) Commission of Inquiry into the University of Oxford which reported in 1966 nor of the (Murray) Committee of Enquiry into the Governance of the University of London which reported in 1972.

[19] See our historical discussion in the previous chapter.

[20] In none of these respects do the colleges at Durham, Kent, Lancaster, and York play as significant a role.

general features of university government applies also to Oxford and Cambridge, and the differences in structure seem steadily to be lessening.[21]

The federal group today contains two institutions.[22] The older of these federations, Wales (formed in 1893), consists of widely scattered and highly autonomous institutions with poor communications between them. (The Council meets in Bloomsbury.) It probably would not continue in being if purely academic considerations were paramount[23], and it might be regarded as a confederation. Until the Charter of 1967 was granted the point of chief interest to this study was the virtual exclusion of the academic staff from the 'executive body of the University', the Council[24], an exclusion which was by then unique in these islands.

The larger of the federations, London, was formed in 1900[25]. It is large[26], and has a uniquely wide variety of constituent units, ranging from very specialized research institutes, to the large colleges or schools which closely resemble autonomous universities.[27]

[21] For example: the Oxford vice-chancellorship is now more powerful than it was, the power of laymen elsewhere is still declining, and the department or institute at Oxford and Cambridge is steadily assuming greater significance in all faculties.

[22] There were, until recently, federal situations at Durham/Newcastle and at St Andrews/Dundee.

[23] The University of Wales Commission of 1964 produced a majority in favour of independence for the constituent colleges, but the report was rejected by the overwhelmingly lay University Court.

[24] The Council was composed of a majority of laymen (or co-opted persons). The minority were appointed by the University Court, on which staff were in a small minority. The Court appointed the heads of the constituent units but not teaching staff.

[25] On the basis of an Act of 1898. The functions of the examining board known until then as the University of London were continued by the new body.

[26] In 1968-9 it listed some 44 units and an overall enrolment of 31,500 full-time students, not to mention the 33,847 registered external students.

[27] Considerable semantic confusion is caused by the fact that London and Oxford and Cambridge are often described as 'collegiate'. But there is no useful basis of comparison between them. The Oxbridge colleges today are primarily tutorial and social units, to which, certainly since the women's colleges admitted men, London has no counterpart. The major London colleges (technically called 'schools') have, for instance, various degrees of direct access to the Vice-Chancellors' Committee, their own laboratories, and their own specialized institutes and units. More important, perhaps, the London schools can have substantial control of their own first degree examinations, while they have an organization, of boards, etc., and above all of subject departments, that is recognizably appropriate to a university. The remaining smaller units of London correspond much more nearly to the specialist institutes and departments of Oxbridge, than to any college except, perhaps, to one or two specialized institutions like Nuffield or St Anthony's.

Constitutionally, it represents various rather uneasy compromises, mainly between the claims of rationalization and specialization on a unitary basis and those of the individual units for independence. In addition, however, the position of external students and the great power of the graduates have complicated the issues. The resulting constitution is highly particular and is of limited general interest except, potentially, in one respect. (It is also, 1973, in process of reform.)

This respect is that the University of London now provides, in effect, a regional Grants Committee (the Court) and a very extensive system of service and specialist support for its autonomous units. This has been built up, despite the strong centrifugal tendencies of some of the major units, partly because most of them cluster so close together geographically. Elsewhere in the country the need for similar support is being felt, and common services are slowly emerging.[28] The appearance of second universities in some towns, the formation of the polytechnics, and the likely up-grading of other institutions, will create many more clusters of important units which will have the same opportunities and needs as the London institutions. It is therefore possible that the London federation will, in time, become of immediate practical interest to others.[29]

What we have labelled the 'unitary' group is by far the largest, consisting as it does of some sixty institutions.[30] Since the bulk of our whole study is devoted to it, the outline of its system of government will be postponed until the next section. Here we will merely offer a brief account of our reasons for treating so many institutions as a single group.

Obviously there are immense differences between the various members of the unitary group in terms of, for example, their size, social and geographical environment, age, history, research activity, emphasis on different kinds of subject (arts, applied science, medicine and so on), or percentage of students in residence.[31] To most university people, moreover, the usual categories of Scottish, civic,

[28] Organization and methods units have been set up in several areas by the joint action of the universities within each region.

[29] There is a close, but not federal, link between the University of Manchester and the University of Manchester Institute of Science and Technology. They are financially separate, but academically united by cross-representation on the appropriate governing bodies. There is no 'superior' body ruling over both units. This relationship provides another possible model for regional co-operation elsewhere.

[30] See, again, our comments in Chapter II above.

[31] See, for example, the interesting analysis in JOHN KING: 'The Typology of Universities', *Higher Education Review*, Summer 1970, pp. 52–61.

major and minor redbrick, and technological convey information, if only a set of impressionistic messages about atmosphere and status. It is also meaningful to group certain charters together on a rough chronological basis, but, as we have seen, the differences between contemporary constitutions may be as significant as the similarities. As our historical survey also indicated, however, particular developments may affect all institutions in some degree, regardless of their age, and not always through formal amendment to constitutions. Today all universities seem to be subject to a new wave of change in a broadly liberal direction, and few are not (or have not recently been) engaged in a process of constitutional creation or review. As a result universities are tending to converge on a single broad governmental ideal. But, even if one were to discount this recent trend, the other differences between universities within the unitary group do not coincide with the difference in their constitutions. (Perhaps, more modestly, we should merely say that we have been unable to detect a consistent coincidence of significant governmental variations with any of the other bases of classification.)

There are, of course, many detailed differences in the systems of government to be found in the unitary group, many of which we mention in the following chapters. But the further our study progressed the more impressed we became by the broad similarities. In large and significant measure, we believe, the vast majority of university staff and students in this country are subject only to variations on a single type of internal government. To its elements we will now turn.

Government in the Unitary Group

Even within this group there are immense variations of detail, some of it important, and of nomenclature. Many of the variations of substance are noted in the relevant sections of this book, but for the remainder of our discussion we will adopt a standard terminology to refer to the main organs of government. In a Note at the end of this chapter we list a virtual glossary of titles and indicate the principal referents of our labels. But, in this section and in the subsequent discussion of the system in action, we will not complicate our account by listing on each occasion the range of bodies to which terms like 'council' or 'senate' refer. They should, therefore, be taken to mean either bodies with those names or the bodies which fill the same essential roles as council or senate. Where the context demands it we use the label in inverted commas to indicate that we are using it in this latter, functional, sense. Our choice of titles is based on those used in Owens College, Manchester, in its 1880 Charter[32] and adopted, since then, by the great majority of English and Welsh unitary universities.

The characteristic structure of government in the unitary universities has five levels, and we use them to organize our outline exposition. Right away, however, it should be emphasized that too much should not be read into the notion of a hierarchy of levels. At least in this stage of the argument 'level' should be understood to refer to something like a 'level of formal competence'. Thus, to say that a body forms, or is at, the lowest level is to signify nothing more than that it is competent to decide only for a small section of the university, which is to say, for a relatively small number of people and/or for a relatively small span of activities. It should not, in particular, be assumed that the 'higher' levels necessarily carry more authority than the 'lower' in every area of their jurisdiction, nor that decisions are necessarily taken at 'higher' levels in any sense other than mere ratification or formal endorsement. Just what the relations are between the various levels is, of course, a major theme of this study; they cannot, therefore, be explored at all fully in this initial description of the machinery of government. Our initial reference to levels is therefore in part a matter of convenience and otherwise signifies only that different bodies have a wider or narrower range within which, legally, they take the official decisions for the university.

In most universities the 'supreme governing body' is still the court.[33] The top level (in the sense mentioned) therefore consists of a large court[34] consisting of local notables, local government nominees, and representatives of various local bodies and institutions of religious, professional, and other organizations, of trade unions (recently, e.g. at Leeds and Warwick), and also of graduates, staff and, increasingly, students (and, less frequently, of non-academic staff). In size they range from the unusually small court of Newcastle or York, around fifty to sixty, to the unusually large 600-odd at Sheffield; 250 is probably the average size, with more modern instruments providing for the small bodies. Court thus provides a

[32] See Chapter II, above, p. 29.

[33] In many of the post-Sussex charters it has been relegated to a purely advisory status, and this was proposed for Birmingham by the Grimond Committee in 1972.

[34] But not, for example, in Durham or the ancient Scottish universities, where the body of graduates (supplemented by current members of staff), has the analogous, but advisory, role. The right to express an opinion is more frequently expressed by the Scottish General Councils than is usual in the Durham Convocation partly, perhaps, because they also elect several members to the Scottish courts (equivalent to the English councils; see below).

means by which usually local society may be associated with the government of the university. Court meets rarely (commonly once a year) and few attend from any distance. Even the traditional courts, though their powers are magniloquently stated ('the Supreme Governing Body . . . shall have absolute power within the University'), can usually only exercise their powers indirectly. Typically, 'control over the Senate (must be) through Council and not otherwise'.[35]

The senior executive body, however, is council; it too has a predominantly lay membership, but it is both smaller and more active than court. The Robbins Committee's investigations revealed that the numbers of members on councils in 1961-2 ranged from sixty-three at Aberystwyth and fifty-five at Sheffield to twenty-nine at Manchester and fourteen at the London School of Economics, with nine councils having a membership in the forties. The old Scottish equivalent, court, was much smaller, St Andrews being the largest at eighteen.[36] The new charters of the 1960s usually prescribe numbers in the middle thirties, with only Loughborough over forty, but with Newcastle, York, Lancaster, and Heriot-Watt below thirty. Thus English councils have been getting rather smaller.

The academic share of membership has been discussed at length in the previous chapter. Briefly, the proportion is rising from around one-fifth of the membership at the unreformed older civics to over two-fifths provided by some recent charters. Councils meet frequently enough (usually between six and ten times a year) for members to be kept informed about the main issues; even so, it works very largely through its committees. It has powers of legislative initiative, and usually of veto, as well as having access to the bureaucracy through its secretary. As we have seen, however, its legislative powers are increasingly hedged about by requirements that it take senate advice. Council's main effective role lies in its responsibility for finance and the management of the university's physical assets. This has traditionally been very much its exclusive province, and remains so despite the requirement, in some newer instruments, that senate be consulted on academic budgeting.

The third major body is senate. Its chairman is the vice-chancellor and its membership almost wholly academic.[37] It varies immensely in size, from under fifty members to over 200, as also in the extent of non-professorial staff representation. There is a clear tendency,

---

[35] See, for example, the Sheffield Charter, S. 9, and S. 12:5.
[36] See the Robbins *Report*, cited above, Appendix IV, tables 5, 7, 10, and 12.
[37] The librarian is normally a member, and occasionally an official (as at Exeter and Lancaster).

however, to move away from the virtually standard senate, to which all professors belonged *ex officio* and a few others were selected, to a body in which all staff grades are represented, but not in proportion to their numbers, and in which only the holders of certain offices (not ranks) are *ex officio* members.[38] Even where the charter does not make explicit legislative reference to the fact, senate is generally regarded as the supreme authority on academic questions other, usually, than the making of appointments. Like council it usually makes extensive use of committees in exercising its authority.

The next level consists, typically, of the faculties. These groupings of related subjects usually comprise all the teachers in those subjects. As a body each faculty meets for advisory discussions, but its direct powers are usually limited to the election of the dean[39] or of representatives to council or senate.[40] The executive of the faculty is the faculty board, which normally includes a substantial proportion of non-professorial staff. The powers of the faculty boards are formally advisory to senate or delegated by it and extend mainly to matters affecting the courses and examinations in the faculty, including the appointment of examiners. A few, however, may also advise on staff appointments[41] or elect members of senate.[42] There may also be similar sub-faculty bodies within a faculty, usually set up by ordinance.

Traditionally, the next step beyond the sub-faculty has been to the department, a body very seldom legislated for at all, and left wholly to the discretion of its professor, who was responsible for the development and conduct of all teaching and research in his subject. This is still the case in most, and especially in the older institutions, but the situation is changing and difficult to categorize.[43]

In many of the newest universities the organization of teaching and curricula is left, below the senate level, to bodies with labels like 'school' and 'board of studies' rather than faculties and departments. No standard usage for these labels has yet developed. The purpose behind these changes seems to be, first, to break down the barriers which have developed between the traditional subjects and faculties

---

[38] The *ex officio* members are likely to include, normally, the deputy or pro-vice-chancellor(s), deans, and heads of departments. The membership and powers have been discussed in Chapter II above and the subjects are returned to in Chapter IV below.

[39] E.g. at Birmingham, where the deans sit on council.

[40] E.g. at Liverpool; S. 24.

[41] E.g. at Liverpool; S. 27:7.

[42] E.g. at Newcastle; S. 25:1(b).

[43] The more modern developments were touched on in the historical survey in Chapter II and are further discussed in Chapter IV.

by setting up new combinations and, second, to legislate for greater non-professorial participation at the lowest level of government.[44] It is not yet clear, however, how far these new institutions in fact constitute governmental innovations when compared with some of the older faculties and departments (and especially with those which have also provided for wider participation in taking their decisions).

Beyond, or beside, these 'levels' we have three university-wide organizations. The first of these, traditionally, is the convocation, the organization of alumni (or graduates as they mostly are today). It is sufficient to say here that the graduates have little organizational significance in the unitary sector.[45] It is, however, worth remarking, in the light of the development of the assembly which we discuss below, that in many places staff in all grades have for long been heavily represented on convocation, and could probably have dominated its proceedings had they wished.

Next there is the student organization, usually the union or students' representative council, whose role is increasing. Despite the immense amount written about the student movement, little of it concerns government, and less of it concerns the actual practice of student involvement[46], but it is increasingly common to find students represented on council, many committees, and senate.

Finally, an essentially modern development, found chiefly at the newer universities, is the assembly of all staff.[47] This may be said to symbolize the transition towards a view of the staff as a group of equals, a view which has already been mentioned in our historical chapter. Its functions are very limited (it may have some electoral rights[48]) but the analogy with the Oxford Congregation is obvious enough. This, however, is only to list the main actors; for the remainder of the book we will examine their roles in more detail.

Note on Terminology

As we have already warned, we have adopted a uniform terminology for our account of university government despite the fact that no

[44] But at one large traditional university we were assured that the term 'school' had been adopted mainly for its cosmetic effect in the prospectus.

[45] They often have power to elect to council and court, however.

[46] But for an authoritative history see SIR ERIC ASHBY and MARY ANDERSON: *The Rise of the Student Estate in Britain* (Macmillan, 1970) pp. 51–6. See also ANNE DENNIS: *The Changing Role of Students*, University of London Ph.D. Thesis (Economics) 1969, and R. B. EUSTACE: 'Student Participation', in M. L. SHATTOCK (ed.): *University Administration in a Period of Expansion* (British Council, 1970).

[47] For its earliest appearances, see Chapter II, above.

[48] E.g. at Aston, where the Assembly elect four members of Council, and at Warwick, where the election is to six seats on Senate.

such uniformity is to be found among the sixty and more institutions with which we are concerned. In this Note we set out the terms we use along with their close or approximate equivalents. The list of equivalents includes the major examples but is not necessarily exhaustive.

1. *Constitutions*. *Charters* is used to refer to all the main documentary constitutions or instruments of government. It is normally used to denote both the charters themselves and the associated statutes. Under this heading are also included, when appropriate, Acts of Parliament (for example, in the cases of the universities of Durham and London) and the Statutes at Oxford and Cambridge. Specific reference will be made, where necessary, to subsidiary rules like ordinances and regulations.[49]

2. *Organs of government*. *Court* corresponds to Convocation at Aston and Heriot-Watt, Conference at Stirling, and General Convocation at Strathclyde. In certain respects parallel functions are performed by, for example, the Governors of Bedford College, Imperial College, and the London School of Economics (all of them schools of the University of London), and by the General Councils at the ancient Scottish universities.

Council corresponds to Court at the Scottish universities and the Senate at Queen's University, Belfast. It approximates, functionally, to Hebdomadal Council at Oxford, Council of the Senate at Cambridge, Standing Committee at the London School of Economics, and Court at the federal universities of London and Wales.

Senate corresponds to the Academic Council at Belfast and Stirling and to the Professorial and General Academic Boards at York. It approximates to the General Board at Oxford and Cambridge, Academic Council at the University of London and, at LSE to the Professorial and Academic Boards.

Faculty and faculty board refer, respectively, to the whole body of staff and to the executive committees within each faculty. Where we wish to refer also to the 'new' *schools* and *boards of study*, etc., we refer, where appropriate, to *faculty-level* bodies; and similarly with *departments* and *subject-level* bodies.

Assembly (of most or all academic staff) corresponds to Academic Congress at Strathclyde, Heriot-Watt, and Salford, to Academic Council at Dundee, and to the Academic Staff Association at City. It is the approximate counterpart of General Board at Manchester, Academic Board at LSE (but see also under 'senate' above), Congregation at Oxford, and Regent House at Cambridge.

[49] Ordinances may normally be made by council only, regulations by any authorized body, but usually by senate.

Convocation (of graduates and some or all staff) is used to refer collectively to bodies which are only roughly similar, but which are sufficiently unimportant, governmentally, for the differences to be of small consequence in this context. The bodies include Convocation at Oxford, Senate at Cambridge, the Graduates Council at Dundee, the Graduates and Former Students Association at Strathclyde, and General Council at the ancient Scottish universities (but see, also, under 'court' above).[50]

3. *Officers and Officials*. *Chancellor* is equivalent to the President at the University of Manchester Institute of Science and Technology and to the Patron at Birkbeck College.

Chairman of council is the equivalent of the President at Reading and Liverpool and, until 1927, of the Vice-Chancellor at Birmingham.

Vice-chancellor is the equivalent of the President and Vice-Chancellor at Belfast; the Vice-Chancellor and Principal at Birmingham since 1927 (Principal until 1927); the Principal and Vice-Chancellor at the ancient Scottish universities, Dundee, and Heriot-Watt; Principal at the other Scottish universities and many of the London schools (colleges); and to the Rector, Director, Provost, and Master at, respectively, Imperial College, LSE, University College, and Birkbeck College, London.

Assistant vice-chancellor approximates to the Deputy Principal at Birmingham and the Vice-Principal at Bradford, These are full-time administrative posts which should be distinguished from that of *deputy*- or *pro-vice-chancellor*, a post filled, part-time and for a limited period, by a member of the academic staff elected by 'senate'.

The bureaucracy is the professional full-time administrative staff normally headed by the *registrar* (sometimes, secretary) or jointly by him and the *bursar*, the senior financial official. We refer to all members of the bureaucracy as *officials*. None of these should be confused with the *administration*, a term used to include all those who administer the affairs of the university; it therefore includes certain lay members of 'council', the 'vice-chancellor', and many academics as well as the bureaucracy.[51]

[50] In many universities the label of *congregation* is applied to a wholly formal body convened for the conferment of degrees. (The term seems to have been taken from the Ancient House of Congregation at Oxford.)

[51] See the discussion at the beginning of Chapter VII, below.

Chapter IV

TAKING ACADEMIC DECISIONS

The secular trend, we have argued, is towards increasing academic self-government especially, but by no means only, on academic issues. This means that the academic staff expect to decide, without serious risk of internal veto or contradiction by non-academics, a wide range of questions which may be labelled 'academic'. These include questions like: Who shall be admitted as a student, awarded a degree, appointed to the staff, or promoted, and according to what standards of judgement? What courses will be provided, in what subjects, by whom, for whom, and leading to what qualification? and, what research projects will be undertaken, by whom, and subject to what provisos? Decisions on these questions are, of course, subject to over-riding constraints imposed, above all, by the availability of finance. But within these limits the power, that is the ability effectively to decide, rests essentially with the academic staff of the university with respect both to policy and to particular cases. It does not rest equally with all of them, however, nor are all such decisions taken by the same individuals or groups or by the same procedures. In this chapter, therefore, we offer a somewhat abstract portrayal of the governmental processes. We will, this is to say, focus on decision-making by academics about academic matters largely in abstraction from other actors and from other kinds of decision.

The traditional Department and Faculty

Knowledge is frequently said to be a 'seamless web' and its professional guardians are as frequently referred to as members of a 'community of scholars'. In fact, of course, the 'web' is divided and sub-divided into disciplines, subjects, and yet further specialized areas of interest, and the 'community' is divided not merely between universities and other educational or research institutions but also, within them, into groups and sub-groups bearing titles like 'faculty', 'school' and 'department'. Academics, even if we confine ourselves to those who work in British universities, tend consequently to think of themselves both as members of a particular academic community and as members of a particular professional group consisting of all architects, historians, geneticists, or the like. These two memberships may involve conflicting ambitions and forms of behaviour, most commonly (if not wholly accurately) described in terms of the opposing pulls of teaching and research. But the demands of the two memberships also overlap, for the university is organized, at the teaching level, into similar disciplinary groups. These groups, especially where the traditional single-subject department is found, constitute the building blocks in the great majority of British universities today (somewhat less so in Oxford, Cambridge, and those newer foundations which have striven consciously for academic and organizational innovation). We will therefore look first at the traditional departmental system.

The new entrant into the profession will normally be appointed as lecturer in Spanish or electrical engineering and also as lecturer in the department of Spanish or electrical engineering. Thereafter, even if he moves to another university, he is unlikely to move except to another department of a similar title. Once appointed the recruit will find his academic existence largely defined by 'his' department. It is there that, among other things, he will first learn the ropes, will have the most intense and constant interaction with colleagues, and will find the students with whom, in all probability, he has the closest contact. It is within the department, therefore, that he must first establish himself as a scholar and teacher. It is from amongst his colleagues that the proposals must originate for the confirmation of his appointment after initial probation and, later, for promotion, just as his reputation among the profession will spread, initially, from his colleagues and students. Through the department, this is to say, the academic is related both to his university and to his section of his profession.

To complete this picture of the overlap of memberships at this level, it is necessary only to add that the success of its individual members, whether that success is measured in terms of good teaching, distinguished publications, or administrative competence, will in some degree be reflected in the standing of the department as a whole, both within the university and in the academic world at large. Tension is not thereby avoided, however. Quite apart from questions of individual temperament, or of the fact that different departments and universities place different weights upon different kinds of performance, it is still the case that publication is the principal route to recognition outside (and thus to mobility between institutions) and that teaching and administrative skills are likely to be appreciated most fully in a man's current university. Tension is likely to exist also between departments and their universities; a departmental policy designed to increase its reputation within the discipline need not coincide with university policy. Politically speaking, as we have already pointed out[1], decision-making within the university must thus take account of the dual call on a scholar's loyalties if the university is not to risk losing (or failing to recruit) the individuals upon whom its work and reputation must depend.

Where they exist, therefore, departments tend to be the focal point for the intellectual life of the academic staff in any university. (To a somewhat lesser extent the same may be said about students, given the prevalance of the single-subject honours degree.)[2] And the larger the university, the greater the role of the department, for it becomes more difficult (and possibly less necessary) to meet 'outsiders'.[3] For most students and many members of staff, indeed, it may not be an exaggeration to say that the subject-department *is* the university. And, in the sense that the job of the university is the actual carrying on of teaching and research, the subject-level bodies, such as departments, are the essential university: everything else is no more than a supporting service or a practical convenience.

Departments are also of major administrative and governmental importance. Most obviously each department decides, subject only to general approval by other university bodies (on which it will be represented), how it will organize its own work and how best to utilize its own resources of time, labour, equipment and money for teaching and research.[4] But it is not only for the academic staff that it is an administrative unit. Officials find some such subject-level organization to be essential.[5] Established posts, equipment, secretaries, travel grants and so on are frequently allocated on a depart-

---

[1] In Chapter I, above.

[2] It is a common complaint amongst students taking joint degrees that they have no proper 'home', no single reliable source of concern and decision.

[3] In the staff clubs or senior common rooms of some of the largest universities, it is often possible to guess a man's subject entirely from the company he keeps (and even, sometimes, from the table at which he sits).

[4] Collective, departmentally organized, research is less common in subjects outside the natural sciences.

[5] A memorandum from a young official at one of the non-departmental universities asked: 'Who are we to assign responsibility for the new calculators to? Presumably they are not for the Professor personally, but for all the statisticians. Would it not be convenient to call them something like "department"?' Soon afterwards, as it happened, his final question was answered in the affirmative.

mental basis, directly, or indirectly through a faculty structure, and the department is responsible for the proper use of the resources put at its disposal. In the application by each university of the various ratios prescribed by the University Grants Commission—for example, those between staff and students or between senior and junior ranks of staff—the general tendency is again to use the department as the significant unit.

Finally, it is the department that serves as the basic unit of representation in academic government, it is the university equivalent (depending upon the national system with which comparison is being made) of the ward, the electoral district, the commune, or the party cell. But it is only the electoral equivalent—in other respects it is much more important than national political grass-root organizations.

The department is more important than these national constituencies only in part because of its greater immediate responsibilities, its 'front-line' role in organizing and pursuing the essential university purposes of teaching and research. Underlying the status of the department is its crucial characteristic of being authoritative in its own field of learning. In areas where compatibility with general university policy or resources is relevant, departmental initiatives or decisions must be reviewed and validated by 'higher' authority.[6] But their academic authority brings with it a substantial degree of academic autonomy and, in the evolution of university decisions, ensures that immense care is normally taken to seek the views of each subject. There is an important sense, therefore, in which the 'higher' bodies seek validation from the 'lower'. Whatever the precise boundaries of departmental autonomy, its existence makes of every university a 'federal' structure rather than a strongly centralized system.[7] Academic freedom, if only in the sense of mutual respect for the integrity of each subject organization, is thus a principle relevant to relations within the university and not only to a university's attempts to protect itself from external pressures.

To talk thus of 'the department' is liable to mislead unless one also examines its internal organization. The most important feature of this is that the members are not equal in rank, status or power. Not only will there be ranks (of professor, reader, senior lecturer, and

---

[6] See the warnings above, in Chapter III, about the need for care in the use of terms like 'higher' and 'lower'.

[7] Cf. the verdict of A. H. HALSEY and MARTIN TROW: The British Academics (Faber and Faber, 1971) at pp. 111–12: 'It is not too fanciful to see the modern university as a federation of departments ... with faculty boards and the Senate as mechanisms for negotiation and arbitration of their divergent interests'.

lecturer), but normally the one professor (or one of several) will be designated as head of department.[8] And although, as we will see, recent years have witnessed some diminution in his position of un-challenged eminence, he remains, nevertheless, *the* key figure in his own department and, largely as a result, *a* key figure throughout university government. To this day, he continues to wield a measure of real power as well as (in part consequentially) a pervasive in-fluence.[9] What are the main bases of his ability to take or mould decisions? What, in other words, are his principal political resources?

The first resource consists of the formal obligations placed upon the head by the university. A senate paper from a southern university emphasizes that the head 'is formally responsible to Senate and Council for the working of the department and for the necessary decisions that are taken, whether directly by himself or through delegation by other members of the departmental staff', and con-tinues by re-emphasizing that 'the responsibility for decisions laid on the professor . . . by Council, through the terms of his or her ap-pointment, cannot be devolved even though the making of certain decisions may be . . . delegated . . .'.[10] In another, more northerly,

---

[8] Some small departments may have as their head a member of the non-professorial staff if the unit is not considered of sufficient size or importance to warrant a professorial appointment. Such a head will lack many of the attributes of power normally associated with the position—one consequence being that the department's bargaining power within the university may also suffer. In the discussion that follows we will concentrate upon the role of the professorial head.

[9] From the huge literature on the subjects of power and influence there is perhaps no more apposite a pair of definitions than those offered (in part with deliberate reference to university affairs) by Lord Beveridge in his autobiographi-cal *Power and Influence* (Hodder and Stoughton, 1953). He defines them thus, on page 3: 'Power . . . means ability to give to other men orders enforced by sanctions, by punishment or *by control of rewards*; a man has power when he can mould events by an exercise of will. . . . Influence . . . means changing the actions of others by persuasion, means appeal to reason or to emotions other than fear or greed; the instruments of influence are words, spoken or written; if the influence is to be for good, *it must rest on knowledge*' (our emphasis). But influence is greater for its resting partly upon a measure of power.

[10] Compare the decision of another senate which, having decided that heads must hold regular meetings of the staff of their departments, went on to point out that 'the Head of the Department will remain responsible for the decisions and recommendations which must be made by the Department and he will not be bound by any vote taken or opinion expressed in any Departmental meeting'. Such a formal responsibility is, of course, compatible with the spirit of a recom-mendation by another university committee to the effect that 'if there is substantial disagreement within a department on some major issue of academic policy we think that the head of that department should inform the relevant (faculty or senate) committee of this fact when he makes a submission to it on behalf of his department'.

university it has been agreed that 'a Head of Department is responsible through the Vice-Chancellor to the Governing Bodies of the University for the standard of teaching and for the promotion of research in an individual subject area'. This document continues by stressing some of the implications of this responsibility: 'It is appropriate for a Head of Department to be in charge of the allocation of staff and other resources, subject to . . . the budget constraint, determined by planning decisions of the University, and the academic programme recommended by the relevant (bodies) . . .'. The professorial head of department thus has the formal backing of the university at least in so far as he acts within the terms of reference of his appointment.[11]

Secondly, not only does a professorial head of department have the normal security of tenure (comparable to that of a judge or civil servant), but he has escaped from most of the pressures for promotion. A chair, in other words, provides the departmental head with a 'safe seat' from which to take decisions.

Thirdly, the head of department possesses the power of patronage (if the term may be used without any necessarily pejorative connotation). This is not unlimited: for junior appointments to his department his selection must formally be endorsed by others even if it will rarely be rejected, while for more senior ones he must normally carry a university committee with him. But the main initiative is the head's, and it is virtually unthinkable that any appointment would be made without his positive recommendation. A similar situation obtains with respect to internal promotions. His proposals will, admittedly, more frequently be turned down by the university, for example, on financial grounds; but here too the initiative is still his, and his recommendations will carry special weight. Again, a member of his staff will almost invariably cite the head as a referee when applying for other posts and will need his support in seeking money for research, while outside requests for authors, lecturers and examiners will commonly come first to the head of department. There are strong conventions designed to ensure that these powers are exercised fairly, and most professors seem to strive for impartiality. Nevertheless their possession cannot but affect the head's relations with his colleagues and thus constitute a significant source of leverage—although their precise importance will obviously vary with the availability of alternative patrons and

---

[11] Both these universities, incidentally, are committed to the view that heads should discharge their responsibilities on the basis of as wide consultation within the department as possible; the documents quoted may therefore be taken as laying down the minimum definition of a head's constitutional powers.

employers, while their extent will vary with the head's own reputation.

The head of department is, fourthly, generally accepted as the chief spokesman for his department within the university, and possibly also its fiercest champion. In the great majority of universities he is an *ex officio* member of senate and, where relevant, of his faculty board, and is always deeply involved in the negotiations for departmental finance. This constitutes a political resource within his department at least in the sense that the success of a colleague's project may thus be crucially dependent on the enthusiasm, as well as the skill, with which the head supports it.

Fifthly, as head and as spokesman, he inevitably becomes a centre of communications between the department and the external world and thus better-informed than his departmental colleagues. To 'know the ropes' is a means of acting with greater effectiveness. This tends to increase the dependence of colleagues upon the head in the furtherance of their initiatives and thus, in turn, swell the flow of information to and through the head.

Sixthly, and in some degree serving to confer legitimacy upon his whole ruling position, is the fact that he will normally have been appointed in virtue of his superior scholarly achievements and professional competence. To the extent that he in fact is learned in his subject (as well as experienced in university affairs), he will have an authority of particular relevance to his immediate colleagues. If, in addition, he happens to be a good administrator, then he is likely to have a significant 'credit balance' of loyalty on which to draw in carrying out his responsibilities and exercising his power.[12]

Once serving as head, finally, he is the more likely to be invited to hold office in professional organizations, serve on all manner of committees, internal and external, or otherwise undertake tasks which may serve still further to increase his prestige and his ability to help his own staff. The power of the professorial head thus rests upon a set of mutually enhancing resources rather than upon any single factor.[13]

The conjunction of formal responsibilities, political resources, and the work of day-to-day departmental administration[14] means that

---

[12] When a professor has not lived up to his early promise, lack of this 'credit' can produce a most unhappy and discontented department.

[13] The non-professorial head of a small department may lack only some of these resources (e.g. status, some forms of patronage, and, in some universities, an assured seat on senate), but his remaining resources will also be weakened. See p. 62 above, f.n. 8.

[14] Which will include allocating secretarial time between other members of the department as well as paper-work, correspondence, student problems and other such tasks which do not bear directly on the political relations amongst members of staff.

much of the autonomy of the department has coincided rather closely with the autonomy of the professorial head. This coincidence may be lessening today when the trend (about which we have more to say below) is toward a more collective style of decision-making; but the professorial head of department remains one of the most important actors in university government.

It may here be objected that the most important element in the relationship between a head and his department is the head's own personal qualities. That the personality of any head is important we would not deny. It may, indeed, make an immense difference to the whole atmosphere and style of a department as well as materially affecting the extent to which it 'gets its own way' within the university. But the importance of any one person is dependent on the institutional environment and in particular on the nature of the body which he heads. The respect accorded to heads of department may be as much to the office as to the person. In universities, as elsewhere, those on whose behalf a person speaks may be as important to the listener as who is speaking. It must be conceded, however, that serious personal weaknesses in a head may both demoralize his department and undermine his own position. When a head does thus forfeit his authority, however, he is increasingly likely[15] to find himself relieved of some or all of his responsibility or, more rarely, to resign. The emphasis here, as elsewhere within the book, is therefore upon the general context rather than upon individual peculiarities.

To complete this account of the traditional department we must look at the faculty structures into which departments normally are grouped and which complement the department organizationally. Indeed from the point of view of a senate, faculties may be of greater formal importance than the departments, if only because business from the latter usually comes before senate through (or from) the appropriate faculty board. To use the faculties as a channel of communication with the individual subjects (as well as independent initiators of business) is both an administrative convenience, especially in the larger universities, and a device normally justified on the ground that members of the same faculty are more competent than others to co-ordinate and appraise the activities of the constituent departments.

Organizationally, each faculty board usually consists of all heads of department and professors, plus, sometimes, all readers and senior

---

[15] Because of the modern trends towards the appointment of more than one professor in a department and the other changes which we discuss below, all of which make it easier to 'defuse' a critical situation than used to be the case.

C

lecturers, as permanent *ex officio* members, along with no more than an equal number of other members of staff, supplemented, where appropriate, by the heads of related centres of institutes and by others whose work may be closely linked to that of the faculty. In the larger universities a board may easily have more than a hundred members and commonly will have fifty or above. The board is chaired by a dean who serves part time, is usually drawn from the ranks of the professoriate, and may be assisted in his administrative work by one or more sub-deans (frequently drawn from the ranks of the non-professorial staff).[16] Increasingly, the work of the boards is assisted (or complicated) by full Faculty meetings attended by all but the most junior members of the affiliated departments, but rarely having the power to do more than seek information and tender advice.

A department may belong to more than one faculty, but the underlying assumption is that departments should be grouped on the basis of some academic kinship which they do not share with every other in the university. It may be that they provide courses which together constitute the preparation for a specific profession or vocational qualification (as with faculties of law, medicine or theology); or that they are believed to teach complementary subjects (as in a faculty of arts); or that their methods and data are closely interconnected (as with the faculties of natural and possibly social sciences). In any case it is assumed that they will draw upon the same group of students, build upon similar bases of pre-university education, and be able to comprehend each other's work sufficiently to justify the common admission of students, regulation of examinations, and design of broad degree structures.

In general the tasks of deans and faculty boards extend beyond those of acting as a channel of communication between departments and other governing elements within the university and of providing common services for their members.[17] They also serve as the embodiments of the 'larger view', but an informed one, on the proposals and activities of each department. Thus, although there are considerable variations in the closeness with which faculty boards and deans involve themselves in departmental questions, it is usual for them to participate in the appointment and promotion processes, to review (and not merely to transmit with formal approval) the content of new

---

[16] In some of the professional faculties, and especially in medicine, the load may be such as to call for a permanent dean who may be virtually a full-time 'official', though his background is likely to be academic.

[17] Although one former vice-chancellor was wont to insist that 'a faculty is an administrative convenience—only!'

courses (in greater or lesser detail), the methods and conduct of examining, and the allocation of research supervisors, and carefully to appraise any proposed new venture. To some extent, of course, these functions arise naturally from the desirability of ensuring that students receive comparable treatment, and are educated to comparable levels, throughout a faculty, or of trying to secure roughly equal conditions of work for members of staff; but as we have implied, faculty boards also act in some degree on behalf of senate in co-ordinating the work of the departments.

In most universities, furthermore, dean or boards also serve as budgetary units, assisting both in the preparation of claims for finance, and less frequently, in the allocation of resources.[18] When, moreover, universities talk of achieving or maintaining a proper academic 'balance', it is normally a balance between faculties that they have in mind. But, in this respect as in the others, faculty is essentially an intermediary body—a provincial level of government, one might say—exercising authority either on behalf of others (senate on one side, the departments on the other) or interstitially. Since most of its business, apart from the straight administration of the common services it renders to its members, originates elsewhere, in the departments or in senate and the central university administration, the ultimate authority for all decisions lies with these other organs. In one university a professor told us that he and the other professors rarely attended meetings of their faculty board: 'I can leave that to my juniors and the dean; if necessary I can always block a decision in my own department or fight it at senate, but no really important decisions are ever taken in faculty'. This view is probably untypical, but its judgement upon the relative importance of faculty would be widely accepted as a reasonably good caricature.

In one other respect the faculty structure is of importance. The faculties are the constituencies for election or appointment to university committees and governing bodies, whether these be senate itself, major committees of senate, or committees of deans charged with general political and planning functions.

This system of, as it might be labelled, department-faculty government is not universal in British universities, nor has it been free from criticism. But certain advantages may be claimed for this traditional

[18] Practice varies widely in this area. In Birmingham, for example, faculties have extensive responsibilities in these areas. Elsewhere, on the other hand, the faculties (while serving as accounting units for the university) may do little more than co-ordinate departmental claims for finance. Commonly, the faculty board structure serves as a convenient framework within which informal meetings of professorial heads of department make important allocation decisions, by agreeing on a 'carve-up' of available money or new teaching positions.

form of organization. To group kindred subjects, it may be argued, is to ensure that the degree of supervision necessary for consistency and co-operation will be exercised by sympathetic and by more rather than less understanding colleagues. By combining the subjects also strengthen their voice and bargaining power within the university as a whole. At the basic subject level, moreover, fellow professionals will naturally seek one another out and their competence, it is arguable, will be greater for the fact that one person bears a clear responsibility for a subject's vitality and development. It has been said that it is the job of a departmental head to keep 'freshness in the teaching'[19]; and many feel that such a job is even less likely to be performed adequately by a committee than by a specially chosen individual. Nevertheless, most of the newest foundations 'were highly conscious of the separatist and narrowing dangers of powerful and isolated departments when they experimented with new school and faculty structures'[20] and have departed from it nominally or in more important respects. It is clear too, that the founders of these universities were influenced by the most serious academic criticism, namely, that the traditional system hindered innovation and imposed excessive barriers in the way of new subjects or of research and teaching that attempted to straddle department and faculty boundaries.

One result of the system of departmental organization is that the teachers of a 'new' branch of a subject frequently find it difficult to expand and develop unless they are permitted to set up a new and independent department. This is because, unless by chance the head of their present department shares their particular special interest, their case for resources may not be made with sufficient strength at the university level and they may lack the scope they seek both in teaching and research, for their expansion will be in direct competition with the rest of their department. Once independent, however, they can argue their own case for university funds and may find it easier to attract research grants from outside. But, precisely because recognition as an independent department makes it easier for a subject to develop, the demand for that recognition will encounter opposition at the faculty level from the existing departments most likely to suffer from its competition. Thus, it can be argued, the structure is an inherently conservative force.[21]

---

[19] 'JAMES DUNDONALD' (pseud.): *Letters to a Vice-Chancellor* (Arnold, 1962) p. 109.

[20] HALSEY and TROW: *op. cit.* p. 112.

[21] Understandably, new departments are most easily established at times of rapid overall growth.

Some of the sins allegedly inherent in 'departmentalism', however, are rather to be attributed to the exercise of faculty supervision. Faculties rest on assumptions about the common characteristics of their member departments, and departments claim to embody a unique competence within their own subject: these two principles conflict or, to put the point more moderately, it is within a faculty meeting that the department's claim to autonomy is weakest. It is there, rather than on senate, that others will feel competent to challenge, judge, and, if need be, veto innovations. It is there, too, that there may be the greatest incentive to do so, lest the innovation be regarded as a precedent in the faculty. When, in particular, subjects wish to develop in ways which emphasize their differences from their faculty bed-fellows, the need for faculty approval may become an intolerable brake. It is for this reason, among others, that groups of departments will, on occasion, attempt to form a new faculty or sub-faculty—and, in doing so, run into much the same problems as does the attempt to form a new department.[22]

Other criticism of the departmental structure properly focuses on the power of the professorial head as the source of rigidity and arbitrariness. One-man rule is often the source of effective and rapid change, yet the criticism has weight, as a few examples may make clear. In one of the older universities there was general agreement on the need for separate chairs of modern and mediaeval history and the autonomous development of economic and constitutional history—except on the part of the single professor of history. By exploiting his authority on faculty and senate he was able to block these developments until his retirement. One of the chairs subsequently created was filled by a former member of the department, himself a leading critic of his conservative and autocratic predecessor. Shortly after he took up his new responsibilities, his former peers (now his junior colleagues) found, on reading the new edition of the university's prospectus, that the whole structure of the degree, and hence their own teaching commitments, had been transformed. The whole process, which included securing the approval of faculty board, was completed without their having had any inkling that reform was being considered, let alone their being consulted.

The variety of practices, and their dependence (in many institutions) on the preference of the individual head, is well illustrated by

[22] The most obvious recent examples are found in the lengthy and sometimes bitter disputes which, in more than one university, have preceded the formation of new faculties of social sciences from departments formerly contained within a faculty of arts. Other cases have, however, occurred in the legal and medical fields.

a survey of departmental organization carried out among non-professorial staff at another university by the local branch of the Association of University Teachers. While only one department did not meet regularly as a group many kept no minutes, most meetings were entirely for purposes of discussion or information and not actually to decide, and in few was there any discussion of general university policy or of finance. Most respondents reported that proposed examination questions were often changed by the head of department without consultation. Interestingly, a number of respondents expressed extreme anxiety lest their answers be traced back to them, in some cases to the point of refusing even to identify their own department (thus rendering their replies virtually useless). This attitude does not amount to evidence of tyranny by a head of department; nevertheless one of the most striking features of the survey is this demonstration of anxiety about the possible use of arbitrary academic power.[23]

School, Board of Study, and the 'new' Department

Before the wave of new constitutions in the 1960s the only indigenous alternative pattern of faculty and subject organization was that to be found in Oxford and Cambridge. There the division of responsibilities between colleges and university, whereby the colleges taught for university-run examinations but appointed their own staff, had led to a system in which the main subject areas were defined by the examination rubrics (known as 'schools' at Oxford) and in which the generality of teachers played a greater governmental role than in other universities.[24]

The Oxbridge pattern has thus escaped the criticisms of professorial autocracy and excessive departmentalism levied at other institutions. Not, it must be noted, that it thereby escapes all the weaknesses alleged to exist elsewhere. In particular it has not demonstrated greater flexibility nor a greater readiness to innovate or to take speedy decisons. On the contrary, change seems to be even more difficult in these universities than in most others.[25] No university with the possible exception of London has been subject to as

[23] The survey was completed in the late 1960s.

[24] See the brief accounts in Chapters II and III above at pp. 26-7 and 48-9.

[25] Professor H. Butterfield, for example, has claimed that 'in the older universities . . . those who set out to remodel the whole pattern of the syllabus often find that mountainous labour and tedious controversy produce only meagre and marginal results' (*The Universities and Education Today*, Routledge and Kegan Paul, 1962, p. 110). Lord Annan remarked that 'the agonies of paralysis produced by this system have to be seen to be believed' (*Encounter*, June 1963, p. 12).

many Royal Commissions and other official investigations in order to overcome internal resistances to reform. And, after all, it was experience of the University of Cambridge that led Francis Cornford to produce his caustic account of academic obstructiveness and of such tactics as appeal to the 'Principle of Unripe Time'.[26] Nevertheless it seems clear that admiration of this model combined with criticisms of the traditional department-faculty structure to inspire some of the variant structures in Sussex (especially) and elsewhere.[27]

Sussex has established a system of schools which have no departmental underpinning. But in many respects they are more like traditional faculties, or even departments, if with different subject components, than they are like an Oxford honours school. Each school is headed by a dean, who is also a subject professor, but who in some ways is much more powerful than deans elsewhere. He exercises powers in the spheres of appointment, promotions, academic administration, and planning which are comparable, throughout his school, to those exercised by a professorial head within his department. In the natural sciences the general resemblance to a department is very marked.[28] But outside the natural sciences, it is more common for a subject to be taught in more than one school than it is for a department to belong to more than one faculty. Since, moreover, the schools devolve the running of individual courses to individuals or small committees, the structure facilitates (or even encourages) teaching and research across the traditional faculty and subject boundaries.[29] Under the system members of staff are, however, still appointed as lecturers in or professors of a particular

[26] See F. M. CORNFORD: *Microcosmographia Academica: Being a Guide for the Young Academic Politician* (Bowes and Bowes, 1908, reprinted 1964). To be fair, one must remember that similar accounts have been offered of politics elsewhere by, e.g. Machiavelli, Bacon, and Sir Henry Taylor. See, too, the Preface to the 1964 edition by W. K. C. Guthrie.

[27] Something between a quarter and a third of all university teachers are graduates of Oxbridge, and the proportion is higher in the arts and social studies. See the figures quoted in HALSEY and TROW: *op. cit.* pp. 225–6. The proportion of the initial senior appointments in Sussex which went to Oxbridge people was more than double this national figure.

[28] Lord Fulton told the Franks Commission, 'We have got the laboratories, of course, and someone has to be responsible for them . . . (but) we do not use the word department in order to encourage ourselves in well-doing' (Oral evidence, O.14, p. 8).

[29] Hence the university's claim to have 'redrawn the map of learning'. See D. DAICHES, ed.: *The Idea of a New University* (Deutsch, 1964), especially at pp. 60–80. On p. 68 the influence of such Oxford Schools as 'Greats' is explicitly acknowledged. On the new universities' experiments in general see H. J. PERKIN: *Innovation in Higher Education. New Universities in the United Kingdom* (OECD, 1969), pp. 145–9.

subject, and by 1970 the university had been forced to give official status to the hitherto informal subject meetings, permitting them, for example, to submit proposals directly to the schools.

The other new universities have also departed, in one or more respects, from the traditional pattern. Lancaster, Essex, and East Anglia retained the department, but have dispensed with faculties, although the latter two have substituted a series of Sussex-like schools. Kent and Warwick made no formal provision for departments, but set up faculties or schools and boards of study (meaning quite different things by the latter).[30] In York there were established boards of study (one for each examination rubric), but neither school nor faculty, so that as in Lancaster there are no intermediary organizations between the boards and 'senate'. Bradford and some of the other former colleges of advanced technology also use the language of school and board of study; but Brunel has departments grouped into faculty-like schools and Bradford's boards of study have deans. The variations are numerous; but everywhere the pulls towards departmentalism have asserted thamselves, and subjects even use the label of 'department' in, for example, Kent, Warwick, and York (where also the status, if not always the formal title, of head of department is accorded to a professor in each subject).

These new forms of organization are best understood as attempts to achieve three ends which have not always been explicitly distinguished: to encourage inter-disciplinary teaching and research; to discourage the subject-centred introverted department; and to 'democratize' academic decision-making. The schools system clearly may help in the development of links between subjects, especially if the school is armed with sufficient authority (as it is in Sussex). But, except where a subject is itself included in several schools, there is no reason to expect greater co-operation across school boundaries than there is across traditional faculty ones. Experience to date has also indicated that it is easier to prepare the outline of an inter-disciplinary course than it is to teach a course in a genuinely interdisciplinary way, and that the majority of students, when presented with the choice, prefer to concentrate their energies on one subject or only a small number of different subjects.[31] It has also yet to be established

[30] In Warwick, boards of study are primarily responsible for research and each embraces several schools (each of the latter embracing several subjects). In Kent there is a board of study for each degree course, several of which are available in each faculty.

[31] This latter point has emerged clearly in those universities, e.g. York and Lancaster, where virtual single-subject curricula are also available. And, in June 1972, the Vice-Chancellor of Sussex was reported to have said that the Sussex innovations had run into a certain amount of student resistance.

that to erect a new umbrella organization of subjects is more productive of inter-disciplinary work than is the York and Lancaster solution of doing away with all intermediary organizations and leaving each subject free to negotiate such joint degrees with others as it wishes, provided only that 'senate' approval is obtained. In both Lancaster and York, it is worth pointing out, members of staff are also members of colleges, in the hope of encouraging inter-departmental co-operation through informal contacts.[32] It is interesting that Sussex rejected the possible contribution that a college system might have made to their purposes, just as it forms an important part of the Oxbridge system.[33] It remains an open question whether the best organizational forms have yet been found to foster the inter-disciplinary goal. What is less open is whether inter-disciplinary work is considered to be an ideal by most academics; the resurgence of the department suggests that it is not.

What has prevented the intended eclipse of the department is, put at its simplest, that the factors which have sustained the traditional departmental divisions continue to operate in any circumstances.[34] Almost all applicants for posts will have specialized in one subject. Once appointed, specialists will wish to talk to one another, and many will seek a secure continuing 'home base'; and not even the new collegiate universities seem to have invented one more appealing than the group of subject specialists. Academic pressures apart, to use the subject as the basic administrative unit continues to have the advantages of continuity and definition. One official of a university (in which departments had no legal status) said to us, 'Something like a departmental system is already in existence, and indeed if it were not administration would be impossible'. The only viable alternative seems to be the heavily burdened dean; but not even that has prevented the emergence of the subject committee in Sussex. The board of study (where it encompasses but one subject), the subject sub-committee of a school board, or whatever is the most appropriate nucleus, has thus tended everywhere to assume (or assert) the functions of the department—but not necessarily in quite the traditional form.

One of the most significant university developments of the 1960s has been the increased governmental role accorded, belatedly and still inadequately some would say, to the non-professorial

---

[32] In neither university, any more than in Kent (which is also collegiate), do the colleges have the academic functions of Oxbridge ones.

[33] And, for that matter, that they persevered with the practice of appointing professors to *subjects* and did not merely appoint undifferentiated 'fellows'.

[34] See the analysis given at the beginning of this chapter.

staff.[35] The demands for change and the beginnings of change long pre-dated the foundation of the newer universities, and the movement for reform has not been confined to them, but some advantage was taken of the opportunity provided by the framing of over twenty new university constitutions, as we have seen[36], and it may be that this further stimulated the developments taking place in the older universities. Thus, in several of the new charters, the basic academic decision-making units, whether they be school, faculty, board of study, or department, allow for greater non-professorial staff participation than had hitherto been common outside Oxbridge or the LSE. But the most significant movement has not waited upon new constitutions nor formal amendments to old ones. Throughout the university system increasing numbers of 'senates' have requested (occasionally required) that decisions at the subject level be taken either by or after consultation with the main body of teachers.[37] At the same time the multiplication of professorships, now almost universal in the larger departments, has had a deflationary effect upon professorial power and status. Even where a permanent headship remains (and almost invariably where the position is either abolished or opened to regular elections) the practice of government has moved in a collective direction and professors are being required to act less unilaterally and much more like the chairman and spokesman of the whole department. It would be a considerable exaggeration to say that the general position of the professorial head of department had been undermined; most of the resources available to him are still available. But he has become a less commanding and god-like figure within his own department even where the headship does not 'rotate' between professors.[38] None of these internal departmental changes need reduce the compartmentalization of subject-teaching, but it undoubtedly allows for greater flexibility by multiplying the number of those who are entitled to initiate proposals and who must be listened to.

Nowhere, therefore, have the academic and administrative forces which were expressed in the traditional department-faculty structure

[35] Certain aspects have already been touched upon in the historical chapters above; others are discussed later in this chapter and in Chapter IX.

[36] See above, Chapter II.

[37] Both Leeds and Southampton, for example, require that all members of each department meet regularly and be consulted on a wide range of issues; Birmingham and Manchester are in process (1973) of adopting similar provisions; and Leicester set up a Senate committee in 1972 to review the powers and duties of heads of department.

[38] See the further discussions of the role of professors later in this chapter and in Chapter IX below.

been dissipated. On the contrary, as we have suggested, many of the new structures are little more than disguised variants upon the old. It may therefore be that recent innovations have served only to demonstrate the inherent strength of the department and faculty concepts, as well as their capacity to survive through internal evolution.

Senate

The Senate, according to the Universities of Durham and Newcastle-upon-Tyne Act, 1963, 'shall be the *supreme* governing and executive body of the University in all academic matters and shall, subject to the powers reserved to the Court and the Council by these statutes, take such measures and act in such manner as shall appear to it best calculated to promote the interests of the University as a place of education learning and research'.[39]

This provision has for a great many years been generally true of all British universities, whatever the actual wording of their constitutions and whatever the actual title or composition of their 'senate'.[40] More recently the restriction to academic matters has become less strict and senates are acquiring financial powers even in formal theory.[41] Halsey and Trow go further when they say that '. . . not too much must be made of formal constitutions. In practice the effective ruling body of all the modern universities is the Senate. . . .'[42] However, the proviso about the powers reserved to court and council must not be overlooked, and we will have more to say about them in the next chapter. In certain areas and circumstances lay influences may be important. Nevertheless it may safely be said that no decision on academic questions will be taken except by senate, on the initiative of senate, with the concurrence of senate, or by delegation from it. Academic authority resides, without serious challenge, in senate.

The traditional senate[43] consists of all the professors, plus a growing minority of others, meeting between six and ten times each year (and most commonly monthly in term time) under the chairmanship of the vice-chancellor. Senate, in other words, is the regular coming together for purposes of discussion and decision, of those

[39] S. 26; emphasis not in the original. For further comments on the word 'supreme', see Chapter III above, pp. 52-3.

[40] See, for example, the pre-war verdict of LINDSAY and others: *The Government of Oxford* (Oxford, 1931) p. 19, that 'within its own sphere, the Senate is virtually supreme'.

[41] See the historical survey in Chapter II, above.

[42] *Op. cit.*, p. 111.

[43] See our Note on definitions at the end of Chapter III above.

with the heaviest and most specific responsibilities for the essential work of the university. The minority of members referred to are of two kinds. There are firstly, historically as well as in exposition, those who also are members *ex officio*. They include, usually, non-professorial heads of departments, the university librarian, and one or more wardens of halls of residence. The second and somewhat more recent kind are co-opted, nominated, or elected for limited terms of office in order to represent explicitly defined constituencies. Especially since the end of the Second World War, senates have thus come to include members of the non-professorial staff, their numbers being limited either absolutely or in terms of some proportion of total senate membership (25 per cent is a common figure, and a smaller proportion is not unknown).[44] Most recently of all, in an increasing number of universities, student representatives have also been added to the effective, if not always formal, membership of senate.[45]

Even had the categories of membership not been extended, university expansion alone would have enlarged the average senate through the development of new departments and the greater number of departments with two or more professorial members. In 1939 few senates contained more than thirty members (almost all of them professors). By 1970 few had less than fifty members and the larger ones had three to four times that number—examples of the latter including Birmingham, Leeds, Manchester, Edinburgh and Glasgow. The demands for greater participation, and the expansion in higher education, are not yet exhausted; senates are therefore likely to continue to expand unless the bases of membership change. The issues with which senates are confronted have become more complex too, in the wake of university expansion, the pressures for economy, developments within subjects, greater public concern with what goes on inside universities, and the tensions introduced by the evolution of more militant student attitudes. Not surprisingly, it is no longer uncommon for senate sessions to last five hours and more, or even to be adjourned and resumed on a second day. As a result universities in recent years have become increasingly concerned about the role of senate, and the way in which it conducts its business. In particular,

[44] The trend, however, is to a higher figure. Lancaster's revised Statutes (1971) lay down a minimum of 'three-tenths' for those members 'who are neither professors nor students' (S. 11 (1)). That some minimum be established was insisted upon by the Privy Council. (See the forthcoming history of the university being written by Mrs M. E. McClintock to whom we are indebted for this information.)

[45] For a further discussion of certain aspects of non-professorial staff and student drives for representation, see Chapter IX below.

considerable attention has been given to means of ensuring that senate's time is spent on matters of important principle rather than 'routine', so that its 'supremacy' should not be eaten away by trivia.[46]

The following is a typical account of the effects of growing agenda upon enlarged senates operating with unreformed procedures:

'The haphazard distribution of senate's attention—important matters passing virtually without comment while comparatively trivial things are discussed at length by two or three committees in succession and finally also by senate—results in an all-round reduction in awareness of responsibility for decisions. Both in senate and in faculty boards there is a feeling that a resolution is either a rubber stamp to something that has already been decided elsewhere, or a recommendation which some higher body will scrutinize in detail before accepting. Thus in its progress up the ladder, from department to faculty board to senate to council, a proposal becomes a rubber stamp without at any point being an effective decision—and so responsibility is lost between the rungs of the ladder. This no doubt partly explains the readiness with which senate reverses its decisions.'[47]

This account may be illustrated by a striking example of indifference to principle at another university. There a retiring dean of medicine complained that his senate, during the twenty post-war years of expansion and development, had never once debated any long-term plan for medical education nor, even, the place of the medical school within the university. Significantly, this valedictory remark itself attracted no senate comment.

The nature of senate business, and hence of the procedural and organizational problems encountered at this level, may be illustrated from the following specimen agenda of which we reproduce a slightly shortened version.[48]

[46] The details of most of the procedures adopted are likely to be of interest only to people actually working in the university affected. We therefore make no attempt to summarize them.

[47] From an internal memo written by the registrar of a midlands university as a personal and preliminary brief for an internal committee of inquiry. It was written early in the 1960s and, except in its forthrightness, is typical of many written in various places during the subsequent ten years.

[48] It is a real agenda which formed the basis for an actual senate meeting— but not in precisely this form. We have edited it in order to render fruitless any attempt to identify the particular institution from the nature and names of the items.

SENATE OF THE UNIVERSITY OF NOTOWN
AGENDA for Meeting of September 31, 1961

PART I

1. Minutes of the previous meeting (already circulated); for approval. Business arising . . .
2. Report decisions taken at previous meeting of Council (see enclosure 1)
3. Meeting of Senate Steering Committee 21.9.61 (see enclosure 2) Business arising:
   a) Survey of tutorial system and use of seminars
   b) Hale Committee on university teaching methods
   c) Robbins Committee on higher education
   d) Draft report on entrance requirements
   e) Review of fees
   f) Promotions to readerships and senior lectureships
4. New established posts for 1962–3. Recommendations from the Steering Committee and Faculty Boards (see enclosure 3)
5. Recommendations from other committees and from Faculty Boards (see enclosures 4, 5, 6 and 7) Business arising:
   1 Committee on Publications and Advanced Studies
   a) Regulations for presentation of dissertations
   b) Regulations for staff enrolling for higher degree
   c) Formal application for award of D.Sc.
   d) Proposed new journal . . .
6. Superannuation of University Teaching Staff—letter from the Committee of Vice-Chancellors and Principals (see enclosure 8)
7. Statement from the University Grants Committee about the forthcoming Quinquennium (1962–7) (see enclosure 9)
8. Annual report on academic developments in previous year
9. Course on teaching methods for new members of staff
10. Regulations on residence of full-time graduate students
11. Review of examination results 1960–1

PART II

(There will be no discussion of items marked * unless a member requests it.)
12. Reports of Committees:
   a) Committee on Awards
      * i Awards to graduate students for 1961–2
      ii Regulations for the award of a new grant in Natural Sciences
   *b) Admission Committee
   *c) Publications and Advanced Studies—minutes of two meetings
   *d) Joint Committees (with Council)
      i To appoint Landscape Architect
      ii For promotions to Readerships

  e) Committee on Laboratory Safety
     i Radiation hazards
   * ii Annual Report 1960–1
   *iii Code of Practice
 *f) Committee to administer a memorial bequest: minutes
 *g) Institute of Education, examination results
 *h) Programme of special public lectures
13. Reports of Faculty Boards (we reproduce only one of several):
 *a) Reports of Examiners on Higher Degree dissertations
 *b) Nomination of Internal and External Examiners
  c) Proposed new post-graduate course
 *d) Re-sit examination results
  e) Exemption from particular course requirements . . .
14. Prizes: recommendations for awards and draft regulations for newly established prizes
15. Report on Admissions for 1961–2
16. Arrangements for 'social' functions
17. Any other business
(On other occasions there might also be business from committees dealing, for example, with the library, student health services, or student discipline.)

Various important features about the working of senate emerge from this agenda. The first is the sheer range of matters which come before senate. In this case, as in many universities, an attempt has been made to distinguish in advance between those items which are likely to be important and controversial, those which are unlikely to be either, and those which seem (subject to challenge by any member) to be matters for routine validation. In this agenda Part I included the first category of items while in Part II the purely routine items were marked with an asterisk. Secondly, it is noteworthy how many items on both parts of the agenda originated elsewhere than in senate itself: in its own committees; in faculty boards (including items which, in turn, had originated in a department); in the university administration, which may well have drafted various reports and proposals for dealing with particular items as well as having prepared the agenda itself; and outside the university altogether, like items 6 and 7 and several of those under 8.

It is clear, finally, that senate must depend thus on the initiatives of others; for unless business not only originates elsewhere, but is substantially 'processed' before senate is called upon to decide, membership of senate would have to be full time. In handling the business that comes to it from others the important distinction, however, is not so much that between routine and non-routine items as that between senate's appellate and original jurisdiction.

Senate's appellate jurisdiction covers those items originating from the active or executive agents of the university (faculties and departments for the most part). Much of this work is in fact 'routine' in the same sense that the vast bulk of the teaching and research work of the university is routine. It takes place within a framework of already established regulations and policies. The responsibility of senate here is to retain the ability to ensure that it continues to take place within that framework and to resolve awkward cases, such as the application of established policy to a new or unclear situation.[49] To frame university policies, on the other hand, falls within senate's original jurisdiction; senate must itself become the executive agent. Processing is, however, as necessary here as elsewhere, and not only to save time; it is delegated to the senate's committees.

These committees are of various kinds, each kind ideally standing in a somewhat different relationship to its parent body. There are, for example, committees with virtual power to act on behalf of senate, found most commonly in areas of decision which turn almost exclusively upon expert knowledge (e.g. on laboratory safety), or which require a combination of confidentiality, informality, and relative detachment (e.g. on individual student cases, whether of discipline or welfare), or which involve both these types of consideration (e.g. committees to appoint or to promote). So long as such committees act within their terms of reference and all their members endorse the decisions, their recommendations normally become senate decisions without further argument.[50] Other committees, which need to include representatives of the various subject areas rather than more specific experts, will be charged with the task of formulating rules and regulations in defined fields (e.g. higher degrees), and these will normally combine this role, for convenience's sake, with that of watchdog and adjudicator over initiatives taken by others within the rules. In performing the first of these roles, however, the committee is not acting as an executive agent; it is rather exploring a situation, both to sound opinion and discover relevant information, in order more clearly to define the issues calling for resolution. In general, senates are like other large assemblies in requiring committees to review, to investigate, to draft, to prepare for the future, and

[49] To validate a set of examination results, for example, is a matter of routine because the examiners attempt consciously to apply rules and thus to make decisions acceptable to senate. All senate requires is the formal opportunity to intervene, if necessary, to ensure that everyone, and especially students, may rely upon the observance of the rules.

[50] There have been many exceptions in the late 1960s and early 1970s with respect to student discipline; but in all the examples known to us this has been in situations where machinery for dealing with individual cases has in fact had to deal with problems of collective law and order.

to thresh out compromises between conflicting interests and attitudes. It even, in some of the larger ones, needs a committee to nominate members to the other committees. In both large and small senates examples can also be found of committees which are not needed, but are either the relics of past needs or serve merely to side-track individuals and issues.

In a celebrated passage[51] the academic propensity to use committees has been subjected to caustic comment by Mr Charles Carter, Lancaster's Vice-Chancellor. In it he says that

'It is important to begin by recognising that many academic persons enjoy having their days broken up by activities other than teaching or research. Many also believe themselves to be wiser, more intelligent and more honest than their colleagues, and in every way vastly superior to the morons they employ as professional administrators, so it is no more than public duty requires if they ensure their own participation in the maximum number of decisions, and in the execution of the maximum number of administrative tasks. So committees grow large and numerous, the weight of paper increases, and the air resounds with cries about the folly of large committees and unnecessary paperwork; the chief complainants being, of course, those who would be most insulted to be left off a committee, and who are most assiduous in reminding the administration of the need for things to be in writing. There is mercifully a natural check to this process. Life must go on, and cannot always wait for a committee: so people with a taste for management meet in caucuses and decide things, subsequently making sure that the minutes of appropriate committees can be construed as authorising what has already been done. The situation becomes one which is very common in industry: the informal structure of management has diverged from the formal structure, and informal lines of communication, for getting things *done*, are no longer the same as the formal lines for getting them authorised.'

(He then pointed out that the University of Birmingham at that time made use of a network of some eighty-six committees; but he gave no indication of what would be the right number or where the 'real' decisions were taken.) To this thrust certain universities can offer no answer other than '*touché*'.[52] It is a commonplace of academic

---

[51] A review of Sir Robert Aitken's *Administration of a University* printed in the *Universities Quarterly*, March 1967, pp. 257–9.

[52] Another vice-chancellor recalled to us, with obvious horror, a professor who had once boasted to his membership of twenty-six committees.

gossip in many universities to assert that senate (or faculty, or assembly, or even a departmental meeting) is a mere 'talking shop' while the 'real decisions' are taken behind the scenes. Nevertheless Mr Carter's picture cannot be accepted—and probably was not intended—as an accurate representation of every senate.

We can provide a different account that also is based on observation, but of different universities. There senate meetings are not unduly prolonged[53]; the committees are relatively few in number and are structured and appointed with due recognition of the different functions performed in different contexts[54]; senate is frightened neither to delegate nor to challenge the use made of delegated authority; in the case of those committees called upon to prepare the major academic policy proposals, it is recognized that 'to enjoy the confidence of Senate . . . (they) must (i) be fully representative, (ii) have rotating membership, no member holding office for more than three (or four) consecutive years, (iii) not retain or acquire any executive power' (i.e. any power to do more than recommend what action should be taken by others)[55]; and amongst the academic staff there is no major sense of grievance or frustration, but rather a widespread agreement that senate is a reliable centre of general debate and supervision. In part this state of affairs is the product of appropriate organization, but we cannot avoid the conclusion that it is also the product of particular circumstances and personalities—of, for example, the presence of sufficient numbers of Cornford's 'good business men' who can, among other things, detect the important question of principle in a long committee minute or appreciate the need for, and possibility of, action without full agreement on the ultimate verities. There does not, however, seem to be any clear correlation between the effectiveness of senate and the number of its members.

It must not be forgotten, either, that such validity as there might be in any particular allegation of mere talk, may in fact be an indication only of the competence and assiduity with which committees have done their work. In most, perhaps all, senates there will certainly exist members whose approval seems essential if an initiative is to succeed, or whose own initiatives succeed more often than chance can explain; but it is not always possible to determine whether this is because they are effective 'operators' or rather

---

[53] One such body expects to end its business well within three hours, its range of extremes, during the past ten years, being 2¾ hours and, proudly, forty minutes.
[54] See our own rough categorization above.
[55] The quotation is from the midlands registrar whose criticisms were reproduced above, though our description is not based upon his senate.

because they think more deeply about senate business than most of their colleagues do and carry weight because they are respected.[56]

Universities are in any case increasingly aware that 'the committee system of government is (or may be) in danger of running riot'.[57] One of the most usual results of the internal reviews to which we have alluded has been, in fact, to streamline the committee structure. There is one further important type of committee, frequently associated with these reviews either as instigator or as product, of which increasing use is being made in the search for order in the conduct of senate business. This is the executive committee—though it is rarely called by that title.[58] Typically it will be chaired by the vice-chancellor, include his deputy and the deans as *ex officio* members, and complete its membership with varying numbers of others elected by senate, usually with an eye on a balance of academic interests, and including at least one member of the non-professorial staff. Its essential task is to prepare the business for consideration at each meeting of senate. We have called this 'one type' of committee, but it would be more accurate to see it as a preparatory committee which may perform a range of functions. In some universities its functions are minimal, being confined to little more than the organization of the agenda paper and supporting documents. Elsewhere, however, it acts more like a traditional executive body, extending its functions to the point where it marshals and summarizes evidence and arguments on the major items, and often formulates suggested solutions and answers. In these ways it attempts to put the issues into a manageable form, possibly to give a lead in the making of academic policy, and, perhaps of greatest importance, to introduce coherence and continuity into the work of senate, at least with respect to the most fundamental or general issues. Its importance is attested both by the duration of its meetings (normally a full day) and by the fact that there is usually competition for election to it. It may also be worth noting that, although some universities do not use this device, in no university where such a committee has existed has it been abolished (and in at least one university serious consideration has been given to a proposal to set up two such committees, each dealing with a different area of business). As a means of securing speedier and more systematic decision-making at senate

---

[56] It was about one of this last kind that a vice-chancellor said to us: 'I know I have lost if . . . speaks against me in senate'.

[57] From the Tyczak *Report* on the University of Warwick, quoted in E. P. THOMPSON: *Warwick University Ltd.* (Penguin Books, 1970) p. 137.

[58] It is so named at Birmingham, but is more likely to be named the standing, steering, general purposes, or business committee.

level, the executive committee has proved its worth. By critics, however, it is regarded as compounding, not solving, the problem of fitting senate to exercise its supremacy. In what sense, they ask, can senate 'decide' when, in order to cope with its business, it must surrender more of its initiative to yet another committee?

To this question there are essentially two possible answers. The first, and most fundamental, is to suggest that the critics' question is itself based on a misunderstanding of senate's role in university government. That role, it may be argued, has never been to initiate but has always (in so far as it played any significant part in government) been confined to the co-ordination, validation, and criticism of the initiatives and decisions of others.[59] If this argument be accepted, then no further justification for an executive (or any other) committee is required than that it watch over the ever-increasing flow of initiatives from elsewhere and call senate's attention to those that merit consideration.

It can be answered, secondly, that the critics exaggerate senate's alleged lack of power by overlooking or misunderstanding the nature of its control. The fact is that senates still possess the opportunity to intervene and, largely through its committees, to obtain the information necessary to effective intervention. It is also important to remember that senate is composed of 'insiders', of people who are themselves engaged in the administrative as well as the scholarly work of the university. In consequence, senate agreement cannot be taken for granted. This fact is known to others throughout the university. These others therefore must try to make only those proposals that senate will accept. Thus, through Carl Friedrich's 'rule of anticipated reactions', senate ensures that others act, normally, by the preparation of acceptable initiatives. This form of control is not destroyed by the use of filtering and reviewing committees whose own work must also be acceptable to senate.[60] It would of course be foolish to assert that every senate will always be able to keep track of all the activity, or to grasp the main thrust of policy, in its university; but our conclusion is that, broadly, senates today both can and do.

Quite apart from questions about the distribution of power or

[59] *Cf.*, for example, L. S. Amery's view of Parliament's role in the British constitution. It is 'not to legislate or govern, but to secure full discussion and ventilation of all matters . . . as the condition of giving its assent to Bills . . . or its support to Ministers'. See his *Thoughts on the Constitution* (Oxford University Press, 1947) p. 12. Such a role in no way detracts from Parliament's legal supremacy (sovereignty).

[60] See our discussion of the bureaucracy (in Chapter VII) and of oligarchy (in Chapter X) below; in both places we return to these issues.

authority within them, senates themselves are widely regarded as oligarchic institutions which deny influence even to many members of the academic staff. The basic criticism is that 'all British universities, with two possible exceptions (Oxford and Cambridge), are run by small groups of people, and the great majority of their respective teaching staffs have very little, if any, share in running them'.[61] Writing over ten years later, moreover, Halsey and Trow reported that, according to their survey of British academics, 'over a third of all university teachers fully agreed with the suggestion that "a serious disadvantage of Redbrick universities is that all too often they are run by a professorial oligarchy".'[62]

The newer constitutions, as we have already indicated, have gone some way towards modifying the traditional preponderance of professors in senate membership, though none has adopted the 'universalist' approach of Oxford and Cambridge. (The closest some have come is to establish largely advisory assemblies of all staff.)[63] Some even retained *ex officio* membership for all professors, albeit along with guarantees of substantial NPS membership (50 per cent in Sussex, for example)—and where, as in Essex or Brunel, the number of departments is kept low this solution is compatible with the further aim of limiting the total size of senate to well below one hundred. Lancaster, however, amended its original statutes in 1971 and, among other changes, replaced the provision for *ex officio* professorial membership by one in which only the holders of certain offices (among them college principals, chairmen of boards of study, heads of departments, and the chairman of the students' representative council) are assured of a seat.[64] But no university has accepted the full logic of the arguments against *ex officio* membership by establishing what could be called a fully representational senate[65] in which, among other things, it is possible for professors to be in a minority.[66]

[61] G. E. AYLMER: 'University Government—but by whom?', *Universities Quarterly*, November 1958, pp. 45–54.

[62] *Op. cit.*, p. 118; and see their fuller discussion at pp. 375–98.

[63] See our accounts in Chapters II and III above. At LSE membership of the Academic Board has been extended to all academic staff, but the Board does not possess the full range of normal senate powers.

[64] Members of NPS are eligible for appointment to most of these offices and, as we have already noted, also benefit from an assured minimum representation.

[65] Even at Warwick, East Anglia, Durham and Newcastle, for example, the senates include a small *ex officio* component; e.g. the vice-chancellor and his deputy or deputies, and deans.

[66] On the other hand, it is also possible for professors to constitute a majority, if they are elected to the relevant positions. In Newcastle they have in fact done

York possesses a unique, bi-cameral, 'senate' which deserves special mention. The General Academic Board (GAB) has a central membership of forty people (at least eight of whom must be professors) elected by and from all members of the academic staff, to which has been added a small number of students and limited contract staff elected by the relevant constituencies. All serve for a limited term. The only *ex officio* members are the vice-chancellor (who takes the chair) and his deputy. It has the same general powers as the typical senate except that, by the Charter, these powers are shared with a second chamber to which is reserved the powers 'to advise the Council upon all academic appointments' and 'to receive, comment upon and transmit to the Council all recommendations and reports of the General Academic Board'.[67] This second chamber, the Professorial Board, consists entirely of *ex officio* members: the vice-chancellor (in the chair) and his deputy, the professors, the librarian, and the heads of colleges.[68] Almost all items of business are first discussed in the GAB (Professorial Board meetings therefore tend to be shorter[69]), and disagreements have hitherto been settled by reference back to GAB. The great majority of 'senate' committees are joint ones, the GAB by convention always nominating members of the NPS. There is no steering committee, partly perhaps because there is a strong Planning Committee[70], and the system has ensured a steady turn-over in the groups most closely connected with policy formation (only in the first few years did the then small Professorial Board act as an influential 'council of elders').[71]

One other variation deserves notice. Into its traditional 'senate' the University of Stirling has introduced a body called the Academic

---

so—the constitutional provisions permitting a Senate which included only ten professors or, at the other extreme, only six members drawn from the non-professorial staff, from a total of between thirty and thirty-three members.

[67] Statute 10.2.

[68] The Professorial Board at Warwick is sometimes thought also to be a second chamber of Senate; but in fact it is a committee of Senate rather than a partner. See our Appendix on the University of Warwick, below.

[69] On average one to one and a half hours compared with about two hours for GAB.

[70] Of the kind described in Chapter VIII, below, as a central planning agency. It is responsible to both Boards for proposing ways of allocating resources.

[71] Coming from York we are slightly embarrassed to give so much space to its 'senate'. But see also H. J. PERKIN: *op. cit.*, p. 144, for the comment that York 'is the only New University to break out of the orthodox pattern in the higher reaches of government'. In York itself there continues to be some surprise that no other university has shown any sign of imitating an arrangement which to date has apparently satisfied the conflicting criteria of wide participation, an assured position for the more experienced staff, and efficiency.

Board. This consists of the vice-chancellor, the academic members of 'Council' and the chairmen of the Boards of Study (which are similar to faculty boards elsewhere).[72] The function of this body are to '(1) . . . exercise such powers and duties of the Court ("Council") or the Academic Council ("Senate") as may be delegated to it, and shall discharge such other functions as the Court or the Academic Council may prescribe or authorise. (2) The Academic Board may consider and discuss any matter pertaining to the University and may convey its opinions to the Court or the Academic Council.'[73]

This seems to have been envisaged as a form of combined steering committee for both 'council 'and 'senate', apparently with general policy most in view. It clearly could become, in effect, bearing in mind its statutory and separate constitution, the effective governing body of the university. Having no lay members, and having the fields of both 'council' and 'senate' in its purview, it could then be a body comparable only to the hebdomadal council or the council of the senate in the ancient English universities.[74]

In concluding this account of university senates three further comments will be offered. The first is to explain why we referred above to 'a fully "representational" senate', and not merely to a 'representative' one. The point is that the position of professors on the traditional senate is ambiguous. It appears, on the one hand, as if they owe their membership solely to their rank and status. But their membership and role seem also to owe something to the belief (implicit more often than not) that they are the most effective, because most senior and most responsible, representatives of their subjects (much as, it may be argued, deans owe their *ex officio* membership to their being the most responsible representatives of faculties or schools). To deny the term 'representative' to the traditional senate is therefore to neglect an important characteristic of its membership.

It has been borne in upon us by numerous informants, secondly, that to introduce non-professorial staff into senate without introducing corresponding changes at the subject level is to accomplish relatively little. That rather curious and not wholly rational fear of retribution which was manifested in the survey of departmental procedures, reported earlier, extends beyond the department. It

[72] The members of 'Council' and the chairmen must be equal in number. S. 13:1.

[73] See S. 13:4.

[74] We are in no position to say, however, to what extent, if any, it has assumed this role. At Sussex, under the reforms proposed in the McKinsey Report, the Joint Planning Committee seems intended for a position similar to the Stirling Academic Board: but it has lay members.

seems to be unreasonable to expect non-professorial members of senate, especially when they are in a minority, to speak up loudly and boldly in the presence of their superiors in power.[75] Where on the other hand, non-professorial senators are also enfranchised at the subject level, our evidence suggests that they are less inhibited on senate.

Underlying the difficulties facing those who seek a strategic reform of senate by radically altering its basis of membership, and this is our third comment, are a minor and a major problem.

The minor problem is this. If senate is fully elected on a university-wide and egalitarian basis, how will the electoral process operate? Even in Oxbridge, with long experience, a well-established egalitarian tradition, and 'ready-made' sub-communities in the colleges, voting must often either consist of a choice between 'unknown' candidates or favour the 'established' figures. It is, in any case, clear that many scholars there play little real part in university government and that the more senior men are (in one sense of the word) over-represented. Elsewhere, the more hierarchical tradition may reinforce any tendency to vote for the better-known and thus produce as great an over-representation of the more senior members. It is likely, too, that candidates will be forthcoming only if elected office carries with it some genuine influence upon events. The end result, therefore, could well be very different from those apparently envisaged by the most ardent proponents of 'democracy'. If the subjects were to be the constituencies, thus ensuring that candidates were well-known to their electorate, the senior members might again benefit, if only from their disciplinary prestige. An incidental result would, of course, be to strengthen the pressures towards departmentalism which, we have suggested, are already so pervasive; it would certainly be no easier for an elected subject-representative to take 'a university view' than for a professorial head of department to do so.[76] The only way in which, presumably, an egalitarian electoral system could produce results radically different from those hitherto experienced, is if a 'party system' were to emerge. To date, however, the issues seem too

[75] One witness, an exceptionally outspoken lecturer, told us of the wrath visited upon him (for one of his utterances in senate) by a professorial colleague who was outraged by his 'disloyalty and impertinence'. Our informant has since graduated to the position of an MP in regular trouble with his whips.

[76] In York's GAB, where the staff members are elected by all staff (with no constituency divisions), some anxiety has been expressed both about the relatively large number of professors elected, though they have always held a minority of seats, and about the inconvenience to departments when they happen to have no spokesman on the Board. To date, however, majority opinion has been opposed to the introduction of any system of formal subject representation.

unrelated, diverse, or trivial to serve as the basis for such an evolution —and this, to judge by experience in Germany and the USA, may be as well.[77]

The major problem is most conveniently stated in question form, thus: If the rank of professor connotes a real difference, in responsibility or distinction or both, then it would seem proper to recognize this difference in the academic government of a university; but how can it be acknowledged in a fully elected and 'egalitarian' senate? If, on the other hand, senates are to be egalitarian, is there any justification for continuing to acknowledge distinctions among academics, of rank, title, responsibility, or salary? To this issue we will return in later chapters.[78] We mention it here only to make the point that resistance to senate reform may sometimes stem from more than mere conservatism or love of power.

[77] See MARTIN TROW: 'Reflections on the Transition to Universal Higher Education', *Daedalus*, 99:1, Winter 1970, and the editorial in *Minerva* X:3, July 1973.

[78] See Chapter IX and our general discussion in Chapter X.

Chapter V

COURT, COUNCIL, AND LAYMEN[1]

There are two areas in which the charters or Acts of universities (outside Oxbridge) are particularly misleading. One of these is the description of the role and powers of the vice-chancellor[1], discussed in Chapter VI below. The second covers both the role and powers of the court and council[1], which are on paper the most powerful bodies in university government, and also those of the laymen[1] who provide a majority of their members and their chairmen.

The first of these laymen is the visitor (usually the Sovereign, though a formal appointment has not always been made). The visitor has complete powers of inspection[2], and an appeal function, as between members of the university, which may exclude recourse to the courts.[3] 'The principle is that at common law the court has no jurisdiction to deal with the internal affairs or government of [a] university for these have been confided by the law to the exclusive province of the Visitor.'[4] The powers of inspection seem never to have been exercised in recent times[5], while in the case of *Rex v. Aston University Senate* (1966) the court was apparently willing, in principle, to intervene despite the 'exclusive province' rule (no visitor had been appointed). There thus may be some doubt whether the formally great powers of the visitor are still effective;

[1] We use these terms as they are used in most English universities. See our Note 3 to Chapter III above.

[2] In the case of the Sovereign the office is exercised 'through the Lord President of Our Council' who may 'direct an inspection of the University, its buildings, laboratories and general equipment and also the examinations, teaching and other work done by the University' (Manchester, Charter, S. IV).

[3] J. W. BRIDGE: 'Keeping peace in the Universities. The role of the Visitor' LQR, 86 (1970) p. 531, on which these paragraphs are largely based. Where a visitor is not appointed 'the Courts treat the Crown as the Visitor'. *Att.-Gen. v. The Dedham School* (1857) (quoted on p. 535).

[4] *Thorne v. University of London* (1966) 2 Q.B. per L. J. Diplock, quoted by BRIDGE: *ibid.* p. 540. See also *Herring v. Templeman and others*, reported in *The Times*, February 16, 1973.

[5] H. W. R. WADE: 'Judicial Control of Universities' LQR 85 (1969) p. 469.

certainly we met no one who suggested that they are important to a study of contemporary university government.[6] At a time when appeal mechanisms are being widely discussed, one reason for the failure to use that provided by the visitorship may be that today the arbitration might not be accepted as appropriate or unbiased.[7] The existence of the visitor's powers of inspection, beside which the UGC's powers of enquiry pale, is, however, another indication of the extent to which the independence of the British universities is a matter of convention.

The most visible of the laymen is the chancellor, whose position is very largely honorific and ceremonial. When present, he presides over the court and (if he is a member) over council, though very seldom for the conduct of ordinary business. He confers degrees and occasionally makes speeches of which some notice may be taken by the press, thus serving as a useful university spokesman. Vice-chancellors are fond of quoting these speeches (which, not uncommonly, they may have drafted).[8]

It would be very hard to obtain any authoritative statement of the qualifications and role of the chancellor. The old requirement of 'an honourable protector' is still relevant, and access to the national political system at a high level is still often a consideration, though probably less so than in the last century, when there were fewer institutions and no collective groups such as the Committee of Vice-Chancellors and Principals. Thus prominent politicians, especially prime ministers or those who are also local magnates, are often chosen.[9]

Beyond that, local influence may be thought useful, as may ability

[6] The Registrar of the University of Leeds, for example, told us (in 1972) that no use of the right of appeal had ever been made there to his knowledge. He felt that the existence of such an 'umpire' might nevertheless be of some value.

[7] Hence, possibly, the resort to its own Chancellor when Lord Radcliffe was invited to enquire into the affairs of the University of Warwick in 1970, or to a lay member of its own Council when Mr Taylor enquired into those of the University of Lancaster in 1972.

[8] In the last century the chancellors of Oxford and Cambridge were at times quite active, e.g. Prince Albert in curriculum reform, Salisbury in college taxation; see, e.g. J. W. ADAMSON: English Education (Cambridge, 1964) pp. 178 and 422. More recently Lord Halifax was asked for help and advice from time to time by Oxford.

[9] Politics has entered, overtly, into consideration in the past. At Oxford in 1925 there was opposition to Lord Asquith on the grounds that he had 'placed the trade unions outside the law' and 'put pressure on the King to create a number of new peers'. However, 'Absolutely the only . . . (Conservative) . . . Oxford candidate of distinction—a quality not absolutely necessary, but very desirable—was Lord Cave . . .' (C. B. GRUNDY: Fifty-five Years at Oxford (London, 1945) p. 142).

to encourage benefaction (if only by appearance on the letterhead) and to shed reflected glory. Thus in the last century great peers (usually politically active ones) were often appointed, while today royalty, leaders of industry, or men distinguished in scholarship or the arts are more often found. One criterion is almost absolute— public honour. In 1969 all the cancellarial officers then appointed were titled except Mr Harold Wilson (Bradford) and Mr Harold MacMillan (Oxford).[10]

One other possible function is worth mentioning. A crisis of an unfamiliar or embarrassing sort is likely to arise at some time in the life of any institution whose life-span is measured in centuries. Should the vice-chancellor become unbalanced or some other private scandal occur, the value of a distinguished, disinterested, yet concerned, head in whom to confide could be great, especially to the chief actors who cannot advertise their difficulties. By definition, evidence of this will be very rare, but we are confident that this function is performed from time to time, while its mere possibility is not wholly insignificant.[11]

The most important of the laymen is the chairman of council, who is often a pro-chancellor. It would perhaps be easier to discuss his position after describing that of his council, for his importance is very largely that of a chairman. As with all such positions, much depends on the person, but we take it that any chairman anywhere, from China to Peru, can and normally must play a significant part in the work of his committee. Lord Franks remarked to one of us that the power of an Oxford head of house was little more than that of a chairman, and Sir Kenneth Wheare told the Franks Commission that that was so also of the Oxford vice-chancellor.[12] The chairman of council, however, is in some respects in a weak position. He is by definition an outsider, he has at the table the vice-chancellor who is far more *au courant* and in fact often virtually conducts the actual business, and there are likely also to be one or two experienced pro-vice-chancellors. Not perhaps surprisingly, we met, or heard of, chairmen whose part was limited. But others were deeply involved,

---

[10] *Commonwealth Universities Yearbook* 1970. Apart from royalty, there were five ducal chancellors. At York Lord Harewood was royal, a local magnate, and prominent in the arts. On the educational and career backgrounds of chancellors from 1935–67, see PETER COLLISON and JAMES MILLEN: 'University Chancellors, Vice-Chancellors and College Principals: A social Profile', *Sociology*, 3(1), January 1969, pp. 77–109. Interestingly, one of the few discernible trends seems to be towards appointing academics (including the heads of Oxbridge Colleges) as chancellor.

[11] *Cf.* the role of the chairman of council discussed below, p. 93.

[12] *Report* S. 483.

extremely knowledgeable, and a force in all general affairs and even in some major academic affairs, such as a new medical school, where much of the 'facilitation' that we discuss in a moment is in any case required.[13] One or two are also active nationally, like the late Lord Simon of Wythenshawe[14], who was most active at Manchester, notably in pressing forward the immensely difficult establishment of the Jodrell Bank radio telescope. Some are ex-academics, others independent scholars.[15] One we talked to had 'let go' an obstructive vice-chancellor (clearly with the support of the academic staff).

This is a very intimate area of affairs, one where the traditional deep discretion of British public service is strong, if only because the relationships are so personal.[16] But it can be said that the universities look first and foremost for a strong commitment to university values and a belief in the tradition of university government. A man who shows signs of wishing to 'systematize' the university is unlikely to be invited to serve.[17] In service, he is expected to exert himself to forward the interests of the university externally (which is likely to mean locally) and to make business smooth internally. Probably his greatest service can be to the vice-chancellor personally; as a disinterested but concerned and knowledgeable confidant to a man whose job must inevitably be solitary and lonely. His position is in some ways perfect for this purpose. He is not part of the university, but he can be told a great deal, and he has the incentive that should anything go wrong, he will be deeply involved, and may be held responsible. All this is a very formidable specification, and requires much time as well as application, patience, and judgement to meet. It is not surprising that universities have even more difficulty in finding good chairmen than vice-chancellors, and are grateful when they succeed.

Two other laymen are of major importance, the treasurer and (very often) the chairman of the committee dealing with sites and buildings. We discuss both these committees below, and here again,

[13] See e.g. the obituary of E. Bramall, sometime Chairman of Sheffield Council and a former lecturer, in the Sheffield *Reporter* 1970.

[14] A founder and editor of *Universities Quarterly*, 'few people . . . had a clearer vision of the problems which lay ahead of universities' (R. A. C. OLIVER: *Universities Quarterly*, 14:2, February 1960, p. 185). In 1958 he called for a Royal Commission on the universities (*ibid.*, 13:1 pp. 9–22).

[15] Sir E. Collingwood was elected FRS while serving at Durham. See also f.n. to p. 115.

[16] See our quotation from Lord Percy on p. 12.

[17] Some of the ex-CATs had certain difficulties with their chairmen on becoming universities.

as with the chairman of council, the body largely defines the man. These two secondary chairmanships are more technical, and less likely to call for deep commitment to university values. The treasurer has a major financial responsibility, but some treasurers leave virtually everything to their bursar. Most, however, devote much time to the job, and give considerable support (occasionally surveillance) to the bursar. The chairman of the sites committee is in a similar position, though this can be the more exacting job because the range of activity, from negotiating planning permission[18], or briefing architects, to choosing contractors, is very wide. One buildings' official remarked to us that a full-time chairman would help, and, significantly, he thought it should be an academic, because that would bring automatic knowledge of academic priorities and needs. Occasionally, an academic does indeed do this job, but a more general view is that the technical requirements of the job outweigh the academic.

In addition to these three laymen, there will normally be a few others, usually chairmen of committees, or people interested in welfare or sport, who devote substantial time or effort to the university and whose views are respected. It would be difficult to be sure, but we doubt if any university has more than ten laymen who are sufficiently closely and continuously concerned with any aspect of affairs to be able to contribute generally (who are 'useful' as more than one vice-chancellor or registrar described them), and most much less. In one or two cases there have seemed to be none.

The rest of the laymen serve, as a majority, on the court and council. The laymen's position depends therefore on the role of these bodies, and on their role within them.

Court

The powers of the court, as we have seen, are first legislative. Except in the post-1960 instruments[19], this usually includes legislation 'on its own initiative', but in practice (as far as we know) it is always confirmation of legislation by the council.

Secondly, there may be, especially in the older universities (e.g.

[18] Planning powers give back to local authorities some of the position their representatives on council have lost. For this reason, universities normally take great care to cultivate good relations with the planners. 'Manchester City Council has shown an imagination in thinking and a magnanimity in action which have given it . . . a consistent role not only in city but in university planning,' Sir W. Mansfield Cooper (Vice-Chancellor of Manchester) *Minerva*, x:1 January 1972, p. 158.

[19] Sometimes court retains powers over the charter (e.g. at Ulster), but council may make statutes.

COURT, COUNCIL, AND LAYMEN

Sheffield), formal powers to appoint the vice-chancellor and some other officers; but in practice this too is reduced to confirmation. Third, there are powers of election, usually of the chancellor, and often to seats on council[20] and in some cases for other purposes.[21] We have heard of no contested elections for chancellor outside Oxbridge, and contested elections to council are extremely rare, so that, in the historical survey in Chapter II, we have treated these council members as co-opted (in fact they are likely to be chosen by the chairman of council, the vice-chancellor and maybe one or two others). Lastly, there is the right to approve the university accounts and the annual report delivered by the vice-chancellor.

Though courts have in fact made very little use of their powers, it would be rash to conclude that they are therefore superfluous. They have only just been introduced into Scotland. The vice-chancellor's annual report often receives more attention from local press (and from court members) because it is ceremonially presented than it would otherwise[22] and mere court membership itself may help to arouse an interest leading later to willingness to serve on council committees. These are probably the only functions that would occur to most experienced university people, who seem to regard them as just about justifying the small cost, in money and time, of the court to its university. One English vice-chancellor, however, told the Robbins Committee that 'the advantages . . . are . . . far out-weighed by the disadvantages', which latter were not specified.[23]

In a more recent review of the university's constitution a northern senate agreed that 'while we would not wish to establish a Court if none had been established, we do not think there is any powerful reason to suggest that the Court should be abolished'. This same

[20] Lay seats, though occasionally members of staff are elected to them.

[21] E.g. at the University of York, three members of Court (who may be members neither of the academic staff nor of Council) are elected annually to form an Appeal Board to hear appeals by any members of staff threatened with dismissal. (York, it might be relevant to note, has no visitor.)

[22] 'Annual Meetings of Courts have come to be regarded as something of field-days for Vice-Chancellors;' the Vice-Chancellor of Sheffield in the *Reporter*, 9.4, December 1969.

[23] *Report* App. IV, p. 31. Sir James Mountford, writing a little later, said that 'in a real sense, it embodies that informed public opinion to which the university is in the long run accountable', *British Universities* (Oxford, 1966) p. 130. Compare the view of Lord Morris of Grasmere when Vice-Chancellor of Leeds: 'The policies of Council and Senate must . . . manifestly be seen to be acceptable (to Court) . . . there are usually at any one moment at least one or two issues on which Council and Senate must take care to anticipate and take account of its known views'. *Yearbook of Education* 1959, p. 275. We found no support for this view, ten years later.

senate, by way of more positive justification, added that 'the abolition of the Court would make the Council a self-perpetuating body,
since the Court elects the majority of lay members to Council . . .'.[24]
The Birmingham Senate, however, suggested to the review body
chaired by Mr Jo Grimond that court should be reduced to 'an
advisory body existing largely to foster good will for the university
in the outside world'.[25] This is the type of advisory 'court' recently
introduced in Scotland.[26] Lancaster recently enlarged its Court,
because, *inter alia*, 'a large number of proposals are made of people
who would be interested to become members . . . and attendance
at meetings is good'.[27] The mere existence of court's constitutional
power may nevertheless be significant on occasion. In a consensual
society such as is a university, even the possibility of public dissension is distressing (journalists love to laugh at 'dons' disagreements).
We have already noted the effect on the constitution of Leeds of a
proposal to use its Court to improve the position of non-professorial
staff[28], and students have found their membership may make a useful base for making their point. One dean, in a rural university,
even remarked that if ever he were faced with an attempt at interference by laymen on council, he would threaten to raise the matter
at the court. This threat, he felt sure, would be sufficient. At another
English university, the threat to mobilize court against a proposal
concerning staff terms of service was sufficient to dissuade the
council from putting it up. Hitherto, cases of this sort have been
too rare for court to be a significant factor in the power balance;
yet it cannot wholly be disregarded as a last defence for some substantial interest in the university. At a time of sharpening disagreements the powers of court either to advocate or to oppose radical
change are likely more frequently to be invoked; and it could then be
the turn of laymen, rather than of staff, to attend in force. It would
not then greatly matter whether the court was the 'supreme governing
body' or merely advisory: either way it would provide a remarkable
forum for the confrontation of ideas.

[24] But at another major civic university an analysis of the role of court included,
as a reason for retaining it if the Charter were amended, the fact that the choice of
council members was effectively by pro-chancellor and vice-chancellor, who thus
were easily able to ensure high quality on council.
[25] *Guardian*, April 17, 1971.
[26] In 1943, 'Bruce Truscot' thought 'It is intriguing to imagine what havoc this
enormous body could work. . . . Fortunately there is no fear of that'. But he
thought it would be worth while abolishing it. *Redbrick University* (Penguin
Books, 1951) p. 84.
[27] Vice-Chancellor's comments on proposed changes in the Charter 1969, p. 2.
[28] In Chapter II, above.

Council

The British system of university government is often described by commentators, and was so seen by most of those we interviewed, as dual or two-tiered; dual, that is, as between council and senate. Now, institutional duality does not necessarily imply a dual interest base. The Franks Commission described as a 'revolution' the subordination of the Curators of the University Chest to the Hebdomadal Council in the years after the Second World War.[29] The Franks Commission was quite right; there was an astonishing degree of dualism at Oxford, but the members of the bodies concerned were all resident dons, all indeed drawn from the same smallish segment of senior dons; and the two bodies concerned shared the same chairman.[30] The dualism outside Oxford by contrast seems to rest in part upon a very real difference in the composition of the bodies concerned and thus in the forces and considerations to which they are most vulnerable. It makes considerable sense to refer to council as the 'executive committee of court', which of course it was intended to be in the nineteenth-century foundations; it too has a majority of non-academic members, and it is constitutionally equipped with an extensive array of executive powers. In the opposite corner is senate—and the boxing metaphor might at first sight seem appropriate. But, as we hope to show, there is less dualism between councils and senates than there was between Council and Curators at Oxford, and little more significant difference of interest.

There is, in legal terms, an element of subordination in senate's relations to council. But it is more realistic to see the situation in terms of a separation of powers, even a system of checks and balances—to use the conventional language of constitutional description—in which, however, the separation favours senate, and the 'checks' include the presence on council of members elected by senate, but no council representation on senate.

As we have seen in earlier chapters, the power of council has declined steadily in the last century and a half, but not even the most modern charter does full justice to the situation as it is today.

<hr />

[29] *Report* S. 464.
[30] 'Conflict between Council and the Curators of the Chest is by no means out of the question', A. D. LINDSAY *et al.*: *The Government of Oxford* (Oxford, 1931) p. 28. A President of Trinity (J. R. H. Weaver), who had served many years on the Hebdomadal Council, remarked to one of us, of the inter-war years, 'The Chairman of Council was terrified of the Chairman of the Curators, and the Vice-Chancellor was afraid of both'. The General Board, roughly equivalent to senate, seems to have been less important, perhaps because it was newer and because it cut closer to college affairs. See *ibid.*, pp. 26, 38–40.

D

For that we have to turn not so much directly to the charters, as to authoritative comments upon them.

Two recent reviews of the situation provide reasoned accounts from which to begin a more detailed examination of the work of council. The first refers to the University of Warwick. According to Lord Radcliffe;

'It is the Charter itself that sets up the Council to be the "executive governing body of the University", exercising "general control over the conduct of the affairs of the University" (clause 12). It is true that this authority is to be "subject to the provisions of this our Charter and of the Statutes" and "subject to the powers of the Senate as provided" in the Charter and Statutes—but it is difficult to feel that the reservation gives any great freedom to the academic side. For, while it is certainly intended that the Senate shall be "the supreme academic authority of the University" (Statute 19), regulating and superintending the education and discipline of its students, this responsibility itself is to be "subject to the powers of the Council as provided in this our Charter and Statutes" (Charter clause 13), and in fact under the Statutes there are a great many matters, substantially of academic content, which can only be regulated and controlled if the Council is prepared to adopt and enact recommendations coming forward from the Senate for the purpose. This is what is meant by the prescription of the Charter that the Council is to be the executive governing body of the University. To my mind it underlies the importance of the academic point of view, formulated in the Senate, being fully and effectively deployed before the Council.'[31]

The other, a commentary on Birmingham University by Sir Robert Aitken, its former Vice-Chancellor, comes still closer to describing the actual situation. After pointing out that under the Charter the Council of the University of Birmingham has 'the government and control of the finances of the University and of the discipline, practical affairs, business and work of the University', he continues with the judgement that, generally speaking, 'it is the effective governing body and can make Regulations'.[32] Offering a brief gloss on the former position, he continues:

[31] LORD RADCLIFFE: *Report*, Pt. II (University of Warwick, 1970), S. 15. But despite this Councillor Tom Taylor, in his report on Lancaster, called for clarification of the legal powers of council (*Report*, p. 16).

[32] SIR R. AITKEN: *Administration of a University* (University of London Press, 1966) p. 10. Lord Morris, in 'Organisation and Control of Universities in the U.K.', *Yearbook of Education*, 1959, p. 275, says council is able to 'exercise continuous and effective autonomy'.

'Custom and practice have established a firm division of responsibility between Council and Senate which makes Senate a partner rather than an agent of Council. Decision on purely academic matters lies with Senate, and the resulting recommendations are all accepted by Council without challenge or discussion, so long as they do not involve expenditure that would outrun income. . . . On non-academic matters on the other hand discussion and decision take place in Council, which is nevertheless open at all times to receive representations from Senate. . . . This division of powers, as a normal working arrangement, has become entrenched as a principle; only in the gravest crisis would there be resort to Council to overrule Senate.'[33]

The description of the situation put forward by Sir Robert Aitken can be taken as substantially true in all those British universities which operate the two-tier system of government, at least with respect to academic decisions. In other areas it is less certain that 'only in the gravest crisis' would council overrule senate—we give some rare examples below—but even there senate will not be treated as a servant. Thus Sir Eric Ashby, also a former vice-chancellor, in asking us to 'consider the power given to the Council of the University to "give directions"[34] to the Senate', continues by indicating that 'no one fears that the Council at Sussex, or elsewhere in England, ever would give directions'.[35]

Another pointer to council's role is given by the contrast between the items with which it is called upon to deal and the time it takes to deal with them. Some indication of the former is provided by an account—a 'précis [of] the Minutes of a recent Council meeting'—published in the report of a working party at York.[36] The items covered were these:

'Confirmation of Estates and Buildings Committee minutes.
Confirmation of Finance Committee minutes.
Confirmation of Catering Committee minutes.
Appointment of member of Council to Court.

[33] R. AITKEN: *op. cit.*, p. 11.
[34] See our discussion of the 'litany' of statutory control powers in Chapter II, above.
[35] *Universities: British, Indian, African* (Weidenfeld and Nicolson, 1966) p. 336.
[36] *The Role of Students in the Government of the University* (University of York, 1968) pp. 10–11. The report is reproduced in Volume VII of the *Report on Student Relations* of the House of Commons Select Committee on Education and Science (HMSO, 1969) pp. 142 *et seq.*

Report of resignation of a member of the administrative staff.
Confirmation of an administrative staff appointment.
Report of Professorial Board appointment to Council.
Academic staff resignations and new appointments.
Report of forthcoming O. and M. unit investigation.
Confirmation of external examiners.
Confirmation of amendment to lodgings regulations.
Consideration of the university's attitude to "campus employment".
Report of General Academic Board decision to avoid timetabled activities on Wednesday afternoons.
Leave of absence for a member of staff.
Report of a modification of a combined course.
Report on admissions for 1968–9 and demand for places.
Report on research grants awarded.
Uses of university seal on official documents.
Consideration of a disciplinary matter concerning a member of the university.'

Neither the minutes nor the agenda appeared in this form, of course, but the list nevertheless provides an accurate picture of the nature of the business transacted—in an hour at most, despite the fact that each set of committee minutes probably ran to several pages and included a number of recommendations for specific decision. Other councils will meet for longer, and some meetings will cope with a longer agenda, but York's experience is not unusual[37], and indeed some councils with as great formal powers meet less often. Elsewhere, in a civic university, the committee structure of council was streamlined and the timetable of meetings changed for all the main university bodies in order to give lay members of council at least the impression that they had a significant role in governing the university.[38]

It would be as great a mistake to conclude from these facts that council is everywhere, and in everything, a mere 'rubber stamp' as it would be to accept the view of some student and junior staff radicals that 'the UNIVERSITY COUNCIL is the real body of power on the campus' or 'the real power in the University, com-

[37] The most extreme example of speed is the London federal Senate which may dispose of up to one hundred printed foolscap sheets in under fifteen minutes, but this body, though lay- and administrator-dominated, is not typical.
[38] So we were informed by one of the officials immediately concerned. And a lay member of more than one council, a former civil servant, remarked to us that 'you might try to find out what we are supposed to do'.

posed of local oligarchs, academic mandarins, and the professional manipulators of the administration'.[39] What is true, however, is that councils have for long been emasculated, by convention, on purely academic questions, generally indulge less in debate than do senates, and make full use of their committees.

About the supremacy of academics in academic decision-making no more need be said here, except that it has implications for the actual conduct of council meetings. In particular, it means that it is not in the interests of the academics, neither those on council nor the others, that council should be asked to arbitrate between them. They wish to present a united front. One result of this is that the academic members tend to speak little at council meetings, for they do not care to appeal to the layman, even if they may not like what is proposed: they prefer to confine their advocacy to the preparatory processes we are about to discuss. As the York Report put it, council should not be asked to arbitrate 'on any matter which it would prefer to see resolved at Committee or (academic) Board level'. Similarly, when discussing student representation on council, the Report says that 'it would be inappropriate to ask council with its strong lay membership, to place itself in the position of arbitrator in debate between academic and student members of the community'.[40] Not all academics would agree in this particular instance, but almost all would agree with the sentiment; as would, in fact, practically all lay members. This aversion from controversy in itself must further reduce the actual role of council, for it leaves the laymen to make the running, and they, as we shall see, are neither well-equipped, nor anxious, to run.

For the most part, therefore, discussion in council takes the form rather of exposition or explanation than of argument leading to decision.[41] A great deal of the talking is done by the chairman, and still more by the vice-chancellor, filling in the background, relating one item to another, providing gossip. Many academic members told us they valued their membership chiefly for this briefing, this informed background, which enabled them to see the university

[39] To quote from broadsheets issued by two extreme left-wing student societies. Their view is of course encouraged by the fact that the committees dealing with residence, catering, or athletics are usually council committees (though usually with an academic majority), so that council seems to be 'the boss' in areas of the most immediate day-to-day significance to students, areas from which so many student grievances have originated.

[40] Op. cit., p. 11.

[41] An AUT witness told the Franks Commission that the Liverpool Council 'has only made one decision since I have been on it, and that was a trivial detail'. Oral evidence O.16, Dr Chapman, p. 32.

entire, and so gave their own opinions greater weight at other bodies.

Even in comparatively recent times, however, informed observers have continued to ascribe real importance to council. When 'Bruce Truscott', writing during the last war, turned to council, 'we come down to exceedingly hard brass tacks . . .'.[42] Though much of the 'hardness' was later eroded by the appearance of relatively plentiful finance, and by the loss of much university autonomy in salary matters, Sir Charles Morris (then Vice-Chancellor of Leeds) writing in 1958 could still say that Council 'plays a direct and active part in initiating as well as finally determining, the decisions of the University'.[43] A little later Robbins said it 'actively controls finance and external relations'.[44]

The solution to the paradoxes of council's role, it would seem, must lie in the use made by council of its committees. Their purpose, after all, is to discuss in detail and to reach an agreed solution, so that, in a situation where there are no political parties, those who were not present and do not know the detail will not wish to challenge most recommendations. This will happen when the actors trust each other, so that a councillor need never doubt that a recommendation, whatever its source, was reached responsibly. Even where the trust is not complete, academics have, we have seen, little incentive to re-open the discussion; while laymen are busy people and seldom anxious to indulge in those discussions of principle that, on other bodies, are so dear to some academics.

The key committees of council are the ones dealing with appointments, estates or building and development (development usually in the sense of physical development only), and finance. In these committees, if anywhere, lie the seats of non-academic power within the university. With the exception of the appointments committees they include, as often as not, a majority of lay members meeting under the chairmanship of a lay member, and are in all cases accountable to a body with a lay majority. Since these control the necessary means to academic development, it is no wonder some students and a few academics, especially junior ones, suspect that

[42] 'BRUCE TRUSCOT' (pseud.): *Red Brick University* (Penguin Books, 1951) p. 84. But 'Truscott' thought that graduates would be more suitable as governors than laymen, an opinion shared by few academics (*ibid.*, p. 295).

[43] C. MORRIS: *loc. cit.*

[44] *Report*, S. 662. A northern vice-chancellor, in evidence to a university committee reviewing the constitution in 1963 wrote '. . . Senate did not normally send forward recommendations that were incomplete . . . and . . . never placed council in a position where it had to make its own decision on a matter initiated by Senate'.

universities may be run by and for the non-academic establishment, and no wonder either that even the sober Radcliffe Report refers to the 'possibilities of tension and conflict' within the system.[45] Let us therefore now look more closely at the role of these committees.

With the exception of such dignitaries as the chancellor and prochancellors, all appointments (as we have noted) are made formally by the council, but in almost all cases on the basis of a single nomination from some other unit. This unit, not uncommonly, will be a committee of council itself in the case of chairs and the most important administrative posts. An exception to this is the practice for long adopted by the 'council' of one Scottish university, namely that of themselves interviewing two or three people nominated for a professorial appointment by an appointment committee.[46] The final choice thus was made by the council as a whole.

There are various categories of appointment, in which councils do not play a uniform role. Thus it is customary on the appointment of a new vice-chancellor for the appropriate committee to be a joint committee of council and senate, the precise balance of membership varying from university to university. For the appointment of professors the selection committee will again usually be a joint one of council and senate, but almost certainly with a majority drawn from senate (including of course those members of senate who are also on the council).[47] Increasingly frequently, however, especially in the newer universities, these appointment committees will be entirely composed of senate members.[48] The chairman of the professorial selection committee is likely to be the vice-chancellor (who for these purposes may be counted primarily as an academic). In the appointment of other members of the academic staff, it is rare for council to play any part other than that of the final and purely formal ratification of recommendations originating in departmental or faculty committees; and where there is any genuine review of such decisions, it will be by senate or by a committee reporting to senate.[49]

[45] Op. cit. Pt. II, S. 16.

[46] This used to be common in England. For a period before the last war, for example, a candidate for a post at Sheffield might be interviewed not only by a selection committee of Council but also by Senate and by the Faculty Board. (Private communication from Dr Chapman.)

[47] It is very rare for NPS members of council to serve on professorial selection committees.

[48] One or more academic assessors from other universities may also be members of professorial appointment committees—the practice varies between universities.

[49] But see the note on a Birmingham committee at the end of this chapter.

Council tends to play a larger role in the appointment of senior administrative officials like university secretaries, registrars, and bursars. The selection will normally be made by a council committee on which lay members will predominate and which may be chaired by a lay member. Since a major qualification for these offices is administrative ability, and another may be the ability to work closely with lay councillors (as a bursar must work with the lay treasurer), the predominance of laymen seems not inappropriate. On the other hand, most academics would consider another essential qualification to be an ability to work with and understand the academics whom these officers are also appointed to serve; it is therefore increasingly the custom for academics to be on administrative selection committees.[50]

Council's 'power to appoint', therefore, boils down to a right of representation on the selection committee for senior appointments and a virtually moribund power to veto.[51] In the older civics this restriction on its role is conventional only, but at least since the Second World War it has become, with increasing application, statutory. In almost no case does the initiative rest exclusively or at all with the lay members. In the appointment of a vice-chancellor perhaps, the initiative will be fairly equally divided amongst all members of the selection committee, any one of whom will be free to put forward names for consideration and even to make delicate enquiries of potential candidates. When it comes to what might be called the semi-official enquiries, the letters, however, will usually be written by the chairman of council[52], but only on the approval of the whole committee. In all other appointment committees, even those for senior officials, the 'running' is more likely to be made by the vice-chancellor than a layman and, in the case of academic appointments, the laymen are unlikely to play any part at all until candidates are interviewed—and this is true whether or not a post is filled by public advertisement.

In all modern universities the overriding concern in making appointments is, however, with those procedures which seem most

---

[50] In more modern charters senate has the right to be consulted about senior appointments to the administration. See the historical survey above, Chapter II.

[51] Once a selection committee has communicated its choice to the successful applicants the latter will normally plan on that basis without waiting for formal ratification by council. In no case that we have come across has a successful applicant been landed in an impossible situation by a 'premature assumption of office', though occasionally a candidate with two offers in hand may prefer the one that is formally unconditional, and this can give rise to talk of council interference. Such is council's veto power.

[52] Or by the registrar in his name.

likely to lead to the selection of the best available candidate—and this aim is common to laymen and academics alike, however they might otherwise differ. From this follows the care taken over references and the use of assessors as well as the various 'weightings' given to lay and academic members depending on the type of appointment being made. But even from this point of view, there are no obvious grounds for totally excluding all laymen from the sacred groves of academe.

It is clear that laymen will tend to bring different skills and possibly different criteria to the business of appointing than will their academic colleagues. The important factor, however, is that the laymen acknowledge this, and in most cases appreciate too that their skills and criteria will be more relevant in the case of administrative than of purely academic appointments. An academic much experienced in university appointments told us that in his experience lay members of professorial appointment committees normally played little or no part. When, however, it came to the appointment of what might be called 'semi-professional' academics like lawyers and doctors, he added, legally and medically qualified laymen often proved their competence to take a full part in the discussion. Our informant could remember only one case where a layman attempted to go beyond his brief or his competence, and in that case he was a nuisance but not a determining factor. 'Bruce Truscott' in his discussion of redbrick universities was able to produce some rather more scaring examples (though 'very few').[53] We, however, were unable to discover recent parallels, and little belief in their possibility.[54]

It is clear, too, that no one could say with any confidence that lay members do worse, by the strictest academic criteria, than selection committees drawn exclusively from the senate occasionally manage to do. It is, indeed, possible that laymen would even have been less likely to prefer the 'safe' but narrow scholar to the venturesome intellectual, but from a non-academic occupation, as head of a new programme (to mention one case known to us) or (to mention another) to be impressed by the interview 'showman' who soon proved incapable of holding together, let alone inspiring, a department of ten people. Laymen may also, perhaps by their mere presence, ensure that the procedure is not marred by petty professional jealousies or undue considerations of 'clubbability'. These examples of academic failings are not to be taken as representative— but unreformed Oxford is not without relevance as a reminder of

[53] *Op. cit.*, p. 87.
[54] Except occasionally among those who had not served on a committee but who no doubt had read 'Truscott'.

what can happen to a self-perpetuating group.[55] Laymen, on the evidence available to us, need neither be feared nor despised as members of a selection committee any more than they should be seen as indispensable.

Council's exclusive legal right to 'hire' remains intact, and only by convention must it accept the recommendation of others; but its right to 'fire' (which might be regarded as part of the appointment power) was hedged around with constitutional limitations even before the passage of the Industrial Relations Act, 1972. Most charters[56] now state the only reason on which a member of the academic staff may be dismissed as being 'for good cause', which is then normally defined to mean either incapacity or scandal.[57] Since the Second World War statutes increasingly lay down sometimes elaborate procedural rules for the exercise of this dismissal power, rules which include, in the most recent charters, such things as the right of the academic to appear on his own behalf or to appeal possibly (as we have seen at York) to a specially constituted appeal board. Council thus cannot, by any stretch of the imagination, or in any significant sense, be said to govern universities through an effective power of patronage.

In any university the committee which deals with its physical development may seem to the outsider to be pivotal for the whole growth, character and evolution of the university. Those who decide what buildings are to be set up, where and in what order, it would seem, inevitably also decide what academic activities are possible. Moreover, decisions about what architects to employ or what general character the building should have, will influence the whole ambience of the university in more subtle ways. Logically, of course, the reverse also holds; those who decide upon the nature of the academic activities and the priorities with which they will be pursued determine what buildings are necessary.

In fact, the buildings committees[58] operate between two major

---

[55] The Robbins *Report* saw both laymen and external referees as possible safeguards against 'scandalous or corrupt' appointments. S. 711.

[56] Usually in the statutes, but occasionally in ordinances.

[57] Idleness is seldom specifically included in the definition, though no doubt covered by e.g. 'misdemeanour in office'. The ex-university colleges favour a deemed resignation of anyone 'convicted of felony' or 'found lunatic' so that dismissal procedures are not relevant. 'Scandalous, immoral or disgraceful' conduct was specified till York (1963) omitted it, since when it has been progressively emasculated, e.g. Essex and Surrey omit 'immoral', Stirling omits altogether; but the Open retains all.

[58] Known, in different universities, under a variety of titles including buildings, sites, estates, and development committee.

constraints. On the one hand there are the academic policies and priorities, which in our experience are invariably decided elsewhere. On the other hand there is the simple availability of sites and planning permissions, and the availability of funds, whether from the University Grants Committee or from the proceeds of a private appeal. What is more the UGC, in having to decide between competing projects for funds from different universities, of necessity must question the purpose of particular buildings, the need for them in one university compared with the need elsewhere, and thus the relationship of any project to the academic profile of the university, not to mention such more mundane matters as cost limits and value for money. Between them these constraints leave to the buildings committees comparatively little room to manœuvre, at least in policy terms. Most of their work, therefore, tends to matter of detail and of seeking the best means whereby physically to translate the academic intentions of the university. It is true that the much publicised saga of the Union building at the University of Warwick suggests otherwise, but it will suffice to comment that this story (as published) shocked people to the extent it did in large measure because of its rarity.[59]

Nevertheless the buildings committee is one which can make the greatest demands on its laymen, partly because it is the committee with the most direct external relations with architects and professional advisers and with local authorities and their planning officers. This is clearly an area in which full use can be made of lay and local experts, and where the expertise they offer will not only be technical but also political. Local political influence may greatly help a university which is in process of redeveloping a whole area in competition with other potential users. National influence may even be useful: one chairman of council told us how he was able personally to persuade the minister to intervene with a nationalized industry over a major site issue. Again, questions of building priority often turn on technical and physical feasibility, and sometimes, when the issues are finely balanced, a strong line on a site committee may be decisive; we heard of a recent case at Oxbridge[60],

[59] THOMPSON: *Warwick University Ltd* (Penguin Books, 1970) pp. 65–70 and 128–30; the account given there is not universally accepted, but it was to it that people reacted. See our Appendix.

[60] Immediately after the Second World War, to give a different example, the preparation of Oxford's development policy fell, by default, to the committee dealing with building rationing. (At least one of the members, the future Lord Murray of Newhaven, had qualifications and a contribution which looked as much lay as academic.) There seems to have been a similar situation at some redbricks at that time.

and no doubt cases also occur where laymen are involved, though architects are probably far more influential. It may look therefore as if the buildings committee decides on academic planning, but when the question is pressed it is clear that the committee does not normally take such decisions, even if occasionally the decision is taken formally at one of its meetings. It must not be forgotten that there are academic members of the committee and that these are often key members of senate. Even in these cases, therefore, it would be to strain accuracy to say that the decision is taken *by* the lay members. In any case the key figures in the work of the buildings committee tend, increasingly, to be the vice-chancellor, the relevant university official, and, if less commonly, the lay chairman. The first of these brings to the work the prestige and knowledge of his office as well as his role of authoritative interpreter of academic purpose.[61] The buildings officer brings to the discussion an unrivalled experience gained from close and detailed liaison with the UGC as well as from his immersion in the local situation, not to mention his roots in an enlarged and increasingly professionalized body of university administrators.[62] The lay chairman possesses the influence naturally accruing to any chairman as well as that deriving from whatever personal qualities and relevant extra-mural qualifications he may possess; but, like his lay colleagues, his role may be affected by the extent to which 'building committee is above all a committee where detailed homework has to be done before a meeting . . . (and the extent to which) universities are indeed much too complicated for laymen to have much influence at a technical level'.[63] It remains true that the layman who knows how to make use of bulk buying or how to let building contracts, or who is familiar with the reputations of quantity surveyors and management consultants, can provide free an important service for which industry and commerce would pay: but the university nowadays is in the position of the firm which respects, but does not depend on, its consultants' advice.

About finance committees a not dissimilar account must be given. Once again the room for independent decision-making is much more limited than at first might appear, even although it remains important in certain respects. Finance committees operate within the same constraints as do site committees, namely the influence of the UGC on the one hand and the requirements of academic policy on the other. True, the formal list of functions performed by the finance committee is far from insignificant. It is probably the one

---

[61] See the fuller discussion in the next chapter.
[62] See below, Chapter VII.
[63] To quote the judgement of a senior university official of wide experience.

committee to look closely at the budget as a whole; it must endorse the final submissions to the UGC, both for recurrent and capital expenditure, and authorize the distribution of funds once received; it must try to ensure that funds authorized for one purpose are not improperly used for another, and above all it must keep the university solvent. In all cases, of course, the committee operates subject to the approval of council, which is invariably forthcoming, and with the help of the university's financial officials. But its responsibility seems both wide and basic.

To help put the finance committee in its proper perspective let us look first at the heads of university expenditure and the proportions each head bears to the total. It would probably be invidious to take the budgets of individual universities; it is also not necessary, since the general point can be made just as well with reference to the expenditure of all universities grouped together. The figures in the following table are taken from a report of the UGC and apply to the year 1966–7.[64]

	£m		%		%
1. Administration	12·576	or	6·7	(1961–2)	6·8
2. Academic salaries, etc.	66·614	or	35·2	(1961–2)	35·9
3. Departmental wages	18·761	or	10·0	(1961–2)	9·7
4. Departmental and lab. maintenance	14·354	or	7·6	(1961–2)	7·5
Sub-total:	99·729	or	52·8	(1961–2)	53·1
5. Libraries, museums	7·855	or	4·2	(1961–2)	4·1
6. Building repair and maintenance	7·858	or	4·2	(1961–2)	3·1
7. Rates, insurance, light, heat, porters, etc.	18·403	or	9·9	(1961–2)	10·6
8. Other expenditure	17·230	or	9·2	(1961–2)	11·3
9. Expenditure from research grants and other specific income	25·202	or	13·3	(1961–2)	11·0
Total expenditure	188·853			(74·550)	

The room to manœuvre in relation to most of these items is remarkably small at any given time. Thus item 9 is largely self-balancing except to the extent that a research grant does not meet

[64] UGC: *University Development 1962–7* (Cmnd 3820 of 1968) p. 40; because of 'rounding off' the individual items do not add up precisely to the 'totals'. All figures are, however, as given in the original.

all the actual expenses generated by the project. Academic salaries constitute the largest single item—but the level of salaries is fixed by national agreement, and to postpone filling vacancies produces relatively small savings. Wage-levels for most non-academic ancillary staff are nowadays determined by collective agreement with trade unions. To postpone other kinds of expenditure—on repairs, maintenance—can be done only if it has not already been done too often. What this means is that at any one time, merely to maintain a university's existing commitments may consume something over 95 per cent of the next year's available income—and possibly well over that figure.[65] This, however, is to talk of the scope available to the university; it is not directly to define the internal role of council and its finance committee, only to point out that it cannot under any circumstances be vast.

In those universities which have significant endowments (a tiny minority) finance committees, acting possibly through a sub-committee, play the major role in managing the capital.[66] Finance committees may also be active in raising money from private sources, through a public appeal or otherwise, though probably no more active, as a group, than the vice-chancellor (who is invariably a member). In preparing submissions to the UGC, however, the finance committee normally plays a much less important part than the vice-chancellor or the main academic bodies, if only because it rarely initiates new expenditure. If one leaves aside the effects merely of inflationary cost rises (considerable as these have been since the mid-1960s) pressure for additional expenditure comes from academic proposals to expand existing activities (possibly reflecting a shift in student preferences) or to undertake new ones, from the desire (or need) of the officials for additional staff and equipment, or from the consequential need for increases under other budget heads such as maintenance. The articulation and aggregation of academic demands are exclusively a matter for the academic decision-making process, guided, it may be, by an academic committee and/or the vice-chancellor. Where finance committee may come into its own is in reviewing the claims of the administration, in making sure that consequential expenditure is taken adequately

---

[65] One bursar told us, and many others agreed, that he regarded 4 per cent as the maximum uncommitted income on which decisions were required, even in a period of rapid expansion. More recently the combined impact of inflation and government policy have reduced this to a minus figure—which of course demands the most difficult decisions of all.

[66] In 1966–7 endowment income amounted to 1·5 per cent of total income for all universities except the former CATs (whose inclusion reduces the figure). UGC: *op. cit.*, p. 38.

into account, and that, in other technical and detailed ways, the submission makes financial sense as a whole. So far as one can tell, however, the persuasiveness of the submission in the eyes of the UGC depends upon the academic purposes for which money is sought, upon the unit costs in a particular university as compared with those in other universities, upon the impact of the vice-chancellor and senior officials (who conduct most of the detailed negotiations with the UGC), and upon the standing of the university in terms of academic reputation, administrative competence, and general probity.[67] Clearly finance committee is in no position to influence all these factors, even indirectly, and over none has it complete control; it is not, therefore, the key actor in a university's relations with the UGC.

In obtaining money for research, from whatever source, finance committee tends to play an even more restricted, if important, part. Research grants, normally, are solicited by academics and awarded to them for specific purposes; finance committee is concerned simply to ensure that the grant adequately covers the real cost to the university—or at least that the additional costs are bearable; but even here, as often as not, it leaves the actual vetting of grant applications and awards to the vice-chancellor and the officials, and in no way is concerned to appraise the inherent desirability of the research in question.

Once the university's income is known, the use to which it should be put is very largely decided in advance either (as we have seen) by existing commitments, or by the conditions attached to its grant by the UGC. Real decisions therefore have to be made only about the distribution of any untied surplus remaining after existing commitments are met or about the incidence of cuts should that 'surplus' be a negative one. And the first decision made in every university, so far as we have been able to discover, is upon the proportion of this uncommitted sum which should be set aside for academic developments and how much should be retained for other purposes.[68] The determination of the amounts required for the latter seems to be one of the very few decisions of potential importance to be taken exclusively 'at council level'. Commonly the figure will

---

[67] These generalizations about persuasiveness are impossible to document, and derive from a mixture of observation and the speculations of others. On this question, as on many other aspects of university budgeting, see the further discussion in Chapter VIII, below.

[68] By 'academic purposes' we mean those items included in heads 2, 3, 4, and 5 in the table of expenditure given above, p. 109, and by 'other purposes' those under heads 1, 6, 7, and 8.

be established by the bursar in consultation with the registrar, the chairman of finance committee and, of course, the vice-chancellor.[69] To a large extent the determination will be semi-automatic given prevailing wage rates, insurance premiums, building costs and the like. Nevertheless there is scope for members of finance committee to the extent that they possess relevant experience with which to assess or define appropriate criteria of prudence—a matter possibly demanding great technical skills in a time of inflation (e.g. in creating, or encouraging bursars to create, 'secret pockets' of reserves)—or to scrutinize the claims of the university administration itself for staff, equipment and day-to-day expenditure. In fixing the amount to be devoted to these non-academic[70] activities finance committee neither has a completely free hand nor does it operate in a political vacuum: many administrators take a perhaps perverse professional pride in keeping their expenses down, increasing resort is nowadays had to the assistance of outside consultants or to one of the university O. and M. units set up in the 1960s, and the whole climate of opinion is affected by the traditional academic resentment of administrative spending (a resentment likely to be voiced by the academic members of finance committee). Even so, the sum thus allocated both reflects a significant degree of discretion on the part of laymen and significantly affects the amount of, and so even the course of, academic development.

To say that finance committee, normally with a majority of lay members, affects academic development is not at all the same thing as to say that it thereby contravenes the conventions of academic self-government. The decisions it takes are taken, firstly, on the basis of financial or administrative but not academic judgements. Moreover, once the size of the 'academic' slice of the cake has been established, further division between competing academic claims is left to academics or, possibly, to a joint senate-council committee on which the academic voice is most heeded.[71] And, to the extent that the academic budget does come before finance committee (either in the form of the draft submission to the UGC or of the annual estimates), it is set out under very broad heads like 'new posts' which convey little or no detailed information and therefore

---

[69] At one London college, a new 'registrar' told us, the work had in effect been done by a 'subordinate of the "bursar"'; and another remarked, 'I've just put the draft to the "vice-chancellor"; he has no comment.'

[70] 'Non-academic' only in the sense that the activities in question do not consist of teaching and research; we do not wish to suggest that they are not essential to the life of the university.

[71] See the further discussion in Chapter VIII, below.

neither invite nor receive detailed examination.[72] In any case, much of the need for non-academic expenditure is generated by the academic policies of a university, while much of the remaining administrative costs are generated by the need for information on the part of the UGC, the impact of legislation, the pressures for efficiency, and the call for new budgetary techniques. Conversely, it may matter less which body ensures that expenditure does not outrun income than that some body does, the task itself being inescapable. Significantly, academics who wish to press a case for additional funds invariably will lobby not the finance committee nor any of its lay members but the vice-chancellor, who is not only likely to be the most influential single member of finance committee (in many universities second not even to its chairman) but is also at least as much a spokesman for the academics as for the laymen or officials.[73]

Once the broad allocation of funds has been agreed by council, on the recommendation of finance committee, the latter's day-to-day work consists primarily of ensuring that adequate accounting procedures are followed so as to make certain that expenditure will only be incurred within the limits authorized by finance committee and, ultimately, by the UGC and House of Commons; of adjusting the budget to unexpected changes in circumstances; and, where relevant, of managing the university's investments and/or overdraft.

The task of finance committee—and one which it takes very seriously—is therefore to assess the financial solvency of its university, to watch over its financial methods, to oversee the efficiency of the administration, possibly to try to attract new funds, and generally to facilitate academic policy by ensuring that no unnecessary financial risks have been taken and that no avoidable financial obstacles will be erected. In so doing it may, on occasion, have to rule that some proposed new venture cannot be undertaken, or some existing one be pruned, but in so doing, it may be argued, it does no more than mediate the facts of economic life to those who are less directly and less intimately familiar with them.

Examination of the three key council committees suggests, then, that one is not presented with any 'seat of power'; instead one finds

[72] On one occasion a finance committee almost overlooked the need to give formal approval to the budget as a whole; pre-occupied with matters of business detail it at first forgot and latter approved without discussion the total annual expenditure of over £2 million.

[73] See our discussion in the next chapter. The director of an audio-visual centre, a non-academic whose expenditure had to be met from general university funds rather than those earmarked for any particular academic unit or project, was surprised even to be asked whether he would lobby finance committee.

focal points for different decision-taking processes in none of which do members of council have wide discretion. Least of all do the lay members nowadays occupy positions from which to dictate policy to subordinate academics. And, if it is true that laymen constitute the majority in council and in most of its committees, it is also true, and possibly more important, that the academic members are the knowledgeable 'insiders', that opinion is not necessarily divided only along lay/academic lines, and that the most authoritative figure may well be the vice-chancellor. Even on finance and buildings committees a decision may in fact be taken on the strength of the contributions made by academics. Their presence there, we were told by an experienced university administrator with a commercial background, is 'invaluable' because they are more intelligent and critical than most of the clients with whom architects and others normally deal; architects, for example, and laymen generally derived great benefit from 'being forced to explain their proposals in detail and to relate them to fundamental principles'. On the other hand, he continued, academics are sometimes too 'idealistic' when confronted with economic and commercial problems so that the presence of laymen was also essential, if only because 'they know the nuts and bolts of £ s. d.' It is also important to remember that friction between a body like finance committee and academics, where it exists, is not simply the product of lay membership of the former, as we have seen at Oxford.

Perhaps the most remarkable feature of relations between laymen and academics in most universities today is the lack of conflict between the two groups. Even in the spheres of finance and physical development, academic self-government is the general rule and the conditions for its maintenance are satisfied. These conditions have been defined by Sir Eric Ashby in the following terms:

'In a university where non-academics participate in its self-government, and where they are in fact in the majority on the body where sovereignty resides, it is essential that non-academics should identify with the university, and not consider themselves representatives of interests outside the university. It is essential, too, that all academic decisions should be delegated to the academics themselves, who must always be regarded as members of a society, not employees. Without this internal coherence and internal balance of power, a university may be free of intervention from outside, and yet have its autonomy betrayed from inside.'[74]

> ' *Op. cit.*, p. 296.

The process of identification with the university on the part of laymen, to which Sir Eric Ashby refers, normally comes about in the day-to-day interactions of the main actors within university government, assisted by the fact that often the academics will constitute a majority of those present and voting at meetings of council or some of its committees.[75] Much depends, of course, on the skill and tact of the senior academics within a university and particularly on the educative function of the vice-chancellor in dealing with laymen. Not untypical was a vice-chancellor in a northern university during the last war who, we were told, set himself to reduce the power of council in academic questions because 'he was an academic snob who regarded laymen as tradespeople'. The process will be helped too by the initial selection of laymen, especially the co-opted group which can be and is chosen from people who understand universities and who are often, in practice, the most active group. Fortunately for universities, many laymen regard it as an honour to be invited to join a council. But in time even those who are appointed by, for example, local authorities or other non-university agencies tend to adapt themselves (where necessary) to the academic environment. And those who remain most 'alien' tend not to be placed on the most important committees. Even in the nineteenth-century heyday of lay power, the laymen were seldom a homogenous group with a clear policy. They have always included, as well as men primarily interested in commerce and industry, powerful groups interested in scholarship and education, or in moral and social purposes, and they still do. These groups have always been as likely to ally themselves with the vice-chancellor or the academics as with other laymen.[76] That aside, it is clear that, whatever the committee or the area in which laymen participate, nowadays laymen lack the political bases from which to make effective use of the powers provided by the charter. In a number of ways one can map the relative decline of the layman. For one thing a modern university is a much more complex institution and, particularly since the Second World War, it has been undergoing very much more rapid change. It is thus much more difficult for non-academics to have the detailed knowledge without

---

[75] This is generally the case in the more rural (and smaller) universities, but not in the cities.

[76] Many of the laymen to whom we talked were themselves scholars; one had been driven by the great depression from All Souls into industry, and these, and others, were extremely anxious to keep industrial values out of the university, perhaps in compensation. Another group has been interested in moral and social influences, as witness the donor of halls of residence. There are also religious groups.

which effective intervention, and certainly authoritative intervention, is impossible. Academics themselves have increased their prestige within society at large; jokes about absent-minded professors have almost died out, science professors run departments the size of a good business, and some social scientists and technologists are called upon to advise whole industries.[77] Nor do laymen have the same responsibility for providing funds. Individual and enterprising academics are much more likely (partly because they are more likely to succeed) to go out themselves to seek funds from the research councils or from foundations and industry. The main bulk of finance now comes through the UGC rather than from private funds obtained from or through individual members of council, or from public money in the form of rate contributions from local authorities. There is no longer the danger, ever present up to 1939, that the laymen might suddenly be called on to ensure that, say, salaries be paid.[78] Even between 1962 and 1967 the proportion of funds coming from local authorities declined and from the UGC increased. In 1962–3 1·9 per cent of university income came from local authorities as opposed to 70·1 per cent from the UGC. By 1966–7 however, the proportion of contributions from local authorities had declined to 0·8 per cent while the UGC contribution had risen to 73·8 per cent.[79] It is not only of course that the UGC provides more money than the groups personified by lay members, it is also that with public money come greater degrees of public supervision of expenditure. As laymen have thus ceased to provide either the degree of financial support or the sole source of public audit which once they did, their influence over university decision-making has inevitably declined. (Too much may however be made of this last factor. The overall decline owes more to the other factors we mention.)

Finally, the growth of university administration as a profession has served to rival the power of the laymen at least as much as, and in our view rather more than, it rivals that of the academics.

Writing in 1958 Sir Charles Morris (as he then was), at the height of his success as Vice-Chancellor of Leeds, said that 'there can be no question that (the universities) have been moving quite

[77] At one midland university we were told how little the laymen regarded their academics until well into the 1950s (without attempting to interfere academically). Their attitude changed about the time that one of the economists was found to be advising, nationally, on the future of an industry important locally, and being paid for doing so.

[78] See, e.g. A. W. CHAPMAN: *op. cit.*, Chapter 28, on the effects of the depression in Sheffield.

[79] UGC: *op. cit.*, table 19, p. 38.

considerably in the direction of greater academic self-government in recent years, and especially since the Second World War. . . . Academics have not needed to ask themselves any searching questions about the matter because, belonging as they do either historically or spiritually to Oxford and Cambridge, they have assumed by instinct that such a move is . . . right. . . . The laymen have concluded from experience that a mixed academic and lay government is good for universities only so far as it can secure a very high degree of independent control by academic persons of all academic affairs.'[80] This, coming from a university where lay involvement is as vigorous as anywhere, may of course have contained an element of wishfulness, but a decade later we found plenty to suggest that the movement had continued steadily in the same direction.

As both a footnote to and as some substantiation of the general analysis which we have just put forward we might mention the two kinds of decision which alone have come to our notice as clear indications of council autonomy or discretion. They are firstly, that councils naturally continue to be sovereign in fact as well as in name over their own committees. This normally is not of very great significance, but has played an important part, on occasion, when universities have had to contend with the demands of students for participation on all university bodies. This is not to say that laymen have been the only members of council opposed to student participation, far from it; some councils have been less resistant than senates to the inclusion of student members. Indeed, in one university it was council which decided 'without any prior consultation with any academic body'[81] to include student members on a committee appointed to select a new vice-chancellor.[82] The second example we can point to is the decision at, for instance, the University of Bristol not to increase fees charged to overseas students. It was Council that took this decision in the face of a recommendation in the other direction from the Bristol Senate. It is worth noting that these cases—student power, and overt government interference—are new problems, outside the area over which the tradition of non-interference has been built up. Rather similarly, student disruptions have sometimes forced council to occupy, in the sudden emergency, and in virtue of their responsibilities for

---

[80] SIR CHARLES (LORD) MORRIS: *op. cit.*, p. 265.

[81] Professor E. Grebenik, in a letter to the *Universities Quarterly*, 24:4, Autumn 1970.

[82] A contrary example—where council rejected a senate decision to include students on a joint selection committee—could also be cited. Interestingly, this second example stimulated protests from neither senate nor students.

university property and discipline, a position of wholly unfamiliar importance and decision (which we discuss further in Chapter IX). The rarity of these cases of interference can perhaps best be judged from the anxieties expressed to the IAU Conference on university autonomy by Dr H. Butterfield, sometime Vice-Chancellor of Cambridge, in 1965. He said no more than: 'I have known cases where . . . the proper autonomy of universities has been overruled by lay elements *in the government* in the appointment to teaching posts'.[83]

In conclusion it may be asked, if our general account be accepted, what need there is for a council in a modern university, and what functions are or may be usefully performed by lay members?

At the general level council would seem to justify its existence in terms of the need to have a focal point for the executive and managerial tasks involved in running any major organization. Most academics, furthermore, would recognize the possible utility of separating the preoccupation with executive and managerial functions from consideration of the real stuff of university government, namely its academic policy, provided only that the former remained substantially subordinate to the latter.[84] Secondly, as we have indicated from time to time, it does seem useful to associate and use outside experience particularly on the business side of the university. Apart from anything else it is hard to understand why any sensible academic would wish, for example, to be chairman of a catering committee.[85] Thirdly, we should mention (without necessarily endorsing) a view put to us by more than one experienced academic in the course of our interviews. They made the point that as a consequence partly of the rapid growth of universities and the creation of new chairs, and as a result also of the increasing tendency for senates to be 'representational', senate decisions were more likely to be the product of shifting majorities and an inexperienced membership, and thus less likely to form part of a consistent and coherent policy. In such circumstances, they suggested, there was a particular need for the stability provided by an independent reviewing body

[83] IAU: *University Autonomy*, Papers 7, Paris 1965, p. 70 (emphasis added). It is possible he was referring to Regius chairs, which are in the gift of the Government.

[84] Interesting, in this connection, is a set of reform proposals drawn up by a group of radical staff members at one of the large civic universities. Having argued the case for a 'single-tier' system of government under which sovereignty would reside in a body of academics, they nevertheless suggested that a powerful finance committee of that body should contain a substantial lay membership.

[85] There are moves at Leeds and Sussex to extend lay activity into senate committees.

like the lay-dominated council. Fourthly, it is often said that laymen protect the institutional autonomy of the university, on the theory that if responsible local citizens are satisfied with affairs, then governments will have no excuse for interference—better King Log than King DES. Thus Lord Morris said in 1958, 'In the public arena academic self-government . . . will finally have to be defended . . . by laymen.'[86] The planners of at least some of the new universities thought likewise. Dr Sloman thought that the laymen were 'watch-dogs for the community'[87], and at York they looked to 'non-academic government' for 'adequate safeguards for the proper expenditure of public money'.[88] Lord Robbins also told the Franks Commission that laymen protect the university from Government interference.[89] But when closely cross-questioned on the whole question of accountability by the Committee of Public Accounts, none of the various groups of academic objectors, in their curiously imprecise evidence, thought it worth arguing far along these lines. The Committee of Vice-Chancellors and Principals gave it no more than an oblique reference.[90] Lord Murray praised the financial skill of universities—'no deficit financing, no supplemental votes'—but doubted if laymen did much more than 'give public confidence'.[91] The warmest comments came from Lord James, who was not objecting to accountability.[92]

Turning rather to the role of the individual layman it may be suggested that he has three functions within a modern university, of which the first is that of the 'service' of expertise and knowledge. This can be tapped, on the university's terms, at will, with very little obligation beyond a willingness to keep the laymen generally and mildly confidentially informed. 'Expertise' may not be merely technical. We constantly met administrators and staff who mentioned the value of the intelligent, experienced outsider, in mediating between academic factions, asking questions from a detached standpoint, or illuminating a problem with outside knowledge. (This is a service academics often give on other bodies.) The service rendered consists essentially of making possible the intentions of the university, like a curler sweeping the ice before his partner's stone, affecting the range but not the aim. For this purpose most

---

[86] Op. cit., p. 266.
[87] A. E. SLOMAN: A University in the Making, p. 79.
[88] Report of the Planning Committee (Chairman, Lord Robbins).
[89] Oral Evidence Pt. XI, p. 178.
[90] Special Report of the Committee of Public Accounts, Session 1966–7, on Parliament and Control of University Expenditure, Sir Charles Wilson, Q. 180.
[91] Ibid. Qq. 779, 799, 800.
[92] Ibid. Qq. 550–3.

universities find it difficult to recruit capable members. A substantial number, possibly as many as a half, are merely 'lay figures'. The direct representatives of 'society', the local government appointees, supply most of these 'lay figures'.[93]

Among the business laymen, employees or executives of national or regional firms are rare. We were several times told that they tended to be unsuitable, partly because they are not their own masters, and must work relatively regular hours, and perhaps do not feel independent of their company. Much more important, they are seldom either local men or likely to spend their lives in the locality. They may therefore lack local pride and concern. We were often told that the disappearance of the local firm is drying up the supply of suitable candidates, to the point, one northern registrar remarked, of making it doubtful if the council could continue to be significant. Certainly there is a shortage of independent but important business and professional men available for service in some of the rural universities.

The fact that neither employees nor landed magnates are much able to help (with notable exceptions) may indicate the chief qualities needed: knowledge of finance, construction, planning, or management; independence; the ability to spare a great deal of time; and the motive to do so when little beyond 'being in the know' in a great idealistic enterprise (rather than any degree of control), is offered in return for a real grind. This may account for the presence, in the very small group of lay members who are deeply involved, of heads of firms, and of professional men, notably important solicitors.[94] No doubt because they are best able to regulate their own working hours and have time, there are retired people in some numbers. This may also explain why the 'representatives of society' tend to be drawn from a narrow range of that society, though hardly why there are so few women. It is, however, a point of the very greatest importance that it would only be sensible to select laymen primarily on a basis of 'representativeness' rather than of ability to provide service if, counter to the trends of the past century, they were to take a greater part in the direction of the university.[95]

Nevertheless the second main function of the laymen is to be in

[93] For a comment on this at Warwick, see the Appendix.

[94] We have not attempted any sort of statistical analysis, which would depend on quantification of very elusive factors.

[95] Similarly, it is sometimes suggested that writers and artists, or trades unionists should be appointed. See, e.g. LSE *Report* of Machinery of Government Committee, Minority Report 1968, and E. P. THOMPSON, ed.: *op. cit.*, p. 161. Leeds, in 1969, in fact decided to invite the TUC to suggest people who might be elected to its Council by Court.

some sense representatives of society able in some way to certify as plain men that all is reasonable in the 'ivory tower'. This function is served, explicitly, by the local government nominees to be found on nearly all councils, but implicitly by all laymen.[96] They have to be made to understand generally in broad terms what the university is doing and how it proposes to do it; it is their function to say whether it has been made at least to sound self-consistent. Simply because they are outsiders, they force the university to articulate its assumptions: it is a valuable discipline for officials and initiators to have to draft papers with the uninitiated in mind. As the layman learns more about the university which he has joined, he can begin to see whether the assumptions have indeed been articulated. Sir Phillip Morris, when Vice-Chancellor of Bristol University, took it a little further in telling the Franks Commission that 'their presence frequently induces much better behaviour in one's colleagues and thus they (the colleagues) make a better contribution'.[97] Moreover the layman performs this service in the knowledge that he has a real responsibility: he knows that if things go wrong he may have to defend what has been done to the outside world. The layman endorses the judgement of the academic community (however defined) and validates it as an act of the university.

Thus the layman facilitates and validates. His third function is to defend. He is supposed to protect the institution's autonomy. It has been argued that it is reasonable for the society which supports higher education financially to wish to control it, but it is also argued that the lay presence on council is the best instrument of (or, possibly, substitute for) social control. This is of course an argument that could be turned to justify greater interference by laymen, although, as we have suggested, in fact it seems rather to be a defence of academic self-government. Universities and the laymen walk a tight rope here; no one, least of all contemporary laymen, in most universities, would wish to return to the position of genuine lay ascendency of the kind which was known before the First World War. But on the other hand, 'if the greater society in which the university lives provides the resources, makes its demands and wishes to express its control through lay membership of the

[96] Many (perhaps most) of the local government nominees will have little time to render great service to the university, although amongst those who do have time may be found individuals whose experience enhances their value to the university. But it is often difficult for someone accustomed to local authority procedures, and who may be constantly attuned to his party and electorate, to adjust his thinking to a university environment.

[97] Oral evidence O.2, p. 22. We have heard that students can perform a similar function.

university government, then it becomes dangerous to allow an erosion of the lay role beyond a point. Too great an erosion will see—and has, of course, seen—a resort to other and nastier methods. If the lay members in university government prove to be weak and useless, society will employ its own government more directly.'[98] It may be that the erosion as we have described it has reached that point. We have seen that no one thought it worth while trying to tell the Public Accounts Committee that public control was effective, or that finance committees are a substitute for the Comptroller and Auditor-General. This is somewhat surprising, for the whole tenor of the enquiry on both sides was that universities are well run. It may thus be the case that the more the layman identifies with the university, the better he understands the role the academics think he should play, and the more real the academic self-government, then the less can the layman claim to represent society, and the less is he able to stand between the university and those who think academics over-privileged and under-aware.

Apart from the suspicions of some students and junior staff (to which we have already alluded), there seems to be general agreement on the fact of academic self-government. Only with respect to events at the University of Warwick (which we discuss in the Appendix to this book) has there been serious public criticism of lay 'power' in recent years—and this was voiced only by some members of that University. This is not to say, however, that the situation meets with comparably widespread approval. On the one side, for example, laymen are seen (presumably critically) as 'closely linked to the protective systems set up by the academic body in support of a collective and all-embracing elitism'.[99] On the other side, a report on the University of Lancaster by Mr Tom Taylor (a local government nominee on its Council) suggests that the disturbances there in 1972 revealed, if they were not in part caused by, the undue weakness of Council. He therefore recommended that there should be lay representation on the academic Development Committee and stronger lay representation on the Buildings and Finance Committees. Furthermore, he concluded by saying that 'there should also be continued or greater opportunities for Council to debate and discuss the broad *educational* strategy of the University, including its future development (physical *and academic*) as well as matters of staff and

[98] BERNARD SCHAFFER: 'Committees and Co-ordination' in RUTH ATKINS, ed.: *University Government*, published by the Federation of Australian University Staff Associations, pp. 59–60.

[99] JOHN DUTTON in a review of Halsey and Trow's *The British Academics*, published in *Higher Education Review*, 4 (1), Autumn 1970, p. 84.

student welfare generally'.[100] It is, of course, never entirely safe to assume that conventional limitations upon the exercise of legal powers guarantee that the latter will never be used. Conventions simply describe the conditions on which the legal powers may be retained and the ways in which they must be used under given political circumstances.[101] It may well be that the effect of public reactions to left-wing student and staff attempts to 'politicize' universities, combined with other radical critiques of universities as socially isolated 'elitist' institutions, has been to change the relevant political circumstances. The reactivation of councils' reserve powers with respect to all major decisions, a possible consequence of such a change, would please many who are suspicious of academic men, but otherwise would bring satisfaction only to those who appreciate the ironies of life.

Note on a Committee at the University of Birmingham

Much of our discussion covers the relation of actual practice to the formal position described in this chapter, a subject on which remarkably little has been published. One interesting aspect of actual practice has however been described in Sir Robert Aitken's account of the government of Birmingham University[102], and recorded in the *University Calendar*.

We have remarked that virtually all council committees include academics. But in the instance we now discuss it was not so. The Finance and General Purposes Committee, the chief committee of Council, with delegated power to make junior academic appointments, excluded academic staff. According to Sir Robert it excluded the Vice-Chancellor as well: and this must for very many years have been almost unique in this country. However, the Vice-Chancellor, the Deputy Principal (another 'administrator'), two officials, and eight academics 'attend by invitation but have no

---

[100] *Report* of the Taylor enquiry, University of Lancaster 1972, pp. 16 and 17 (our emphasis). The *Times Higher Education Supplement*, July 21, 1972, in its editorial comment suggested that 'it will . . . be useful if the university council plays a more central role in deciding policy, and so perhaps bring [*sic*] a layman's coolness to the sometimes hot-house atmosphere of an academic institution'. As we pointed out in our historical discussion, it should be remembered that the formal powers of the Council at Lancaster are less than those granted by most other charters. In particular they omit powers in academic matters.

[101] See the discussion of constitutional conventions in G. MARSHALL and G. C. MOODIE: *Some Problems of the Constitution* (Hutchinson, 5th ed., 1972) Chapter 2.

[102] SIR R. AITKEN: *Administration of a University*, 1966.

vote', and this group is listed in the *Calendar* as attenders, not as members.[103] This arrangement in itself illustrates, in an unusually public form, the process by which power has been shifting away from laymen, who in the case of Birmingham were originally very active and still had greater than usual powers.[104] But this arrangement has been modified further. Sub-committees of the FGPC have been set up on which sit various of those entitled to 'attend' the FGPC, plus others, including a third consisting of official and academic staff appointed by academic bodies. One of these sub-committees 'consists of one nominee from each Faculty Board with the Vice-Principal (an academic) and the Deputy Principal under the chairmanship of the Vice-Chancellor',[105] but includes *no* full members of the parent FGPC. This sub-committee, representing an extension of a committee unknown even to Sir Kenneth Wheare[106], 'has to satisfy itself that an appointment is *financially provided for* and that the *conditions*, particularly the *salary*, recommended, are *appropriate*. It can then authorize the issue of a letter of appointment.'[107] Thus the whole of the appointment, with its financial implications, was in effect made without reference to any member of the committee to which Council had delegated power to appoint.

Formally the procedure is most illiberal; informally (that is without alteration of the Statutes) the published practice goes beyond the liberality of the Privy Council's Model Charter of 1963, and is not easily distinguished in principle from that at the Open University.[108] It is perhaps typical of published or public comment on university government that this result, through the use of a double delegation of power, is not immediately noticeable even in Sir Robert's lucid prose, which must be read rather carefully to be sure of the actual position.[109] There is a yet further illustration of informal amendment in that, after Sir Robert wrote his account, the

[103] The *Calendar* (1966–7, p. 39), however, also carries a general note to the list of committees that 'the Pro-Chancellor, the Vice-Chancellor and the Treasurer are *ex officio* members of all Committees and Sub-committees of the Council'.

[104] See Chapter II.

[105] *Ibid.*, p. 50. *Calendar* 1966–7, p. 39.

[106] *Government by Committee*, 1955, pp. 9 and 194–5.

[107] SIR R. AITKEN: *op. cit.*, p. 50. (Emphasis added.) Curiously, professorial appointments appear to have been made, in effect, by an equally independent body, but one which was formally a committee of Senate, not of Council, *op. cit.*, p. 43.

[108] See Chapter II, p. 35, f.n. 41.

[109] It is typical of problems of investigation in this field that though the people concerned are usually willing enough to talk, they are very shy of writing. A draft of the foregoing account was submitted to an apparently appropriate quarter, but the discussion had to be telephonic.

membership was further modified. The proportion of academics among those attending at the FGPC table rose from a little over a quarter to a third, by the addition of NPS representatives (one of whom, in his turn, was an observer on Council). Two student representatives were also added. On the appointments sub-committee just discussed, there were now 'two members nominated by the NPS' (who were not the same as those entitled 'to attend by invitation' at the FGPC table). This must be one of the finest examples of the British urge to fight new causes under old banners. What is perhaps surprising is that even in the heat of the Atkinson case[110], no one was deceived, nor even attempted to deceive, by the banner; and the responsibility was laid where it belonged, with the academic staff.

[110] In 1970 a faculty appointing committee recommended that a vacant lectureship in sociology be filled by a Mr Atkinson. The recommendation, exceptionally, was not ratified. It was believed by many people that the refusal was motivated by dislike of Mr Atkinson's political (left-wing) views, and considerable controversy resulted. The point of concern to this study is that the decision not to appoint was taken by other academics—at least in this sense, therefore, academic freedom was not infringed.

Chapter VI

THE VICE-CHANCELLOR

To most students and to some disaffected staff, and particularly to those from other countries, vice-chancellors[1] are the very embodiment of 'the administration'. This is not new. In 1841 the Vice-Chancellor of Cambridge was described as '. . . the chief and almost the sole administrative officer of the University' with an immense list of office duties.[2] Vice-chancellors are listed under the heading of 'Administration' in the tables of membership of university governing bodies printed in the evidence to the Robbins Report.[3] Yet almost all vice-chancellors to whom we have talked resent the label and in 1966, according to one study, more than three-quarters of British vice-chancellors were recruited from the ranks of academics.[4] To be more specific Mr Szreter reported that out of fifty-four individuals studied by him only twelve had not been university teachers at some previous stage in their career and of those twelve, three had spent a period in universities doing research. All but one were academics in the sense that they were graduates of a university.[5]

These two perspectives of the office are reflected in ambiguities

[1] See our definitions at the end of Chapter III, for a discussion of the positions of vice-cancellarial officers. In the present discussion, we include the typical 'vice-chancellor' or head of a quasi-university such as Bangor or Bedford, but much of what we say also applies, *mutatis mutandis*, to the analogous officer at Cambridge or Wales, and, in particular, to the present officer at Oxford. Similarly with the two halves into which the office is divided in the London federation.

[2] G. PEACOCK: *Observations on the Statutes* (of Cambridge) 1841, p. 136. The duties included petty book-keeping; but it seems to have been possible to neglect them on the grand scale, as for fox-hunting.

[3] *Report* of the Committee on Higher Education (Cmnd 2154 of 1963), App. IV Pt. I, Tables 4–13.

[4] R. SZRETER: 'An academic Patriciate', *Universities Quarterly*, winter 1968, p. 17. Szreter includes in his total the heads of the larger London schools whom we also treat as vice-chancellors.

[5] The exception held a professional qualification regarded as equivalent to a degree.

built into the role. Thus the older charters style the vice-chancellor 'chief academic officer', reflecting the position in the last century when the position of the officer was more like that of a headmaster. Since 1948 charters have recognized the emergence of administration into academic life, and he has been styled 'chief academic and administrative officer'.[6] The vice-chancellor is often brought in from outside, but his deputy or deputies are normally chosen from (and sometimes today, by) the senate. On the other hand, the top unambiguously administrative officers, the senior permanent officials like registrars and bursars, are council appointments, and they are still generally responsible not to the vice-chancellor but to council.[7] The dual nature of the vice-cancellarial post is seen again in a recent development. At Birmingham, where the Vice-Chancellor also has the (original) title of Principal, he now has an aide who is not a registrar, but an *alter ego* called Deputy Principal, who is certainly not a conventional official (he has a seat on the main governing bodies) but whose duties are also unlike those delegated to an American 'vice-president for business affairs'. His duties are some of those normally carried out by the vice-chancellor 'shared in whatever manner best suited both'[8], thus calling attention to the wide and largely unspecified role of the chief academic and administrative officer as compared with that of the permanent officials. A similar post existed for a few years (1968–72) at Warwick.[9] Though vice-chancellors are deeply, no doubt mainly, concerned with seeing that the organization works, and so are often counted as administrators for crude statistical purposes (such as Robbins'), it would be quite misleading to overlook the older part of their title of 'chief academic officer'.

They are therefore best seen as university 'centaurs'. For, although their day-to-day activities within the university may conveniently be described as 'administrative', they are expected to be, and in fact often are, academics in purpose and outlook. The author of a

---

[6] Nottingham Charter S. 6. The office is almost as often described as 'principal' as 'chief'.

[7] In many recent cases the 'registrar' is responsible to the vice-chancellor, e.g. Sussex and Stirling, though not the Privy Council's Model Charter. At Brunel he is responsible to Council for policy and to the Vice-Chancellor for administration. See the discussion in our next chapter.

[8] SIR R. AITKEN: *The Administration of a University* (University of London Press, 1966) p. 56.

[9] There are posts of full-time deputy to the vice-chancellor in several of the ex-CATs, alongside those of registrar. These posts were, however, carried over from a different style and system of government, and we do not know how far they will become a permanent feature.

set of fictionalized 'letters to a vice-chancellor' even advised him: 'Be seen in the library, as a user, set aside one day in the week when you will read and write. . . .'[10] Most vice-chancellors would regard this as a counsel of perfection, but among others, Briggs (Sussex), Dainton (Nottingham), Carter (Lancaster), Caine (LSE), Knox (St Andrews), and Ashby (Belfast and Cambridge) have all managed to combine office with continuing scholarship.

The actual duties of a vice-chancellor have never been made explicit. The committee set up to advise the Trustees of Owens College in 1849 suggested they should 'seek an experienced person and define his duties as little as possible'.[11] The first redbrick charters followed this advice very literally.[12] The Privy Council's Model Charter of 1963 gives the vice-chancellor 'a general responsibility to the Council for maintaining and promoting the efficiency and good order of the university'. But it would be misleading to take this too literally. It is true that many people outside the university, and even inside it, regard the vice-chancellor as though he were in fact responsible for efficiency and good order. It is clear too that the vice-chancellor is thereby empowered to interest himself in and to examine any aspects of affairs within the university. He may even be answerable in this area, in the sense that he must normally attempt to explain, defend, or justify to the outside world what goes on within his university. What is untenable however, is the view that the vice-chancellor properly deserves full praise or blame in this context, as he might if he were armed with sufficient power personally to maintain, or for that matter seriously to undermine, efficiency and good order; but he is not so armed.

For the most striking thing about the position of the vice-chancellor is that he is granted virtually no powers by the constitution of any university. Indeed many instruments, especially those written before the First World War, and in Scotland, give no powers 'of any sort, kind or description to tell anybody to do anything about anything'.[13] This too is an old tradition. Mark Pattison was 'unable to define the powers of the vice-chancellor. Probably no definition is possible.'[14] Since 1918, a few powers have usually been specified, typically these three:

[10] 'JAMES DUNDONALD' (pseud.): *Letters to a Vice-Chancellor* (Arnold, 1962) p. 42.

[11] H. B. CHARLTON: *Portrait of University* (Manchester, 1951) p. 33.

[12] Birmingham and Manchester did not even make him 'chief academic officer'. The revised Liverpool Charter of 1961 did little more than that. See below, p. 137, f.n. 42.

[13] Sir P. Morris (Bristol) to the Franks Commission, O.2. p. 20.

[14] *Suggestions*, p. 37.

'The vice-chancellor may refuse to admit any person as a student without assigning any reason, and may suspend any student from any class or classes and may exclude any student from any part of the university or its precincts. He shall report any such suspension or exclusion to the Council and the Senate at their next meeting. . . .

The Vice-Chancellor may resign by writing addressed to the Council.'[15]

Thus, no vice-chancellor has absolute powers over any person or event in his university. Some light on this may be gained from the situation at LSE, typically untypical on this point. There the 'vice-chancellor' (Director) has, comparatively, considerable formalized powers[16], but our informants in the School (who had limited experience in other universities) were almost unanimous in saying that the existence of these 'powers' made no great difference, unless possibly a psychological one, to the running of the School.[17]

Despite the unspecified nature of his positive activities, nevertheless the vice-chancellor is normally the most important single figure in any university. He may, for better or worse, affect the whole climate of a university. His actions, his personality, his strengths and weaknesses, and his attitudes are a frequent topic of academic conversation and gossip. There are numerous more serious testimonials to his importance. The names of vice-chancellors are included, not infrequently, in the Honours Lists (amongst the fifty-four individuals studied by Szreter, fourteen were either knights or peers).[18] Writing in 1931, a group of senior dons said that at redbrick universities 'the authority of the vice-chancellor is, of course, very great. In ordinary routine matters, in practice, even where not

[15] Keele S. 6:4 and 5. It may be noted that refusal to admit does not have to be reported. Some sixteen post-1918 charters have similar provisions (Reading has an appeal against non-admission), and two have slightly more extensive powers (Surrey and Bradford). Five omit refusal to admit. Six (and one draft) give no powers, or only power to resign. Actual power of expulsion usually lies with council, though increasingly with senate.

[16] We say 'formalized' not 'formal' because there is no charter to give them to him, or indeed to make him exist at all. He is unique in not being a statutory officer.

[17] It is clear that the four directors since 1918 would agree with this, though Lord Beveridge might have disliked the possibility of delays if the powers were abolished; see, e.g. his *Working Constitution of the LSE* (private, 1937) pp. 78–80. Sir Alexander Carr-Saunders had little use for formal powers, and provided none for colonial vice-chancellors. See the 'Asquith' *Report* of the Commission on Higher Education in the Colonies (Cmnd 6647 of 1945).

[18] *Op. cit.* Six of these were 'vice-chancellors' of London colleges and the principal of the London federation. Three of the titles had been earned outside the university system.

E

by legal right, he is supreme.'[19] Sir Philip Morris (Bristol) in his evidence to the Franks Committee, refers to the 'pivotal' role of the vice-chancellor and his peculiar ability to 'organize catalysis'.[20] The *Report* of the Robbins Committee gives extended testimony to the importance of the role of the vice-chancellor, saying that:

'It would be difficult to overstate its importance, particularly in a period of expansion, which calls for imagination and continuous initiative. . . . There are certain duties of which the Vice-Chancellor cannot divest himself. He is at once a member of the governing body and Chairman of the main Academic Councils. He must therefore be at the centre of all discussions involving broad questions of internal policy or relations with the outside world. He must represent his institution in all formal or informal relations with the University Grants Committee; he must be present at meetings of the committee of vice-chancellors and principals; he must keep in touch with potential benefactors, and he must be aware, in general, of developments in the various branches of learning. . . . No other enterprise would impose on its Chairman the variety and burden of work that a modern university requires of its vice-chancellor.'[21]

More briefly, and perhaps a shade more hyperbolically, it has been said that 'a vice-chancellor plays many parts. He is the high priest of the hierarchy of teachers and students and the managing director of a large State-supported institute. In his own domain he is the final arbiter of all academic policy and in a wider field he exercises a profound influence on the educational planning of the whole country.'[22]

Despite his dearth of constitutional powers, the vice-chancellor is thus clearly an important figure, and one with constant and varied demands upon his time and attention. Every morning he is the target for a vast correspondence—for example, from the UGC and the Committee of Vice-Chancellors and Principals; from the anxious and suppliant parents of would-be students; from all manner of outside bodies keen to extract (free) services from the university or render (paid) ones to it; from cranks, critics, and (occasionally) encouragers;

[19] A. D. LINDSAY and others: *The Government of Oxford* (Oxford, 1931) p. 19.
[20] Oral Evidence, O.2, p. 13.
[21] Report S. 676.
[22] SIR CHARLES ILLINGWORTH: *University Statesman* (Outram, 1971) p. 91. In this biography of Sir Hector Hetherington, Principal and Vice-Chancellor of the Universities of Liverpool (1927–36) and Glasgow (1936–61) one might expect the great personal impact of a Scottish principal to affect the estimate of a vice-chancellor's role.

and from those hoping he will address some local or national group or organization. For some the vice-chancellor can serve only as a 'box number', but he must answer them all, if only to maintain the good name of the university, and many can only be answered after extensive consultations or several committee meetings. The letters read (and some answered), the rest of a vice-chancellor's morning will typically be spent 'largely in seeing people at, for example, half-hour intervals: professors grinding axes, junior members of staff with a bright idea to have (say) art shows in the hall foyer, the technicians' shop steward, and the student president, besides outside visitors, UGC officials, and members of the public'.[23] To this list must be added regular meetings with officials to plan, to approve, or to prepare for the next meeting. The morning ends, as often as not, with what politicians like to boast of as a 'working lunch'— though in a university it is not a rare enough occurrence to warrant special nomenclature. The afternoons pass in chairing committees or other meetings—they must be in the afternoon as the academic members usually teach and/or run their own departments in the mornings. In the evenings the vice-chancellor is free—to attend city dinners, make speeches, or act as host to various social gatherings, all of which constitute virtually inescapable public (and public relations) obligations. In between times he must read and digest, when he is not drafting, documents and papers. And this is to note his internal activities only. His centrality and the wide extent of his work is evident, but it is still to be explained.

No more than in the case of a British prime minister can one account for the role of a vice-chancellor by reference to the legal rules. One must therefore look, in the second case as in the first, to the political relationships that the rules establish or merely permit— that is, to the political resources which he can mobilize or exploit.

Notably, to pursue the comparison with the prime minister one step further, the vice-chancellor lacks the resource of an organized and coherent party following. But there is a sense in which he shares the support accruing to a prime minister because of the manner of his selection. By means which have changed over the centuries, the selection of a prime minister is governed by the constitutional rule that 'the new Prime Minister must command the support of his own party and the confidence of the House of Commons'.[24]

---

[23] To quote a personal letter from a former vice-chancellor.
[24] To quote the formulation to be found in HAROLD NICOLSON: *King George the Fifth* (Constable, 1952) p. 117. See, too, the general and detailed discussion in SIR IVOR JENNINGS: *Cabinet Government* (Cambridge University Press, 3rd edition, 1959) pp. 20–58.

If one disregards the reference to party and for 'House of Commons' substitutes (in this order) 'senate and council', then the same convention applies to the selection of a vice-chancellor. The precise procedures vary. In some universities he is selected (i.e. nominated for appointment by council) by a committee of council (on which the senate members of council are invariably represented), in others by a joint committee of council and senate, and in the older Scottish universities he is appointed by the Crown (Secretary of State for Scotland).[25] Recently, in Leeds and York, students have also been involved in the selection process.[26] Whatever the procedure, however, one of the principal concerns in all cases is to find a man who can be expected to have and retain the confidence of the academics as manifested, particularly, through senate. Without the support of senate (of which he is chairman) a vice-chancellor, as we will see, may be incapable of positive action; with it his voice will be strong in council and in committee. That he should be chosen with this in mind is thus his first political resource, and his others are significant in part because they help to obtain and secure senate backing—for such backing can never be taken for granted. To an even greater extent than is true of a prime minister, a vice-chancellor must earn his influence by working to maintain the allegiance of those who, not too fancifully, may be seen as the source of his selection.

That the vice-chancellor is, by charter, the chairman of senate is not only particularly appropriate, it is one facet to his general chairman's role within the university, a role which constitutes his next, and possibly most obvious, political resource. In every university he will also take the chair at all important senate committees and it is generally understood that he may, if he so wishes, be a member of, or chair, every non-council committee. He will also be a key member of council committees (as we have already seen[27]) and, in the older Scottish universities he is usually *de facto* chairman of council (court) and the general council of graduates. Lord Boyle was sure that 'by far the most important aspect of a vice-chancellor's work is his attendance at senate and academic committees'[28], but it would be less significant were he not in the chair, or were the powers of a chairman less than those common throughout most of British public life. In fact, however, in universities as elsewhere he is usually 'very much of an executive chairman proposing decisions rather

---

[25] And in Cambridge by election from or rotation of the heads of colleges.
[26] In another university the council rejected a senate recommendation to include students.
[27] See Chapter V, above.
[28] *New Academic*, June 1971, p. 8.

than someone to arbitrate between debators'.[29] It is accepted that the chairman should have great influence over the order in which items appear on the agenda and when or if they appear at all. He is expected to contribute freely during the discussion and to exercise some discretion in the recognition of others who wish to speak. In many committees too it is seen as his duty to attempt to formulate conclusions, to summarize discussions, and to suggest lines of action. Lord Boyle thought that 'you've got to help decisions to emerge, and sometimes to guide them along'; a vice-chancellor cannot be an autocrat, but he should not be 'waiting to be conducted by the orchestra'.[30] If, moreover, the committee is charged with certain executive functions, it is normally understood that, subject only to a report at the next committee meeting, the chairman may take decisions on behalf of the committee between meetings. With skill, therefore, a chairman can use his prerogatives to influence the outcome of committee deliberations and would indeed be widely regarded as failing in his job if he did not do so.[31] As Sir Kenneth Wheare told the Franks commission in referring to his tenure of his office of Vice-Chancellor at Oxford '. . . almost all that any wise man wants can be got from the use of the power of chairman'.[32]

The line between influence and domination may sometimes be hard to draw. Principal Sir James Irvine, for example, exercised as complete an ascendency over St Andrews University as any vice-chancellor of any university. Writing of Irvine's work on committee, his widow says that:

'he prepared the business of every meeting with great care . . . his agenda paper was covered with red and blue circles and underlinings and marginal notes of the possible objections or support he expected from members of the committee. . . . The result was the business went through quickly and easily and each man left the room with the feeling that he had contributed to the successful findings of the meeting . . . very few people at the committee realised that Jim had led them, or driven them, with a golden but inflexible rein.'[33]

---

[29] JACK STRAW (then President of the National Union of Students) in *Students Today* (Young Fabian Pamphlet No. 17, 1968) p. 24. Significantly, perhaps, the vice-chancellor of his university, Sir Roger Stevens, claimed (on an Open University programme) to be more an arbitrator than an initiator, a view shared by others. [30] *Loc. cit.*
[31] See SIR KENNETH WHEARE: *Government by Committee* (Clarendon Press, 1955) pp. 36–42. [32] Report S. 483.
[33] MABEL V. IRVINE: *Sir James Irvine* (Blackwood, 1970) p. 72.

About Sir James a less affectionate author might have echoed a verdict on A. D. (Lord) Lindsay's style as Master of Balliol College and Vice-Chancellor of Oxford. He, it has been said, 'could also be high-handed and rough with opponents. (Once) when every vote went against (him) he smiled and said genially "Well, we seem to have reached an impasse".'[34]

As chairman of senate, vice-chancellors in many universities have the additional right virtually to nominate (in form, suggest) members of senate committees—for it is difficult openly to oppose such a suggestion.[35] This, too, is an important source of influence, though rarely as sinister or manipulative as it may seem at first sight. On the contrary, it is a not uncommon belief about committees that 'senate will not accept their views with confidence if their membership is determined in the haphazard way of calling for spontaneous nominations in a full meeting of senate'.[36] In any event a vice-chancellor who exercises this power cannot ignore the interests and expectations of others. Wheare has also pointed out; 'what a chairman can do . . . depends in the last resort . . . upon what a committee will stand. They can limit or nullify him at any time if they have the will to do so.'[37] A skilful chairman can, of course, by the way in which he conducts the discussion, sometimes prevent the opposition from concerting its actions and thus, so to speak, forestall the formation of the will to nullify. But the point is very important: in all his work, the vice-chancellor must keep within the limits of what the committee will stand, and what the committee will stand depends, more than on any other factor, on the reputation of the vice-chancellor. As 'James Dundonald' said, 'don't try to juggle too deliberately with agenda items, or obstinacy will settle in like Scotch mist'.[38]

Closely linked with the role of chairman is another very important resource. The vice-chancellor forms a focal point, usually the focal point, for communications. There are at least two aspects. One is communications with the outside world. The vice-chancellor is the official channel for communication between the university and the University Grants Committee; he is, as his title would suggest, a member of the increasingly important Committee of Vice-Chancellors and Principals; and he continually represents his university else-

---

[34] D. SCOTT: *A. D. Lindsay* (Blackwell, 1971) p. 222.

[35] In some universities names are put forward by a nominating committee, also chaired by the vice-chancellor.

[36] From an internal document approved by a redbrick senate in 1961.

[37] *Government by Committee*, p. 39.

[38] *Op. cit.* p. 15.

where. This ambassadorial role (it contains elements of those both of foreign secretary and head of state) is an important source of influence within his university. Though it may contribute to the misunderstanding of outsiders about the nature of the vice-chancellor's role (he is seen as ruler more than emissary), internally it does ensure that major university initiatives which impinge upon or depend upon the outside world shall be communicated through him. Thus he acquires the opportunity to discuss ideas at an early stage when they are most amenable to modification and amendment. He is also armed in internal discussions with the ability (not wholly unique) to estimate the response of outsiders. This is not to suggest that vice-chancellors would deliberately misrepresent outside reaction; but since the vice-chancellor is only human it is impossible for outside reactions not to be selectively edited by his perceptions. On occasions too, as the university's representative outside, it may prove to be impossible for the vice-chancellor not to commit his university, and even to do so in advance, on a particular issue.

Internally, as a member of a variety of committees, the vice-chancellor is in a strong position to steer business in particular directions, to facilitate or make more difficult the passage of particular proposals, and, if he is allowed to get away with it and is so minded, to hinder proposals by ensuring that they get ensnared in the committee system. But here again, 'Dundonald's' 'Scotch mist' is never far off, and the typical vice-chancellor is not machiavellian in the use to which he puts his chairmanship and communication role; rather its importance is that he is always consulted by people before they make proposals formally. His advice is not only sought but usually heeded, and in the process the vice-chancellor becomes more and more informed about everything that is going on in the university and (if sufficiently capable) he can end up uniquely well informed about the university's activities and the way in which they impinge one upon the other. Just because the vice-chancellor is thus particularly well informed, it becomes yet more worth while for others to consult him and thus ensure that he becomes even better informed. Knowledge in this context may not be power, but with this degree of knowledge, normally unrivalled, the vice-chancellor is uniquely well placed to influence policy formulation within his university.

Another important resource is also to be construed partly in terms of communications. As chairman of senate and a major figure in council the vice-chancellor is generally regarded as the most important link between the two bodies. Certainly, as we were told by all the vice-chancellors whom we interviewed and by many others, this linking function is a major source of vice-cancellarial influence. Various relationships seem to be involved. Those between the vice-chancellor and senate, already mentioned, ensure that he speaks on council as the chief representative of the academic constituency. He is also the member best informed about the university's affairs. It therefore matters less than it might at first seem that he is not in the chair at council meetings. It was said of Sidney Webb that 'where Sidney sat, there was the Chair'. The vice-chancellor's position can provide something of what Webb had solely by personality, and at many councils the vice-chancellor does in fact share some of the privileges of the chair, for instance in being in effect the opening speaker on each item if he so wishes. Moreover, in the selection and appointment of a vice-chancellor council plays an even greater part than senate, formally at least, and regardless of the weight given to academic opinion; the laymen are therefore inclined to back 'their' man's judgement, especially as he is better informed. In council meetings, too, the senate group of members will be reluctant to dispute with the chief academic officer before outsiders. The vice-chancellor, as a linking figure, is thus crucial (and is acknowledged to be so by most experienced academics) to the maintenance of those relations between council and senate that permit the latter its predominant part in university government.

It is sometimes suggested that the vice-chancellor does not so much unite council and senate as play them off against one another in a university variant of the old political ploy of 'divide and rule'. It was put graphically to us by one professor like this: 'the vice-chancellor dissuades senate from pressing a policy he does not like by saying that council would not like it; and dissuades council from interfering by saying that senate would object'. But this is to over-simplify the picture, if only because it ignores the strong senate group on council who, however reluctantly, can either dispute the vice-chancellor's view or press senate policy on council. It is true that, on occasion, a vice-chancellor will cite the likely reaction of council as an argument in senate, or vice versa.[39] In our view, however, the essence of the usual situation is better captured in the following quotation from an official document circulated within a Yorkshire redbrick in 1963: 'Council relies on the vice-chancellor to advise senate in such a way that it would not send forward any recommendation which it would be impractical to implement'. The

[39] At Warwick, for example, it is reported that on one occasion 'the Vice-Chancellor said that the laymen on Council . . . were not pleased when past decisions were re-considered'. E. P. THOMPSON, ed.: *Warwick University Ltd.* (Penguin Books, 1970).

converse also applies, *mutatis mutandis*. But the vice-chancellor can only advise, for all that he is known to speak with authority about the attitudes and likely responses of both laymen and academics. If, moreover, conflict should occur between council and senate, the limits to his powers become apparent. So far from being able the more effectively to rule over a divided university, he will have to side with one body or the other in order to maintain his position—and in such a situation to choose council is probably to 'ride for a fall'[40], at least in the long run. Under normal circumstances, however, a vice-chancellor can derive some personal room to manœuvre from the complex relations between council and senate, is likely to find that his linking role is one of the more demanding aspects of his job, and certainly benefits from the additional information it brings him.[41]

Despite the fact that the vice-chancellor of the major redbrick universities does not commonly have the legal title of 'chief administrative officer'[42], he nevertheless occupies this role in practice. It constitutes another political resource, even if he, unlike the stereotypical tycoon, cannot issue orders to university officials as though they were mere subordinates in a hierarchical chain of command. For, as we shall discuss in greater detail[43], the officials may typically be answerable not to the vice-chancellor but in law to council and in practice to the bodies they service. The vice-chancellor nevertheless has closer and more frequent contacts with the senior officials than, normally, does anyone else in the university. Moreover, because the university bureaucracy has at least a hierarchical appearance, he may well be seen by the officials as a factor in their career prospects. Thus the vice-chancellor can ensure that he is kept informed at the bureaucratic level as well as in all other spheres, and be confident that most officials would be prepared to assemble data, prepare memoranda, or order an agenda if directly requested by him. Indeed the imperfection of the bureaucratic hierarchy may itself help the vice-chancellor, who may the more easily deal directly with junior officials and use them as substitutes for, or as in several cases we heard, in opposition to, their seniors.[44]

[40] To borrow the phrase used to us, in this context, by a vice-chancellor.

[41] Many academics find, on ceasing to be a member of council, that they miss only one aspect of this service: the sense of knowing most of what is happening in the university.

[42] Except at Liverpool where under the 1961 Charter S. 6 he is 'principal' administrative officer.

[43] See Chapter VII below.

[44] We were given a vivid description of one distinguished vice-chancellor who, on a national body, openly dealt, at meetings, with the deputy secretary across the secretary. We heard elsewhere that he acted similarly, if more discreetly, at home.

The principal significance of the vice-chancellor's close (and often personal) working relations with the bureaucracy is that he not only extends his own sources of information but can also stimulate the officials to assemble, process, and analyse particular kinds of data rather than others, and thus influence committees throughout the university to approach their problems in particular ways. He may thus be able to ensure that alternatives are considered which might otherwise be neglected and that all the decision-making organs within the university address what seem to him to be the real problems and issues, and to do so adequately and appropriately briefed. This process of selection must involve some omission and it may be hard to say when omission becomes suppression. As the biographer of Sir Hector Hetherington has put it, 'there were doubtless occasions when Hetherington would slur over bits of evidence which might, in his view, have distorted the debate'.[45] But again there are limits. No vice-chancellor wishes to acquire a reputation for deliberate manipulation or suppression of relevant evidence, and very few will risk acting in a way which would substantiate it. The point is simply that a capable and imaginative vice-chancellor can do much to establish the criteria of relevance generally accepted within his university. Even this capacity is not unique, however, and may well become more widely shared by both officials and academics as new information-based administrative techniques[46] come into greater use. It is, however, unlikely that the vice-chancellor will ever cease to obtain some political leverage from his position as chief administrator, both in the ways just outlined and as the chief beneficiary of the need for executive delegation felt by all deliberative bodies.

Like those other influential members of the university, professorial heads of departments, vice-chancellors also wield what may be called the power of patronage. Despite the size of some universities it is the rule rather than the exception for a vice-chancellor to be on every professorial appointing committee and at least to take note of the more junior levels, promotions included. Appointments must of course initially have the agreement of an entire appointing committee, and in general must appear to meet the prevailing professional criteria. Nevertheless this is an area in which a vice-chancellor may exercise a creative influence upon the whole life of the university. This derives in part from the custom that, particularly in the case of professorial appointments, it is the vice-chancellor who should make the most extensive and authoritative enquiries about

[45] SIR CHARLES ILLINGWORTH: *op. cit.*, p. 148.
[46] See Chapter VIII, below.

actual or possible candidates. In addition some at least know how to establish a preponderating influence in the deliberations of committees. We were assured, on several levels, that the rise of at least one of the major English civics to academic distinction was due to the intense care taken by its vice-chancellor after the Second World War: 'He always knew more about the candidates than any one else on the selection committee,' remarked his registrar. To quote from the biographer of Sir Hector Hetherington again, 'Hetherington was well aware that even the most knowledgeable of committees needs guidance, and he saw to it that the guidance was properly given . . . it is probably true to say that every one of the professorial appointments made during his Principalship accorded with his own choice. He was almost equally assiduous in the appointment of lecturers.'[47] In another Scottish university, a more than usually autocratic principal was generally believed systematically to wield the power to appoint (in particular, *not* to appoint and *not* to promote) in order to rally voting support in the senate or to limit the clarity with which possible opposition was voiced. These more extreme examples derive, however, from the older Scottish universities where generally the principal has tended to exercise a more personal sway than vice-chancellors elsewhere, and where in particular 'council' (court) has normally governed more positively than in England and very much on the advice of the principal. It is more usual for the vice-chancellor to use his patronage in isolation, as it were, from what might be called the power game, and genuinely to seek the best man. Nevertheless, whatever his own criteria, it is unavoidable that some others within the university will seek to hasten their promotion by paying special heed to what they take to be the vice-chancellor's wishes.

The powers of patronage also extend, as in the case of the head of department, to lending (or not lending) his personal support to approaches to outside donors for funds. (It should be noted in this context that the private foundations and the government research councils normally require the signature of the vice-chancellor or registrar on all applications.) Lastly, the power of patronage extends also to the writing of references for members of staff who may be seeking translation and promotion to other institutions. The

---

[47] ILLINGWORTH: *op. cit.*, p. 94. It was in a Scottish university, too, that one appointment at a very junior level was vetoed by the principal because the recommendation was to appoint a woman. In the upshot the whole process of advertising, sifting and interviewing was gone through once more, but this time with the principal taking part. This was less surprising in the 1950s than it would be now.

general point is perhaps worth making again that in all these respects, as in the case of appointments, a vice-chancellor who departed frequently or obviously from the kind of decision which merit indicates risks undercutting his own capacity to influence events through these (and other) means: a vice-chancellor who is known to use the powers of patronage as a political weapon is likely to find that he ends up merely by destroying his own 'credit', and sooner rather than later.

A further resource is financial. In the past the vice-chancellor's control of the budget might be almost total, where the finance committee (on which no academic served) normally accepted his advice with little question, though it might have been discussed beforehand with the treasurer, and bursar.[48] We heard of vice-chancellors who, well into the 1960s, budgeted by summoning their heads of departments one by one to discuss their claims, and then drafted a budget which regularly emerged unaltered in council minutes. As recently as the mid-fifties, a London 'vice-chancellor' remarked to one of us, 'I can't understand all these elaborate arrangements: I have a piece of paper in my desk which says what we have, and when someone comes to ask for some money, I open the drawer and I have a look.'

In the larger universities the budget was generally more 'open' than this; and increases in the size of universities, the growth of information-based methods, and even more, the establishment of development committees have very greatly reduced the solo budgeting function of the vice-chancellor. But in any case the vice-chancellor cannot avoid having some influence on affairs through the financial decision-making process, if only because, as we have already noted, he is the official and primary source of communication between the university and all its sources of finance, notably the University Grants Committee. Traditionally, too, he is the person who has been most continuously and intimately concerned with attempts to raise money from private sources. And, once having raised them, a vice-chancellor may be able to exert considerable influence upon the way the money is used, either through the internal decision-making process or by the advice and guidance he gives to that potential donor. (One vice-chancellor told us that he would have given a great deal to have had a discretionary fund available for disbursement on research and other academic projects. In this way, he said, he could encourage the potentially most creative departments and professors within his university. He clearly lacked

---

[48] Ironically, in such a case, the university would appear on paper to be wholly lay-dominated.

such a fund, but there have been other vice-chancellors who in effect did not suffer from this handicap.) Even more, the vice-chancellor is central to the whole modern budgetary process, serving on all the committees and sub-committees involved, and chairing those of senate, as well as having the administrative position we have already noted. In this area, too, it is easy to exaggerate the scope given even to a determined man. It is therefore important to remember that his influence can, at most, extend only to that small percentage of the budget which constitutes 'new' money—and that is the area in which others also are vitally interested.

From administration we must turn to his position as 'chief academic officer'. Very few vice-chancellors have much to do with the routine—and that is no derogatory word—of academic work. But his central position gives him the ability to exercise the influence we have noticed in the key areas of appointments and fund-raising. There is a more general academic duty. He is the only person charged with the interests of subjects which are not professed in the university. Lively and progressive academic staff may bring forward the claims of new or neglected subjects, but they are likely to keep close to their own fields. New fields may also have friends outside the university, as in the Foundations. But the responsibility for the unborn and the embryonic must rest chiefly with the chief academic officer, and it is indeed here that he may often make his main mark. Similarly, 'those parts of the work of the School which are least specialized are his particular sphere'.[49] These again, are the areas for which the staff have least direct responsibility, but which may be vital to the university as a whole. The vice-chancellor, by representing these areas, on the one hand gains as it were his own territorial sovereignty, like a professor's department, and on the other, becomes the natural (as well, usually, as necessary) ally of innovators within the university.

There remain three other general forces or factors which strengthen the vice-chancellor's hand. One, on which we have touched already, is the strong desire of many staff that the vice-chancellor should himself take certain decisions. Of course the expectation is that he will use his discretion within conventional limits of propriety and acceptability. Nevertheless and particularly on difficult problems of choice, as between the conflicting claims of different individuals or departments, many universities expect the vice-chancellor to assume the responsibility and the odium of these difficult decisions which, if thrown into the general arena, might disrupt relations between colleagues.

[49] W. BEVERIDGE (later Lord): *op. cit.*, p. 9.

The second general factor is that the vice-chancellor is appointed to retiring age, and may well serve for twenty or more years. When he is young, he can expect to outlive his more senior colleagues, and increasing years will give increasing weight to his knowledge and experience. This is of the greatest importance when related to the responsibility just mentioned. Two ways in which the time factor strengthens the hand of a vice-chancellor may be distinguished. The first can be illustrated by the story of a Welsh college principal who disagreed with the professorial head about the future development of a science department. The principal is reported to have said, once deadlock had been reached, 'Well, I can afford to wait: you will soon wish to go back to your research'. He was right; the professor did and the principal carried his point. The second, and possibly more fundamental, way was clearly articulated by a committee set up to review the government of a midland university. 'Any vice-chancellor', it reported, '. . . may expect at some time or other to fall foul of the academic staff or the students or the council or the general public. If a Vice-Chancellor is made vulnerable to pressures from one direction, he will be vulnerable to pressure from many others. The long-run interests of academic freedom therefore seem to us to require that a Vice-Chancellor's security of tenure be upheld rather than undermined.'[50]

Finally, there is the mere fact that the vice-chancellor is the vice-chancellor. However genial or informal, he cannot avoid a hierophantic status. However little of deference may be left in the scholarly community, the office still carries its aura.

Together these resources, each of which is the more potent for the existence of the others, mean that it is not impossible for an able vice-chancellor to discharge the wide and open-ended responsibilities laid upon him by charter. From them he can draw the knowledge, position, and capacity continuously to influence the policy and general running of his university. Nevertheless, as we have tried to suggest, his resources are highly conditional and must be used in full awareness of the limitations imposed by the university setting.

A military commander once ventured this comment on university organization: 'It's quite easy. Here you have the GOC, and reporting to him you have an A and a G and a Q and in no time you have an organization chart for a university which I am quite sure would run perfectly, at least if it weren't for the academics.'[51] Just so—

---

[50] From an internal university document.
[51] Quoted in J. A. L. MATHESON: 'The general Framework of University Government', *University Government*, Federation of Australian University Staff Associations, n.d., p. 10.

there is the rub. Lord Annan, a London 'vice-chancellor', remarked that 'University College is very strong departmentally in the administrative sense—that is to say that the heads of the forty-six or forty-seven departments are really the great barons and the Provost is like King John perpetually signing Magna Carta at Runnymede'.[52] 'The change (to being a vice-chancellor) for the Principals of the former CATs was quite striking: they had, most of them, to alter their whole style of administration[53] and in no authoritarian direction, either. As W. J. M. Mackenzie put it long ago, 'if leadership there must be, the Duke of Plazo Toro is likely to be a more popular model than the grand old Duke of York'. He went on, 'but we should *much rather* state the problem in quite different terms, as that of a Chairman in a body of equals'.[54] Or, as a very senior and important vice-chancellor put it to us, 'professors don't see the vice-chancellor as their superior, just as a man with a different job'. They may indeed greatly dislike that job, for traditionally professors have deeply despised administration; other than their own, at least.[55] Though this attitude is probably most usually found amongst old-style heads of departments it links up two major strands in the traditions inspiring the redbrick universities: the German tradition of professorial autonomy, on which the growth of research was based, and the Oxbridge tradition of magisterial equality, on which teaching was based.[56] Either tradition can create a climate hostile to central authority. Together, and especially in association with a more general English tradition of hostility to bureaucracy, they form a powerful and restrictive element in the climate of opinion in which vice-chancellors must work.[57] One academic consequence is the low standing given to the vice-chancellor, even if he has an academic background, in debates about syllabuses, curricula, and other such questions which are thought to be the preserve of department, faculty, or school (and on which even senate may be reluctant, or

[52] Open University programme, 'University Government' (Soc. Sci. Unit 27) 1970. And see the complaint by Lord Morris quoted in our Appendix on the University of Warwick.
[53] T. BURGESS and J. PRATT: *Policy and Practice* (in draft) p. 8:34.
[54] 'The Professor as Administrator', *Universities Quarterly*, August 1953, p. 329 (our emphasis).
[55] See ILLINGWORTH: *op. cit.*, for some account of Hetherington's difficulties with 'the Group of the New Testament' at Liverpool. One Welsh dean used to be heard saying, 'Haff you heard what ploody Hector iss up to now?' pp. 34–5.
[56] For the great influence of Oxbridge see HALSEY and TROW: *British Academics* (Faber and Faber, 1971) Part II, on 'The English [sic] Idea of a University'.
[57] It might be said that almost the whole of the case against the administration put in *Warwick University Ltd.* would be unintelligible except in terms of these traditions.

unable, to comment). Nor are British vice-chancellors expected to have a 'philosophy' of education in the way which seems to be standard for an American university president.

The vice-chancellor's dependence on others is the heavier for his inability to get rid of members of staff (even officials) who oppose him or simply withold their full-hearted co-operation. Since long before the Industrial Relations Act, 1972, academics traditionally have enjoyed security of tenure, and in most universities it is felt that the same consideration should be extended to at least senior members of the professional administrative staff. Only in this way, it is felt, can the senior officials give sufficiently courageous, dis-interested, and reliable service to the university.[58] It is, of course, possible in the last resort for a vice-chancellor, with allies, to dis-place particular individuals; an incompetent head of department, for example, can sometimes be persuaded to devote himself to a life of research or to permit the establishment of a second or even third chair within the department, and thereafter to institute a system of rotating chairmanship. It may also be possible to encourage an academic to seek a post in another university. It is not unknown either for senior officials to have been persuaded to accept posts outside, but even when one is available no one can be removed merely because he has incurred the displeasure of the vice-chancellor. We pointed out, at the beginning of this book, that an essential ingredient in political situations is the need to secure agreement on policies without disrupting the relevant group. Vice-chancellors, we may say, are therefore constrained to act purely politically and not in any way like a military commander, managing director, or even an abbot. Vice-chancellors, furthermore, are themselves not entirely indispensable. It has been shown on occasion that a uni-versity can not only survive during a protracted interregnum, it can even take important decisions.[59] Moreover, even in normal times, no vice-chancellor can alter the fact that every major decision must, at some stage, be at least ratified by a committee or governing body in which he can easily be outvoted. From this ultimate consti-tutional restraint there can be no escape.

The resources or sanctions available to a vice-chancellor are thus resistable by men of integrity and resolve (or of ordinary obstinacy) and, given time and a degree of determined and concerted action,

[58] The same considerations in national government have served to make the position of a senior civil servant equally secure. See, too, our next chapter.

[59] E.g. at Reading, the decision to abandon the traditional objective of a small pastoral community, and instead to expand into the big league, came during the long interregnum which followed Sir J. Wolfenden's translation to the UGC.

none of the vice-chancellor's views, powers, influences or objections are insurmountable. Of course academics are not always capable of taking the time or of concerting their effort sufficiently to obstruct a skilful and able man whose general purposes and style commend themselves to a university as a whole.[60] But one must regard with some suspicion any attempt by academics to suggest that their vice-chancellor completely runs the university and is to blame for all mistakes; this cannot be unless a sufficient number of academics are prepared to go along with the vice-chancellor or to bury themselves in their own parochial concerns, thus leaving an open field to, it may be, an over-ambitious or even unscrupulous vice-chancellor.

The first point that must therefore be made in an attempt to summarize the role of the vice-chancellor is that, if he is to get anything done, *he must have allies.* All his transactions reflect his constitutional dependence on the votes of others. Crucial to any definition of his position, too, is the fact that the constraints upon him are direct, while his positive resources are only indirect (in the sense that they amount only to means of influencing those with the voting power). All the vice-chancellors we talked to, moreover, pay more than lip service to the notion that university government must be government by consensus.[61]

In seeking allies and support the vice-chancellor may be said to have one weapon and two advantages. The weapon is that degree of bargaining power, possibly amounting (at times) to polite blackmail, rooted in his ability to grant or withhold certain favours and to facilitate or not to facilitate business—and the degree of enthusiasm with which he greets some request can be important, if by no means invariably.[62] This is, of course, the kind of bargaining position most frequently exaggerated by others, if only implicitly. Many a vice-chancellor has benefited from the desire of suppliants to play safe and avoid any risk of giving offence, an attitude all too easily rationalized into overestimates of his power (or underestimates of his integrity). The bargaining power is nevertheless real, if finite.

Of the two advantages possessed by a vice-chancellor the first is

---

[60] A similar judgement can be made of cabinet ministers, a fact to which more than one recent prime minister owes his relatively long tenure of office.

[61] The emphasis on consensus may mean that votes are comparatively rare, as they are also said to be in British cabinet meetings; but this is more a tribute to than a denial of the power residing in those who possess the preponderant voting strength.

[62] Among the examples of requests we gave earlier in this chapter, he could do virtually nothing to secure the admission of any parent's 'favourite son', even if he wished to, but, if he so wished, something to facilitate an art show, and often a great deal to blunt a professorial axe.

his particularly favoured position—as chairman, chief administrator, and focal point for the flow of information—to prepare his own initiatives and to steer the initiatives of others. He has the time, the information, and the bureaucratic support, as well as the opportunity to assess the likely responses of others, to prepare initiatives which have a fair chance of being accepted, and a location within the governmental system which permits him to feed in his ideas at the most favourable time and place. Put more crudely: he is in a particularly favourable position to do the essential homework[63] on which effective influence depends, especially in universities 'whose resident senior members combine a deadly power of dialectic with astonishing stamina and obduracy in debate'.[64]

A vice-chancellor has the advantage, secondly, of his uniqueness, and by 'uniqueness' we do not mean anything so simple as the fact that he is a presidential and not a collegiate figure. What we have in mind, rather, is that upon him more clearly than upon any other individual in the university is placed an unmistakeable responsibility to speak for and think about the university as a whole. As Lord Fulton put it to the Franks Commission, '. . . somebody has got to lie awake at night feeling responsible, not for inventing the shape, but for seeing that there is a shape'.[65] He may, we have suggested, be regarded as in some degree a representative of senate on council and of council on senate, but otherwise he is uniquely not a representative of any outside interest nor of any departmental, faculty, or other lesser interest within the university. His job, manifestly, is to represent and guide the university as a whole, owing allegiance only to the university as a whole, and formally accountable only to council and court, the legal responsibilities of which are similarly defined. Implicit in this responsibility, as well as a necessary condition of constructive influence, 'the vice-chancellor has got to have, and be known to have, a position and a view'.[66]

The 'cash-value' of this second advantage is that it vests him with an initial credit balance of confidence, demonstrated most clearly in the natural tendency of others to turn to him, as we have already noted, at times of stress or when an unpleasant internal arbitration is required. This balance of credit is, of course, reinforced by the ordinary practice of delegation to the chairman to

---

[63] 'Ploody Hector' literally got up too early for his opponents at Liverpool, and, no doubt, Glasgow. He worked before breakfast. (ILLINGWORTH: op. cit., p. 35.) And see Sir Eric Ashby's description of a vice-chancellor's budgetary role quoted in Chapter VIII, below.

[64] To quote from NOEL (now Lord) ANNAN: Life of Leslie Stephen.

[65] Oral evidence, O.14, p. 24.

[66] Sir Philip Morris to the Franks Commission.

which, also, we have already referred; but it also exists independently, as an initial furnishing of office and, as universities try to ensure, in virtue of the personal distinction of the incumbent. Upon this confidence a vice-chancellor may draw in all his activities, and the outstanding man will even add to his credit, but he must draw upon it with care, for it is highly vulnerable. More than one case was brought to our attention in which a vice-chancellor, by a single major misjudgement, either of the merits of the case or of the political attitudes within the university, has squandered his credit balance of confidence at one go; and once gone, such confidence is difficult or perhaps even impossible to rebuild quickly, if at all. Once confidence has gone, moreover, many of the resources which we have seen as converging to reinforce each other, now pull apart. Once this has happened, for whatever cause, the vice-chancellor's power over events becomes at best negative, and he may not wish to continue in office. Three specific cases since 1945 were quoted to us where a vice-chancellor who had either lost the confidence of, or fallen out of sympathy with, his staff was let go with little stir, and there are no doubt others.[67] The vulnerability of his credit balance is thus closely linked to his ultimate dispensibility.

With a carefully conserved credit balance of confidence, however, and if the resources available to him are used with both vision and courage, there is no doubt that a vice-chancellor can induce his colleagues to take decisions which add up to a coherent policy and provide a sense of direction for their university. There is no doubt of this because it has been done. The last word here, on both the scope and its limits, may be given to Sir Hector Hetherington. 'I can think of many vice-chancellors who have influenced their universities, but only one who really made his university. On the whole, influence, not making, is our job. It is the big professors who really matter; and if you can collect your share of them you do the main part of your job.'[68]

It follows from this account of the job that, in any particular case, the impact and role of a vice-chancellor will depend considerably upon his individual style and capabilities. It is understandable, too, that the search for a new one should often be a protracted and agonizing business.[69] Given the importance of the confidence factor,

---

[67] The much publicized resignation of Mr Goronwy Rees is *not* one of the cases to which we are referring.

[68] ILLINGWORTH: *op. cit.*, p. 93.

[69] And, perhaps, that it is not customary to seek candidates by public advertisement. (The Open University and the Universities of Coleraine, Stirling, and York are the notable exceptions to this custom.)

and that this means, above all, the confidence of senate, a vice-chancellor must not only be a man of integrity (otherwise the confidence would wither under the close and constant scrutiny to which he is subjected), he must be capable of securing the respect of the academic community. (This is one obvious reason why the majority of vice-chancellors have been academics.) As one experienced former vice-chancellor put it to us: 'to be an FRS or an FBA gives any vice-chancellor a flying start'—but, equally, it is not essential so long as the incumbent can show that he is sympathetic to academics and 'able to understand what academics are after'[70]—a task at which many 'outsiders' have been conspicuously successful. Desirable, too, are such qualities as the ability quickly to switch attention from one subject to another—a quality nurtured in, for example, the higher reaches of government service—and a robustness, both physical and mental, to withstand the considerable stresses of office. (Our notes of interviews on the subject are full of such phrases as 'nervous exhaustion' or 'a hell of a strain on the character'.) Of major importance, too, is the statesman's 'ability to size up men and situations'.[71]

It is not to be wondered at, therefore, that some vice-chancellors, able and worthy men, leave relatively little personal imprint on their universities other than the important legacy of an institution which continues to function. For them the role has been largely that of facilitating the conduct of business. Others work, through personal preference and temperament, with such an absence of fuss and drama that their contributions as quiet persuaders and facilitators are frequently undervalued when not entirely overlooked. Yet others, as we have seen, have quietly been 'allowed' to retire prematurely or have lapsed into virtual disuse, for any one of numerous possible reasons (misjudgement, weaknesses of health or character, or a tendency to think of themselves too much as managing directors or super-administrators). Fortunately this last category is small. But the history of British universities contains many others, the strong men, who have genuinely given shape, direction, and impetus to their university—and in these cases it is no mere convenience or courtesy to talk of 'their' university. They have done so, moreover, mainly because they have used the resources of the post with clarity of purpose and force of personality, sustained over a reasonable period of time, not by any ruthless exploitation of a power to command.

If, in particular, a vice-chancellor assumes office at a time of

[70] To quote another former vice-chancellor, in an interview.
[71] Ibid.

anxiety, even crisis, about the whole future of the university, he may well be able to establish an unrivalled ascendancy within his institution. Possibly the outstanding example is to be found in the position created for himself by Sir James Irvine during his long tenure as Principal and Vice-Chancellor of the University of St Andrews (1921 to 1952). Of few could it be said, by a successor who did not know of him other than by repute (and that almost twenty years after his death), that his 'mark . . . is not only upon the fading memories of men but is set upon the developing university'. Of fewer still, today, could it be said: 'I have been told that professors trembled when called before him. I have also been told that they felt that this was only right and proper.'[72] This is an extreme case, possibly unique in this century, and unlikely to be repeated even by others with a comparable tenacity of purpose and ferocity of will to guide an almost unlimited flexibility of method. Even at the time of his death in 1952, the university was a small one, small enough for him, as it were, to carry all the major items of its business in his head. Moreover much of the time in which he held office, and in particular the earlier years, came within a period when the primary source of funds for development in any university came, and had to come, from private donations. Irvine in fact was personally immensely successful in raising funds (and not only for his university); not surprisingly, nor exceptionally, he had the first say over their disposal—more exceptionally, he also had the last.

These reflections raise the question whether even a less exceptional degree of leadership will be possible for any vice-chancellor in the near future, as universities grow in size and as they become increasingly dependent upon the public purse for development resources. It is true that one consequence of the increasing dependence on the Exchequer for funds has been the growth in influence of the Committee of Vice-Chancellors and Principals, the collective spokesmen for British universities in their dealings with government and other large national organizations (including the National Union of Students). The position of vice-chancellor may be somewhat enhanced as the sole representative of his university on this committee. But it is the internal position of a vice-chancellor which most concerns us.

To quote once more from the Robbins report, 'no other enterprise would impose upon its Chairman the variety and burden of work that the modern university requires of its Vice-Chancellor'.[73] Accept-

[72] Principal J. Steven Watson in his Foreword to MABEL V. IRVINE: *op. cit* None who knew 'Jimmy the Princ.' (Irvine) would be disposed to dispute these reports.   [73] Report S. 676.

ing this as true it would seem plausible to argue that the burden will become excessive as universities grow in size. But it is far from obvious that this point has yet been reached. Even before the Second World War, when the largest redbricks were well under 2,000 students, and much less complex, the vice-chancellor was thought to have a full-time job, and sometimes to require significant help from a pro-vice-chancellor. As universities have grown, there has been constant anxiety on the vice-chancellor's behalf. Even since Robbins was writing student numbers have doubled. Nevertheless, though there still is anxiety, no one has actually given up yet, and schemes to share the vice-chancellor's burden are as likely to be found in small as in large universities. The largest unit in the country, Edinburgh, appears to see fewer problems than some of the new universities. This is probably highly significant: in general the vice-chancellorship is not a divisible post. All that can happen, it may be argued, is that peripheral autonomy grows as the vice-chancellor loses touch with less vital areas. More to the point, there is every sign that vice-chancellors from all sizes of university continue to be active in public life outside. There are times when one thinks that to head a university is almost an essential qualification for chairing government committees of enquiry, royal commissions and the like. Indeed, the vice-chancellor of a medium-sized university told us in 1967 that his was a job which could and should be done in 'three days of the week', otherwise he would find himself doing the job of registrar and bursar.[74] (One must add in fairness that although he was widely regarded as a 'good' vice-chancellor, within his own university there were some complaints that he was absent a little too often.)

But there are straws in the wind on the other side. In almost all universities there has been increasing resort to the institution of deputy or pro-vice-chancellor. More and more universities have at least one, and in some cases three, such part-time deputies who can, for example, take the chair or receive outside visitors for the vice-chancellor, even if they cannot take his decisions for him. In the University of Birmingham, as we have noted before, the vice-chancellor also has a full-time deputy who may, in effect, be put in charge of certain areas of university business. It may be significant that this appointment, initially experimental and for a limited period

[74] Sir H. Hetherington, when Principal of Glasgow, 'held office as Hon. President or Vice-President of over fifty educational or charitable societies and as a member of a hundred more, and was a willing participant in their activities'. An account of his more important outside interests occupies pp. 100–132 of ILLINGWORTH: *op. cit.*

in order to reassure an anxious senate, was soon ratified as permanent by the senate. In the University of Sussex a different tactic is exemplified. There the 'private office' of the vice-chancellor has been enlarged beyond the traditional secretary (sometimes reinforced by a typist) to include the Development and Information Officers. Clearly increasing size in the university will require some differences in practice or technique. Thus when, as in such universities as Glasgow or Edinburgh today, there may be two hundred or more new academic appointments within a session, it is impossible for the vice-chancellor personally and closely to take part in all interviews. At most, it would seem, such a vice-chancellor must confine himself to personal participation in the appointment of professors and, for the rest, to a concern with the general procedures and criteria used. Similarly, where there may be sixty or more autonomous departments or subject boards, it is much more difficult for a single man to consider their activities or their budgeting in detail, although it still may be possible for him to allocate funds as between the claims of different faculties or in connection with major new proposals. Much, that is to say, will depend upon the size of the main accounting units. Nevertheless the point remains valid. In a large university, too, where the number of academic staff may run into four figures, it becomes impossible for a vice-chancellor to know anything of importance about more than a very small proportion of his academic colleagues. Perhaps, it may be said, the desire to do so is a misplaced hangover from olden days; it might be that it is the job only of university porters to know the academic staff on sight.[75] If so, the loss will be slight—but many present-day vice-chancellors, and others, would regret the passing of the older sense of community which only personal knowledge can bring.

Size also threatens the right of all heads of departments to personal access, a right commonly also extended, in the smaller universities, to every member of staff who feels he has a grievance or an inspiration. Of the professors a formidable and influential registrar told us that 'they are willing to come to me and probably be satisfied with what I can say, but only as a convenience, and if their right to see the Vice-Chancellor is not in question'. He, as did others, therefore doubted how far additional administrative appointments would relieve the pressure upon a vice-chancellor's engagement diary. It was partly with this accessibility in mind, too, that a management consultant told a Yorkshire university: 'It is wrong to think of the vice-chancellor as the apex of a pyramid. He stands

---

[75] See the suggestion by Professor Bernard Crick in the *Times Higher Education Supplement*, October 15, 1971.

slightly above a wide horizontal line.' The larger the university the wider is that line; there must therefore come a time when it is impossible for one man, however devoted or efficient an administrator, to span it.

It is, of course, very much easier to state these problems than even to sketch the solutions. All we can do here is briefly to indicate the directions in which British universities seem to be groping. In principle, and in very broad terms, there are three. The first we have already touched upon. That is the multiplication of deputies or other immediate aides. This, if extended further, would be the 'managerial' solution—to increase the degree of hierarchy and elevate the vice-chancellor to an apex. If extended far enough it might also be the American presidential solution with its corollary of a large number of full-time assistants, vice-presidents, and deans[76] all with considerable discretionary powers, and all acting as a screen between the president and the academic staff, not to mention the students. This is the solution most feared in universities, and most antagonistic to the historical movement to academic self-government. Because it would curtail the right of access and make it almost inconceivable that the vice-chancellor would still be accepted as 'senate's man', British universities are unlikely to experiment much further in this direction.

More in keeping with the established style of university government is the second direction of change—towards, as it were, putting the office into commission, or, to express it differently, collectivizing parts of the vice-chancellor's role. Two forms of this may already be discerned. The one is mainly political; most typically, regular meetings of the vice-chancellor with his deans are used much like meetings of the nineteenth century national cabinet, as occasions for settling disputes upon detail and for deciding upon general policy. The vice-chancellor remains pre-eminent, but his burden is shared, responsibility (and, with luck, confidence) is more diffused, and it becomes worth the while of others to seek access to more than the one man. Together, moreover, the members of the 'cabinet' can more readily deal with a widened administrative span than could any individual. As far as we know this device has yet to be formally institutionalized in any even of the existing larger universities. Nor could it be called a major innovation, since it may be seen as a mere formalization of the long-standing need of vice-chancellors to be 'supported by up to eight wise men', as Sir Philip Morris put it to the Franks Commission. The other form is the establishment of

---

[76] Comparable, possibly, to the deans of British medical schools now.

strong planning committees charged with the tasks both of formulating academic strategy and of taking all major decisions upon the allocation of resources. Under a variety of names such committees are becoming increasingly common. It may also be significant that one of the earliest, at the University of Sheffield, was instituted during a vice-cancellarial interregnum, a possible indication of the role that it was designed to perform. About these committees we have more to say in a later chapter.[77] But they could, clearly, provide a means of reducing the vice-chancellor's burden and, in one area at least, of moving him some distance from the front line.

The third possible solution is perhaps less a solution than a means of avoiding the problem. It is, in a sense, to admit defeat either by radical devolution (in practice even if not by statute) to faculties or schools, and thus to their deans, of which there are signs both in some of the new and in some of the major civic universities, or by insisting that the effective administrative span of a vice-chancellor serve as an absolute limit upon the size of any unitary university.[78] There are, as yet, no examples of this insistence, nor any agreement upon the numerical value of the limit to be imposed, but it is an answer which would commend itself to many within the academic world, if only as yet another argument against expansion.[79]

At the present time, however, it remains the case that vice-chancellors do not govern their universities, but that without vice-chancellors of vision and energy universities may sometimes drift. In an earlier chapter we quoted 'James Dundonald's' view that 'it was the job of a departmental head to keep freshness in the teaching'.[80] He continues thus: 'Who but the poor vice-chancellor can keep life going in the whole concern?'[81] To this question there is, at present, no satisfactory alternative answer.

---

[77] Chapter VIII, below.

[78] One way of implementing such a policy would be to establish new autonomous units within a broad federal framework, possibly on the model of London. Alternatively—and some of the London units seem to prefer this—more new autonomous small universities could be established. And for example, it may in fact be as expensive to establish (and maintain) one university of (say) 24,000 students as three universities each of 8,000.

[79] See A. H. HALSEY and MARTIN TROW: *The British Academics* (Faber and Faber, 1971), especially pp. 243–275, for evidence of academic resistance to further growth.

[80] See Chapter IV, above, p. 68.   [81] *Op. cit.*, p. 109.

Chapter VII

THE BUREAUCRACY

This chapter is about the group we have called in our definitions the 'officials'[1], the group concerned with servicing the decision-making process. What we say applies, principally, to the senior (often graduate) staff of the registrar's department and some of the senior financial officials.[2]

The temptation to refer to this group as the 'administration' must be strongly resisted. In the first place the 'administration' must include the office of vice-chancellor, a subject to which a chapter has already been given. Secondly, and much more important, it is quite wrong to see the 'administration' as composed of the professional bureaucracy only. For, despite the growth of the bureaucracy, a very substantial amount of administration is done, and is likely to continue to be done, by the academic staff. We have already dealt with those administrative functions of heads of departments which, analagous to some in the vice-chancellor's role, constitute important political resources.[3] But academic staff also undertake a great deal of labour which is similar to, and often identical with, the work of the bureaucracy. These chores include such things as organizing field-courses, negotiating with outside lecturers, admitting students, timetabling, or issuing book lists. As such tasks become larger and more routine, they are progressively taken over by bureaucrats or even by computers, but much always remains to be done[4], and because what remains will usually include the new or

---

[1] In Chapter III, above.
[2] Some of the registrar's staff may in fact play little part in policy matters. Occasionally important officials may not be in any department, but in the vice-chancellor's office.
[3] See Chapter IV, above.
[4] Professor W. J. Mackenzie has argued, with great strength and conviction, that to carry out some administrative tasks is inseparable from any, and certainly from any good, teaching and research. 'The Professor as Administrator: a Comment', *Universities Quarterly*, Vol. 7, pp. 333–41.

not yet routine, its importance is disproportionately large.[5] Sometimes this administrative work is institutionalized, and academics act as secretary to bodies (though today this is rare above the departmental level).[6] There can be no doubt that one reason for this has been an appreciation, even an over-appreciation, of the political value of a secretaryship. Another reason has been a traditional dislike of bureaucracy; though it may be more realistic to emphasize a lack of funds. It may also happen that the person who is able to spend the most time on a given administrative subject, say the preparation of a major new scheme, is not an official but an academic. As one professor, who had just organized and put through a great expansion of his department, remarked to us: 'universities do not take decisions; they tolerate initiatives'. (By 'universities' here he clearly meant their governmental and administrative machinery.) Several registrars confessed that they had no time to keep up with the detail of all such schemes; as one remarked, 'I'm responsible that the boring parts work as well'. Moreover, academics often chair committees, which is likely to involve them in an essentially administrative chore. In any event, all academics who wish it are likely at some stage to find themselves administering alongside, and often directing, the professional bureaucracy.

Thus, the 'administration' (in the proper sense of 'those who administer') is 'not a cohesive group with well-defined membership (like Mr Gladstone's administration) that runs the place'.[7] It should not be seen even as a group of professionals so much as a diverse and shifting group in which the bureaucrats are in a numerical minority. The majority includes numerous 'amateurs' ranging from regular officers, sometimes almost full-time administrators, such as pro-vice-chancellors or sub-deans, to academics filling offices (often

[5] The Robbins *Report* put the overall expenditure of staff time at about 10 per cent (excluding meetings of examiners and advice to students); see App. 3, Table 63. See also *Report of an Enquiry into the Use of Academic Staff Time* (Committee of Vice-Chancellors and Principals, 1972). This, regrettably, if understandably, does not show time spent on administration separately.

[6] In London the federation-wide subject committees (Boards of Studies) which were, and appear still to be, key bodies in the academic system, normally had academic secretaries who regarded the federal bureaucracy warily if not with hostility, at least in the early stages of their tenure. In the last century the secretary of the senate was often a professor; at the University of Glasgow it has recently been decided that the Clerk of Senate should remain so.

[7] To quote the comment given by an ex-registrar on our early ideas; because of the Gladstonian connotation he thought 'administration' an unsuitable word altogether.

extremely time-consuming) such as subject-chairman, course-convener or chief examiner.[8]

The bureaucracy's lack of a monopoly is complemented by the relatively low status traditionally allotted to it. This is partly a product of the historical development. Though at most redbricks there has always been a devoted, and powerful, administrator[9], whose tenure was often far longer than the vice-chancellor's, yet he was a solitary; and he was generally reluctant to employ any assistants. At Oxbridge the tradition has always been even more strongly against a central bureaucracy.[10] The strong anarchic element in the outlook of academics in this country has always tended to the view, as Merton College, Oxford, has put it, that 'education in general and university education *par excellence* are worlds in which the administrator should be kept in his place'.[11] This view has largely prevailed. Thus Sir Eric Ashby has claimed that 'our British system . . . almost eliminates the administration as a power point'.[12] (The word 'almost' should, in our view, be stressed.)

The bureaucracy in fact was not professionalized until quite recently and the registrar typically was a former lecturer of limited academic distinction chosen very much *ad hoc* and with as much eye to ethos as to expertise.[13] No longer, however, is it remotely possible to run a university with 'three men and a boy' helped by two typists and the vice-chancellor's secretary. There has therefore grown up since the end of the Second World War, and particularly since the mid-fifties, a large new career in university administration. This

---

[8] The group may extend even beyond the academic staff, to chaplains, wardens of residences, architects, and, of course, to the active lay members of council.

[9] At Sheffield in the 1920s and early 1930s the staff depended for their increments on the registrar, who ruled with extreme strictness within certain areas. See A. W. CHAPMAN: *The Story of a modern University* (Oxford, 1955).

[10] It is said that the 1922 Royal Commission was unable to investigate Oxford as they intended because there was no means of obtaining information.

[11] From the (Franks) *Commission of Enquiry* (Oxford, 1966), Written Evidence, Part XIII, p. 35. Note also '. . . the old unreflecting Oxford fear of an efficient official service . . .' *ibid., Report* S. 551; or, '. . . the fact is that the word "administrative" falls like a chill on all academic hearts', D. G. James (Vice-Chancellor, Southampton) in the *Universities Quarterly*, May 1953, p. 248. Even in the United States 'at the larger and more prestigious schools it has been necessary, traditionally, for management innovations to be introduced with considerable diplomatic finesse, to allay the suspicions of faculty'—F. E. ROURKE and G. E. BROOKS: *The Managerial Revolution in Higher Education* (Johns Hopkins Press, 1966) p. 13.

[12] *Masters and Scholars* (Oxford, 1970) p. 11.

[13] His few assistants, even if graduates, were usually of much lower calibre. Registrars were almost always recruited from outside the office.

reflects not only the greater numbers of people involved[14] but also the increasing specialization of function within the bureaucracy. Before the war no university had its own architects, its separate planning or public relations officer, or a multiplicity of financial officials; by now they are almost universal. This burgeoning of officials has of course led to many new problems into which we cannot go here. Suffice it to say that a new dimension in the work of senior officials is that of personnel management within their own structure, of attempting to see that service in a university bureaucracy provides an adequate career structure for young entrants, and that nationally the development of this new profession continues to offer genuine opportunities to able graduates. Though senior officials are still to some extent recruited from outside[15], it has nevertheless proved possible to maintain a bureaucracy that is strongly committed to the university and, in particular, to the principle of academic staff self-government.

The bureaucracy has thus expanded[16], but not obviously more so than the increased complexity of their work and of outside demands (especially for information) might seem to warrant. More important, however, is whether this growth indicates a corresponding inflation of the role of officials within university government. What, then, are the actual powers and functions of registrars, bursars, and the like in British universities today? Most obviously university officials advise, they implement, they record and file, they 'keep the papers moving', they formulate issues and arguments, they count, they inform, and they render all necessary services to their masters, but they have to act in accordance with decisions which they have no formal power to determine. Their position is best illustrated by their relationship to the committee structure of the university. They attend committees, in many cases they supply the briefs and docu-

[14] For example, one recent conference of junior non-financial administrative staff was attended by over 400 people, and each year there are several national conferences of university officials.

[15] Oxford has appointed its last three registrars from the home civil service. In the last decade there has been a notable influx from the overseas civil service, and even of overseas vice-chancellors. There have been some other outside entrants, though seldom from industry or commerce.

[16] The UGC's *Annual Surveys* for 1968–9, App. V, Table 1 and 1970–1, App. III, Table 1 show a steady rise in the proportion of total university expenditure accounted for by administration. It rose from 7·5 per cent in 1961–2 to 8·2 per cent in 1969–70. Earlier, however, there was a decline in the proportional cost of administration (see M. L. Shattock in the *Universities Quarterly*, 24:3, 1970, p. 312), and it appears that the older and larger institutions had lower proportions than the newer and smaller (DES, *Statistics of Education, 1967*, Vol. 6, Table 65).

mentation without which committees would not know what they are deciding, and they are expected to see that committee decisions are carried out; but they are seldom full voting members of the most important committees.[17]

This account clearly resembles that commonly given of the constitutional role of the higher civil service, and university officials are sometimes referred to as 'civil servants'.[18] We do not, however, recommend this usage. It does not tell one enough about the actual influence of the officials, nor does it do full justice to the fact that members of university committees are better informed about, and more closely involved in, university affairs than a minister can nowadays hope to be in most of the work of his department. It is in any case doubtful how far the role and nature of a university committee can properly be likened to those of a minister, if only because it is not easy to determine who, precisely, are the 'political masters' of a university official and where exactly his duty lies.

It is not even easy to establish the formal duties of officials. Charters provide that the registrar shall be appointed by the council (though recently senate has been brought into the process).[19] His duties, normally, are to be such as council 'shall deem fit', but councils rarely deem by formal pronouncement. The Privy Council's Model Charter (which was more specific than most other instruments) made the registrar 'responsible for providing secretarial services for the Court, the Council, the Senate, and for the administration of the Universities' but did not say to whom.[20] The Sussex charter (and it was the first to do so) subordinated the registrar to the vice-chancellor, but only for 'finances . . . buildings . . . and

---

[17] Librarians and other quasi-academic officers may be found on certain committees. An official may be a member of what might be called the more social committees, certain highly technical ones, or even an *ad hoc* advisory committee. We know of few current cases of membership of a major policy-making body or committee. There are the slightly curious exceptions at Birmingham, mentioned in the postscript to Chapter III, and another at Belfast. At the University of Lancaster the Assistant Academic Registrar, Secretary to Senate, was elected by the Senate in 1971 as one of its members on Council—perhaps significantly, he was also secretary to the local branch of the AUT—and the University Secretary has been co-opted to Senate. At an earlier date the Secretary of LSE did sit on some such committees, but not, and from this point of view very significantly, since the last administrative reorganization.

[18] See, e.g. Sir Kenneth Wheare's view of a registrar as '. . . a cross between Secretary to the Cabinet and Permanent Secretary'. See the *Report* of the Franks Committee, S. 486.

[19] See Chapter II, above.

[20] S. 11. The vice-chancellor, by contrast, is not given any specific administrative responsibility. (S. 7.)

general adminstration' and not as secretary to the governing bodies.[21] This distinction is made in the six charters which thereafter included this subordination.[22] In 1966 the Vice-Chancellors' Committee submitted to the Committee of Public Accounts a memorandum which stated that the officials 'are strictly the servants of the governing bodies, lay and academic, with whom decision lies', and made no reference to any relationship with the vice-chancellor.[23] We asked many registrars whether they saw themselves as responsible to council (or senate) or to their vice-chancellor. Almost all had some difficulty in answering, partly of course because they had difficulty in conceiving of a conflict. One extremely senior adminstrator simply replied to us that a man faced with such a conflict ought to be looking for another post. But all, on a little reflection, gave the answer made by the Vice-Chancellors' Committee just quoted. It seems clear that the duty of a secretary of council (performed by the 'registrar') must in the last resort be to his council rather than to a single member of it, unless possibly its chairman. In fact the legal position, save in that last resort from which communities of scholars traditionally shrink, is probably not very important. Personal factors are more so.[24]

In practice the registrar is often, perhaps normally, a close confidant of the vice-chancellor, kept well informed, and able to assist in forming the vice-chancellor's own opinion as well as to act for him in dealings with others. In many matters staff and outsiders would prefer to see the registrar before making an appointment with the vice-chancellor. They may never wish to go further, feeling that their case is in better hands than their own. This is so partly and most obviously because of the registrar's specific administrative duties, but also it is so because the relationship of a registrar to his vice-chancellor is often a very subtle one, akin in many ways to a personal assistantship or even to that between the president and general secretary of a major trade union. This sort of relationship, as we have noticed in Chapter VI, provides great support to the vice-chancellor as well as inevitably increasing a registrar's own influence.

[21] S. IX.

[22] E.g. Stirling S. 6. Of these Brunel, in addition, makes the 'Secretary General ... responsible to the Council for implementing those policies of the Council affecting the finances of the University' (S. 9.3).

[23] *Special Report* on Parliament and Control of University Expenditure (HMSO 1967) Appendix 8, S. 10.

[24] Overseas, especially where nationalism is deeply involved, the legal position can be important. At University College, Nairobi, for example, there was a separate Council letterhead on which the names of the Chairman and Registrar (with the title of Secretary), but not that of the principal, appeared.

W. M. Childs, the first Vice-Chancellor of Reading, wrote that 'I recall [the Registrar's] helpfulness in counsel before all else . . . he helped me to clear my mind on many occasions'[25], and many modern vice-chancellors would endorse this.

This Childs-like relationship is, however, not invariable. We saw little more than half the country's registrars, and these often only once, but even so we found evidence of difficulties. One registrar was greatly offensive when his vice-chancellor peered round the door and another cut him dead in the corridor. Elsewhere registrars clearly had little rapport with their vice-chancellors, had been left to routine duties, or had even been passed over, in effect, for one of their own juniors. At least two had had to pick up threads from a vice-chancellor who was beginning to lose interest or was unable wholly to cope. There were also differences of policy. One told us of his alliances with the vice-chancellor's opponents on senate and another was in deep doubt over his vice-chancellor's failure to keep council fully informed financially. One ruefully showed us his draft on a major matter of organization: he plainly expected his vice-chancellor to pay it little attention. Two others were later forced into resignation; one, in alliance with the chairman of council, forced his vice-chancellor to resign. The scope for friction is obvious enough. For one thing, the roles of vice-chancellor and of registrar have enough similarities for a vice-chancellor always to be in appreciable danger of being overtaken in some areas by a good registrar, and of having to take over others from a bad. A new vice-chancellor, in particular, may have to make his position very clear. Moreover both officers are extremely busy, and a vice-chancellor is often away a great deal; they may thus have little time to consult.

We have dwelt rather long on the disharmonies partly in explanation of our remarks in Chapter VI about the limits to the vice-chancellor's control of the bureaucracy, and partly to emphasize that the registrar is no man's 'creature'. His responsibilities are chiefly to the bodies he services. He also has close dealings with the staff, especially the senior and more active staff, as well as the more active lay members of council. For all of them he is likely to show a high regard. Thus his duties, both legally and functionally, do not lie exclusively on a single vertical line.

A similar account may be given of the other senior officials. They, too, tend to see themselves as the servants of the whole academic community and to regard their central loyalty as being either to the institution in general or to some part of it which, for them, embodies

---

[25] *Making a University* (Dent, 1933) p. 114. Significantly, however, 'he was in agreement with me . . . in the policy of independence'.

a community interest. There is, for example, a strong tendency for officials to identify with committees they service; especially is this so amongst the more junior ones and those who are seconded to work with a faculty or other academic unit. They may then prefer, for ideological reasons as well as personal ones, to take instructions from their chairman or committee rather than from their professional superior. Their disregard for their career prospects sometimes astonished us; some, for example carried this to the extent of withholding information from the central administration or a superior.[26] Such committee loyalty is not, however, entirely confined to the junior officials. Thus one deputy registrar in a new university, who was most loyal to the vice-chancellor, none the less remarked 'the vice-chancellor likes to decide things for himself, but when I think the committee should know about something I see that it goes on the agenda', and this we think is a very common attitude.

These imperfections in the bureaucratic hierarchy are in fact closely relevant to its functions. To quote from Jacques Barzun, 'The best administrators for a university . . . must know (and need no reminders) that what they do is mere facilitation.'[27] This is to say that their job is to make it possible for decisions to be taken at the right time, by the right people, and on the basis of the proper information. Similarly, once decisions are taken, the officials are expected to ensure that they are carried out. (Their task includes everything from the provision of chalk in those rooms, and those rooms only, where there are blackboards, to ensuring that the university does not run unawares into financial disaster.) To say that the job of the bureaucracy is to facilitate does not, however, tell one what or whose business they facilitate when, as often happens, the claims of different people and different items of business conflict with one another. One can say only that some discretion remains as to how, and with how much energy, business shall be facilitated.

A crucial element in the process of facilitation is that of being the guardians of established procedures (which must be observed at

[26] The initiative may come from the staff. Several times staff told us they did (or did not) 'trust' the faculty, etc. official to keep its affairs out of the hands of the centre. One of us was for years under instruction from successive chairmen of a committee systematically to deny access to a superior official. Conversely, officials would tell us they could not do their job if they were suspected of being an 'administration man'.

[27] *The American University* (Oxford, 1969) p. 115. The official in the USA is moreover much more an 'administrator' in the sense in which we are using the word. That is, he is more like a responsible member of the government, and less like a mere civil servant. Professor Barzun's judgement thus applies even more to the British situation.

F

least in the eyes of officials, if not always in the eyes of those whose business they administer). The Many officials quite clearly see that their job is to ensure that decisions are taken by the methods and people who, within the university, are supposed (by the charter, or more frequently by council or senate decision and by custom) to take the decisions. Much of this is of course a simple routine business, although not necessarily for that reason one easy to do well, but here too there is a positive task to be performed. In this area above all perhaps may be found officials taking the important initiatives within particular universities. It is no secret, for example, that the elaborate set of procedures and criteria that have evolved at the University of Sussex owe their origin (though not their adoption) to one or two particularly able and numerate officials. It is generally accepted, too, that in any university the more sensible proposals for re-organizing the committee structure or the flow of business will have been discussed in detail with the officials, the experts on this aspect of government.

Friction is unavoidable, it being in the nature of bureaucracies to stress rules and of professionals to stress their own exceptional cases. Academics are inclined, too, to wish some things done at once and to do others (like make returns and submissions) only when, if ever, it is convenient. For the most part, however, the officials' attempts to operate by the rules (most of them enacted by academic bodies), like their loyalty to 'their' committees, in fact serves to maintain the governmental role of academics.

There is another, more positive, aspect to the officials' role as facilitators, and that is the formulation of proposals for consideration. Thus a document on the administration prepared within one of the new universities says that 'the central administration . . . requires a core of professionally qualified administrators and planners to give expert advice as well as to execute university policy'. As Sir Kenneth Wheare told the Franks Commission, 'most of the initiative for conducting the business and bringing it up . . . comes from the Registrar'[28] who was expected to offer opinions and suggestions. The Commission, after commending this exercise of initiative by the registrar, continues: 'similar behaviour should be expected from the other officials . . . they should act as advisers, free to speak and suggest, but not to vote on committees'[29]. Sir

[28] *Report*, S. 456.
[29] *Report*, S. 556. Interpretations of officials' subordinate status as they bear upon their right to speak at committee vary between universities. In some they speak only when spoken to, or even only when called upon by the chairman, while in others they are expected to intervene, especially upon matters of fact,

Philip Morris, emphasizing the same point, told the Commission that 'for an administration to operate successfully, in addition to having the duty of serving, it must also feel itself responsible for formulating proposals for consideration and must have ready ways of obtaining due consideration for such proposals'. No one with any experience of university administration would want to quarrel with these propositions. In fact, the history of most universities would be incomplete without reference to the university equivalents of such civil servants as Edwin Chadwick, Sir Robert Morant, or even Sir Horace Wilson.

In exercising their discretion and in taking initiatives senior officials can draw upon a number of resources from which their impact upon government is in part derived. Of these probably the most fundamental is the information they possess and cannot help but acquire in the course of their normal work. Most obviously, information comes to the bureaucracy in its capacity as university secretariat—the group which handles the paper-work for all the university governing bodies (and, in places, for some at faculty, school or subject levels as well), which is in some degree responsible for much of the correspondence with outsiders, and which keeps the central files. As a university grows beyond the early stage at which consultation may easily take place informally and through chance encounters[30], more must be committed to paper (in the form of minutes, memoranda, and the like), the need for the secretariat also grows and, with it, the extent to which the secretariat becomes privy to all important matters. As a vice-chancellor put it to us, 'everything of importance, at one time or another, flows across Mark's or Daniel's desk' (the people named[31] being the registrar and bursar). There is, of course, some variation in the extent to which senior officials are kept well informed depending, particularly, upon the extent to which they are respected (and thus confided in) by the vice-chancellor and the academic staff. But a senior official who has held office for a long period may, like Walter Bagehot's 'sagacious king', 'acquire an experience with which few . . . could

---

at their discretion. At Warwick there is now (1972) a Senate minute specifically recognizing the right and duty of officials to speak in order to prevent error or to provide relevant information.

[30] The stage familiar to, for example, those who have worked in the 'new' universities from the beginning; it was described to us as that of 'the euphoric Jean-Jacques Rousseau community', but described more commonly by social scientists as the 'pre-bureaucratic' one of largely face-to-face relations.

[31] But not precisely thus.

contend'. And some officials do in fact have comparably long reigns.[32]

It may perhaps be useful to say something about the ways in which the possession of information can confer influence upon officials, even although universities do not in this respect differ much from other types of organization. Most obviously, a well-informed man is likely to make useful proposals, but there is more to it than that. The information available to officials, in alliance with their guardianship of procedures, means that it becomes worth the while of others to seek their guidance, and this not only permits the officials to discuss proposals while they are still relatively flexible, it also makes them better informed. In this respect they share one of the vice-chancellor's resources.[33] The same combination of assets has the further advantage that the senior officials are particularly well placed to feed in ideas or proposals at the point in the structure, and the time, at which they stand the greatest chance of a favourable reception; not the least of their strengths being the opportunity, as close observers of all committees, to know the styles, prejudices, and personalities of the individuals concerned. One assistant registrar, in a judgement echoed by many others, told us that 'one works on the assumption that one will put forward recommendations that will be accepted'. Undeniably this carries with it a clear implication that others do the accepting and thus exercise both an ante- and post-natal control over the recommendations advanced. Nevertheless, to know how, when, and where to initiate may be crucial for success.

As the external constraints upon and the internal complexity of universities grow with expansion, specialization, and financial pressure, so too does the need of decision-makers for adequate briefing both upon the background and about possible solutions to given problems. It is the job of the officials to provide such briefs—though not necessarily or always upon their own initiative or without guidance. In this way too, however, influence may be wielded. In part this is simply because an initial definition of a problem, like an initial policy proposal, has a natural headstart over any other, and if an official's suggestion is permitted by the vice-chancellor or other chairman to go forward to the deciding bodies, its strength is

[32] See WALTER BAGEHOT: *The English Constitution* (2nd ed., 1872) Chapter III. To give but two examples of official perseverance in office: in the first eighty-four years of its existence, spanning the period 1879 to 1963, Sheffield had only three registrars (whereas merely since 1905 there were seven vice-chancellors); and in the London federation, the present Principal has already (1973) served for a quarter-century in that post.

[33] See the previous chapter.

great. In the sphere of resource allocation a suggested solution has a special advantage when it is considered by academics, in that the academics both are interested parties and hesitant about making alternative suggestions which must adversely affect some colleagues. The official's suggestion in this area is thus the more likely to be accepted precisely because it is a judgement between academics. Partly as a result, and in combination with his other resources, the registrar or bursar may become the key man in the budgetary process and in the allocation of resources within the university. This has been most marked in those universities which have had an experienced official in office at the beginning of the period of expansion and who, really for lack of any alternative, became thereafter the main drafter of budgets and quinquennial proposals and the man whose advice carried the greatest weight in the basic divisions of government grants. Beyond any doubt this ability to suggest on occasion has been consciously used to create academic priorities; but in any finely balanced situation an official's predilections, however diffidently held, are likely to be of significant weight. In a somewhat unusual case the registrar at one of the longer established universities lent active support (so he told us) to one academic faction in a dispute about the future size of the institution.

One of the respects in which this last case is unusual is in the official's admission of his own part. More typically, and no less honestly, officials stressed to us how limited was their scope. A Yorkshire official (regarded by everyone in his university as a powerful figure in its government) insisted that 'facts make the decisions; I merely find out the facts'. A London counterpart put it slightly differently when remarking that 'one can only explain; then, once "public opinion" has been formed, decisions take themselves'. Both reflected the feeling, common to decision-makers everywhere, that it is always the situation which decides. As commonly, outsiders do not see it thus—even when it is largely true. Thus we were told in three universities which had at one time prided themselves on being small that the actual decision to 'go big' came almost undiscussed; opinion had been shifting, and suddenly resources were available. In each case, the actual decision appeared to the outsider to have been taken on an official's initiative; it no doubt was technically so in at least two of the cases, but in none of them (that we could see) was it agreed in any sense because of official pressure or manipulation. Clearly, in some situations the official role is merely to digest the relevant factors and then, computer-like, to draw the inescapable (but not always obvious) conclusions. It may then appear, wrongly, as though officials had conceived the policy which they had merely 'printed out'. But one cannot, nevertheless, accept that officials 'merely find out the facts'.

We are sceptical of this claim for reasons familiar enough to many academics.[34] Just what the facts are is not always a simple matter to decide; and it may be impossible easily, if at all, to secure agreement upon what facts are relevant and, if relevant, precisely what they imply. Indeed, and in this sense it may often be true that 'facts make the decisions', the crucial policy debate may turn on those questions. In other words, the situation could also be described by saying that the decisions make the facts. Try as he may to be impartial, an official's own frame of intellectual reference will inevitably affect his perceptions of the facts and his selection of facts to be incorporated in his analyses and recommendations.[35]

There are clear dangers of bureaucratic government here. They are accentuated by the modern trend towards the adoption of more sophisticated 'information-based' techniques of planning and budgeting.[36] These techniques represent an attempt to achieve more rational processes of decision-making, but to the extent that the techniques and principles involved outrun the comprehension of vice-chancellors, academics, or other officials and thus constitute an area of opaque administration, they may confer a significant increment of influence upon the officials concerned. We were not reassured by a young man, recently appointed to a new statistical post in an ancient university, who remarked to us that he doubted if the committee which had recommended the creation of his job had fully realized what he would in fact be able to do. 'I don't think they'll like some of it, but they won't have any grounds for stopping me.' It is, of course, important not to mistake academic resentment for legitimate scepticism. In particular, it is important not to accuse the officials of selecting facts when one means little more than that the particular facts selected are unpalatable. As one senior official put it to us, 'friction (with the administration) is unavoidable because academics are too unresponsive to outside needs and pressures (although the natural scientists are rather better than arts men in this)'.[37] On occasion, too, it may be left to officials to point out some

---

[34] Though, it must be confessed, often forgotten in the heat of debate in committee.

[35] Among other factors influencing his frame of reference will be the range of people whom he normally encounters (and the circumstances in which he does so)—hence the importance to the life of a university of the degree to which officials are accessible both in and out of office hours.

[36] Most of the next chapter is devoted to a discussion of their significance.

[37] As arts men ourselves, we can only hope that we have made the proper allowances.

of the larger implications of a decision for the institution as a whole or, most unpopularly of all, to enforce or to persuade others to accept the unpleasant decisions necessitated by the scarcity of money, time, or whatever else is at stake.

With whatever qualifications may be thought necessary, the conclusion seems inescapable that officials are in a position to help mould the policy of a university. That position is the stronger, too, for the possession, at least by the more senior officials, of a security of tenure as good as that of the academic staff. In some of the newer charters the provisions which safeguard members of the academic staff from dismissal are specifically applied to the registrar and bursar. It may be possible for them to be by-passed in, or reorganized out of business, for some attractive offer to be made from elsewhere[38], or even to persuade a senior official to seek employment elsewhere by making life difficult to the point of humiliation. We even know of a case (but only one) in which a registrar was simply urged to retire prematurely, assisted by a compensatory payment. Few universities, however, can afford to offer a 'golden handshake'. The senior officials, like academics, are thus secure in the knowledge that it would be difficult to move them.

These resources, important as they may be, nevertheless do not confer unlimited discretion or immense power upon any member of the bureaucracy, for great importance must also be attached to the limits placed upon officials by the special context in which they work.[39] The main limitation, of course, is the fact (already noted) that the formal powers of decision are firmly in the hands of others, including the academic members of important decision-making bodies. They are all capable of using their powers quite unexpectedly.[40] As a result officials are well aware that banana-skins can lie anywhere, and some complained to us of the semi-paralysis caused by anxiety not to slip on them. Officials know that their initiatives must be acceptable, and also that they are more likely to be acceptable if they themselves are trusted not to seek power.

[38] An unsuccessful registrar at North Staffordshire became, first, director of studies and then a vice-chancellor overseas. See SIR JAMES MOUNTFORD: *Keele* (Routledge and Kegan Paul, 1972) p. 87.

[39] On this and other points covered in this chapter see R. B. EUSTACE: 'Some governmental features of the Expansion of the British University', in M. L. SHATTOCK, ed. *University Administration in a Period of Expansion* (British Council, 1971) pp. 135–142.

[40] As a minor illustration we can cite the instance of the professor on a very inert council who told us how he had just induced the council to reject an elaborate and no doubt already half-arranged scheme for rationalizing the replication services.

In part because, as we have emphasized, academics also administer, the contacts between officials and academics are constant and often close. This is important in several ways. While it may mean that academics learn to appreciate the bureaucratic imperatives for orderly and uniform procedures, it also means that they acquire the know-how with which to meet (and beat) the professionals on their own ground. This close contact, often extended into the common rooms, is possibly most important as a means of further socializing officials into academic ways and ideals. The task is not difficult. Most senior officials are themselves university graduates and some have even begun their university careers as members of the academic staff. But even those with different backgrounds seem, with a few conspicuous exceptions, soon to work within and sometimes to share the academics' ideals of university government.[41]

As a result, possibly, of a combination of the qualities looked for at the time of an official's initial selection and of consequent learning, our experience was that almost all the important officials we talked to clearly saw themselves, sometimes rather naïvely but always genuinely, as mere facilitators. One registrar, seen by all in his university as central to policy, and who for a period had worked virtually without a vice-chancellor, bid one of us farewell with: 'Remember, influence: yes; power: no.' And though the scholar toad under the harrow might question this statement, there is good evidence that his real interest was not in fact in general policymaking. The statement may, in any case, be accepted as one of intention. In most universities, moreover, officials are helped to realize such intentions by the generally accepted view that overall policy is properly the sphere of the vice-chancellor (to the extent that it is not an academic preserve), and it is one which he rarely cedes willingly to an official.

The university bureaucracy has certainly grown in size as the universities have expanded. In some degree, too, it has grown in importance and influence; but its constitutional and political position does not seem to us greatly to have changed in recent years. Officials still benefit more from the delegation of power to prepare memoranda than from any delegation of power to take the final

[41] Former colonial civil servants, even, get over their initial horror at the apparent chaos of university administration. At worst they see themselves, as one put it, 'like a resident in a princely state tolerating the expenditure on concubines', and they often end in a frame of mind not easily distinguished from affection. See too the judgement of A. H. HALSEY and MARTIN TROW: *The British Academics* (Faber and Faber, 1971) at p. 114: 'The administrative staff of British Universities appears . . . small in numbers and strongly conditioned to subservience to the academic will.'

decisions. In one area only, that of the application of new sophisticated techniques, have we detected any serious new danger of bureaucratic aggrandisement. The only real question here, however, is
whether academics will themselves use or direct the use of these
techniques which, in principle, are as available to them as to
officials.[42] In general, the vast majority of university officials regard
their duty as seeing to it only that the essential decisions are taken,
and taken on the most reasonable grounds possible. They do not
believe that they should themselves take these decisions; but if no
one else comes forward to take them the bureaucrats may have to.

[42] We return to this question in the next chapter.

Chapter VIII

BUDGETING AND THE ALLOCATION OF RESOURCES

How best to allocate resources is one of the two major governmental problems facing universities today.[1] Our main interest is in the allocation of resources within universities, but it is impossible totally to ignore the problems involved in allocations between universities and between them and other areas of public expenditure. This is not only because of the heightened public interest associated with the changes in the relations between government and the universities which took place during the 1960s. There are also certain problems common to public and university expenditure which warrant discussion.

The most direct and obvious link between university and central government expenditure is brought out by the following table of the sources of university recurrent income. It is for 1966–7, the final year of the latest quinquennium for which full information is available at the time of writing.[2]

Source	Amount, £000's	Percentage of total income
1. Parliamentary grants:		
(a) UGC	139,709	73·8
(b) Other departments	2,132	1·6
2. Fees	13,354	7·0
3. Endowments	2,619	1·4
4. Local authority grants	1,622	0·8
5. Donations, etc.	855	0·5
6. Payments for research	21,630	11·3
7. Other	7,274	3·4
	£189,183	100·0

[1] The other, the internal pressures for greater participation in decision-making by non-professorial staff and students, is the subject of our next chapter.

[2] UNIVERSITY GRANTS COMMITTEE: *University Development 1962–1968* (Cmnd 3820 of 1968) p. 38.

If capital expenditure is also taken into account, the contribution of public funds will amount, in many institutions, to some 90 per cent or more of available finance. The starting-point for any consideration of university expenditure and its determination is thus the UGC which, since its establishment, has been the principal channel and filter of year-to-year government involvement with the universities.[3]

The UGC receives its money from the Department of Education and Science (since 1964) but, ultimately of course, on the agreement of the Treasury which, previously, had made annual grants direct to the Committee. The UGC itself decides how, precisely, the grant will be apportioned amongst the universities, although within the limits of overall government policy. Of particular relevance, in the sixties, were government decisions on the total number of students, the emphasis on science and technology, and fees to be charged to students from overseas, a list which seems likely, in the seventies, to cover an increasing number of other issues (among them staffing levels, shorter courses, and other matters bearing directly upon the costs of university education).

The recurrent grant from the UGC to each university, however, has at least until recently been largely free from overt strings, being given in a 'block' whose size was related to the case made by the university in its quinquennial application, but otherwise wholly at the university's disposal (except that the scales of salary paid were fixed).[4] Since the 1950s, and particularly since the award of grants for the 1967–72 quinquennium, the block grant has in effect been increasingly hedged about with restrictions, some of which amount to earmarking for specific purposes. Universities are now told, for instance, whether a particular proposal contained in their application has 'not been taken into account', and informed of some of the general principles of allocation followed by the Committee.[5] There are limitations on the proportion of senior staff that may be appointed, and the total number of students who may be enrolled year by year, and thus on the staff-student ratio. These constraints, which some prefer to describe as controls, are important, and affect internal decisions, sometimes sharply. From time to time, the UGC has also

[3] See, e.g. the brief account of itself given in UNIVERSITY GRANTS COMMITTEE: *Annual Survey for 1968–1969* (Cmnd 4261 of 1970) Appendix II, pp. 36–40. The best general analysis of the role of the UGC is to be found in R. O. BERDAHL: *British Universities and the State* (University of California, 1959); but see also an earlier American study: H. W. Dodds and others, *Government Assistance to Universities in Great Britain* (OUP, 1952).

[4] How far universities might in practice have been allowed to stray is debatable; see BERDAHL: *op. cit.*

[5] See the UGC *Report, op. cit.*, Appendix 12, pp. 220–6.

given additional 'earmarked' grants (for which universities some-times had to compete) to encourage the development of, for example, area studies. Where capital grants are concerned, the UGC imposes (and has done so for longer) much stricter and more direct controls, so that buildings, especially, must confirm to tight cost specifications with strict physical limits, for instance to the amount of space to be allotted to a professor's office.

Even if no weight be attached to the fact that the vast majority of UGC members are present or former academics, the system still permits universities a substantial degree of self-government in financial matters. Universities continue, in spite of the changed role of the UGC, to be substantially free to decide how they will spend their money. Thus within the lines of guidance to which we have already referred, universities are told by the UGC that the general recurrent grant must be allocated within each university by the university itself. Moreover, the initiative for any particular item of expenditure lies with each university, and there is no restriction on the right of a university to seek other funds to finance its activities. It is at least arguable, moreover, that the UGC is, at the very worst, no more restrictive than alternative donors today and in the past, whether these others are local authorities, business men, the church, or royal patrons. Both the processes internal to universities and those external to it (and to the UGC) therefore remain important in the allocation of resources. What is more, there are basic similarities in the nature of the problems with which these processes, in both the universities and the government, have to deal: the fundamental similarity is that in neither case is income obtained by selling the final product(s)—the results of expenditure—in the market. Thus, in the case of the universities, income is largely the result of inducing the UGC to provide the necessary finance[6], while in the case of the government spending departments, it is the result of inducing the Treasury to do the same. In both cases, therefore, the first task of the decision-making process is, broadly speaking, the formulation of claims to support the organization's existing and proposed activities.

Any claim for finance is in principle competitive with any other, while each claim has its consequential implications, say the needs of the bureaucracy or for space. The library may need additional books if a university is fully to exploit the skills of a proposed new member of staff, but money spent on his salary is no longer available for book-buying. Consequently, the claims from different spending units must not merely be aggregated, they must be brought into relationship with each other and, at some stage, arranged in an order of priority.

[6] As we noted above, Chapter V. p. 111.

The point at which priorities are assigned varies: at Leeds, for example, priorities must be indicated within each unit's claim, but such decisions may, elsewhere, be postponed until the size of the UGC grant is known. There is also considerable variation in the extent to which the final submission to the UGC is integrated with long-term strategic intentions, or, for example, is largely a matter of 'present costs plus x per cent for development'. Again, some universities entrust the task of compiling the submission (on the basis of the unit claims) to a special 'quinquennial' committee of senate (sometimes jointly with council), others to a standing committee on planning or academic development, and yet others leave it to the vice-chancellor and senior officials—in some cases subject to endorsement or review by senate and in all, ultimately, by council and its finance committee.

Everywhere the vice-chancellor, officials, deans, and professorial heads of department tend to exercise more discretion in preparing the estimates than in more exclusively academic matters—after all, particular responsibility in financial matters normally rests with them. In a small, but growing, number of universities the process of preparing claims also reflects the newer techniques of expenditure control which we must discuss later.[7] Given academic ambitions and policy, however, it is only a slight over-simplification to say that the articulation of expenditure claims is a relatively mechanical and routine process.

The real, and often painful, problems arise in deciding which claim(s) to translate into authorized expenditures, and how to do so. Once again, the problems faced by the Treasury in appraising the claims of the spending departments before approving the final estimates of expenditure to be submitted to the House of Commons (and equally by the UGC when distributing its parliamentary grant) are of the same kind as those faced by a university when it must apportion its grant among its spending units. The major difficulties relate to the principles by which the claims should be assessed and to the detailed application of these principles. The problems may most conveniently be described in the context of public expenditure, about which more has been written.[8]

[7] See below, p. 185-8.

[8] See, for example, S. H. BEER: *Treasury Control* (Oxford, 1957); G. REID: *The Politics of Financial Control* (Hutchinson, 1967); LORD BRIDGES: *The Treasury* (Allen and Unwin, 2nd ed., 1968); and especially, the only account of the internal politics of public expenditure decisions in Britain, H, HECLO and A. WILDAVSKY: *The Private Government of Public Money* (U. of California, 1973). On the situation in the USA, however, see A. WILDAVSKY: *The Politics of the Budgetary Process* (Little, Brown, 1964).

The overriding constraints upon the Treasury are, firstly, the need to raise revenue by taxes and borrowing for those expenditures which seem unavoidable and, secondly, to restrict expenditure to a level which calls for no greater demand upon national production than political and economic circumstances permit or require. The starting-point for allocating future revenue has, customarily, been the current year's estimates for each department. In the absence of a government policy of 'retrenchment', attention is focused on proposals for new or increased expenditure under any particular head. The amount approved has tended to be the outcome of detailed negotiation and argument about each new or increased item between the Treasury and the spending department—which in fact has meant, in case of disagreement, the outcome of the relative strengths of the Chancellor of the Exchequer and the Minister and, especially, of their relative ability to secure the support of the Prime Minister and, on major policy issues, of the Cabinet. Otherwise, the tendency (if not the invariable practice) has been to authorize general percentage changes —leaving each department to add or excise its own selection of activities, subject to detailed scrutiny of all expenditure in order to minimize waste, even of 'candle-ends' (in Gladstone's famous injunction). With greater or lesser severity, depending upon the exigencies of the situation, funds have thus been allocated on the basis of a mixture of the *status quo*, the strength of the case mustered by any given spending department, political bargaining and in-fighting between officials and/or ministers, the policies to which a government is already committed (on both the revenue and expenditure sides), and the element of political judgement by (especially) the political masters, the Prime Minister and Cabinet.

Having referred to some of the bargaining strategems adopted by spending departments in the preparation of their claims, Samuel Brittan sheds light upon the pressures inherent in the situation when he continues:

'It is tempting to suggest eliminating such nonsense by fixing an overall limit for each spending authority, within which more spent on one subject will mean less on some other one. Those in charge can then, if they are competent, be left to subdivide their expenditure so that no marginal shift from one area to another will increase the total return. The trouble with such a system is that the initial allocation between departments is itself open to argument. Each department will always be able to put up a strong case for more at the expense of other departments; and no central watchdog body will be able to form a sensible judgement of the relevant merits of rival claims, unless it takes a close interest in the composition as well as the total spending of the programmes. Public expenditure can thus be neither entirely allocated from the top downwards, nor built up from the bottom upwards, but must in practice be regulated by a mixture of both methods.'[9]

This method developed to deal with a particular set of circumstances. Among them, and of crucial importance, are the facts that different forces and considerations tend to establish the most desirable levels of, respectively, revenue and expenditure, while the actual amounts cannot be settled independently of each other; there is no market price on most of the services rendered by government while most revenue is 'extracted', not 'earned'; the purposes of government cannot be reduced to, though they may include, the establishment of any particular balance between income and expenditure; and that many of the inputs and outputs cannot (even in principle) be measured fully (some would say, at all) in terms of financial receipts and payments.[10] The method may have developed for understandable reasons, but it has obvious shortcomings—decisions on particular items tend to be taken too much in isolation from each other; too great a premium is placed on existing expenditure in comparison with new proposals; standards of provision and performance may vary widely, and apparently accidentally, over the public service as a whole; there is no way of telling, because the procedures provide no incentive to find out, whether the overall pattern of expenditure is the most efficient one for the fulfilment of the government's objectives; and, consequently, the total and the distribution of expenditure continues to elude control. Hence, recently, attempts have been made to introduce clearer criteria and improved techniques for the control of public expenditure and, above all, to shift the emphasis from finance to the proper use of all resources.[11] But at this point let us return to universities, about whose processes very similar statements may be made.

In general, once the total from the UGC is known, university

---

[9] SAMUEL BRITTAN: *Steering the Economy* (Penguin Books, 1971) pp. 119–20. In these remarks may be found the explanation, if any be needed, of the extensions of UGC guidance already mentioned.

[10] See DESMOND KEELING: *Management in Government* (Allen and Unwin, 1972), where it is suggested that the main differences between public service and business management are that in the former the criteria for resource use 'are more numerous and complex', and that 'a substantial proportion of the resources used by the public service is in systems (in) which . . . the best use of resources is a secondary rather than a primary task' (p. 156).

[11] For brief accounts of these, see, e.g. D. KEELING: *op. cit.*, Chapter 9, and S. BRITTAN: *op. cit.* especially pp. 101–27.

income is allocated to the various spending units (both academic and other) by methods which could almost be deduced from the way in which other decisions are taken and from the roles of the main actors. As we have already noted[12], any additional money available for academic purposes is usually entrusted to senate for detailed allocation between the competing claims, which in practice is to say, to a committee of senate whose recommendations come into effect only after senate approval. Most commonly, this committee, like finance committee in allocating funds between academic and non-academic purposes, will sub-divide the academic allocation between general academic services (the library, for example, and the computer centre) and the main teaching organizations (faculties, schools, etc.) occasionally with only an indication to the latter of the desirable division between expenditure on new posts and other kinds of departmental expenditure (supplies and ancillary staff, for example), but usually with a clear decision about the amounts available for the different kinds of expenditure. These 'block' allocations are then finally broken down in terms of the grass-root spending units of which the department is still the most common.[13]

The nub of the problem, again, is the lack of any simple financial yardstick by which to decide how total income may best be allocated between various types of expenditure. Not only is there no price which can 'measure' the relative worth (as distinct from the financial cost) to the university of, for example, an additional lecturer in a small department of Chinese literature, duplicate copies of the library books in greatest demand amongst undergraduates, two physics technicians, or a small piece of laboratory equipment needed by graduate students in medicine—for there is no 'market' for their output. There is the further difficulty that, even if it could be shown that the financial return for the piece of equipment were greater than that on a lecturer in Chinese, a university might still be right to choose the latter if to do so could be said to produce an academic and cultural balance better suited to the general character and purposes of the institution. There is, of course, no way of being sure that it would. But, and these are the important points, first, it would be perfectly reasonable to think so, and second, argument on this (or

[12] In Chapter V, above.

[13] It is the job of the finance officer or bursar's department of each university, as it is one task of the Treasury in central government, to ensure, thereafter, that expenditure is incurred only on those items thus authorized, and only up to the limits thus fixed. Ultimately, in both central government and (since January 1968) the universities, the Comptroller and Auditor-General must also be satisfied that expenditure is incurred only for the purposes and within the limits authorized by the House of Commons.

any similar issues of allocation) cannot be resolved simply by reference to quantitative evidence or technical calculation; it must be settled by resort to politics and judgement.

The nature of university planning decisions has been described by Sir Eric Ashby in terms on which we cannot improve and which demand extensive quotation. In a lecture entitled 'The Scientist as University President'[14], delivered to an American university audience, he gave this detailed description of preparing a quinquennial estimate which, in essence, applies equally well to the allocation exercise.

'In the task of preparing the quinquennial plan for each university the president is the key man. Now let us watch him at work. The University of Middletown is preparing its quinquennial estimates for the University Grants Committee. The work is entrusted to a committee consisting of the president . . . the honorary treasurer . . ., and the deans of the faculties of arts, science, and medicine: . . . These constitute a syndicate of administrators who have to make decisions of far-reaching importance. Of course, their decisions are made after prolonged consultation with faculty boards and departments and they will have to be discussed and endorsed by the Senate and Council. There will be a lot of dissent, but it is unlikely that any further thinking will be contributed to the work after it leaves the committee. On this committee the president is the only man who 'has the feel' (as we say) of the problem as a whole: he knows how high the bids can be before they become unrealistic, what projects are likely to get support from industry, how co-operative the city is likely to be over the acquisition of sites, and so on. So he carries a correspondingly heavy share of responsibility for the decisions.

Now let us consider one single item in the quinquennial estimates. The University has one unallocated site across the London road. In the papers before the committee there are four applications for this site. The professor of biology, in twenty foolscap pages of single-spaced typescript, presses, rather querulously, the need for a new building; . . . . The Librarian, in two lucid and persuasive pages, asks for a science library on this site; . . . . The refectory committee press strongly for a new cafeteria on the site, ... The faculty of engineering, in half a page put up a confident—not to say arrogant—claim for a new institute of aerodynamics on the site. . . . Five men, none of whom is an expert on biology or libraries or

[14] Published by Washington University, Missouri, 1964, and to be reprinted in a collection of Sir Eric's lectures and papers. We are greatly indebted to him for permission to use this quotation from pp. 5–7 of the original published version. For 'president', of course, read 'vice-chancellor' throughout.

cafeterias or engineering, have to decide what is to be built on this site; and the decision has to be made within a limited time. What is the process of decision-making?

It is clearly of a different order from decision-making in scientific research or scholarship. One difference is that there is a time factor, which can be neglected in science, but which cannot be neglected here: there must be a decision on the use of the site, whether there are enough data for the decision or not. Another difference is that once the decision is acted upon there can be no going back. . . . A third difference is that no one could ever reach a decision on this question solely by logical processes. The president will doubtless provide a pseudological rationalization afterwards to make the decision respectable and to attempt to pacify the losers; but in fact the decision itself will have to be made through an extrapolation beyond logic. It is common knowledge among administrators that if a man relies on reasoning alone in these circumstances he ends in a sticky morass of hesitation, fear, and lack of initiative. Nothing is decided.

But the process of decision can begin logically. There is a sort of Ohm's law in decision-making. Standing in the way of the fulfilment of all decisions there are resistances. If these resistances are too great, action cannot flow and the decision, even if you make it, is not viable. An administrator who makes non-viable decisions is a failure. So the committee must familiarize itself with the resistances. . . .

More likely than not, none of these resistances totally disqualifies any of the proposals. The result of the application of Ohm's law in administration will be that there are resistances to all solutions, but none of the resistances entirely eliminates any of the solutions. The committee then have to go beyond logic. They must first of all carefully try to eliminate any prejudice due to personalities: the querulous biology professor, the plausible librarian, the testy refectory committee, the arrogant engineering dean. . . . Then comes the extrapolation from logic. In solving a problem like this the committee simply cannot use the technique Darwin tried to use before he decided to get married: jot down a list of pros and cons and add them up. They have to get in their minds a picture of the University as a whole, as an architect has in mind his building as a whole, and by the exercise of a non-logical process—call it intuition, judgement, perception, what you will—they have to fit first one solution and then another into the picture and to decide which (to use an Americanism) is the most "purposeful"—I would prefer to risk saying "the most aesthetically satisfying"—for the University as a whole. One thing is certain: after eliminating any solution which is impossible or impracticable, the committee will rely on "hunch", although afterwards the president will cover the committee's tracks with a lucid memorandum weighing one proposal against the other and explaining logically how the decision was made. Of course the decision is not made merely by contemplating, in a Yoga-like state of relaxation, the needs of the University. The president has consulted departments, architects, city planners, the University Grants Committee, his colleagues in other universities. He has to go on doing this until the situation-as-a-whole is developed (like an image on a photographic plate) in his mind. It is an exhausting process and clarity, if it comes at all, will be followed by a noticeable degree of emotional exhaustion. To a scientist accustomed to the austere logic of research, this may seem a dangerously imprecise way to reach a major decision. But even the most distinguished of scientists recognizes the validity of a non-logical approach, provided of course that it is supported by logic as well. Hear what the French mathematician Laplace says: "The principal means of arriving at truth are: induction, analogy, hypothesis founded upon facts and rectified continually by new observations, and a happy tact given by nature and strengthened by experience". "A happy tact" plays an essential part in major administrative decisions.'

In this account the element of judgement is made explicit, that of politics is left implicit and requires supplementation.[15] The allocation of resources might be called an archetypal political problem every bit as much as it is an archetypal economics problem. It is obviously in the realm of public affairs, it must be carried out for any given group as a whole, and all solutions are mutually exclusive.[16] It is only to be expected, therefore, that the principal actors in the process should be those who wield the greatest influence in university affairs generally.

[15] We do not know whether Sir Eric Ashby would agree with the latter.

[16] See the definition of politics given in Chapter 1, above. It meets, moreover, another criterion of the political. As has been argued in H. A. PITKIN: *The Concept of Representation* (University of California, 1967), the activity of politics is appropriate to issues which lie in a middle ground between the extremes of certainty and complete subjectivity, to issues, this is to say, in which there is an inextricable combination of matters of fact and of value-judgement. Politics, the activity of dealing with such issues, 'is a field where rationality is no guarantee of agreement. Yet, at the same time, rational arguments are sometimes relevant and agreement can sometimes be reached' (p. 212). Characteristically, 'politics entails the reconciliation of conflicting claims, each usually with some justice on its side' (p. 218).

The vice-chancellor is always, as in the fictional University of Middletown, chairman of the quinquennial estimates committee—and also of the committee(s) dealing with both the quinquennial and annual divisions between competing academic users (as well as being a key member of finance committee). His role therein benefits from, as it also reinforces, all the resources at his command[17]—and even more so if, as is found in more than one university, the relevant 'committees' are one-man. Apart from his central position within the communication network, external as well as internal, the vice-chancellor, aided by the bureaucracy, has the immense advantage of initiative—for it is he who is best placed to put forward the broad package proposal for reconciling the conflicting claims. In a tight financial situation, moreover, any suggested change in a proposed allocation is possible only at the expense of others—and it may be difficult, not to say invidious, to name those other areas which should be pruned. This is not, of course, to say that the vice-chancellor always gets his own way here any more than elsewhere, nor that he personally dictates the whole direction of university expenditure during the quinquennium. Quite apart from the fact that it may be impossible at this stage to add items which were not included in the original bids, the proposed allocation must be accepted by others. Thus the academic budget, in which the proposals are incorporated, is usually submitted for ratification by the senate and may there be referred back for amendment (we know of no case of a budget's being simply negated). To give but one example, that of a faculty which felt itself to be discriminated against in the proposed allocation: concerted opposition in senate by all the professors in that faculty secured a major revision of the allocation. On the other hand, our informant in the university concerned went on to express considerable doubt whether anything short of such concerted action could have succeeded at this stage; and the fact is that such action is rare if only because of the time required to overcome internal conflicts. The central problem is that the items are all competitive, and any attempt to revise the allocation must mean singling out something which can be cut. Normally, however, a vice-chancellor, and this is itself a constraint upon his descretion, will not propose allocations which even appear entirely to overlook any serious claim by any important section of his university.[18]

[17] See our account in Chapter VI, above.
[18] As a result of the incident mentioned the vice-chancellor lost, permanently, much of the 'credit' on which, as argued in Chapter VI, his influence depends. For he had failed to produce a solution deemed 'fair'—a word of great importance in all budgetary debate.

The other actors who tend to be particularly important in the allocation process, not surprisingly, are the professorial heads of departments, in virtue of their 'subject sovereignty' even if not as members of senate. If, in addition, they are determined, energetic, distinguished and already in command of independent research funds, they may be able to exert very considerable influence. To take an extreme example, one may cite the success of a newly appointed FRS who virtually pre-empted all development funds available to his faculty. This he did by persuading the vice-chancellor of a smaller civic university that the department he had left Oxbridge to head must expand radically to accommodate his research staff and projects. (In fact he also ate into the university's remaining funds as well, for his projects, and their implications, acquired a momentum of their own.) Understandably, he has compared the system of government at Oxbridge unfavourably with that at his new abode. 'The trouble with Oxbridge', he said to us, 'is that there is no one you can get hold of to secure speedy and effective action.' Not even he, of course, could expect a repeat performance—such coups are easiest for the new arrival, before it is difficult for him to withdraw from the post and before he has become integrated with (and dependent upon) his colleagues in other subjects.

In most universities the deans must be added to this list of actors. They are likely both to be the main spokesmen for their faculties or schools in making the main division of academic funds and, once a sum has been allocated to their units, to fulfil a 'steersman's' role in securing agreement on the further subdivisions. But it is not common for deans (Sussex may provide one of the exceptions) to have the formal powers, or the autonomous authority, to rival the vice-chancellor and heads of important departments.

It is in this sphere, perhaps, that the strongest evidence can be found (outside some individual departments) for the widely held belief that universities are run by professorial oligarchies[19] tempered or, possibly, led by the vice-chancellor. It is important, however, not to exaggerate the significance of this evidence for other areas of university government. The fact is that there is, as we have already suggested, a greater need for bargaining and compromise, indeed for 'horse-trading', in the painful process of pruning bids and hammering out a university budget than in other areas of academic decision-making. Such 'in-fighting' is most easily conducted, and with least harm to social cohesion, by relatively small numbers of people each of whom must be armed with some authority, not only to speak for a group's interests but to negotiate and (if need be) to

[19] See the further discussion in the next chapter.

accept defeat. The scope for bargaining, it must also be remembered, is limited—by the terms of the original bids (which in most universities today are based on wide discussion), by any long-term policy decisions for academic development (which need not be taken only by a few), and by the need to secure ratification for the compromises struck. There is usually, in allocating resources, what might be termed a 'functional' oligarchy—but it need not indicate, nor produce, oligarchic government elsewhere, if others in fact make the long-term policy decisions and are both able and willing to review resource use within the university. But in many universities one or other of these conditions is not satisfied. We must now turn, therefore, to look at some of the criticisms of, and recent modifications to, the control of expenditure.

In most universities, at least until recently, there has been comparatively little detailed enquiry into the initial bases of the various academic bids, other than their relationship to the UGC-imposed ratios affecting staffing, and thereafter attention has tended to focus upon the financial totals. As we have already suggested, the whole operation has most commonly been conducted in terms of 'block grants' to a succession of sub-units and, moreover, predominantly in terms only of the division of income increments. On occasion, too, the resulting allocation, and not merely the process of decision, has been carried out in an atmosphere of confidentiality. There are still universities, for example, which follow the once common practice of refusing to publicize the size of the departmental grants (for most forms of expenditure other than academic salaries). This procedure can be justified on the ground that it permits rewards to excellence without arousing ill-will on the part of the less distinguished. But, whatever the justification, the result can only be to discourage general discussion of the underlying criteria and hence effective review of overall academic strategy and its implementation. Lack of such review is, in fact, a further possible criticism of the system. And in the absence of adequate information or publicly agreed criteria (beyond that of 'the *status quo* plus *x* per cent'), combined with the prevailing acceptance of substantial subject, school, or faculty autonomy, it is only to be expected that senate debate on the budget (in those universities where it occurs at all) should, for the most part, be superficial, perfunctory, or devoted to minor details and the ventilation of particular grievances.[20]

The result has not been disastrous—the detailed control exercised

[20] Compare the complaints about the weakening of House of Commons control over finance which constitutes the major theme in A. Hill and A. Whichelow, *What's Wrong with Parliament?* (Penguin Books, 1964).

by finance offices prevents expenditure beyond the budgeted limits (in so far as this lies within the powers of the university) as well as 'saving candle-ends', and, as we have seen, co-operation between universities and the UGC has exerted increasingly tight control over, especially, capital expenditure. The ability and vision of vice-chancellors, moreover, has done much to give shape and direction to the general pattern of expenditure. It was therefore possible for the Robbins Committee to pass favourable judgement. Having looked at the proportions of the age group which actually graduated in Britain and other countries, it said: 'The output in Britain is equal or superior to that in most of the Western European countries shown. We suspect that full comparative investigation would reveal that, on its chosen ground, the British university system is amongst the most efficient and economical in the world.'[21] Nevertheless, too many decisions on expenditure are taken in isolation from others, as if the items concerned were not in competition. Thus decisions about academic staff entitlements may be divorced from decisions about the allocation of secretaries, library purchases in particular subjects, or the staff levels within a section of the administration. This is to say that the different blocks, once allocated, may thereafter be kept so distinct that different levels and standards of expenditure coexist in different parts of the university without its even being realized, let alone taken into account. The underlying trouble, in other words, is that universities, like the central government, have tended to think too much about finance and too little about all resources, too much about accounting heads and too little about the objectives and functions of the whole organization, and too much about new proposals while largely exempting established claims on resources from any comparable analysis.

In central government and, in part consequentially, in universities too, serious attempts have been made, especially since the early 1960s, to meet these criticisms.[22] The success of these attempts have yet to be demonstrated, but the attempts are important, in themselves and in the questions they raise for university government. But let us glance first at the developments within Whitehall.[23]

Under the influence of political and economic pressures upon

---

[21] *Report*, para. 126, p. 44.

[22] In central government the watershed was probably the publication of the (Plowden) *Report on the Control of Public Expenditure* (Cmnd 1432 of 1961).

[23] See the works, already cited (pp. 173-5 above), by Brittan, Keeling, and Wildavsky. The last two give references to additional and more technical literature. See, also, J. BRAY: *Decision in Government* (Gollancz, 1970).

Government spending, of criticism in the House of Commons and the Fulton Report[24], and of the spread of business management thinking into government (initially in, to take the most notable example, the United States Department of Defence), British central government has become increasingly preoccupied with its 'management' function—by which is meant obtaining the most efficient use of resources. The more recent discussions thereof abound with references to new institutions, like the Public Expenditure Survey Committee, and (in this context) novel concepts and techniques. Only these last are sufficiently relevant to require mention here.

Central to this new thinking is the view that the budgeting process, the process of authorizing particular units to spend specified sums of money for defined purposes within a stated period (the financial year), must be supplemented by other approaches which transcend each of these limitations. Expenditure should not be allocated merely to particular accounting heads on the basis of bargaining with the spender, as the Treasury might haggle with the Department of the Environment over a sum for new motorways; such an item must take its place as an element in a long-term programme for inland transport that is assessed with regard to that use of all resources, private and public, which will most efficiently contribute to the general ends of (say) speeding the movement of men and goods, urban renewal, and protection of the physical environment. And the place of expenditure on motorways ideally depends upon a careful costing, not only of motorway construction and the benefits (or penalties) it confers but also of all other possible means of contributing to these ends. It would, admittedly, be too expensive to make such assessments of all expenditure every year; but at all times expenditure should be thought about in terms of such programmes, and all policies should be subject to periodic review and analysis in terms of their costs and benefits, and especially of their cost as measured by the opportunities for different kinds of expenditure which have been foregone in adopting the existing policy.[25] Given such a programmatic analysis, it may be possible to elaborate strategic plans for, say, the general direction of the subsequent five years' expenditure to provide a further guide to the annual budget decisions. Crucial to the full implementation of this series of operations is the possibility, first, of identifying the separate inputs of resources and, secondly, of relating

---

[24] *Report of the Committee on the Civil Service* 1966–8 (Cmnd 3638 of 1968).

[25] See the introduction in 1971, under the auspices of the Civil Service Department, of a system of programme analysis and review (PAR) for this purpose.

them to the relevant results (outcomes) or measurable outputs of the activity in question.

Such, in simple terms[26], are the various strands or elements which make up a full system (if it be a system) of programming–planning–budgeting (PPB)[27]—which is sometimes referred to more briefly as output budgeting. About its use and application controversy continues in government circles, and outside. Into that controversy we need not go at any length. Let it suffice to say, in the context of national government, that public expenditure is not yet, and many would argue that it never can be, fully allocated by these techniques, but that certain kinds of decision do seem to lend themselves to analysis by some of the techniques involved: that to think in terms of, for example, opportunity costs or programmes or the benefits to be achieved for stated objectives by particular outlays, is to create a new administrative style distinguished above all by its need for and use of vastly increased amounts of information; and that any central financial organ is thereby armed with new weapons in its quest for efficiency and economy in the use of scarce resources— including those resources allocated to higher education. Although the multiplicity of governmental objectives and the inescapable qualitative judgements involved in assessing both the inputs and outcomes of government policies seem likely to limit the applicability of these modern principles of business management[28], yet their use seems likely to spread if only because, within their limits, they serve wonderfully to concentrate the mind.

British universities, faced with similar problems, have begun to draw upon the same pool of ideas in their quest for financial 'elbow-room'. In doing so they too have been influenced by the flow of ideas from North America[29] as well as by pressure from outside for information and efficiency[30]; but, as with government, the mere increase in the size of their budgets, of the claims from the separate spending-units, and of the number of such units, might have con-

[26] And, we hope, accurate ones; we claim no expertise in this field.

[27] See KEELING: *op. cit.*, p. 169: 'PPB is a group of sensible propositions (on some of which rational men may entertain reservations) which are neither mutually incompatible nor so logically interdependent as to make it necessary to accept all or none. On this view it is not a system.'

[28] See the passage already quoted from Keeling, p. 156.

[29] See, for example, the interest in such books as (to name only the best known) FRANCIS E. ROURKE and GLENN E. BROOKS: *The Managerial Revolution in Higher Education* (Johns Hopkins Press, 1966).

[30] In this period, as we have seen, the UGC requests for information have grown immensely as it has undertaken increasingly complex efforts to measure and control university costs. In 1970 it published its decision to venture into the field of linear programming, aided by computer—*op. cit.*, p. 24.

stituted sufficient reason for seeking more sophisticated methods of planning and budgeting. Despite immense variations in the extent to which, and enthusiasm with which, different universities have responded to these forces, it is possible to detect sufficiently widespread evidence of change to justify their consideration as new developments in university government.

The first of these new developments is a change in the climate of opinion such that universities, too, are beginning to look beyond mere financial accounting to the real problem of securing a better use of all resources, including time, labour, buildings and equipment as well as money. The manifestations of change vary, but most universities now apply at least a rudimentary notion of opportunity cost in their appointment practices. They have done so, most commonly, by deciding that established academic posts, as they fall vacant, should not be filled without a review of the need for a member of staff in that area rather than some other. In the University of Leeds, for example, all vacancies (since the mid-sixties) are referred to the Vice-Chancellor who may, at his discretion, recommend that they be reviewed by the Development Committee of Senate. The first consequential advice that Senate should not fill a vacancy provoked a long and searching debate, but thereafter the principle won general acceptance, and such discussion as takes place now focuses on the merits of each particular case. In another, midland, university review takes place at the faculty level, thus limiting the range of alternatives with which comparison is made. This device has the further disadvantage (as we would regard it) that the review is conducted by those most concerned—and, possibly for this reason, no post was re-allocated in the first few years of the system's operations.[31] But here the principle at least has been established—only in a few institutions is the principle itself still thought heretical.

Significant, too, are the kinds of argument deployed in reviews of vacant posts. Almost invariably evidence will be adduced about student demand (often with reference to 'A'-level qualifications as well as absolute numbers[32]), the teaching load of staff members, and the existing staff/student ratio—all factors which can be quantified and thus compared with the situation in other subjects. Problems of interpretation and 'weighting' remain, so that the information does not eliminate dispute, but the decision will not, either, be made merely on the basis of pressure from interested parties modified by hunch. Indeed, without the possibility of appeal to some verifiable

[31] The latest time of which we have knowledge.
[32] Thus introducing a notion comparable to the economic concept of 'effective demand'.

evidence and agreed criteria, it is hard to see how such reviews could be instituted or their results command acceptance.[33]

As an extension of this growing practice one may cite the view, voiced with increasing frequency, that all university activities should be subjected to comparable 'zero-based' reviews and be invited to justify themselves as if they were new claims for expenditure. The best-known example of such a review is the decision of the UGC that certain departments of agriculture be closed down during the 1967–72 quinquennium. But in at least two universities other departments have been abolished entirely as a result of internal initiatives[34], and a report on *The Future of Birkbeck College* by its Academic Advisory Committee expressed the view that 'if the demand for a subject is falling off it must be assumed that in this subject Birkbeck is not catering for the needs of mature students, and the balance of studies must be adjusted accordingly, even if it means the "phasing out" of a subject'.[35]

An inevitable accompaniment, and in many cases instigator, of these new attitudes is the evolution of more sophisticated concepts and methods within the central administration of the university.[36] The most elaborate and comprehensive attempt to rationalize the planning and management processes is, almost certainly, to be found at the University of Sussex where, under the guidance of the first Planning Officer (G. Lockwood) and with the support of the first two Vice-Chancellors (Lord Fulton and Professor Asa Briggs), the aim is the 'adoption of a Planning Programming and Budgeting System'.[37] By 1970 the planning process already rested upon, for example, highly developed means of collecting, analysing and disseminating data on all the activities of the university; a clear distinction between, but linkage of, spending programmes and budget authorizations to

---

[33] That the data exists is, in large part, a consequence of UGC demands for information—a further small example of the link between national and university decision-making in the sphere of resource management.

[34] Anthropology at Newcastle and mining at Sheffield.

[35] The 'Ashby' *Report*, p. 28.

[36] Using 'administration', as before, to refer to both the officials and the other administrators within universities. See above, Chapter VII.

[37] See G. LOCKWOOD: '"Institutional Management and Planning" with Reference for illustrative purposes to the University of Sussex', in M. L. SHATTOCK, ed.: *University Administration in a Period of Expansion* (The British Council, 1971), p. 40. This paper provides an illuminating introduction to the Sussex system as it had evolved by 1970. On the whole topic of university management see also J. FIELDEN: 'Management Accounting in Universities' and 'Techniques of Programme Budgeting in Universities' in SHATTOCK: *op. cit.*, pp. 51–61 and 62–68, for a comprehensive treatment, J. FIELDEN and G. LOCKWOOD: *Planning and Management in Universities* (Chatto and Windus, 1973).

the spending units; a devolution of responsibility to various levels, within the overall university strategy, for detailed resource-allocation choices; and regular analytic studies of various aspects of the University's activities, partly in furtherance of the more efficient use of resources, but also, and by no means least importantly, in search of greater clarity and agreement (which are not necessarily always compatible with one another) upon the 'purposes and roles' or 'objectives'[38] of the institution.

In this quest for greater efficiency, universities have turned to management consultants[39], but may also draw upon a growing body of research by economists and others within the university world.[40] It is also to be expected that the organization and methods units set up by various consortia of universities will venture increasingly beyond the relatively limited studies of, for example, the organization of catering, into the more sensitive area of PAR.[41] Meantime, however, the Universities of Bradford, Lancaster and Surrey in particular, and others to a lesser degree, are also pursuing the goal of highly numerate, analytic, programme and resource-oriented university management. The details do not concern us, but certain problems do.

The key problem is that the move towards a more numerate, analytic, and systematic base for decison-making may produce a corresponding shift of political influence into the hands of the officials who are most intimately involved in preparing that base. Thus, in the context of national government it has been suggested that 'if PPB is concerned with information it must also be relevant not only to better decision-making but to power and authority . . . (for) in practice they are found where the information is and are not found where the information is not'.[42] In university affairs, a not dissimilar judgement has been voiced by Dr Loach, when Registrar of the University of Leeds. He said:

'I don't think the Registrar ought to be a part of the policy making process. I would rather see the Registrar as a clearing office—a clearing house with information. Members of the university come and give him the information. He has to get information from

---

[38] LOCKWOOD: *op. cit.*, p. 40.

[39] E.g., at LSE, Sussex, Warwick and Leeds.

[40] See, for example, LOCKWOOD and FIELDEN: *op. cit.*, and, from the Universities of Bradford and Lancaster, the reports published in *Studies in Institutional Management in Higher Education—Costs and Potential Economies* (OECD, 1972).

[41] On the work of these units, 1967–70, see A. J. DALE: 'O. and M. in Universities', in SHATTOCK: *op. cit.*, pp. 69–78.

[42] KEELING: *op. cit.*, pp. 176–7.

outside. And then I think it's important that he should lay the available information before the committees, which are, in fact, to make the decisions. Because the Registrar has a lot of information, *I don't doubt that he could be powerful*; but I don't see it myself as part of the Registrar's duties.'[43]

If, however, an increasing amount of information available to a registrar is generated within his own office, if, moreover, it is processed in ways which go beyond the understanding of the average outsider, and if that data is to play a crucial part in policy-making, then it is hard to see how officials could avoid extending their 'duties' in the way disavowed by Dr Loach, and exemplified by much in American experience. This is not to suggest that we are presented with an official bid for power by the advocates of modern management techniques. On the contrary, the 'new men', like the older, continue to subscribe to the beliefs expressed by Dr Loach and which, as we reported in the previous chapter, characterize the typical university official. John Fielden, for example, concludes a discussion on management accounting thus: 'Many of the tasks will seem to imply an increasing centralization of university decision-making. This must be avoided at all costs and the pre-eminence of devolution and participation must be assured. The increasing sophistication of the central administration will be an improved service to the academic decision-maker, not a shackle.'[44]

The fear of bureaucratic aggrandizement which, in many universities, underlies resistance to administrative innovation is nevertheless not without respectable foundation. There are, indeed, three points on which disquiet may properly be expressed. The first, familiar enough, is that information, in order to become evidence, must be selected and processed in fashions about which there may be legitimate disagreement, but the choice of which is likely to affect whatever conclusions are drawn. Thus, to take a relatively simple and innocuous example, the Vice-Chancellor of Lancaster has pointed out that, depending on the criteria selected, the staff/student ratio at his university could be made to vary, in 1970–1, between $1:8\cdot9$ and $1:10\cdot4$.[45] Now, in most universities, this ratio is the one most widely used as a datum for planning purposes. Exactly what data is

[43] Taken from an interview included in an Open University television programme for the first year social science course (Unit 27), emphasis supplied.

[44] J. FIELDEN: *op. cit.*, p. 58; Fielden is not himself an official, but see the similar stress placed upon wide participation throughout the paper on Sussex by LOCKWOOD: *op. cit., passim.*

[45] C. F. CARTER: 'The Efficiency of Universities', *Higher Education*, I(1), 1972, p. 78.

assembled, how, and for whom are thus issues of more than technical relevance. If they are to be answered exclusively within the bureaucracy, then the traditional academic policy-makers are probably right to worry.

The second point of concern, put crudely, is that administrators may be 'blinded by science', overstep the proper limits of their own techniques, and thus again take a political decision in the guise of an expert one. We would not wish to dispute the judgement that, to quote Mr Charles Carter again, 'no university has unlimited resources. The main interest of the members of the university is in its purposes of teaching, research and the prosecution of scholarship. If there is any way of using the available resources more efficiently for these purposes the members of the university should wish to find that way.'[46] But there are, he goes on to argue, reasons why scientific efforts to measure efficiency (and without measurement, modern managerial techniques collapse) are capable of application only to limited aspects of university life. This is so, crucially, first because it is impossible to disentangle those resource inputs required for teaching from those devoted to research and scholarship, and second because no measurement of worth can be attached to the outputs in these spheres; nor (as he added more recently[47]) is it possible to measure the full contribution of teaching to the students' consumer satisfaction. Not every economist would accept this argument in its entirety[48]—nor do we have to make a judgement upon it. The fact of disagreement among experts is sufficient to establish the point that no outsider can safely rely upon precise measurements of efficiency which extend beyond certain limited spheres. More important, university purposes vary and properly extend far beyond the merely commercial test of a means–end relationship between measurable inputs and outputs. It is clear that numerate analysis and policy recommendation therefore requires to be conducted and controlled by people who both have some comprehension of the limits and are responsive to the full range of considerations and constituencies relevant to university decision-making. This, in practice, means that the modern administrative techniques need to be subordinated to that traditional partnership of officials, academics, and the vice-chancellor which is normally responsible for administration.

The third point about which legitimate anxiety is sometimes felt

---

[46] *Op. cit.*, p. 77.

[47] In an address to the Second International Conference on Higher Education, held at the University of Lancaster, reported in *The Times*, September 6, 1972.

[48] *Cf.*, for example, the more 'optimistic' tone of M. WOODHALL: 'University Productivity', in SHATTOCK, ed.: *op. cit.*, pp. 33–9.

is that any review of resource use from a central, university-wide, perspective may endanger that margin of tolerance, that room to manœuvre, on which diversity, autonomy, and pioneering work within the university is in some degree dependent. There are, for example, great costs, in terms of flexibility and the ability to seize the fleeting moment, in a level of space utilization which requires every meeting to be arranged weeks in advance if it is not to be held at some highly inconvenient hour. A more fundamental problem is raised by Martin Trow when he argues that

'the co-existence of basically different kinds of education within the same institution depends on functional boundaries, structural insulation, and the inattention to and ignorance of details that mark the absence of a tight, rationalized and standardized co-ordination from the center. In this way, as in others, the growing application of systems analysis to higher education threatens educational diversity . . . within the same system.'[49]

Here again, the only possible defence seems to be the intimate involvement in the planning process of academics, that is to say, of those with the strongest interest in the survival of their own autonomy.

Our argument up to this point may be summarized briefly in two assertions. The first is that it would be as mistaken for universities to ignore these modern developments in managerial and administrative techniques as it would be to confuse academic policy-making with resource-budgeting.[50] The second is that there are limits to the extent to which university policies and decisions can be judged merely in terms of their means/ends efficiency or rationality.[51] But,

[49] MARTIN TROW: 'The Expansion and Transformation of Higher Education', *International Review of Education*, XVIII, 1972, pp. 61–82, at p. 81, f.n. 5. The article is primarily concerned with the relations between elite, mass and universal higher education; but the point applies also to other kinds of diversity.

[50] In one of the more surprising of our interviews a senior university officer, an economist, seemed never to have noticed the relevance of the resource allocation problem to his administrative role. But the same seemed true of a former senior civil servant (who had included Treasury service in his career). Their reluctance to view universities from their own professional perspectives was, incidentally, matched by the professor of politics who told us that there were no university politics.

[51] The verdict of a firm of management consultants that the University of Warwick was 'certainly inefficient by normal commercial or industrial standards' (quoted in E. P. THOMSON: *Warwick University Ltd.* (Penguin Books, 1971) p. 129) probably tells one more about the consultants than about the university.

where notions of instrumental rationality are not entirely helpful, recourse may be had to the introduction of procedures for taking decisions which may ensure a reasonable degree of processual rationality. Where no accurate measurement of the 'rightness' of a decision is possible even in retrospect, let alone a set of calculations which will identify a 'right' decision amongst a set of possibilities at the moment of choice, it may yet be possible to point to processes of decision-taking which will go far to lessen the risk of avoidable error or political ineptitude. Herein lies the potential importance of another innovation in university government, the tendency to establish new committees responsible for planning and implementing current and future university policy.

The new planning committees vary in precise form and title from one university to another; nor are they to be found everywhere. But the logic of events is such that most universities seem to be moving, at varying speeds, in the same direction. Meantime, both in new universities like Lancaster, Sussex, York, and Stirling, and in older ones like Reading and Sheffield, recognizable variants have been established.[52] Essential common features include memberships drawn predominantly from academics, a link with council (principally through its academic members), the duty to report to senate in which alone lies the power to authorize action, and a clear responsibility for overseeing the allocation of resources, annually as well as quinquennially, in step with the university's long-term academic intentions.

A composite description, drawing upon the experience of several institutions, may serve to highlight the principal features of this development and the ways in which it relates to the other innovations, and to the problems, that we have discussed.[53]

In the late sixties a new central planning agency (CPA) was established in a number of universities, formally as an advisory committee. Power to act resides where it has always done, but certain decisions are now automatically referred to this committee for evaluation and advice. To ensure that the CPA is not simply a new arena for 'infighting' between organized interests, it does not necessarily consist, as do comparable bodies elsewhere, of deans or the heads of major

[52] Lord Murray of Newhaven, in his 'Introductory Note' to the *Final Report of Enquiry into the Governance of the University of London* (1972), points out that his committee based its 'major recommendations . . . on the establishment of adequate machinery for planning and development' (p. viii).

[53] The following account is based on part of a paper delivered by one of the present authors (G. C. M.) to the Academic Consultative Conference, 1968, on 'Manpower Planning and its Implications for Universities'.

departments, but of senior academic staff who need not hold any of these positions. The committee is served full time by a senior official who acts as research and intelligence officer as well as performing the normal roles of drafter, minute-writer and keeper of the archives.

The CPA may initiate proposals for academic policy, and to it are referred all claims for staff, equipment and accommodation, including the filling of hitherto established posts and the renewal of other existing 'rights'. The essential point is that all claims on resources, whether new or existing, must justify themselves as claims on *university* resources to a body specially established to embody a *university* point of view and to assess each claim by reference to *university* priorities and criteria. A departmental request to fill a 'vacant' lectureship, for example, will be appraised in precisely the same way as a request for a new post; namely, by reference not only to UGC ratios but also to such factors as the existing teaching load, effective demand for places, the demand for its graduates (in so far as this is known), research commitments—in all of which respects the department is compared with others throughout the university—and any long-term decisions to expand or phase out the subject concerned (a decision which will itself have been taken in the light of similar factors). The committee can, of course, only advise senate, but it will back its advice with statistical and other relevant evidence which can, therefore, be disputed only at a comparable level of sophistication and disinterestedness; and in fact its advice has hitherto been accepted with only minor emendations. By thus treating all uses of resources as though they were claims for additional resources the CPA may enable a university to expand certain departments, provide teaching space, and obtain much-needed secretarial help while maintaining morale and the impetus to change merely by, as it were, living off its own fat.

No less important than these material achievements is the fact that a university may thus give itself room to manoeuvre without destroying the essentials of its constitution. The decisions are still made by senate, initiatives are still widely diffused, and authority is still exercised in a manner consistent with the nature of the university as an institution of higher learning. But the general debate is largely about general criteria (or their detailed application) and takes place on the basis of more systematically assembled information systematically brought to bear on those recurrent, and often apparently routine, decisions from which, like a coral reef, universities grow and adapt themselves to their environment. Senate thus has a clear and manageable role. It should be emphasized, therefore, that the task of the CPA is not to pre-empt all decision-making and all policy

G

initiatives, but to act as a new 'lens' through which these decisions and initiatives should be focused. The crucial objective is to ensure that no activity or policy which involves an actual or potential claim upon resources shall be adopted until it has been appraised, in the widest and most clearly defined context possible, within some university committee.

It is, of course, no more possible in university than national government to guarantee, by any procedure or by any system of information-gathering and analysis, that the 'best' decisions will be taken on the use of resources, let alone on long-term objectives. The very reasons why it is impossible to secure agreement on the nature of 'best' are also the reasons why no procedures or techniques can solve all problems. Some improvement may nevertheless be obtained through an attempt to bring the most complete available information, in what seems to be the most usable and relevant form, to bear upon problems at the point in the decision-making process where the most sensible deliberations can occur. The aim is to substitute informed judgement for mere guess-work and, where appropriate, reasoned argument and public debate for mere power struggles—not that hunch and struggle can ever be entirely eliminated from any process of government.

However successful universities might be in putting their own internal affairs in order, their scope continues to be limited—in resource allocation as elsewhere—by the procedures of the government and UGC. It is therefore impossible to conclude this discussion without noting the extent to which the latter have come under increasing criticism. Criticism has focused on, for example, the separation, and at times apparent isolation, of decisions upon capital grants from those on recurrent, or upon the delays in announcing grants; but the main point, perhaps, has been the continuing obscurity of the reasoning underlying the allocations and the nature of its advice to the DES. As one critic has put it: 'if the academic community is intelligently to debate the issues and seek support for the universities' case then the UGC must at once publish its submission to the Government'.[54]

The present problems of resource allocation seem likely to plague universities, and government, for a long time; only future research, perhaps, can say with certainty how far the current quests for

---

[54] ALFRED MORRIS: 'The UGC and the Mystery of the UGC Cake', *Times Higher Education Supplement*, July 21, 1972. For other criticisms see, e.g. J. FIELDEN: *op. cit.*, and the papers given by R. O. Berdahl and by J. Dunworth and A. Bottomley to the Second International Conference on Higher Education, September 1972, at the University of Lancaster.

solutions will succeed. Meantime, however, one may venture the judgement that there is no evidence that the national government holds all the answers, for itself or for the universities, or that the latter are any less competent than the former in dealing with the expenditure problems common to them both.

Chapter IX

CHALLENGES TO AUTHORITY

Almost everywhere, in the second half of the 1960s, established decision-makers were challenged to justify themselves, especially to the younger generation. In the universities authority had first been questioned, many years earlier, by the non-professorial staff, but the most vivid and dramatic challenge came from the students. We will therefore look first at their demands for greater freedom and power.

The Student Challenge

Much of the student unrest and, at times, rebellion has, of course, been directed to problems and issues extending far beyond the confines of the academic world, and many of the reasons for it seem also to be rooted elsewhere. With these wider aspects we are not here concerned; rather we will focus only on the challenge to university authority, to the ways in which it has been met, and to some of the consequences for university government.[1]

The occasions for 'sit-ins', confrontations and riot have ranged from the price of meals in refectories to the right to prevent speakers from airing views unacceptable to some students, the content of the files on students kept by universities, the situation in Northern Ireland and Vietnam, and matters of individual and collective student discipline or of staff appointments and dismissals. At some stage, whether centrally or peripherally, all have raised the issue of the content and sources of university decisions, but have done so in ways seen within the universities to affect both more peripheral and more central aspects of the existing system of government.

---

[1] For an illuminating sociological account of the linkages between the university arena and the wider society, see MARGARET SCOTFORD ARCHER, ed.: *Students, University and Society* (Heinemann, 1972), especially the editor's introduction (pp. 1–35) and the chapter on Britain by Colin Crouch (pp. 196–211); see, too, the works cited therein.

Not surprisingly in this so-called 'permissive' age, one of the earliest and most widespread challenges was directed at the universities' right to regulate what students feel to be their private lives. Beginning, perhaps, with a relaxation in some of the rules (or in their application) in the late forties, when the universities were crowded with returning ex-servicemen, and consummated after Parliament had accepted the recommendation of the Latey Committee[2] to lower the legal age of majority to eighteen, universities have steadily reduced their claims to monitor the social and personal behaviour of their students. Most universities still maintain rules forbidding certain illegal activities (assault, narcotic indulgence and 'dope-peddling', for example[3]), but few now even attempt to forbid private sinning (whether in the form of copulation or non-attendance at chapel). Paradoxically, perhaps, the ending of the universities' overt claim to stand *in loco parentis* has been accompanied by student demands for (and the actual provision of) more extensive counselling and psychiatric services for individuals with personal problems both academic and emotional. But, pre-dating student 'unrest' as well as subsequent to it, few senates have resisted strenuously, or for long, this movement away from discipline, by academics, to the provision of welfare services, preferably by more appropriately trained professionals. Today, certainly, few academics would claim special expertise in the realms of social and sexual relations or morality, and many are happy to be absolved of official responsibility in these areas of their students' lives.

There has also been lessening resistance to student demands for a natural extension of this development, namely, for association with both the legislative and judicial processes involved in the regulation of conduct. Thus, in most universities, students have substantial representation (40 per cent or more) on the committees which govern halls of residence or residential colleges or which, in the few places where they exist, make rules for students in lodgings and flats. In some universities too, there are student members or observers on those committees which investigate individual cases of transgression and recommend punishments for those found guilty.

Possibly the most important development in the disciplinary field however, has been the formalization, and the institutionalization, of

---

[2] See its *Report* (Cmnd 3342 of 1967), and particularly its comments upon the complementary concepts of *in statu pupillari* and *in loco parentis* at p. 114.

[3] Despite constant student complaints that these may involve 'double-jeopardy' [*sic*] or 'double-discipline'.

procedures in an area hitherto regarded as a matter largely for the vice-chancellor (subject to ratification by council or senate in cases where the recommendation was to exclude a student from the university).[4] This process of formalization has served both to insulate the vice-chancellor from premature involvement in any dispute about discipline and, conceivably, to lessen the likelihood of such dispute. It will be recalled that such disputes were important elements in the earliest instances of unrest at Essex and the LSE. At the former the first troubles were undoubtedly exacerbated by the temporary lack of any agreed tribunal or procedures (they were under review), while at the latter 'the Board [of discipline] had not met since 1951 . . . and it was not expected ever to have to meet again'.[5]

Significantly, this evolution has occurred even in Oxbridge[6] where the emphasis on the college community and the personal obligations of tutor to pupil were traditionally construed to include a somewhat paternal concern for almost every aspect of undergraduate life and behaviour. As significant, perhaps, are the two areas of which a slightly different account must be given. There has been, on the one hand, relatively little challenge to the right of universities to terminate the careers of students who are academically unsatisfactory, provided only that the criteria are known and the machinery leaves room for appeal (as is increasingly the case). On the other hand, no generally accepted recipe has yet been found for dealing with cases of mass infringements of university rules by disruptive or violent behaviour. Clearly, in universities as in industry or a political party, disruption or defiance by large numbers is rarely a mere matter of 'discipline', but becomes a political problem requiring to be dealt with by such political means as negotiation and compromise.

In many universities, even before the mid-sixties, it was the practice for the vice-chancellor and/or other members of council or senate regularly to meet with officials of the students' union or representative council either informally or as a formal staff/student committee.[7] With rising tension these assumed new importance as a

---

[4] This is, indeed, the second of three charter-given powers of vice-chancellors. See our discussion above, Chapter VI.

[5] H. KIDD: *The Trouble at LSE 1966–1967* (Oxford, 1969), pp. 3–4. See, too, the discussion in JULIUS GOULD: 'Politics and the Academy', *Government and Opposition*, III, 1, 1968, pp. 23–47, and especially pp. 29–40.

[6] See the well-known Oxford (Hart) *Report of the Committee on Relations with Junior Members* (Supplement No. 7 to the *University Gazette*, May 1969).

[7] In Hull such a staff/student committee had been set up shortly after the end of the Second World War; it had been abolished in the fifties, at the students' request, for lack of business to discuss.

convenient arena in which to seek compromises when issues had arisen, to try to prevent matters of common concern from becoming issues, and to ensure that the increasingly strident voice of the student estate was given an official hearing. Such committees, not surprisingly, multiplied rapidly in response to the newly articulated concern of student organizations with university policy. By the end of session 1968–9, staff–student committees at council or senate level existed in three-quarters of the forty-six institutions covered by a National Union of Students survey.[8] From about 1968, however, the characteristic tone of the meetings of such committees changed. 'Suddenly', as one vice-chancellor told us, 'they stopped being pleasant occasions to which I looked forward.' Instead, they became an arena for stating demands and, frequently, for a search by mandated militant students for those issues which might polarize opinion, lead to confrontation, and thus mobilize and 'politicize' the main body of students.[9] The University of York, exceptionally, in 1968 established its University Committee (of laymen, academics and students) with terms of reference that explicitly include the task of acting 'as a negotiating body in the event of crisis'.[10]

Governmentally, the principal battle-lines came to be drawn round the later issue of participation (as opposed to consultation). That students should become voting members of student 'welfare' committees was conceded fairly readily, most notably in the Joint Statement issued, on October 7, 1968, by the Committee of Vice-Chancellors and Principals and the National Union of Students[11], but also, with less attendant publicity, in the practice of many universities.[12] Indeed, membership of some of these committees, if but only

[8] NUS document EW/110/2 of January 1970. While not entirely reliable, the broad picture emerging from the document seems substantially correct. It does not include the Scottish universities.

[9] See, for example the account of the tactics and aims of the student left wing in COLIN CROUCH: op. cit., pp. 202–8.

[10] To quote from the description in the university's Staff Handbook.

[11] Not that it was universally acclaimed either by academics, many of whom felt that it conceded too much, or by students, many of whose spokesmen felt it to be inadequate. For a trenchant and critical review of the whole movement to student participation see EDMUND IONS: 'Threats to Academic Freedom in Britain', Critical Quarterly, XII, 2, 1970, pp. 113–47.

[12] According to the NUS: op. cit., by 1969 students were members of committees dealing with library facilities in thirty-four institutions, catering in thirty-three, residences in twenty-eight, and sports in twenty-five. These are the committees which most commonly include students. In addition, students attended court meetings, either as members or observers, in twenty-two places, councils in eighteen, and senate in fourteen.

by one student, had long been accepted as normal in some universities, as had full membership of court (in Birmingham, for example, since 1960).[13] Beyond this point, however, when students demanded substantial membership on the main governing bodies and an equal, or even predominant, voice in deciding academic questions, organized student protest ran into two difficulties: lack of support and intensified academic resistance. The support of the majority of students for their left-wing leaders decreased steadily as the governmental demands became more extreme, and as the more moderate ones were met. The militant radicals thus became more isolated as they first encountered strong academic opposition and defences rooted in the very nature of university government.

The first point to emphasize about the response of senior members in universities, however, is that it was not universally hostile. Quite apart from the small minority of academics who shared the student radicals' ideological commitments to equalitarian and communal 'democracy', there were many others not unsympathetic to what appeared to be a natural enough extension of the long-term governmental trend discussed earlier in this book, i.e. towards the goal of a 'self-governing community of scholars'. University opinion had also been accustomed at least to the idea of change in the distribution of power and authority by decades of non-professorial agitation. The partial successes of the latter were relevant too. They meant that the non-professorial staff as a whole did not join the revolt, since they were not as alienated from and by an autocratic and rigid professoriate as was the case in many of the continental European universities worst affected by disruption. Furthermore, the device of extending committee membership to a new interest had first been adopted with reference to non-professorial staff. When faced by the new challenge of the students, universities were thus prepared once again to broaden the governing group by the same means. It was readily perceived that the committee system provided numerous points of access to the decision-making process. Through the gradual extension of membership in various committees universities could therefore (to put it cynically) put up a protracted 'defence in depth', but a defence which all the same permitted a real degree of penetration. This flexible use of the committee system was not, however, a matter of mere expediency—it stemmed also from sympathy and the

[13] See Chapter II, above. As a possible example of peaceful student influence one might cite the claim of a student ex-president that he had, in 1965, won the argument for the construction of an extension to his union building instead of a new undergraduate library.

simple fact that the system had already demonstrated its adaptability.[14]

Resistance, too, was based on conviction—the changes resisted did not seem capable of assimilation at an acceptable cost. We have already noted some of the ways in which non-professorial achievements influenced responses to student demands. Another is also important. These latter demands ultimately went far beyond the familiar proposals made for non-professorial participation in university government. It was not only to non-professorial staff that it seemed indefensible to grant to students what had not (yet) been granted to colleagues.[15] To do so would have been not only to ignore an important interest; it would also have been to surrender a fundamental principle widely cited in justification of the existing distribution of academic authority. This is the principle that authority should reside with the more rather than the less expert and learned. Dispute there has been and is about what precisely this means in a contemporary university, but, as we have seen, it is a principle which has been used to validate the shift of power from laymen to academics as well as to regulate relations between subjects and within them.[16] It is arguable that, in fact, universities have breached this principle by allowing any degree of student participation, other than consultation, in academic decision-making[17]; be that as it may, no university has been prepared publicly to admit to doing so, and few academics have attacked the principle itself. Attachment to it has, therefore, been the ultimate intellectual basis of resistance to demands for full student equality and power.

There have been other important, if more concrete, grounds of opposition which also deserve mention here. There were, first, fears that to include students on any committee would be almost endlessly to protract each meeting—in part because new categories of business would swell each agenda, but mainly because of bitter experience (gained during negotiations with student leaders) of repetitive and often mutually uncomprehending argument. It was feared, second, that the introduction of an organized and permanent adversary (even

[14] One can therefore share Edmund Ions' distaste for Mr Jack Straw's uncharitable and sweeping statement (made in a public lecture, as President of the NUS) that: 'most of the concessions made had occurred out of expediency to stave off student militancy. The response had not only been intellectually dishonest but also foolish.' See IONS: *op. cit.*, p. 141.

[15] On the other hand, as Richard Hoggart has pointed out, non-professorial staff in some places have also been the 'accidental beneficiaries of student unrest'. *Universities Quarterly*, 23 (3), 1969, p. 274.

[16] See the further discussion in the later section of this chapter.

[17] See, e.g. IONS: *op. cit.*

if in a minority) would call for more than usually intensive private majority-building in advance of each meeting, with a consequent reduction in the significance of public discussion and, possibly, of the role of those members of staff excluded from the inner circle. Both these fears were reinforced by the students' political style, with its emphasis on mandating and reporting back, and (as it seemed to staff) its refusal to trust the students' own committee members, let alone any others; and by student expectations of and search for conflict rather than consensus, and the associated use of disruptive and violent tactics. Many academics, too, were aware that students were exempt from the constraints within which university political processes normally operated. Of these constraints a crucial one is the knowledge, amongst university staff, that they may well have to spend most of their working lives together. During that long association, moreover, they may agree over certain issues despite disagreement over others. It is, therefore, often imprudent, to say the least, to engage in open warfare, and necessary to exercise some restraint in debate. Students, however, are not thus constrained—indeed, any individual student may be all too aware that he has but one year of office in which to win a victory, and rarely has any expectation that the staff he denounces today will be colleagues or allies tomorrow. Furthermore, as a spokesman elected by an organization designed specifically to cater for those features of student life which are most distinctive, his duty may well seem to lie in pressing precisely those points where there are the fewest assumptions in common with university staff, and this even when there are no important ideological cleavages.[18]

These objections clearly do not apply with the same force to consultation as to student participation. At all levels of university government (especially departmentally), therefore, and in most universities, staff–student committees speedily became normal features of the academic landscape. If used very extensively, however, they develop into something like a parallel governmental system that is both time-consuming for staff (who have to go over every item of business at least twice—in the staff–student committee and in its parent body) and unsatisfying to students (who may even feel their lack of status all the more acutely for being permitted only to use the tradesmen's entrance to the citadels of power). Universities have

[18] It may be significant that experience of student participation reveals a relative absence of conflict at the subject or departmental level, for it is there, presumably, that staff and student are likely to come closest to having a genuine and basic overlap, or even community, of interest, as well as being the context in which, if anywhere, members of staff will be seen as properly authoritative.

therefore had at least to contemplate committee membership—at which point, it seemed, the essential principles of academic authority would fatally be compromised, unless some line could still be drawn.[19] In practice two types of limitation are commonly to be found in those universities that have agreed to student participation. The first is to restrict the number of students on governing bodies, usually to fifty per cent or less on 'welfare' committees and to a much smaller (if varying) percentage on 'academic' ones. The other is to regard certain subjects—appointments and promotions, examination results and other sensitive academic decisions—as 'reserved': students are not members of committees dealing exclusively with these subjects and must withdraw from discussions of them elsewhere. Here, to date, the line has been held.[20]

Throughout 1972 the President of the National Union of Students (Mr Digby Jacks) made it clear that this line was not satisfactory—because students were in minorities, were not on all committees, were sometimes 'absorbed' into 'the system', and could not fill all the committee seats reserved for them.[21] On a later occasion, while supporting the idea of representation and attacking the suggestion to resort to direct action instead, he again argued for an end to restrictions on representation whether of number ('there is no substitute for votes') or of the 'most serious drawback', the reserved areas of jurisdiction.[22] If this, and student criticism of the 1968 agreement with the vice-chancellors and principals, is an indication of future contests, the end of the relatively peaceful session 1971-2[23] may be an appropriate time at which to note some general results of the student challenge up to that time.

[19] For discussions of attempts to articulate satisfactory criteria by which both to justify and to limit greater student participation see the Hart *Report*, *op. cit.*, pp. 86–93, and the sections of a University of York *Report* quoted at SS. 510–522 of the *Report on Student Relations* of the Select Committee on Education and Science (House of Commons, 449–i, of 1969).

[20] Autumn, 1972. On December 31, 1971 the *Times Higher Education Supplement* carried a headline: 'First steps towards student say in appointments', but it referred, in fact, to attempts by students at the University of Sussex to intervene in the process of filling a chair in international relations, attempts which clearly did not fully succeed to judge by the students' subsequent failure to persuade the chosen candidate to decline the offer.

[21] *Times Higher Education Supplement*, January 14, 1972. See, too, Frances Morrell's 'Hot and cold war', *The Guardian*, October 3, 1972.

[22] *Op. cit.*, October 20, 1972. Direct action was opposed because 'this is based on a phoney industrial analogy. Subtle academic matters cannot be dealt with by negotiation'—a point made frequently by staff.

[23] During that 'lull' there was but the one arena of public discord, the university of Lancaster. Elsewhere, of course, changes were still occurring, but by peaceful means and within the limits we have stated.

Most obviously, students have secured official recognition, in some universities by seats on councils and senates as well as many of their committees, as one of the 'estates of the academic realm'.[24] In all universities, too, decisions have come to be taken with an awareness of and sensitivity to student responses previously much less in evidence. Both academics and officials have, moreover, been forced to reflect upon, and publicly to articulate, their goals and assumptions in a way which can hardly be less than beneficial and, at best, might be an important prophylactic against stagnation and complacency.[25] The acceptance of the NUS as an important and established interest in the sphere of higher educational policy-making (fit to dine with the Prime Minister, be consulted by ministers and the UGC, and enter into formal agreed statements with vice-chancellors) has also been consolidated.[26] In yet another respect, therefore, decisions of importance to each university have come to be taken outside the confines of any one institution.

In part as a natural consequence of this public recognition, but possibly to an even greater extent as a result of student readiness to adopt disruptive tactics in pursuit of their objectives[27], a major result has been an increase in public concern with what were once thought to be the internal affairs of the universities. The earliest and most public manifestation of this new interest may have been the investigation of staff–student relations conducted by the House of Commons Select Committee on Education and Science in 1968–9[28] but, possibly more ominously for the students themselves, it was followed in 1972 by the declared interest of the Government in the internal constitutional, and particularly financial, arrangements of students' unions. The unions may thus come, in time, to recall the story of the Sorcerer's Apprentice—for it is inevitable that universities and the public should attend to the unions' internal organization now that they have established roles in university government.

[24] The authoritative history of the achievement of this governmental status, valuable not least for demonstrating that there *is* a history long pre-dating 1966, is SIR ERIC ASHBY and MARY ANDERSON: *The Rise of the Student Estate in Britain* (Macmillan, 1970). See, too, D. A. BELL *et al.*: 'A Survey of Student Representation on University Senates', *Universities Quarterly*, 27:1, 1972.

[25] It is perhaps not too fanciful to see student pressure as one explanation for increased interest in the questions of training academic staff for their teaching role and of assessment techniques.

[26] See ASHBY and ANDERSON: *op. cit.*, Chapter 5, for an account of this initial recognition, in the fifties when Lord Eccles was the Minister in charge of education, and steady rise in influence even before the late sixties.

[27] Not to mention the alignment of some student leaders with unpopular political causes and the belief that most students are licentious.

[28] See its *Report*, cited above.

They, or some of their members, may also come to regret the closer interest of local authorities in the universities supported from the rates.[29]

Some of the fears about the effects of student participation upon internal university government do not appear to have been justified—there is, for example, no clear evidence that more business is being dealt with behind the scenes. On the other hand the conduct of business in those committees of which students are members has sometimes been affected, although by no means universally so.[30] Many staff members undoubtedly feel inhibited by the presence of students. This is a case not so much of *pas devant les enfants*, but of fear that their statements and arguments may be misrepresented (and, in some instances, just represented) to outsiders by students committed to report back to their constituents. For the same reason it becomes more important that minutes be full and that they spell out very carefully the arguments which seem to have been influential in the discussion. Another result is that the officials who service university bodies are being called upon to prepare fuller supporting papers and to set out data and evidence with much greater care. Inevitably this means that the perspectives of the bureaucracy may come to play a much greater role in the formation of opinion and in the way in which issues are perceived and considered. It may also happen that decisions reflect the political necessities for 'peace' rather than the traditional criteria accepted (possibly uncritically) by most academics.[31]

As we have already indicated in a previous chapter, there was almost a universal tendency on the part of students to overrate the role of council in redbrick universities. This was largely because questions like discipline and amenity in most universities involved council committees, directly and not as the ultimate legal validator of the senate's decisions: but it was also due to a misidentification of council with governing bodies elsewhere. There was a similarly uninformed tendency to exaggerate the roles of the vice-chancellor and

[29] In April 1972 the Education Committee of the East Riding County Council recommended, by a majority vote only, to continue making a grant to the universities of Hull, Leeds, and York. The minority view that universities were failing to deal firmly enough with student 'indiscipline' seems to have been overborne only by the reassurances of those members who were also lay members of university councils.

[30] More than one informant reported to us that the presence of students on, for example, senate had made 'absolutely no difference' to the conduct of meetings.

[31] See R. B. EUSTACE: 'Student Participation in University Government', in M. L. SHATTOCK, ed.: *University Administration in a Period of Expansion* (British Council, 1971), pp. 143–51.

the bureaucracy (seen by virtually all students as 'The Administration'). Ironically, however, the challenge has had the effect of forcing council more nearly into the position it theoretically occupied. The decline in council's position had come about through a long process of conventional delegation of the matters that staff thought important. Almost up to the moment of the explosion, the possibility of physical violence and disruption was almost inconceivable to staff: there had been not the smallest need nor opportunity for the emergence of conventions for dealing with it.[32] Nor, when it did come, were senates particularly anxious to assert any right to a seat which was not one of power, but merely hot. Moreover, as we have seen, some of the immediate causes of trouble, such as catering, were in areas staff tended to regard as peripheral to the main objects of a university; chores such as might appropriately be dealt with by council and the officials. In any case, if only in virtue of its responsibility for university property and, in some universities, for discipline too, council has inevitably had a more active role thrust upon it. (It is perhaps significant that it required a wholly unfamiliar, and non-academic, situation, to articulate university government in an unfamiliar way, with emphasis on its non-academic aspect.) Similarly, the unprecedented nature of the crises, and their extreme urgency, brought the vice-chancellor to the fore in a stance to which he was little accustomed. We know of one university where, at one stage, important decisions were largely agreed beforehand between the vice-chancellor and the president of the union and then adopted by the relevant body at least partly on the ground that peace would thus be guaranteed within the university.

In general, however, 'the student revolt in Britain has probably been the quietest and most restrained of the contemporary outbreaks of protest which have emerged from the student communities of most industrial societies'.[33] Its effects, too, have probably been the least disruptive of the traditional methods and structures of university government, for all its success in winning for students a new and much more important place within the governmental system. The practitioners of student participation, moreover, have not on the whole been those who led the demands (or who now think as these students did), but more 'socialized' students who are prepared to sit on committees and to reach consensus. There seems little doubt that, in a rather undramatic way, student participation has been quietly working rather well in many universities, worthy rather than news-

[32] Well after the riots had started, the Oxbridge representatives at a conference held at York most smugly denied that *they* could ever have any such problems.
[33] Colin Crouch, in ARCHER: *op. cit.*, p. 196.

worthy. But, as we have already indicated, there is reason to think that the story is not over. In particular, two problems remain, either of which could lead to further conflict. The smaller is that of setting a numerical limit to the extent of student participation. It is difficult to justify any particular percentage of committee membership in terms that do not equally justify a rather smaller or a larger percentage. Thus it will always be difficult to defend a present position, especially in a heated debate. A much more fundamental problem is the effect of a large percentage student participation on the self-government by academic staff that has been a main theme of this study. Students may or may not be members of the community of scholars, but they are not, by definition, professional experts. Their claim to control of professional matters from outside the profession thus introduces a new element into the development of university government. It would, of course, be wholly within the British tradition if no very specific answers were given to these problems, and no precise rationale were provided for their practical solutions. In the past, this lack of precision has without doubt helped to ease the layman to the side-lines. It remains to be seen, however, how far students, or the general public acting through central or local government, will continue to accept such uncertainty or how far they will insist on further challenging the authority of academic decision-makers.

The Challenge by Non-Professorial Staff

The requests and occasional demands for non-professorial staff (NPS) participation long pre-dated the demands and occasional requests for student participation and power. Articulated first after the First World War[34], NPS discontent came, throughout the late 1940s and the 1950s, to be a constant preoccupation of meetings of the Association of University Teachers (AUT), both nationally and locally, and of local junior staff associations which increasingly were formed to express NPS views within their own institution.

The background to this movement undoubtedly was the slower inter-war expansion and the faster expansion after 1945 which, in so far as it affected staff, took place primarily at the non-professorial level. After the Second World War especially, NPS members were vitally affected by changes in policy, curriculum, economic circumstances and long-term development, but often in ways which did not seem to reflect their attitudes and interests. Indeed, an important

[34] H. J. PERKIN: *Key Profession*, p. 54. See also our discussion in Chapter II.

feature of this period was their stronger belief that they did in fact possess interests distinct from those of professors or of universities as a whole. This was most apparent in respect of such matters as academic salaries and the prospects and procedures for promotion with which, inevitably, the AUT was often preoccupied; but there seemed also to be a separate interest even with respect to major matters of university policy. Thus, for example, the younger (predominantly non-professorial) members of staff tended to favour university expansion more than did their seniors.

The increasing numerical preponderance of non-professorial over professorial staff was the starting-point of most arguments for changes in governmental structure. Thus a 'Memorandum on Staff Structure' prepared in 1962 by one local AUT branch pointed out that in its university during the period 1898–1962 the total number of staff had increased eightfold, but that the permanent non-professorial staff had increased almost sixteenfold, and that professors, who had formed 31·6 per cent of all academic staff (including temporary assistant lecturers) in 1898–9, formed 21 per cent in 1918 and only 11 per cent by 1961–2.[35] Another local branch, in a northern civic university, wrote that, originally, a few hundred students were taught by 'a small permanent staff of professors' each of whom 'had one or two "assistants" of a temporary character'. By 1961, however, the university had grown to ten times its original size and 'the "assistants" have become permanent academic grades of lecturer and senior lecturer and form the main body of the permanent academic community'. 'But', the document continues, 'they are able to take little part in decision making'. Similarly, a Scottish document pointed out that 'lecturers ... have little authority to influence either departmental or university policy although they carry out a major proportion of the teaching and research in the university'.

Two different kinds of argument are commonly adduced from the fact of numerical increase to press the case for greater NPS representation in university government. Rarely are they explicitly distinguished. Both may be found in this statement: 'Non-professorial representation on the Senate is a reflection of the days when there were *relatively few* non-professorial teachers, *so that* academic decisions were properly taken by professors. Now that lower grades of university teachers are filled with *specialists*, sometimes *solely responsible for a branch of their subject*, it is right that they should be more strongly

[35] The Robbins Committee figures for all universities show that professors constituted 22 per cent in 1924–8 and 12 per cent in 1961–2. See Appendix 3, Part I, table 7.

represented in the Senate'.[36] In the first sentence, the implicit reference is to the argument that no large number of teachers should be unenfranchised; given a general democratic vision of self-government, number is taken to be a sufficient argument in itself. This is quite different from the appeal made in the second sentence to the principle of expertise and responsibility in an academic subject area. Ironically, and perhaps significantly, students (as we have seen) borrowed and developed the 'democratic' argument to claim governing power for themselves and were resisted, by non-professorial as well as other staff, in part by reference to the argument from academic authority. It seems to us, furthermore, that the success of the NPS campaign owes more to the second argument than to their use of democratic rhetoric, as does the fact that their success has, for the most part, been limited.[37]

In earlier chapters we have traced a clear trend in the direction of extending the role of the NPS in government. We have there noted the tendency to assure members of the NPS of seats on councils and senates, a voice (usually strong) on faculty boards, an opportunity to debate any issue at meetings of all academic staff, and a share in increasingly collectivized policy-making at the subject level. NPS, who constitute the great majority of members in the AUT, may also expect to benefit from the recognition (almost universally) of the local AUT branch as 'sole bargaining agency' for the academic and library staffs under the 1972 Industrial Relations Act. In particular, such recognition entrenches, and is likely to make more effective, the right of the AUT to take part in discussions of university procedures for appointing, dismissing, paying, and promoting members of staff, not to mention 'matters affecting university education in general'.[38] Nevertheless there are still wide variations between universities in the governmental role permitted to the non-professorial staff, and nowhere are junior staff on an equal footing with senior. In 1964 over 80 per cent of the non-professorial staff included in Halsey and Trow's sample agreed (either strongly or with reservations) with the

[36] ASSOCIATION OF UNIVERSITY TEACHERS: *Submissions to the Committee on Higher Education* (AUT document G. 184, 1961) para. 11, p. 5, (emphasis supplied).

[37] It should, however, also be noted that few members of the NPS have argued that senates should represent NPS in proportion to their numbers. Most NPS, in other words, themselves temper the 'democratic' argument, possibly in recognition of the resistance it has met, but in part too, it seems to us, because many of them also believe that power in a university should reflect inherent inequalities of professional authority. See our discussion in the next chapter.

[38] To quote from one local association document on this matter.

statement that 'a serious disadvantage of Redbrick universities is that all too often they are run by a professorial oligarchy', and 46 per cent of the professors shared this view.[39] In 1969 Professor Richard Hoggart could write that 'the larger civics are too hierarchical . . . to a degree that seems unbelievable until you meet it'.[40] Even more recently, at a meeting early in 1972, a group of academics cited Halsey and Trow, with approval, when claiming that universities continued to be 'undemocratic'.[41]

For such opinions our own studies lend considerable support, even if we are chary of using such terms as 'oligarchy' and 'democracy'.[42] As we have already stated, it is a fact, that, in all but a small minority of universities, all professors still have a personal seat on senate. Even more to the point, perhaps, is the fact that non-professorial staff have not always made full use of the improvement in their formal governmental position. With unexpected frequency we were told that NPS tended to defer to professors on senate, and to leave to them both initiative and discussion. We have, for example, heard complaints from professors at Newcastle (and also at Durham) that NPS do not play the part intended by the initiators of the constitution. Some professors elsewhere suggested that NPS are bled of their natural leaders by promotion to the professoriate, so that the ability to contribute on senate is impaired. 'They're rabbits' was only one of the more terse comments we were offered. This may not be the whole matter. We talked to one professor at a new university, who could never have passed for a rabbit, of his time as a lecturer at Manchester. Why, we asked, did NPS, who under Statute VI (1) (a) of the 1903 Charter appear to have a majority on faculty boards, not play a larger part in the initiation of academic policy? The question surprised, and then: 'Well, I suppose if we'd devoted all our time to administration we could have made our views heard': (pause, contemptuously) 'of course, that's just what some of the professors did do'. Rather similarly a respondent at LSE, who thought that NPS should be entitled to initiate items on the Academic Board agenda 'if they could get, say, twenty-five signatures', was surprised to read in his current agenda a routine entry to the effect that any member (in the singular) wishing to put an item on should inform the

[39] H. A. HALSEY and MARTIN TROW: *The British Academics* (Faber and Faber, 1971) pp. 377 and 381. Their whole chapter should be consulted, pp. 375–98.

[40] *Op. cit.*, p. 274.

[41] The academic section of the ASTMS, reported in the *Times Higher Education Supplement*, April 7, 1972. The claim also was one reason for the foundation (in 1970) of the Council for Academic Freedom and Democracy.

[42] For our views on university democracy and oligarchy see the discussion in the next chapter.

secretary. On the other hand, at Sussex, where professors do still have *ex officio* seats, NPS appear to play a much more active and vigorous part, as they do at York, where the 'senate' is representational.

For the continuance of the special position accorded to professors it would, however, be quite wrong to suggest that the explanation lies to any very great degree in the timidity of others, significant (and sometimes justified) as that may be.[43] More important is the fact that changes in the composition of senate must normally secure the approval of the 'unreconstructed' senate itself. Those who must agree to wider membership thus include those, the professors, who appear to have most to lose. It is probably significant, therefore, that the most radical of the reforms at senate level have been at the new universities. Durham and Newcastle apart, proposals to give anything approaching full weight to the NPS elsewhere have been a major sticking-point. At one northern redbrick, for example, an initiative in the late 1950s, strongly backed by an able and vigorous vice-chancellor, collapsed in the face of organized professorial resistance, and in all the redbricks there has been the greatest reluctance to deprive the professors of their seats.

Professorial power at the subject level is also of significance, and this is not merely in the obvious sense that NPS members of senate may be reluctant publicly to challenge or embarrass those on whose positive support they may be dependent in other spheres. There is also the simple fact that though senate may be the ultimate academic authority, it is the seat of only certain sorts of power and information. It is of course true that meetings of senate are usually well attended and seats are prized, but none the less much, probably most, purely academic business is decided at levels 'below' senate. This applies also to the faculty level, where NPS are usually well represented (and where the transactions are often considered very dull), but it does not apply to the subject level, usually the department, where the actual work of a university is done. It is interesting that in the university mentioned just above, where the democratic initiative on senate was defeated, some of the steam went out of the discontent amongst NPS when, following the failure to secure major senate reform, the university prescribed changes at the departmental level, changes which met relatively little resistance. Departmental meetings became mandatory, consultation by professors with their colleagues was strongly advised and, within the larger departments, the system of rotating headship was instituted. This last experience suggests,

[43] See, for another instance, the exaggerated caution of respondents to the survey of departmental practices discussed above in Chapter IV.

possibly, that at the root of much NPS concern has been a traditional and natural concern with 'job control'; but it also suggests that one main reason for relative NPS ineffectiveness on senate may be lack of knowledge of the grass-roots. If we are right, then the opening out of departmental affairs to more junior staff through systems of departmental committees may well lead to more pertinent and effective NPS participation in senate deliberations. Here again, the experience of Sussex, with its extremely wide-ranging system of committees on both a 'school' and 'subject' basis, and with relatively effective NPS participation at 'higher' levels, may be significant.[44]

The relative ease with which changes were introduced at the subject level, in the university mentioned above, also suggests that resistance need not stem from a rooted opposition to all change on the part of all professors and that professorial reluctance is therefore not to be dismissed simply as a 'bourbon' reaction. In fact the response of the professoriate has been ambivalent, at times to the point of acute discomfort. It is undeniable, on the one hand, that members of the NPS are, after all, colleagues and fellow scholars, that many of them carry through independent research, and that most of them are trusted perforce to teach and to examine with the minimum of effective supervision. Nevertheless, as we have seen[45], the fact remains that it is the professorial head of department who is responsible to senate and council for his subject, by convention and in some cases by the formal terms of his appointment.

For some professors the acuteness of the discomfort is reduced by the sincere feeling that involvement by junior staff in university politics is at best a distraction during a period of learning the job and/or of greatest research creativity; or, at worst, is an escape for the academically mediocre and the professional malcontent. For most professors, however, the dilemma is sharpened by an intractable practical problem. This is that to give substantial representation to the NPS as well as to professors produces a senate (or indeed a faculty or board of studies) that may be too large for effective working.[46] Such enlargement, many fear, must inevitably diminish the power of these bodies, presumably in favour of the vice-chancellor,

[44] However, one lecturer at a Yorkshire redbrick who told us with enthusiasm of the degree of departmental democracy that had been achieved by 1968, later remarked, 'Lately we've been getting a bit bored with all these committees. There's a move to make the professors take more decisions like they're paid to.'

[45] See Chapter IV, above.

[46] In even the smaller universities today a senate with all professors and a substantial minority of NPS on it, not to mention students, must be at least fifty strong, and in the larger it will be well over 200.

bureaucracy, or a cabal (possibly called the steering committee). So long as all professors are *ex officio* members of all the main academic bodies this objection is difficult to combat. But if, on the other hand, professors are deprived of their *ex officio* memberships, then their whole role might finally be undermined. So, at least, the situation seems to many professors disquieted enough by the changes which have already occurred. It would perhaps be no exaggeration to suggest that the professoriate, in trying to come to terms with fuller enfranchisement of the NPS, is grappling with a 'crisis of identity'.

Even as late as 1950 the title of professor normally denoted a head of department, a member of the only group from which deans and other senior academic offices were filled, and a man (rarely a woman) with tenure as head and senate member which extended to retirement.[47] In the succeeding twenty years each of these characteristics ceased to be distinctive of professors everywhere, while professorial status was more frequently conferred on some who did not hold the title (like directors of institutes or librarians).[48] 'Professor' thus has come to designate rank but not necessarily to indicate function. In the eyes of 40 per cent of Halsey and Trow's sample, significantly, it was no longer a rare mark of distinction; instead, it should be 'a part of the normal expectation of an academic career'.[49]

One of the most commonly remarked paradoxes of the present-day professorial role is that 'a professor is often so overloaded with university and departmental affairs that it detracts from his primary function' of teaching and research (on the basis of which he is initially appointed).[50] As a group, indeed, 'they are least able to research during term'.[51] In response to this kind of tension the hitherto inconceivable has happened on more than one occasion: a professor has resigned his chair in favour of a readership or, more commonly, gladly allowed the headship to rotate away from him. Increasingly, too, for this reason as well as to extend the rights of others, the role of departmental head is being distinguished from that

---

[47] The exceptions, like the holders of non-science Oxbridge chairs and a few non-adminstrative professors elsewhere, did not upset this picture.

[48] And, symbolically, *Who's Who* ceased automatically to list occupants of chairs outside Oxford and Cambridge.

[49] *Op. cit.*, pp. 378–9. Among professors only 29 per cent agreed.

[50] The quotation is from the northern civic AUT branch statement already referred to.

[51] HALSEY and TROW: *op. cit.*, p. 293. Unfortunately the important distinction between professors with administrative duties and those without is not made. Since, however, professors as a group do almost as much research as lecturers, presumably it is the administrative professors who bring down their average.

of chairman of a department or departmental committee[52] or the post of head has been replaced by that of elected chairman.[53] Most commonly of all, almost to the point of being the norm in all but the smallest department, there are two or more professors (amongst whom the post of head or chairman may rotate).[54]

In the multi-chair departments, an interesting practice is to designate the 'additional' professors as professors of some particular area or field within their subject or discipline. This underlines the fundamental reason why the authority of the single professorial head of department has been eroded. That reason is the explosion of knowledge and the associated growth in specialization characteristic of most of the subjects taught at universities (since it is by no means confined to the natural sciences). For purposes, primarily, of under-graduate teaching it has not been thought wise for each new special interest to be institutionalized in a separate department.[55] As a result the traditional head can no longer claim, with conviction, to be the sole authoritative spokesman for his subject. Not only his professorial colleagues, but some of his junior ones too, will normally be more authoritative than he is, at least in the sense of being more expert in some significant part of the subject.

At the same time as professorial heads of department have lost any plausible claim to intellectual primacy over all the main areas covered in their department, their purely administrative functions have become more important. The size of departments has grown, the financial and organizational aspects, in the natural sciences particularly, may assume the proportions of a small business, and a new prominence has been given to the political arts involved in handling (possibly) several dozen academic colleagues, many more technicians, secretaries and other ancillary staff, and hundreds of students. It has thus not only become clearer, it has become important that there is no necessary conjunction of intellectual distinction and managerial flair. In this respect too, therefore, the claim to *ex officio* pre-eminence for any individual professor has been weakened, and clearly seen to be so. Nevertheless, professors are still appointed in

---

[52] The distinction has, for example, been agreed by the Senate of Aberystwyth, recommended to the University of Birmingham by the Grimond Committee, and for long applied by the University of York.

[53] In such new universities as East Anglia and Essex eligibility for election extends to NPS as well as professors.

[54] Seventy-five per cent even of the professors in Halsey and Trow's study favoured the appointment of a second professor in any department with more than eight members. See *op. cit.*, p. 381.

[55] Economy, administrative convenience, and the resistances to the creation of new departments have reinforced this policy.

the belief that they are intellectually distinguished, some are appointed also because of their known administrative ability, and all are expected to be capable of bearing the responsibility placed upon them for guiding and developing research and teaching within their subject. Only a minority patently fail on all counts. As a result few would deny some special governmental role to the professoriate, just as few would now either make or accept the assertion of professorial omni-competence.[56] The issue in most universities, with professorial power as with academic power over students, is therefore increasingly seen as one of balance, of drawing a rationally defensible line, and not one of either/or.

Broadly speaking, professorial opinion seems to be distributed along a spectrum, at the 'conservative' end of which lies the view that all professorial heads of department should retain a seat on senate (but not all professors, nor on a senate composed solely of professors). The more 'radical' end may be represented by the view put to us that 'if he has the final say over appointments, a major say about promotions, continues to be in demand as a referee, and is any good at his job, a professor has all the power he needs to accept responsibility for the development of his subject'. There is no evidence that any substantial number of professors would fall outside these limits. There seem, moreover, to be few members of the NPS who, provided that minimal safeguards exist against unilateral and arbitrary decisions, dispute the advantage of having someone to accept final personal responsibility for the difficult, potentially divisive, and often invidious choices involved in allocating scarce resources, whether these be money or senior lectureships. Amongst the professorial and NPS holders of such views accommodation obviously is possible.

The variety of new constitutional arrangements to be found in British universities today[57] may therefore be seen as different responses to the logic of academic authority, as different attempts to accommodate traditional structures to changed internal circumstances. What they have in common is the attempt to limit the possibility of purely arbitrary professorial decision-making at the subject level, to make it possible (by rotation and election) to remove

[56] Although we were told that a professor at the University of Stirling made it known that he expected all members of his department to vote for his proposed method of dealing with the students involved in the disturbances during the visit of the Queen in October 1972. On the other hand, our informant was clearly shocked by this—and there is no evidence that his colleagues' voting behaviour was affected.

[57] See the discussion, above, in Chapter IV. See, too, the articles by Michael Locke in the *Times Higher Education Supplement*, 14, 20, and 27 October 1972.

an unsatisfactory head by constitutional means[58], and at senate level, to transform the professoriate from a privileged political caste into no more than a special constituency. The role of the professorial heads of department in the government of the university has always, in our view, been a reflection of their departmental role. As the latter has changed with changes in the organization of knowledge, so too must the role of the erstwhile sole spokesmen. Appropriately, as we will argue in the next chapter, these changes have amounted to a clearer recognition of the representative nature of senates and, therefore, to the introduction of more formal institutions of representative government.

In answer to the challenges posed by both students and members of the non-professorial staff, the exercise and the location of authority within universities have both been modified. The process of adaptation is clearly not over, but its direction seems virtually to form part of a new consensus, at least among academics. In any case, the system of government in the universities has satisfied one test of any political system[59]—it has evolved new policies of a kind, and in a manner, that have enabled the universities to survive in still recognizable form—as functioning and coherent organizations.

[58] Some of the most unpleasant episodes in the lives of individual universities have occurred when, in the absence of such constitutional means, colleagues have attempted to force the resignation of an unpopular figure by resort to intrigue, 'leaks' to the press, and systematic personal hostility and non-co-operation. The rarity of these events (so far as we have been able to discover) does not lessen their legacy of bitterness, shame, and lowered morale.

[59] See Chapter I, above.

Chapter X

WHAT KIND OF GOVERNMENT?

The kind of government appropriate to a university must depend, ultimately, on the purposes for which it exists.[1] Thus it was natural for Newman to accord a decisive role to an external body, the Church, since he saw the main purpose of his university as the formation of Christian gentlemen.[2] This particular purpose is not widely accepted today, but traces of a similar view may be found amongst those who demand that universities become the instruments by which society (or some other external agency, such as industry or a political movement) meets certain of its needs. Formal obeisance is paid to this ideal in Aston's Charter[3], and it is at least acknowledged in the preponderance of laymen in university courts and councils.[4] A contrary view, that universities are places in which the individual student can develop his own potential, irrespective of the needs of society or the dictates of scholarship, seems to underly some of the arguments adduced in favour of 'free universities' or of the abolition both of examinations and of rigorous entrance tests. But the main stream of university development, and the most generally accepted frame of reference for discussion of university government, seems rather to assume that the overriding purpose of a university is, in another of Newman's phrases, 'to protect the interests and advance the dominion of Science' (in a broad sense which includes all learning

---

[1] See, for example, AMITAI ETZIONI: *Modern Organisations* (Prentice-Hall, 1964), especially Chapters 1 and 2, for a discussion of the dependence of organizational forms upon an organization's goals.

[2] J. H. NEWMAN: *On the Scope and Nature of University Education* (Dent, 1949) pp. xli and 164.

[3] 'The objects . . . shall be to advance . . . learning and knowledge . . . for the benefit of industry and commerce and of the community generally' (Charter, para. 2).

[4] See, too, E. P. THOMPSON: *Warwick University Ltd.* (Penguin Books, 1970) and the *Minority Report* of LSE's 1968 Machinery of Government Committee, for further example of demands that the 'outside community' should have a say in university government.

and teaching). It is from this basic standpoint that we examine certain possible models of university government.

The most common answers to the question, what kind of government, are 'democratic' and 'oligarchic'. Comparatively rarely is either term clearly defined or precisely used; but it is clear that they are used in both descriptive and prescriptive senses and would not be defined in the same way by all those who use them.

'Democracy', to begin with it, is notoriously susceptible to different interpretations of emphasis and substance.[5] In its application to British universities, however, it is necessary initially to distinguish only the two broadest and commonest usages. They may be labelled the 'populist' and the 'consensual' theories. We will discuss them in turn.

The populist view stresses the popular power aspect of democracy. According to it legitimate government rests upon the active endorsement of the people while the power to take at least the ultimate decisions must also lie with the people at large. Different proponents of this theory will, however, place emphasis upon varying means of establishing and recording the popular will. Some see populism as virtually synonymous with majority rule while others advocate a universalist and communal decision-making process in which all shall participate and from which decisions presumably emerge as does the spirit from a Friends' meeting.[6] Quite clearly neither variant constitutes an accurate description of what happens in any university today, but equally clearly the populist notion of democracy is widely used as a basis for criticism of existing university government by both staff and students. As a statement of the goal for reform, moreover, it has been flirted with by non-professorial staff and the AUT[7] and espoused by the more radical student leaders as well as, it seems, by at least some members of the Council for Academic Freedom and Democracy.[8]

By both its supporters and opponents populism is correctly seen as a radical prescription with which the existing system of university government is incompatible. If applied seriously and honestly, in

---

[5] See, for example, the discussion of the definitional problems in G. SARTORI: *Democratic Theory* (Praeger, 1965) pp. 3–50.

[6] Or, possibly, as a new leader used to 'emerge' from the ranks of the Conservative party.

[7] As we have seen in the previous chapter.

[8] An academic pressure group founded in 1970 largely, it seems, in response to alleged cases of political discrimination against left-wingers in staff appointments at the Universities of Birmingham and Manchester. Its aims are to combat such discrimination and to struggle for democracy throughout higher education. It is linked to the National Council for Civil Liberties.

the form of full 'student power' and a 'one man, one vote' system of decision-making, it implies that there are no governmentally significant differences between any members of the university. It is therefore proper, as some are sufficiently consistent to advocate, that the right to vote be extended to all ancillary and domestic staff as well as, and on the same terms as, students and academic staff. To draw no governmental distinction between teacher and taught, between intellectual and non-academic worker, or between student and employee is, in turn, to assume either that the purposes of an organization are irrelevant to its form or that the professional authority hitherto claimed by and for academics is irrelevant to the decision-making process, or both. The first of these assumptions runs counter to all scholarly studies of organizations and the second carries further implications which are seldom stated. It implies, first, that teachers of different subjects could no longer assert a special subject-authority with which to justify those elements of autonomy, *vis-à-vis* teachers of other subjects and disciplines within the university, which are such a feature of the present system. (Under the 'communal' variant, it might of course happen that any subject minority could block all decisions that it deemed hostile to its interest.) Populist theory seems, too, to re-assert a principle of omni-competence among decision-makers which runs counter to, for example, recent trends to restrict the spheres in which universities attempt to regulate the behaviour of their students. Finally, populist theory, by ignoring the present distinctions between the various people who work in universities, distinctions which rest at least in part upon their different relations to the university's purposes, abolishes any ground for distinguishing universities, governmentally, from any other kind of institution or association. This, of itself, seems sufficient reason to reject the theory, at least in its unqualified forms.

Not all those who use populist rhetoric, one suspects, use it to express a coherent set of positive aims so much as to express disapproval of certain features of the current situation. Even when considered in this light, however, the attitude seems to us to underestimate or misstate the problem of academic authority. Donald Bligh, in a recent discussion of the difficulties to be faced by attempts to 'teach university teachers to teach'[9], pointed out that the enterprise differed from that undertaken by colleges of education, in that universities were, at least for some of the time, trying to teach a subject at its most advanced level, and that there were, generally speaking, no higher authorities than the university teachers in that subject.

[9] 'Untaught Teachers', *The Observer*, November 5, 1972.

With this one might contrast the view of Professor John Griffith (Chairman of the Council for Academic Freedom and Democracy) that 'universities and other institutions of higher education are, *at their best*, groups of people working in certain disciplines at the difficult but mundane task of taking the process of education one stage further than school—and sometimes two stages further'.[10] Against this we would argue that universities have rightly claimed, especially at their best, to provide not one form of higher education only but, in T. H. Huxley's phrase, 'the highest intellectual culture that could be given' and, as such, to embody a particular authority of which account must be taken in assessing their form of government.

A different kind of shortcoming, it seems to us, is represented by another view which echoes much that has been said by populist advocates of 'a new legitimacy', as Dr Stephen Hatch puts it. 'In the past', he continues, 'the university teacher's authority was of a paternal kind: . . . its justification lay in morality and tradition rather than in the consent of those taught, or in any concept by the taught of their own interests. This paternal type of authority cannot be sustained in the modern university. . . .'[11] As we have noted in the previous chapter, however, academics have relinquished much of their authority over students' non-academic lives[12], while to reduce the claim to authority in academic matters to morality and tradition seems to deny any validity to the justification for that authority in terms simply of greater knowledge. At this level at least, it is difficult to see how the authority of the teacher can *derive from* the consent of the taught, even if one accepts the pedagogical commonplace that a willing student is a better learner.

To argue thus against the applicability of a pure populist standard to universities is, of course, neither necessarily to dispute its applicability to other organizations, nor to deny that populism is one essential strand in the western democratic tradition.[13] It is merely to claim that university populism is an inappropriate instance of that transfer of general political attitudes and commitments to the

[10] 'Freedom and the Universities', *New Statesman*, November 17, 1972, p. 720, emphasis not in the original.

[11] STEPHEN HATCH: 'Change and Dissent in the Universities. An Examination of the Sources of Protest', in H. J. BUTCHER and ERNEST RUDD, eds.: *Contemporary Problems in Higher Education* (McGraw-Hill, 1972) pp. 224–32. The quotation is from p. 232.

[12] An authority which was in any case associated primarily with the residential universities.

[13] See the discussion in G. C. MOODIE and W. G. STUDDERT-KENNEDY: *Opinions, Publics and Pressure-Groups* (Allen and Unwin, 1971) Chapter 1.

university context which characterizes academics.[14] And it is inappropriate, we feel, essentially because it overlooks or undervalues a crucial and distinctive source of authority within a university. (As will be made clear below, we do not believe that scholarly expertize is the only source; but it is the one to which populist views most signally fail to do justice.) Clearly, too, the objections advanced against populism do not necessarily hold against the other main concept of democracy sometimes deemed relevant to universities.

The 'consensual' definition of democracy places its main emphasis on the style of decision-making by academics. Thus, when the Franks Commission approvingly describes the government of Oxford as 'democratic'[15], it seems to mean that decisions are taken by a process of discussion and consensus-building among the more or less equal senior members (the resident masters). As a description of the two ancient English universities this is reasonably accurate, and certainly would be accepted as such by most British academics. We almost labelled this version as 'Oxbridge', but did not do so because it would also be widely accepted outside Oxbridge as an ideal for all universities and even as a partial description of most.

It might seem fanciful, in the light of our previous discussions of the role of professorial heads of department[16], to suggest that 'consensual democracy' is an acceptable description of the way in which most universities are run. Nevertheless, even in those universities where professorial power remains strongest and members of the NPS are much 'less equal than others', certain aspects of their governmental procedures lend themselves to this interpretation. In particular, the ideal of rule by consensus underlines the important and widespread feeling that, at least with respect to major policy decisions, no simple majoritarian system can successfully be operated within a university. Instead the stress is placed upon discussion and persuasion as the proper means to securing agreement upon the most important decisions. In this the style of university government reflects the simple fact that, in academic matters, the successful implementation of policy requires the general consent of the academics, at least to the extent that no significant dissenting group should be unwilling even to 'go along with' the decision. In the actual business of the university, teaching and research, results cannot be

---

[14] See A. H. HALSEY and MARTIN TROW: *The British Academics* (Faber and Faber, 1971) pp. 438–50, for a discussion of the correlations of academics' general political attitudes with their opinions on various university issues.

[15] In its *Report* at, e.g. paras. 43, 54, 84, 437, and 440.

[16] Especially in Chapters IV and IX, above.

achieved by commanding people to teach 'better' or even very differently—and only within the more authoritarian departments is one likely to encounter decsion-making by overt command. Even voting is comparatively rare, and is most often resorted to on the more trivial issues or on those where the possible choices have been defined and narrowed sufficiently to ensure that, whichever way the vote goes, the outcome will be tolerable. For this practice there are also 'ideological' reasons. Academic policy, to have any effect, must be actualized at the organizational 'periphery', as we have remarked before. Decisions on policy must therefore be taken—or so it is generally believed—by procedures which not only encourage consultation with and consideration of every affected interest. The procedures must also reflect the fact that only the interests (subjects, departments, etc.) may realize that they are affected, and how. It is important, therefore, that all interests be informed about the issues, and that they be guaranteed a serious hearing before the decisions are taken.[17] This is a recipe for the pursuit of consensus.

Consensual democracy is thus an accurate descriptive label for certain aspects of government in all British universities. In so far as the term also denotes that the consensus should be of equals, the main difference between Oxbridge and the rest, at least until relatively recently, has lain in the definition of full citizenship: the resident masters in the former, the professoriate elsewhere. But, as we have seen, the ideal of a fuller democracy (in this sense) has been one factor in extending at least some of the rights of full citizenship to the non-professorial staff outside Oxbridge as well. In these latter institutions, however, it is clear that continuing elements of 'oligarchy'[18] limit the descriptive accuracy of consensual democracy, even if applied solely to the governmental role of the academic staff. It is also worth remarking that the main thrust of the Franks Commission's recommendations was to strengthen the executive bodies, Hebdomadal Council in particular, in the government of Oxford and thus, some might say, to increase the existing elements of oligarchy there too.

The problems—among them those of establishing an authoritative spokesman for the university in its dealings with others, and ensuring greater co-ordination of initiatives in the academic, financial and other spheres—that led to the setting up of the Franks

[17] We invited a management expert, who had just completed a report on a redbrick university, to detail those who, in his view, must be consulted and heeded on an important non-academic decision. To his surprise his answer was little distinguishable from a conventional list of senate members.

[18] We discuss this label below.

Commission[19] point to one of the main shortcomings of consensual democracy as a prescriptive model for university government. As we pointed out in Chapter IV, above, it may lead to a system in which it is excessively difficult to take the decisions necessary if an institution is to adapt to changing circumstances. All too easily a preoccupation with consensus can create a system which approximates to one of *liberum veto*, where any organized minority operates as a veto-group rather than an autonomous centre of creativity, or, at best, one in which obstructive minorities may demand an excessively high price for co-operation. Even more to the point, perhaps, is the fact that, in the pure Oxbridge model, such minorities may consist of any collection of 'voters', however heterogeneous their motives and interests; unlike the redbrick system, there is not even the possible justification that the relevant minorities are defined functionally in terms of some departmental, disciplinary, or faculty interest. Consensus may refer, this is to say, either to a 'federal' set of relationships (which may have some academic legitimacy) or merely to one where any small grouping, however temporary and fortuitous, may obstruct decisions. In the latter case, not only are subject interests given no special protection, they may even be peculiarly vulnerable.

The other main shortcoming of consensual democracy relates to the criteria by which citizenship should be defined. Among what precise group of more or less equal citizens should consensus be obtained in this kind of democratic system? Is there, in particular, any good reason for extending citizenship beyond the restricted group of equal redbrick professors to all members of the academic staff, or for restricting it to the Oxbridge group of resident masters and excluding students and non-resident masters? Within the limits of the model itself it is not easy to detect any principle on which to base a satisfactory answer. The model is not unique in its failure to supply the rules for its own application or relevance, but in this context at least the failure is important. This is because the main point at issue, as a matter of history, has been and is precisely that of the qualifications for citizenship. It is important also because one test of citizenship (other than that of membership of a college corporation) has in fact become that of academic expertise: hence, in particular, the exclusion of students and non-resident masters from the system of consensual democracy in Oxbridge.[20] The

[19] Like those which led to the strengthening (1967) of the university's ability to control finance and allocate resources at Cambridge.

[20] The clearest acknowledgement is to be found in the *Report* of the (Hart) Committee on Relations with Junior Members. Supplement No. 7 to the *University Gazette*, May 1969. See, particularly, the discussion at paras. 140-9.

'equality' of citizens, in other words, is something which does not result, *ex officio*, from the conferment of political rights, but is the precondition for it and is defined by reference to criteria that are not in themselves obviously 'democratic'. What is more, the ideal must appeal to some outside criteria if it is not to be merely a variant of populism. Regardless of its intrinsic appeal, therefore, consensual democracy is not a sufficient prescription for university government. It is either supplemented by extraneous (and potentially antagonistic) principles, those of college and academic authority, or it is a version of the populist ideal whose proponents have been actively hostile to Oxbridge notions of consensus.

'Democracy' is thus, in our view, a term which should be applied with much greater care than is customary in discussions of university government if, indeed, it should be applied at all. At the same time one cannot be entirely comfortable about recommending that universities should be debarred from receiving (if justified) such an all-purpose political accolade. Within the more traditional ideology of a 'community of scholars' as much as in more modern and radical ideologies it is undeniable that there are ideals, particularly of mutual respect (as among equals) and of government by discussion, that also are central to western democratic thought. Even so, it seems to us that these ideals, within a university, do not depend and have not depended for their validity upon general arguments for democracy[21]; on the contrary, they are ideals which have flowed naturally from the nature of creative intellectual activity. In arguing, therefore, against the appropriateness of 'democratic' criteria, we are not intending to discard those criteria which are common to universities and democratic states.

The other governmental label commonly applied to universities is 'oligarchy'. This label is normally used in a purely descriptive (and disapproving) sense. But there is also a widely-supported prescriptive account of university government which incorporates certain oligarchic features. To this 'republican' model, as we name it, we will turn once we have commented on the more usual oligarchic one.

To describe a system of government as an oligarchy or rule by a few (depending upon one's interpretation of 'rule') means almost anything from the truism that a few people are more politically active than the many others (and hence are more influential) to the assertion that an identifiable small group exercises despotic powers over a mass of subjects. In the first sense it is obviously true of

---

[21] It is arguable, even, that these 'democratic' ideals are historically rooted as much in academic life as in the politics of the larger society—e.g. in Plato's notion of the Academy, but not in his ideal form of the Republic.

universities, but not in the second. The real question, therefore, is as to the nature (and not the existence) of university oligarchy. To that question this whole book may be seen as an attempted answer, but it may be useful to add a few comments addressed more specifically to this issue.

Over and over again we have been told by university officials and by academic committee men, though not always in these words, that their job (and a prime source of what influence they possess) is the preparation of acceptable initiatives. They, the activists in university government, certainly take initiatives—they draft, they brief, they propose at all levels—but in the greatest number of instances their initiatives must, if they are to be effective, be enacted, approved, and/or validated by full and formal meetings of council, senate or, in fewer cases, faculty board or its equivalent. As we have seen, moreover, there is even a sense in which the 'lower level' academic teaching units are expected to validate many of the general policy decisions taken by senates. Conversely, almost all the business of these validating bodies originates elsewhere: the vice-chancellor, the bureaucracy, their own committees and, especially, the basic academic units. And, although the logical form of many decisions seems to be that of the imperative—departments *must* submit returns by a certain deadline, or *must* keep within their budgetary limits, and so on—the psychological mood of the imperative associated with, say, a military command or a directive from a business head office is regarded as ill suited to relations between academics and, increasingly, to some aspects of relations with students. These general features of university government provide the crucial limits within which oligarchies may develop and operate.

The first sense in which, therefore, 'a few' may be said to rule is that a few people are better placed than most to take acceptable initiatives. Those who are best informed, both about a particular issue and about the possible or probable reactions of others, those who belong to important committees, and those with other political resources, clearly are at an advantage. But, as we have seen, the nature of the advantages conferred upon particular people, and the lists of eligible members, vary widely between universities—so too, therefore, does the denotation of 'oligarchy'. A second kind of oligarchy may also be found in many universities, one which might be said to grow directly out of the elements of consensus government to be found in all universities. To illustrate from the academic decision-making sphere, it is a fact that senates and their committees are not uniquely free from the lover of intrigue and 'politicking' (in the pejorative sense). Such men are peculiarly likely to devote

H

greater time and energies to governing than most others. In an organization which stresses consensus, such men may well be able systematically to exploit their own potential veto-power. More typically, the existence of many potential veto-groups, bolstered it may be by an elaborate and somewhat untidy committee system[22], makes it both easier and more necessary than it might otherwise be for an inner clique or skilful 'power-group' to manipulate the system for their own ends or simply in order that some decisions be taken. To establish itself such a group needs only to secure places on several key committees (*ex officio* or otherwise), competently to use its position to acquire the information and influence with which to make it difficult for others to work the system without their co-operation, and to establish their own reputation for 'getting things done'. Such a position, once established, tends to be self-perpetuating, if only because others may lack the time, ability, or inclination effectively to challenge it.[23] As Mr Charles Carter put it, 'life must go on . . . so people with a taste for management meet in caucuses and decide things . . .'.[24] In practice, the only alternative to guidance of a traditional senate by an informal 'oligarchy' (or such guidance as can be offered by the vice-chancellor from the chair)[25] may be to set up an executive committee with a *formal* responsibility for organizing business. This may seem to be no real alternative; it is merely another 'oligarchy'. This device, however, does differ in significant ways from a powerful informal group or clique. In particular, in comparison with the latter a formal executive committee is open, is more easily brought to account because it is dependent (in part) only on a single electoral process, and since it operates by means of comments upon the work of other committees rather than by attempting to guide them from inside, its existence poses less of a threat to the survival, in different areas of business, of alternative centres of initiative and hence of effective opposition. In both cases the principal source of leverage of the group is that it comes to

[22] See the complaint of a students' union president at Bristol: 'When you ask a question, it always seems to be some other committee that has the answer'. Quoted in MERVYN JONES: 'Students and the Gap', *New Statesman*, September 29, 1972, p. 427.

[23] For an argument that this is the major kind of power in certain organizations see TREVOR NOBLE and BRIDGET PYM: 'Collegial Authority and the receding Locus of Power', *The British Journal of Sociology*, xxi (4), 1970, pp. 431–45.

[24] From the passage quoted more extensively in Chapter IV, above.

[25] See Chapter VI, above, for a discussion of the forces defining the scope for vice-cancellarian leadership. Vice-chancellors may often work in conjunction with a dominant group, but others have been as much limited by one as has senate as a whole.

meetings well informed and with a clear objective, while potential opposition may be fragmented and less well prepared. But it is also true that their initiatives, like any others, must be acceptable to the major university interests and that, in the last resort, this influence depends upon the forbearance, indolence, or lack of interest of others. When all is said and done, senate members as a whole have the voting power to 'pack' any committee[26] and to reject any proposal from any source.

Within senate, therefore, the extent of oligarchy is limited by basic structural factors, and its significance will vary according to whether a small and influential group is informally or formally constituted, whether its members are nominated, elected or *ex officio*, whether the membership is stable or forced to rotate, and whether its jurisdiction is wide or narrow. Its significance will differ, too, if it exists primarily because of a common recognition of the convenience offered by a division of labour in government or, alternately, if it is the product of in-built inequalities of power. Similar analyses can be made of all instances of 'oligarchy' in universities, whether of a particular committee or, more usually, of a professoriate; and, significantly, complaint seems most frequently to be directed to the one clear case of in-built, structural, inequalities: that of the traditional professorial heads of department and their dominance in senate.

Many would accept the judgement that university government is, and even must be, oligarchic in certain respects, but would deny that all major decisions are taken by any single small group. This view, implicit in some of the criticisms made of arguments for university democracy, seldom is clearly articulated. For it we have therefore had to coin the label 'republican', even though it has probably been the most influential picture of how universities are and should be governed. Its essentials may be summed up in two propositions. The first is that decisions on any issue should be taken by those who know most about it, and the second is that those who know most will vary according to the nature of the issue. We call this picture 'republican' because the first proposition echoes Plato's *Republic*, and because the second bears some resemblance, in its practical application, to the system of checks and balances and

---

[26] But see the opinion of the midlands senate document on committees already cited in Chapter IV, above, that 'Senate will not accept their views with confidence if their membership is determined in the haphazard way of calling for spontaneous nominations in a full meeting of Senate'. The need for concerted behaviour is once again made clear: the issue is whether or not it be taken on behalf of senate.

separation of powers incorporated in the Constitution of the USA.[27]

That we believe the republican view to have considerable descriptive validity should be evident from the detailed discussion which has filled most of this book. At numerous points the existing system is intelligible only on some such assumption about the basic presuppositions of those who operate and have helped shape the system. The right to take decisions, generally speaking, has either been vested in or has gravitated to those who are informed or learned in relevant ways, or who are at any rate believed to be so. There is, admittedly, an ambiguity in the notion of being informed or learned. Within the university context it may mean learned in the sense of being scholarly or an expert in a particular academic field. It may also mean, as it does in any organizational context, informed about the particular business in hand. The difference may be important— an official, for example, may have confidential information which assists him in steering a proposal through a committee, whereas academic reputations, and thus authority, must rest on some public display of learning. The whole movement to academic self-government has rested, however, upon the claim that scholarship (professional expertise) is the primary source of authority within universities, if only because no other source is as intimately rooted in their very nature and purpose. It is only a natural extension of this that other kinds of knowledge, provided only that they are relevant, should be accepted as another source of authority and not only, as a matter of fact, a source of power or influence. All other sources of authority (as hierarchical office) are seen as subordinate. It has followed, too, that the more academically learned have normally been granted a weightier role in government than the less learned (junior staff and students), or those whose knowledge is of another kind (officials and, on academic questions, laymen). As we have argued, too, serious encroachments upon the 'prerogatives' of the professoriate have taken place only at a time when (and because) professorial authority is patently less superior to that of other academics than it was once reasonable to assume.

Were academic knowledge the only criterion of authority 'republicanism' would be far less persuasive. But this is not so. Universities, in this system of government, allow both for different areas of academic expertise and for certain non-academic kinds of com-

---

[27] Many of the US Founding Fathers were adamant that they were establishing a 'republic' and not a 'democracy'. The former, according to them, was a system of government of and by free men, the latter was government by a mob (by the 'canaille' as Jefferson put it).

petence. Senates, as we have seen, both represent and defer to particular subject competences, while departments, schools, and faculties
are normally hesitant to intervene in the affairs of others. And
academics generally, while jealous of their academic sovereignty,
yet have accepted that special financial responsibilities should be
exercised by laymen deemed to be experienced in appropriate fields
and, if with some reluctance, that students be granted some authority
in areas in which they can properly claim to be informed. Members
of the bureaucracy, though sometimes suspect, also may establish
themselves as respected and influential figures—to a significant
degree because of their knowledge, experience and good sense. If,
furthermore, it be granted that, as we suggested earlier, the preparation of acceptable initiatives is the characteristic means of
influencing (even 'taking') decisions, then it may also be said that
clearly to have 'done one's homework' is a characteristic source of
influence within universities. Both as a description and an appropriate criterion of judgement this view of universities as 'republics
of learning' has obvious strengths. But despite this, and despite the
fact that it seems even to be an implicit orthodoxy in academic circles,
it provides only an incomplete, some might even say utopian,
account of university government.

The republican model as thus stated, fails[28] because it does not
leave room for the other forms of power and influence or for the
political activity also present in the normal life of every university.[29]
If it is true that authority is accorded to the possessor of relevant
knowledge, that information is an important source of influence,
and that the general governmental ideal is one of a consensus at-
tained through rational argument among the possessors of knowledge, it is also true that decisions are affected by bargaining,
obstinacy, pertinacity, selective briefing, threats of non-co-operation
and all the other 'skills' and weapons traditionally associated rather
with the politician and negotiator than with the scholar. Resort to
such methods is not to be explained, or possibly explained away,
merely in terms of individual deviance, institutional failure, or some
accidental conjunction of circumstances. Such politicking may, for
these reasons, play a larger part in some places and times than in
others, but every institution is faced with problems, the solutions to

[28] As does the more sociological 'collegial' model of university organization to
which it bears certain resemblances.

[29] Cf. the criticism of the 'collegial' model by a sociologist: it 'fails to deal
adequately with the problem of conflict'. J. VICTOR BALDRIDGE: Power and Conflict
in the University (Wiley, 1971) p. 14. See, too, his general critiques of this model,
and of the Weberian bureaucratic one, at pp. 8–15.

which cannot properly be decided merely by reference to learned authority, verifiable information, or rational argument. The archetypical problem is that of resource allocation[30], but comparable problems arise whenever choices must be made between alternatives that are not fully commensurable or between policies rooted in incompletely reconcilable perspectives and interests. It is clear, too, that inequalities of power and influence are inexplicable in terms of differences in competence only.

As the republican model recognizes, the issues on which decisions have to be taken are of different kinds. But they do not differ only with respect to the *type* of knowledge that is relevant. They may also be ranged on another kind of scale. At one end are issues to which experts can provide the one right answer, or about which only experts can seek agreement on what is probably the right answer (as with many academic issues). At the other end of this scale are issues which can reasonably be left to individual preference or some other more or less arbitrary device in which there can be no legitimate claim to superior expertise (as with the colour of an academic gown, or the range of beers to be sold in a university bar). But a large number of issues fall between these extremes; they demand decisions which can properly be taken only by reference both to evidence or special competence and to matters of evaluation or opinion, and in which the two elements are inseparably interwoven in varying proportions. Hence the need for judgement and for politics.[31]

In this respect, as in others, universities are like states and other kinds of institution. The distinctiveness of universities lies, not in the absence of politics, but in the extent to which university problems are bunched towards the 'expert' end of the scale and in the extent to which professional autonomy is accepted as a necessary condition for the highest levels of academic work. Together these mean, as the republican view insists, that special governmental rights and responsibilities should be accorded to the academic staff; but, as is recognized most clearly by the proponents of the populist and consensual views, there is no unchallengeable expert authority on every act of university government. It follows, too, that it is not only easier to govern a university if in fact there is a general consensus on the fundamental value-judgements about academic work; it is also appropriate to minimize overt conflict by accepting the claims of different groups to autonomy within their own areas of expertise. But, as the consensual model does not sufficiently acknowledge,

---

[30] See the discussion in Chapter VIII, above.
[31] See, again, our discussion in Chapter VIII, above.

there may be genuine conflict about the legitimate extent of that autonomy, and about the precise boundaries of each area of expertise (whether academic or other). Such conflict is not susceptible to solution merely by experts and scientific argument.

Of universities, even more than of other political units, it may be said with Professor Hanna Pitkin that 'political life is not merely the making of arbitrary choices, nor merely the resultant of bargaining between separate, private wants. It is always a combination (of them) and common deliberation about public policy, to which facts and rational arguments are relevant.' The sentences that follow immediately upon those just quoted are also relevant to any serious discussion of university government. Professor Pitkin continues: 'but this is precisely the kind of context in which representation as a substantial activity is relevant. For representation is not needed where we expect scientifically true answers, where no value commitments, no decisions, no judgements are involved. And representation is impossible . . . where a totally arbitrary choice is called for, where deliberation and reason are irrelevant.'[32]

There are those who would dispute the applicability of these definitions of politics and representation to university life. A few academics may find it difficult to accept that their own judgements do not always constitute 'scientifically true answers'. There is a slightly larger number of students, and a small minority of staff, who claim that deliberation is irrelevant to relations between them and 'the authorities', because the latter are imprisoned in a rulers' ideology. But most members of universities, we believe, would accept the broad account just given, if with varying emphases, as they would the suggestion that some university decisions, but not all, should properly be taken only by (or by representatives of) a particular group of competent professional scholars. Argument will, of course, continue as to the nature of the decisions and groups—as they do with respect to the role of non-professorial staff for example—but this does not affect the principle. In any case, the fact of representation has long been incorporated into university government.

By representative government we mean a system under which those who govern, and who thus are responsible for the interests of any particular institution, should not only be responsible for but also responsive to the governed. As Professor Pitkin has put it, 'representative government requires that there be machinery for the

[32] HANNA FENICHEL PITKIN: *The Concept of Representation* (University of California, 1967) p. 212. Our discussion of politics in universities in the previous paragraphs also owes much of its formulation to this book. See, generally, Professor Pitkin's discussion on pp. 209–240 of the work cited.

expression of the wishes of the represented, and that the government respond to those wishes unless there are good reasons to the contrary' in terms of the interests of the represented.[33] But, as we have seen, this relationship is appropriate only to the taking of decisions which are neither like the scientific solution to a purely technical problem nor like a mere expression of taste (in which no one has the right to choose for another).

Within such a framework it is clearly possible to accommodate both the authority of the expert, and the limitations to its relevance; the need for argument and the fact of conflict; the role of evidence and information, and the need for judgement. While accepting the necessity for responsiveness, this account also directs attention to the need for care in the delineation of constituencies and the dependence of the right to decide upon the nature of the issue in question. It also takes for granted that there is, if only for reasons of convenience and as a matter of fact, some division of labour within the political system; in this respect it might be said to encompass the oligarchic model. To conceive of university government as a form of representative government thus has the advantage of enabling one to take account of the persuasive elements in the various models we have discussed.

None of the main models that we have discussed, the democratic, the oligarchic, or the republican, may be rejected as a total travesty or irrelevance. Traces of each may even be detected in the government of almost any university. Of them we feel that the republican model comes nearest to providing a satisfactory and comprehensive picture of internal university government, if only because it puts proper emphasis on the characteristic source of authority in a university. Nevertheless, as the other models more clearly recognize, scholarship cannot be and is not the only source of authority. In many areas it may simply be irrelevant—academics may have no special competence in the choice of architects, may be utterly lacking in practical judgement on budgetary or organizational issues, or may be devoid of imagination outside their own special fields. (It may, of course, happen that particular academics possess these skills; but, if so, it is not necessarily *because* they are academics.) They, too, must therefore be made responsive through mechanisms which ensure the representation of other interests and perspectives. Furthermore, since we are talking about forms of government and the inescapability of political decision-making on issues which defy

[33] *Op. cit.*, pp. 232–3. See, too, 'the representative system must look after the public interest and be responsive to public opinion, except in so far as non-responsiveness can be justified in terms of the public interest' (p. 224).

the search for scientific certainty, it is important to ask whether a wide or narrow range of interests and perspectives are entitled to participate. Academics are thus not uniquely and superlatively equipped to govern universities; but, and this is the crucial point, on the central activities of a university and on the conditions necessary for them to flourish, none can reasonably claim to be better equipped. The supreme authority, provided that it is exercised in ways responsive to others, must therefore continue to rest with the academics for no one else seems sufficiently qualified to regulate the public affairs of scholars.

Appendix

THE UNIVERSITY OF WARWICK

In the spring of 1970 students of the University of Warwick (or more accurately, some of them) occupied part of the administrative offices in the University and subsequently publicized some of the items they found in the files, especially those kept in the Vice-Chancellor's office. As a result of this the governmental machinery of the University of Warwick became a matter of public complaint and dispute, some of which was published. If only because so very little on our subject has been published, we could not fail to make some comment on this affair, though without attempting any judgements, for we are provided with a rare opportunity to discuss some of our formulations in the context of published material. Our direct knowledge is small, and our comments are largely based on what has been published since the disturbances. We have referred, chiefly, to the account in *Warwick University Ltd.*[1], written at great speed during the course of the events, all of which we would hesitate to accept unreservedly, and to the somewhat circumscribed Part II of the *Report*, also written at speed, by Lord Radcliffe.[2] It may no doubt be that this evidence is highly subjective. Lord Radcliffe was unable to produce evidence 'sufficient to enable me to pass judgment' and fell back on 'some impressions I have gained'.[3] But in this study we have had—partly for the reasons which surprised Lord Radcliffe by their force—to regard perceptions of what happens as important, and, as we have seen, they are in a sense the basis of our whole study.

First, it is worth noting that the new University of Warwick, which had been open some five years at the time, had been promoted against the background of a desire for closer association between a university and 'industry'[4] by a body on which industrialists were prominent. At some of

---

[1] E. P. THOMPSON, ed.: *Warwick University Ltd.* (Penguin Books, 1970). Dr Thompson was at the time a Reader in history at the University.

[2] LORD RADCLIFFE: *Report as to procedures followed in the University with regard to receiving and retaining of information about political activities of the staff and of students*; and *Report* Part II (an enquiry into 'improper administration in the conduct of the University's affairs') University of Warwick, 1970. Some other papers were published locally.

[3] *Report, op. cit.*, paras. 3 and 6.

[4] THOMPSON: *op. cit.*, pp. 1 ff.

the CATS, this sort of situation led to attempts to introduce distinctly authoritarian constitutions, all of which, as we have seen in Chapter III were significantly defeated, sometimes after major disputes. At Warwick one might have expected to find an interest in industrial and commercial organization reflected in a management style of government. There seems never to have been any intention of that, and the Charter, on the criteria discussed in Chapter II[5], in fact provides one of the more 'liberal' and egalitarian of recent constitutions.[6] In this constitution staff were to have (after the Academic Advisory Committee disappeared) a minimum of over a third of the seats on Council while a lay majority was not mandatory.[7] Three of these staff seats were reserved for non-professorial staff. Whether such reservation is 'democratic' is a point of interest discussed in Chapter IV. Since most of the academic members are elected by Senate, which is itself unusually 'democratic', this point of interest is rather relevant to Warwick, and is further discussed below in this context. The powers of this Council, compared with those of the traditional universities, were very limited. For instance, Senate itself (rather than a joint committee) must be consulted on the appointment of the Vice-Chancellor[8], and Senate must recommend the appointment of all academic staff.[9] More novel, Senate has financial functions, most notably the initiative in determining conditions of appointment[10] for academic staff, and it must be consulted in 'any question of finance which directly affects the educational policy of the university'.[11] Viewed against the traditional powers of councils down to the early 1960s, even against the revised Liverpool Charter of 1961, the powers of the Warwick Council are, indeed, limited, and a wide field is formally opened to Senate.

[5] Especially pp. 33 and 42-3.
[6] An attempt to quantify 'liberality' presented to the BSA 1970 Conference suggested that of the 'new' universities only Lancaster's was more 'liberal' and that, of the other charters granted earlier than Warwick's, only the Durham and Newcastle Acts were more 'liberal'. R. B. EUSTACE: 'The origins of self-government of University Staffs', presented to the Annual Conference of the British Sociological Association, 1970.
[7] S. 15: (1). Disregarding the Chancellor. The size of the Council can be varied widely, so that it appears that, legally, thirteen out of a total of only nineteen members could be academic. Until its dissolution soon after the 1970 disturbances, however, the Academic Advisory Committee occupied two of the academic seats.
[8] S. 5: (3).
[9] S. 17: (12). Thus Senate has the initiative (as against Council) even in the appointment of professors, and Council a veto only. Council has power to 'review' the work of the university (5.11:5) but has none of the rest of the 'litany' of directive powers discussed in Chapter II. All academic powers are exercised only 'on the recommendation' of Senate (though Senate has, curiously, no rights in relation to statutes) (Ch. 19:2; S. 17:6). Thus Council has no power of academic initiative.
[10] S. 17: (11).
[11] S. 17: (20) and, as a Senate power, 'to advise the Council on the allocation of resources for teaching and research'. S. 19: (18).

The Senate itself was one of the first to be 'supreme' in academic matters.[12] In composition, Senate shares the general trend towards egalitarianism in that professors have no *ex officio* seats; though they have a reserved constituency, and are entitled to a majority of the seats in the 'faculty' constituencies.[13] This in practice seems to provide a professorial majority of about three-quarters, a result not in fact much more egalitarian than that achieved by less 'liberal' constitutions. The lack of an *ex officio* seat for professors is none the less a significant factor, which would become more so as the staff grew, and already in 1969–70 over a third of the professors were excluded. The Senate was interesting in another way. The Warwick Senate, of some thirty members, is not too large for effective deliberation. Being representational, and having financial functions, it clearly looks less like a traditional senate, and when the Statutes were being drafted was apparently seen as more like the Oxford Hebdomadal Council.

In addition, professors have seats on another innovation (which has no Oxford parallel), the Professorial Board, which is 'responsible for advising the Council, through the Senate, on matters affecting the appointment, duties and conditions of service of all members of the academic staff'.[14] This Board is not a 'second chamber' or 'upper house' like that at York, as we have seen.[15] In other words, though it may, like the Assembly (see below) elect to Senate and discuss any university business, it contributes little to formal professorial power.

Three other relevant points about the constitution may be made here. First, the constitution gave the Vice-Chancellor the near-standard responsibilities for 'efficiency and good order' discussed in Chapter VI, and the three powers commonly given to vice-chancellors by charters granted since 1945.[16] It was however one of the first to make him responsible not merely to Council, but also to Senate.[17] Second, there were no permanent heads of departments. There were in fact no departments, but there were Schools, which, governmentally, look pretty similar, and these had Chairmen elected by the members of the School.[18] Third, there was an Assembly of all academic and some other staff. This had the power to 'discuss and declare an opinion on any matter whatsoever relating to the university'; and to elect six members to Senate (in 1969–70 one-quarter of Senate). Warwick's was one of the first Assemblies, and remains one of the few with powers.[19] In addition to the legal requirements the constitution had

[12] S. 19.

[13] S. 18: (1).

[14] Ch. S. 14.

[15] See above, Chapter IV.

[16] S. 5: (4) and (5). The three powers are (a) to refuse admission to a candidate without giving a reason, (b) to suspend or exclude a student pending reference to Senate, and (c) to resign. It will be seen that inclusion of the power to refuse admittance had no obvious connection with any business or managerial orientation.

[17] S. 5: (4).

[18] S. 23: (2). Some of these arrangements have since been made more traditional.

[19] See discussion in Chapter IV, above.

been informally modified by 1969–70 by the inclusion on Council of two student 'observers'. These students received the papers, etc., but had no vote: they attended the meetings after October 1969.

None of this can be described as radical innovation, but it was clearly the intention (reflecting the Oxford provenance of some of the chief figures involved) first to give to staff a formal strength as against the laymen still unusual in the system; and second, within the staff, to give junior members a formal position as against the professors that is much less usual in the system.

In practice, however, the result was unusual in a different way. According to the account given by the university's critics there were three principal occasions on which the Council disagreed with a recommendation of the Senate. The first case, which was the proximate cause of the riot, concerned the allocation and control of a new student union and social building.[20] The convolutions of the story need not detain us; the essential point is that at the final stage Council seemed to override the recommendation of the Senate. On the second occasion Senate had made a recommendation that the chairmanship of the 'departments' should rotate and should be filled by election from and by the members of each department.[21] On the third occasion the Senate unanimously recommended the rejection of some of the recommendations of a report on the university administration submitted by a firm of management consultants.[22] Nevertheless Council decided to appoint a permanent full-time Assistant Vice-Chancellor, a type of officer only found elsewhere at Birmingham and at some ex-CATS, who would operate outside the bureaucracy headed by the Registrar. (It is suggested that the resignation of a number of senior university administrators, including that of the Registrar, was affected by this decision.)

Elsewhere in the book we have looked at some of the comments of the management consultants' report and disagreed with the picture there given of the actual and ideal government of a university.[23] Here one must note, in these cases at least, that the relationship between Council and Senate differed from the account we have given of the normal procedure. To some extent at least the understandings and conventions prevalent in other universities were not fully observed on these occasions. These instances of Council's treatment of Senate (which are not in principle disputed, though much of the detail could no doubt be presented in a very different light), are unusual and could in another university have led, metaphorically if not actually, to a riot indeed—but of staff. These cases are of interest primarily in so far as they indicate the fragility of the existing system.

It is not our intention to allocate responsibility for the Warwick state of affairs, even if we could, but rather to indicate some of the circumstances which seem to have existed at Warwick (but not usually elsewhere) which

[20] THOMPSON: op. cit., p. 49.
[21] Ibid., p. 62. The book refers here as elsewhere, no doubt for simplicity, to 'departments', though technically there were none.
[22] Ibid., p. 85.
[23] See Chapter VIII.

throw into relief some of the preconditions for the satisfactory working of the two-tier system of government within British universities.

Part of the story, it might be thought, is that the University of Warwick was a new university and had therefore had little time in which to establish the conventions and the habitual procedures which operate elsewhere. On the other hand this can only be part of the story. In others of the new universities, in which similar constitutional provisions exist governing the powers and relations of council and senate, no comparable crisis or friction has occurred. Nor has it occurred under the many charters granted after 1945, including those of Sussex and York, which give a much greater position both to council and to laymen. E. P. Thompson and his collaborators have suggested that a major explanation is that the university was from the beginning anxious to act as a service organization for industry and to this end co-opted on to the university Council a large number of businessmen, many of whom furthermore were leading executives of national firms (a kind of origin which we have suggested above is comparatively rare elsewhere).[24] Clearly there were senses in which this was so—there *were* company executives on Council, and they *did* facilitate the creation of posts with titles like 'Institute of Directors Chair of Business Studies'. Some of the documents published show that some at least of the business laymen saw the university as an administrative structure less radically different from a large industrial organization than would most academics. In the absence of the whole story, it is not possible to say how far the conclusions drawn from these facts are themselves valid. It is, however, reasonably clear that the business laymen had not been inducted into the university in quite the way that Sir Eric Ashby envisaged in the comments quoted above in Chapter V.[25] It appears too that the contacts, particularly the informal contacts, between the average member of the academic staff and the laymen had been less frequent and intimate even than is usual elsewhere.[26]

Perhaps it is worth remarking that in any university which was developing strongly on a side well represented among laymen on council, one could expect to find an undercurrent of suspicion of undue influence. We have heard something of the sort elsewhere in relation to the subjects of education and of law; and, in a different form, of social administration.

Nor may it be irrelevant that the Chairman of Council had held a chair at a major university, and one with an exceptionally authoritarian tradition

---

[24] See Chapter V.

[25] This is not perhaps of itself surprising. Sussex felt it advisable to invite the Principal of London to lecture to an audience that included prospective lay members of Council on 'The Governance of a University' (1958, unpublished; Sir Douglas Logan kindly let us see his notes for this lecture). But, five or so years later, fears of over-enthusiasm among laymen who had participated in the promotion of new universities had not been borne out by experience.

[26] According to Dr Thompson, the Vice-Chancellor invited to official lunches before Council meetings only the lay members and none of the academics. If true, this would be unusual. *Op. cit.*, p. 61.

of government.[27] We have some evidence that an ex-academic layman may feel less inhibited from close involvement, and even actual direction, than a 'pure' layman; this is an important comment on the functions of laymen in all similar positions, for instance in hospitals.

Lastly the administrative style may not have been one commonly found in the system. For instance, management consultants have not usually been allowed to comment on the general governmental processes of the university in the way that Tyzack's appear to have done (and in at least two cases where we have interviewed consultants they have been much dissatisfied with their brief in this respect).[28]

There remain the staff. We have seen that they had an unusually powerful position under the constitution, and that participation by juniors was unusually well provided for. But the Senate allowed itself to be overridden more than once in a short period and Council clearly played a more distinct part than in many universities where it has larger formal powers. There were some special circumstances, such as the very great turnover of Senate membership, due partly to the creation of new 'faculties', which must have made the formation of clear Senate attitudes difficult. Warwick was a new university, growing rapidly, and enjoying a rapidly increasing reputation in certain fields[29] and great success in attracting good students.[30] These are not conditions likely to dispose staff to be critical of, or indeed to concern themselves greatly with general government, though in fact at Warwick they played a sufficient part in the governmental process for the Tyzack Report to assert that 'the Committee system is in danger of running riot'.[31]

From our point of view, interest in the allegations of undue outside interference lies in the fact that they came from a university where staff powers and participation were unusually well provided for, so that they raise general questions about the conditions in which staff can best govern themselves.

We have also noted the importance to senatorial power of the 'entrenched position' of senators who acquire influence by long experience and immovability. At Warwick the term of Senate service is three years.[32] A representational senate must be more or less ephemeral in membership, and so the less able to entrench itself; this after all is one of the arguments

[27] Imperial College, London.

[28] The effect has of course been greatly to reduce the interest of their experience for the purposes of this study.

[29] For instance in French and in mathematics, which latter, in 1969–70, provided seven out of twenty-seven professors.

[30] Ivan Yates said that it had overtaken Sussex. *Observer*, September 26, 1970.

[31] *Report* quoted in THOMPSON: *op. cit.*, p. 139. However, Thompson himself says 'The academic staff, all of us, throughout the early history of the university were struck by a paralysis of the will . . . in any general exertion of control over their own institution' (p. 155).

[32] Of 'appointed' members, i.e. those elected in the various 'constituencies'. Only the Vice-Chancellor and Librarian had permanent seats (there could be others). S. 18: (2) and S. 7: (3).

advanced for representation, and, normally, radical critiques of university government aim at reducing entrenchment. But entrenchment is a defence against outsiders, as also against the vice-chancellor and the bureaucracy.

A perhaps even more significant question is raised where professors do not have *ex officio* seats, and are not permanent heads of departments.[33] What are the likely consequences of taking away the governmental and disciplinary resources (discussed in Chapter IV) that traditionally have converged to provide the professoriate with a predominant position? Here again, it may be that the defences against outside pressures will be weakened; and in particular, that the supply of persons who feel able to participate effectively will be affected. Warwick does not provide conclusive evidence, either way, because it was so new, but the task of a vigorous vice-chancellor who wishes to innovate is clearly easier when there are no professorial barons well placed to stand up to him. It is also questionable whether more junior, or less well-placed, staff can be in a position to exert that degree of authority which has meant that most vice-chancellors must see their role at least as much a chairman's as a manager's. There is some practical evidence that a more 'democratic' constitution may leave a freer field to the full-time administrator, who is faced with less concentrated power resources.

What seems to have underlain the difficulties at Warwick were, firstly, a disagreement between the laymen and the academics as to what constituted an academic decision and what constituted an administrative decision, and above all about the proper role of laymen and academics in the taking of so-called administrative decisions. Furthermore, whether from lack of time or opportunity or for other reasons, these two views had not been clearly argued out, nor had they been adequately accommodated into the standard consensus about the priority of academic considerations and of the judgement of academics upon academic issues. There are signs too that on some issues at least academic opinion was not only divided but was known to be divided and thus of necessity carried less weight. In other words the process we describe in Chapter V, of interpreting the academics and laymen to each other and of ensuring that any disputes within the university do not reach the point of apparent confrontation between lay and academic opinion, was not successfully carried out. We have noted this task of interpretation as part of the vice-chancellor's function[34], but whether the failure was here, or in the (possibly inherent) weakness of Senate, or in both, is another question.

No doubt, however, a vigorous and innovating vice-chancellor will appear to manipulate committees and take procedural advantages. In the chapter on the vice-chancellor's position we discuss how it is that an officer with virtually no governmental powers is none the less able to discharge

---

[33] At the time, there were no departments, in theory, but they were perceived (see above) and some professors seem to have perceived themselves as permanent heads. Lately (1972) departments have been formalized and headships turned into elective chairmanships.

[34] In Chapter VI.

the responsibilities which the charter imposes on him. He has the choice—
which more than a few vice-chancellors take—of being primarily a chairman, anxious only to extract the 'sense of the meeting', and to act upon it.
Or he can attempt to lead and exercise initiative; in short, to have a
policy. In our intensely traditional and conservative academic system, this
latter is not a straightforward task, partly because by definition it involves
attempting to discriminate between subjects and between persons. If some
of these are new, they will by definition have no place in the decision-
making process, and innovation and change have therefore to rely heavily
on the vice-chancellor. In the process, a good deal of abrasion occurs,
sometimes very heated, and we hope we have not given the impression that
we think otherwise. Part of the vice-chancellor's role is to see that the
abrasion does not ignite the structure. Sir Charles (now Lord) Morris has
said, 'Everything in British universities is against you: you try to do something and the university is against you: the press is against you. Then
there is a storm from everyone inside the university who says we ought
not have done this. But look what happens if you are willing to have a
storm and stand up in the storm. It will fade away.'[35] Part of the reason
why it will fade away is that if the vice-chancellor's policies are good, time
should show them to be so. We frequently met academics who remarked,
of some decision or other, 'I was strongly against the Vice-Chancellor, but
in the event I now think he was right'. If the policies are not good, if the
vice-chancellor's judgement is not borne out, then the vice-chancellor is in
a difficult position. Now at Warwick an unprecedented element was introduced: the student intervention denied to the Vice-Chancellor his
normal appeal to time. We have discussed elsewhere[36] the effects of student
impermanence on the time scale of decision-making; but here is another
time effect which in future may always have to be present in the vice-
chancellor's appreciation of his situation.

The troubles at Warwick have not been entirely typical of British
universities but are nevertheless of interest to students of university
government. They show what can happen when the conventions found
elsewhere are not fully established and, perhaps, indicate some possible
effects of the contemporary challenges to authority within the universities.

[35] Gulbenkian discussion, reported in the *Universities Quarterly*, 17: 2, March
1963, p. 141.
[36] In Chapter IX.

SELECT BIBLIOGRAPHY

This list covers most of the main works consulted that are directly relevant to a study of university government and staff autonomy. We have not included the extensive literature that is less directly relevant, or which is interesting precisely because it does not deal with these subjects. The list covers little of the literature on administration, in the narrow sense (e.g. 'PBBS'); or of that on the student movement (comparatively little of which, however, is relevant to this study). The historical section represents a very brief, and even more arbitrary, selection. A very full bibliography, with some annotation, *The History of British Universities 1800–1969* (excluding Oxbridge) by Harold Silver and S. John Teague (Society for Research in Higher Education, 1970) would have saved us much labour had it been available earlier. No references to the English-speaking universities overseas are given, because the great size of the documentation is disproportionate to the use made of it here, though the history of universities in the Empire is in fact often very relevant to an estimate of contemporary 'best practice' at home.

In one or two cases, we have noted reviews where they add to the work criticised, or have included some of our working notes on contents. Names of publishers of the older works are not always given.

Abbreviations

BUA	= *British Universities Annual*	*THES*	= *Times Higher Education Supplement*
HER	= *Higher Education Review*	*UQ*	= *Universities Quarterly*

General

ROBERT AITKEN (Sir): *Administration of a University* (London, 1966). Reviews: C. F. Carter (Vice-Chancellor, Lancaster) 'An intolerable degree of complication?' (*UQ* 21: 2, 1967, p. 257). *BUA*, 1967.

W. S. ANGUS: 'The Growth of the University in the last fifteen years' (*Aberdeen University Review*, Vol. XLII, 2 No. 138, Autumn 1967). Discussion of the formation of the building and development plans.

W. S. ANGUS: Regarding the Registrar's Office (unpublished, 1969).

NOEL ANNAN (Lord): 'The Universities' (*Encounter*, April 1963).

ERIC ASHBY (Sir): *Masters and Scholars* (OUP, 1970) XII—discussion of university government.

ERIC ASHBY (Sir): 'Decision-making in the academic World' (*Sociological Review*, Monograph No. 7, P. Halmos (ed.) (Keele 1963).

ERIC ASHBY (Sir): 'No cosy Consensus' (Review of Duff-Berdahl Report on university government in Canada) (*UQ* 21: 1, 1966, p. 110). Comments on British University Government.

ERIC ASHBY (Sir) and A. K. STOUT: 'Self-government in modern British Universities' (*Science and Freedom*, No. 7, 1956).

ERIC ASHBY (Sir) '. . . and Scholars' (LSE, 1964). Need to consult students— their responsibility and reasonableness.

G. E. AYLMER: 'University Government—But by whom?' (*UQ* 13.1, 1958, p. 45). Role of academic staff in administration—need for participation by junior staff.

D. A. BELL: 'A Commission on University Government' (AUT *Bulletin* No. 31, March 1970).

E. BOYLE (Lord): 'Talking to Simon Hoggart' (*New Academic*, May 1971).

E. BOYLE (Lord): Statement to Court of University of Leeds, 1970 (*Annual Report*, Leeds 1971). Position of vice-chancellor.

J. W. BRIDGE: 'Keeping Peace in the Universities. The Role of the Visitor' (*Law Quarterly Review*, Vol. 86, 1970).

ASA BRIGGS: 'The "Distinction" of Sussex' (*THES*, December 31, 1971). Effects of internal decision-making: the financial pressures from outside.

S. CAINE (Sir): *British Universities. Purpose and Prospect* (Bodley Head, 1969). Chapter 6, student participation; Chapter 7, 'The Government of Universities'.

B. G. CAMPBELL: 'The Constitution of Oxford' in M. L. Shattock (ed.), below.

A. M. CARR-SAUNDERS: *English Universities Today* (LSE, 1960).

RENE CASSIN: 'Principle of Independence in University Teaching and of Academic Freedom' (*Communication* 56, January 1968).

DAVID CAUTE: 'Crisis in All Souls' (*Encounter*, March 1966).

D. G. CHRISTOPHERSON: in *The expanding University*, Niblett (ed.) (below) —size and government of Durham.

P. COLLISON: 'University Chancellors, Vice-Chancellors and College Principals: A social Profile' (*Sociology*, Vol 3,1, January 1969).

F. M. CORNFORD: *Microcosmographica Academica*, Being a Guide for the young academic Politician (Bowes and Bowes, 4th ed., 1949).

J. DRÈZE and J. DEBELLE: '*Conceptions de L'Université*' (Institut Administration-Université, Fondation Industrie-Université, Bruxelles 1967, in series on 'L'Enseignement universitaire et la Preparation des futurs Dirigeants'). An account of five ideas of a university. 1. Newman, 2. Jaspers, 3. Whitehead, 4. Napoleon, 5. Soviet Russia. S. 4 modern French system of university government. S. 5 modern Russian system of university government.

AUSTIN DUNCAN-JONES: 'Thoughts on the Government of modern Universities' (*UQ* IX, 1954–5, p. 245).

'JAMES DUNDONALD' (pseud.): *Letters to a Vice-Chancellor* (Edward Arnold, 1962).

'JAMES DUNDONALD' (pseud.): 'Advice to an Alderman' in J. Lawlor (ed.): *The new University* (Routledge and Kegan Paul, 1968).

PHILIP EDWARDS: 'Lines and Veins' (*Essex University Review* No. 1, 1968). A plea for departments.

ROWLAND EUSTACE: 'The Layman in University Government' (*Essex University Review*, No. 2, 1968).

ROWLAND EUSTACE: 'The Government of Scholars' in D. Martin (ed.): *Anarchy and Culture* (Routledge and Kegan Paul, 1969).

ROWLAND EUSTACE: 'Some administrative Effects of Expansion' in M. L. Shattock (ed.), below.

J. FIELDEN: *Analytical Planning and improved Resource Allocation in British Universities* (University of London, 1969). American PPBS (planning, programming and budgeting system) and its potential in Great Britain.

M. P. FOGARTY: 'A Society of equal Colleagues' (*BUA*, 1963).

GEORGES GUSDORF: *L'Université en Question* (Payot, 1964).

A. H. HALSEY and M. TROW: *The British Academics* (Faber, 1971). Reviews: J. Ben-David, *Minerva* X: 1, January 1972. John Dutton, *HER* 4: 1, Autumn 1971.

H. HETHERINGTON (Sir): *The British university System* (Aberdeen University Studies No. 133, 1954).

M. HOOKHAM: 'Enquiry into the structural Organisation of Universities, 1967' (*Communication* (IAUPL) 59, October 1968).

E. W. HUGHES: *The Internal Government of Universities* (Association of University Teachers (J1379), 1964). Description of and reasons for 1963 statutes of University of Newcastle.

EDMUND IONS: 'Threats to academic Freedom in Britain' (*Critical Quarterly*, XII, 2, 1970).

D. G. JAMES: 'Reflections of a lapsed Professor' (*UQ* 7, 1953, p. 247).

CARL JASPERS: *The Idea of a University* (Peter Owen, 1965). Chapter 9—the university and the State, including functions and qualifications of a vice-chancellor. Academic self-government of limited value.

MALCOLM KNOX (Sir): Address to General Council of St Andrews, June 26, 1966.

MAURICE KOGAN: 'Freedom and Participation in the Universities' (*THES*, May 12, 1972). (With M. POPE) 'Dynamics of Polytechnic Government' (*THES*, May 19, 1972).

A. D. LINDSAY et al.: *The Government of Oxford* (Oxford, 1931). Chapter II —constitutional outline in other universities.

R. MCCAIG: 'Institutional Changes in British Universities—Reactions to Social Pressures' (*The Australian University*, 5: 1, April 1967). Developments in university government and administration.

D. G. MACRAE: 'The departmental Zoo' (*New Society*, November 13, 1969).

SELECT BIBLIOGRAPHY 245

W. J. M. MACKENZIE: 'The Professor as Administrator' (*UQ* 7, 1953, p. 333).

PETER MANN: '1965-6: The academic Year in retrospect' (*BUA*, 1966).

P. MEREDITH: 'The departmental Reality' (*UQ* 17, 1962, p. 54).

GRAEME C. MOODIE: *The Universities: A Royal Commission?* (The Fabian Society, 1959).

CHARLES MORRIS (Sir): 'Organization and Control of Universities in the UK' (*Yearbook of Education*, 1959).

JAMES MOUNTFORD (Sir): *British Universities* (Oxford, 1966).

W. R. NIBLET (ed.): *The Expanding University* (Faber, 1962). 6. 'Departmentalism and Community', discussion led by Brian Gowonlock.

TREVOR NOBLE and B. PYM: 'Collegial Authority and the receding Locus of Power' (*British Journal of Sociology*, XXI: 4, December, 1970).

JOSE ORTEGA Y GASSET: *Mission of the University* (Routledge and Kegan Paul, 1946).

W. B. PALMER: 'University Government and Organisation' (*BUA*, 1966).

E. G. PHILIPS: 'Do we need two Types of Professor?' (*UQ*, 1952-3, p. 261). Need for administrative professors to make possible intra-department democracy.

G. PORTER: interviewed by Basil Peters (*New University*, January 1968).

JOHN PRATT: 'Who governs the Governors?' (*HER* 2.3, Summer 1970). Comment on DES Circular 7/70 and on progress in democratising university government.

RADCLIFFE (Lord): *University of Warwick*. Pt. I *Report as to Procedures followed in the University* (University of Warwick, April 1970). Pt. II *On Propriety of Administration* (University of Warwick, May 1970).

H. E. S. RHETT: *Creating University Communities. Four new Universities in England* (Cornell University Ph.D. thesis, unpublished, 1969).

A. P. ROWE: 'Redbrick and Whitewash' (*UQ*, 1959-60, p. 247).

A. P. ROWE: 'Freedom and Efficiency' (*Science and Freedom*, No. 16, 1964). Role and powers of academic staff in administration, with discussion by Bruce Williams and Percy Smith. No. 17—further discussion.

M. L. SHATTOCK: 'A changing Pattern of University Administration' (*UQ* 24: 3, 1970, p. 310).

M. L. SHATTOCK (ed.): *University Administration in a period of Expansion* (British Council course on University Administration 1970, British Council, n.d.). The best available collection of essays on university administration generally. Those relating more directly to government are listed individually.

ALBERT E. SLOMAN: *A University in the Making* (BBC, 1964).

NEIL SPURWAY: *Authority in Higher Education* (SCM Press 1968).

R. SZRETER: 'An academic Patriciate—Vice-Chancellors 1966-7' (*UQ* 23:1, 1968, p. 17).

JAMES A. TAYLOR: 'The Idea of a federal University' (*BUA*, 1964).

E. P. THOMPSON (ed.): *Warwick University Ltd.* (Penguin, 1970).

'BRUCE TRUSCOT' (Edgar Alison Peers): *Redbrick University* (Penguin, 1951).

DOUGLAS VEALE (Sir): 'University Administration' (*Fortnightly*, 1951, Vol. 170).

BARBARA WOOTTON: 'Reflections on resigning a Professorship' (*UQ*, 1952, p. 36).

COMMITTEE ON HIGHER EDUCATION: *Report* ('Robbins Report') (HMSO Cmnd 2154, 1963).

DEPARTMENT OF EDUCATION AND SCIENCE: Study Group on the Government of Colleges of Education *Report* ('Weaver Report') (HMSO, 1966).

COMMITTEE OF PUBLIC ACCOUNTS. SESSION 1966–7: 'Parliament and Control of University Expenditure', *Special Report* (No. 290, HMSO, 1967).

ASSOCIATION OF UNIVERSITY TEACHERS: 'Representation of teaching Staff on University Governing Bodies' (*Universities Review*, Vol. 16:1, 1942). *University Government and Organisation* (AUT, 1965).

INTERNATIONAL ASSOCIATION OF UNIVERSITIES: University Autonomy (IAU papers 7, Paris, 1965). 'University Autonomy' (IAU *Bulletin*, supplement to Vol. XIII, No. 4, 1965). 'The Administration of Universities' (IAU papers 8, Paris, 1967).

ASSOCIATION OF UNIVERSITIES OF THE COMMONWEALTH: 'Who should determine University Policy?' (Eighth quinquennial Conference *Proceedings*, AUC, 1959). 'The Place of the Layman in University Government' (Ninth quinquennial Conference *Proceedings*, AUC, 1964).

HOME UNIVERSITIES CONFERENCES: 1958 'The Size of Universities and University Departments, and the Need for new University Institutions'. 1959 'Administrative Problems in expanding Universities' (Association of Universities of the Commonwealth).

UNIVERSITIES QUARTERLY: 'University Administration: an Enquiry by *Universities Quarterly*' (1949, p. 796). 'The academic Organisation of Studies' 19.3 (1965, p. 150).

BIRKBECK COLLEGE: *The Future of Birkbeck College* ('Ashby Report') (London, 1967).

UNIVERSITY OF BIRMINGHAM: *Consultative Document prepared by the Review Body appointed by the Council of the University* (Birmingham, 1972). *Report of the Review Body* (Birmingham, 1972).

UNIVERSITY OF MANCHESTER: Charter Revision Committee *Interim Report* (Manchester, 1965). *Final Report.*

UNIVERSITY OF LIVERPOOL: Petition to Privy Council for 1961 Charter and Statutes.

LONDON SCHOOL OF ECONOMICS AND POLITICAL SCIENCE: *Report* of Machinery of Government Committee. Minority *Report* by David Adelstein and Dick Atkinson (LSE Mimeo, 1968).

Historical References

ERIC ASHBY (Sir) and MARY ANDERSON: *Universities: British, Indian, African,* A study in the Ecology of Higher Education (Weidenfeld and Nicholson, 1966).

ERIC ASHBY (Sir): 'The academic Profession' (*Minerva*, VIII:1, January 1970).

ERNEST BARKER (Sir): *British Universities* (Longmans, Green, 1946).

H. H. BELLOT: *University College London* (1929).

E. M. BETTENSON: *The University of Newcastle-on-Tyne 1834–1971* (Newcastle-on-Tyne, 1971).

W. H. BEVERIDGE (Lord): *The London School of Economics and its Problems 1919–37* (George Allen and Unwin, 1960).

W. H. BEVERIDGE (Lord): *The working Constitution and Practice of the LSE and PS* (printed privately, 1937).

E. G. W. BILL: *University Reform in Nineteenth Century Oxford* (Oxford, 1973).

SIDNEY CAINE (Sir): *The History of the Foundation of LSE and PS* (LSE, 1963).

ARTHUR W. CHAPMAN: *The Story of a modern University: a History of the University of Sheffield* (Oxford, 1955).

H. B. CHARLTON: *Portrait of a University* (Manchester, 1951).

W. M. CHILDS: *Making a University* (1933). History of Reading University: The Vice-Chancellor's Work.

B. COTTLE and J. W. SHERBORNE: *The Life of a University* (Bristol, revised edn., 1959).

W. S. COX: *Charter, etc., of the Queen's College, Birmingham* (1873).

G. N. CURZON (Lord): *Principles and Methods of University Reform* (Oxford, 1909).

GEORGE ELDER DAVIE: *The democratic Intellect* (Edinburgh, 1961).

W. H. DRAPER: *Sir Nathan Bodington* (1912).

PERCY DUNSHEATH and MARGARET MILLER: *Convocation in the University of London* (Athlone Press, 1958).

E. L. ELLIS: *The University College at Aberystwyth 1872–1972* (Wales, 1972).

ROWLAND EUSTACE: 'The Origins of Self-government of University Staffs' (Paper to British Sociology Association Annual Conference 1970).

EMERYS D. EVANS: *The University of Wales* (Wales 1953).

G. C. FABER: *Jowett* (Faber, 1957).

STRICKLAND GIBSON: *Statuta Antiqua Universitas Oxoniensis* (Oxford, 1931).

M. B. HACKETT: *The Original Statutes of Cambridge University* (Cambridge, 1970).

F. J. C. HEARNSHAW: *A centenary History of King's College London* (Harrap, 1928).

H. HETHERINGTON (Sir): *The University College at Exeter* (Exeter, 1963).

THOMAS LLOYD HUMBERSTONE: *University Reform in London* (George Allen and Unwin, 1926).

C. ILLINGWORTH (Sir): *University Statesman*. The Story of Sir Hector Hetherington, G.B.E. (G. Outram, 1971).

MABEL IRVINE: *The Avenue of Years*. Life of Sir J. Irvine (Blackwood, 1970).

LAW (Chancellor of Lichfield): *Materials for a brief History of the Advance and Decline of the Queen's College Birmingham* (1869).

G. LEFF: *Paris and Oxford Universities in the thirteenth and fourteenth Centuries* (John Wiley, New York, 1968).

JOHN D. MACKIE: *The University of Glasgow 1451–1951* (Jackson and Son and Co., 1954).

JAMES MOUNTFORD (Sir): *Keele. An historical Critique* (Routledge and Kegan Paul, 1972).

A. T. PATTERSON: *The University of Southampton 1862–1962* (Southampton, 1962).

M. PATTISON: 'Review of the Situation' in *Essays on the Endowment of Research* (1876).

M. PATTISON: *Suggestions on academical Organisation* (*with especial Reference to Oxford*) (1868).

G. PEACOCK: *Observations on the Statutes* (of Cambridge) (1841).

PERCY OF NEWCASTLE (Lord): *Some Memoirs* (Eyre and Spottiswoode, 1958). Chapter XII 'A University'.

R. S. RAIT: *The Universities Commission 1889–97. A Review.* (Aberdeen, 1898).

R. S. RAIT: *The Universities of Aberdeen* (Aberdeen, 1895).

HASTINGS RASHDALL: *The Universities of Europe in the Middle Ages* (a new edition, F. M. Powicke and A. B. Emden (eds.) (Oxford, 1936, 3 vols.).

W. RHYS ROBERTS (ed.): *British Universities* (Manchester, 1892). 'Notes and summaries contributed to the Welsh University discussion by members of the Senate of the University College of North Wales'.

DRUSILLA SCOTT (Lady): *A. D. Lindsay* (Blackwell, 1971).

J. R. SEELEY: *A Midland University.* Address to the Midland Institute, 1887.

GOLDWIN SMITH: *The Re-organisation of the University of Oxford* (1868). The case for government reform largely based on mediaeval precedent.

E. J. SOMERSET: *The Birth of a British University. A passage in the life of E. A. Sonnenschein* (1934).

JAMES STUART: *University Extension* (1871).

A. I. TILLYARD: *A History of University Reform from 1800 to the present Time* (Cambridge, 1913).

M. J. TUKE: *History of Bedford College for Women 1849–1937* (Oxford, 1939).

E. W. VINCENT and P. HINTON: *The University of Birmingham* (Birmingham, 1947).

WILFRED WARD: *Life of John Henry, Cardinal Newman* (1912).

S. WEBB: 'London University: A Policy and a Forecast' (*Nineteenth Century*, 1902). Discussion of structure of government.

C. E. WHITING: *The University of Durham* (The Sheldon Press, 1932).

A. C. WOOD: *History of University College Nottingham* (Oxford, 1953).

UNIVERSITY OF DURHAM: *Statute enacted by the Dean and Chapter with the consent of the Bishop for the University established in connection with the Cathedral Church of Durham. With Regulations passed under its authority by the Senate and Convocation of the University* (1836).

UNIVERSITY OF LONDON: Papers in the University Archive in the University of London Library.

ASSOCIATION OF UNIVERSITY TEACHERS: *Universities Review*, Vol. 16, No. 1, 1942.

UNIVERSITY GRANTS COMMITTEE: *Report 1923-4* (HMSO, 1925).

Student Participation

E. ASHBY and M. ANDERSON: *The Rise of the Student Estate in Britain* (MacMillan, 1970). Review: E. Shils (*Minerva*, October 1970). Answer to review by E. A. and M. A. (*Minerva*, IX:3, July 1971). Comment by J. Drever (*Minerva*, July 1971).

D. ADELSTEIN (ed.): *Teach Yourself Student Power* (Mimeo Radical Students' Alliance, 1968).

W. BELL: 'Student Participation in the Government of the University of Glasgow' in M. L. Shattock (ed.), above.

COLIN CROUCH: *The Student Revolt* (Bodley Head, 1970).

E. J. DEARNALEY: 'Elephants or Marmosets?' (*Solon*, 1963, 6 19–22).

ANN B. DENIS: *The Changing Role of Students in Relation to the Government of British Universities 1935-68* (University of London Ph.D. Thesis (Econ.), 1969).

ROWLAND EUSTACE: 'Student Participation in University Government' in M. L. Shattock (ed.), above.

ANTONY FLEW: 'Participation and Principles in Higher Education.' (*Solon* 1.1, October 1969). The principles of student participation; the argument against it on professional self-government grounds.

JAMES OF RUSHOLME (Lord): *Authority in Education* (mimeo, unpublished, 1968).

GRAEME C. MOODIE: 'Student Dissent in Britain and America' (unpublished MS. of talk on Zurich Radio, 1967).

BENEDICT NIGHTINGALE: 'The Student Schism' (*New Society*, February 16, 1967).

F. PARKIN: 'A Student Revolution?' (*New Society*, March 23, 1967).

AUT/NUS: *The Student in a College Community* (AUT, 1968).

AUT: 'The Student in University Government'. Policy Statement (*Bulletin*, March 1968).

COMMITTEE OF VICE-CHANCELLORS AND PRINCIPALS. Joint Statement of Vice-Chancellors and Principals Committee and NUS on Student Participation in Government. Reprinted in *Minerva*, Vol. 1, VII, Autumn 1968.

NATIONAL UNION OF STUDENTS: *Student Participation in College Government* (NUS, 1966).

UNIVERSITY OF OXFORD: *Report of the Committee on Relations with Junior Members* ('Hart Report') (Supplement No. 7 to *University Gazette*, May 1969).

UNIVERSITY OF YORK: *The Role of Students in University Government* (1968). (Reprinted as Evidence to *Report* of Select Committee on Education and Science below.)

SELECT COMMITTEE ON EDUCATION AND SCIENCE: Session 1968-9. *Student Relations, Report and Evidence*, 7 vols. Sessional paper 449 of 1969.

INDEX

Academic freedom 61
Academic staff in university government 38-43, 232-3
see also non-professorial staff *and* Professors
Administration 57, 154-6
Aitken, Sir Robert 98, 123
Annan, Noel (Lord) 143
Appointments 63, 103-6, 118, 131, 138-9
Ashby, Sir Eric (now Lord) 7, 23, 99, 114-15, 128, 156, 177
Assemblies of staff 41, 55
Association of University Teachers (AUT) 70, 207, 208, 209, 218
Aston, University of 32, 35, 36, 55, 56, 217
Atkinson Case, the 125

Bagehot, W. 163-4
Barzun, J. 161
Bath, University of 32, 35, 42
Belfast, *see* Queen's University
Birmingham, University of 29, 31, 34, 35, 36, 38, 39, 43, 52, 54, 57, 67, 74, 81, 83, 96, 98-9, 123-5, 127, 128, 150, 200, 214
Boards of Study 42, 54, 72-5
Bologna, University of 26
Boyle, Lord 132, 133
Bradford, University of 32, 35, 42, 43, 57, 72, 129, 188
Briggs, Asa 128, 187
Bristol, University of 29, 31, 39, 117, 226
Brittan, S. 174-5
Brunel, University of 32, 72, 85, 127, 159
Bryce, James 29

Bureaucracy 21, 137-8, 154-69, 190, 205-6
Butterfield, Sir H. 118

Caine, Sir S. 128
Cambridge, University of 26-7, 29, 31, 45, 46, 48-9, 56, 57, 70-1, 126, 132, Trinity College 46
Carr-Saunders, Sir A. 13
Carter, Charles 81-2, 128, 189, 190, 226
Caute, David 12-13
Chairman
  of Buildings Committee 93-4, 108
  of Council 92-3, 101
  of Finance Committee 93-4, 111-12
Chairmanship as power-source 132-5
Chamberlain, Joseph 31
Chancellor, the 57, 91-2, 95
Charters, University 20-1, 32-3, 44, 56
City University 32
Coleraine, University of 32, 43
College system 48-9, 73
Colleges of Advanced Technology (CATs) 32, 43, 143, *and see under separate names*
Commission of Inquiry into the University of Oxford (Franks) 48, 97, 130, 162-3, 221, 222
Committee
  of Inquiry into the Government of the University of London (Murray) 48
  on Higher Education (Robbins) 45 102, 127, 149, 183
  of Public Accounts 119, 122, 159
  of Vice-Chancellors and Principals 49, 119, 134-5, 149, 159, 199

IN THE GULF

By Arthur H. Blair, Colonel U.S. Army (Ret)

TEXAS A&M UNIVERSITY PRESS

The paper used in this book meets the minimum requirements
of the American National Standard for Permanence
of Paper for Printed Library Materials, Z39.48-1984.
Binding materials have been chosen for durability. ∞

LIBRARY OF CONGRESS CATALOGING-IN-PUBLICATION DATA
Blair, Arthur H., 1927–
    At war in the Gulf: a chronology / by Arthur H. Blair. — 1st
ed.
        p.   cm.
    ISBN 0-89096-507-2
    1. Persian Gulf War, 1991—Chronology.   2. Iraq-Kuwait
Crisis, 1990–1991—Chronology.   I. Title.
DS79.72.B58   1992
956.704'3'0202—dc20   91-33371
                                                                      CIP

To the best-led, best-equipped, best-trained,
and best-motivated men and women
this nation ever put into the field of battle

Contents

Illustrations

Acknowledgments

For material assistance in preparing this narrative of Desert Shield and Desert Storm, I am indebted to the U.S. Army War College, particularly the Strategic Studies Institute Special Report *Desert Shield and Desert Storm: A Chronology and Troop List For the 1990–1991 Persian Gulf Crisis* by Lt. Col. Joseph P. Englehart, USA; to the Department of the Air Force for its white paper "Air Force Performance in Desert Storm, April 1991"; to the Department of Defense Still Media Records Center for photographic support; and to the Department of the Army for additional data, photographs, and the maps of the Kuwait Theater of Operations reproduced from *Army Focus: June 1991.*

At War in the Gulf

1 Prologue

At 0800 hours 28 February 1991, the Coalition forces halted offensive operations against the few Iraqi forces that remained intact after their invasion of Kuwait at 0200 hours 2 August 1990. After a devastating Coalition air campaign which began at 0230 hours 17 January 1991, the ground operations of Desert Storm commenced at 0400 hours 24 February. The total defeat of Iraq by the United Nations–sponsored Coalition in such a few days and with so few allied casualties seemed almost incredible. Many of the weapons used by the Coalition had never been tested in combat, yet proved to be extremely effective. Some of the members of the Coalition forces had been virtually antagonists on the eve of the fighting but fought together in what became a common cause, and a previously ineffective world body, the United Nations (UN), proved that it could function cohesively against aggression.

If the speed of the military victory is almost unbelievable, the success of Pres. George Bush and his administration in forging the Coalition arrayed against Iraq is equally remarkable considering the complex social, political, and economic factors that affect the nations of the Middle East.

If there is one factor that unites the Arab countries of the region, it is an implacable hatred of the nation of Israel. Since that nation was created after World War II, it has enjoyed the support of the United States, and it has lived in a virtual state of war against all the Arab countries in the area. Thanks to Pres. Jimmy Carter's Camp David Accords, Egypt has managed to make some sort of peace with Israel, but even this is a fragile one. Palestinians, who see themselves as victims of Israeli aggression, are scattered in almost all the other nations of the Middle East and, owing allegiance less to the leaders of the nations in which they live than to the cause of a Palestinian state, help create an unstable situation for their host governments. Armed opposition against Israel, through such groups as the Palestine Liberation Organization (PLO), has been a constant. Moreover Iraqi president Saddam Hussein provided a safe haven for some of the more fanatical terrorist groups, and Syrian president Hafez al-Assad has also been viewed by the United States as having supported worldwide terrorism.

Saddam Hussein attempted both before and after the invasion of Kuwait to focus world attention on this Arab-Israeli conflict to pave the way for his planned annexation of Kuwait and, after the invasion, to break apart the Coalition by comparing Israel's seizure of the West Bank and the Golan Heights with the Iraqi annexation of Kuwait. In addition, during the air war he fired SCUD ground-to-ground missiles into Israel in an attempt to goad Israel into entering the war, an act which would have seriously strained the Coalition. Israel, however, abstained from any military actions against Iraq, keeping the Arab-Israeli factor from becoming a disruptive element.

In a larger context, the Arab-Israeli conflict is but one part of what can be called Pan-Arab Nationalism. When the victorious Allies of the First World War carved up the old Ottoman Empire and drew the boundaries of the nations of the Middle East, they did so with an eye more to their own national interests than to those of the peoples of the region. This arbitrary division gave little regard to either ethnic or religious groupings in the region which might have created countries of peoples with common interests and aspirations. Instead, Kurds found themselves scattered among what became Iran, the Soviet Union, Turkey, Syria, and Iraq. Similarly, the national boundaries that were drawn paid little regard to the two major sects of the Muslim religion, the Shiites and the Sunnis, who found themselves scattered across and mixed within many different nations. As a result, the common bond of the people was less to nations than to the movement called Pan-Arab Nationalism, a force which was temporarily subordinated when Iraq invaded Kuwait but which is still a major factor in the postwar region.

Pan-Arab Nationalism holds that Arabs are one people, some 170 million strong, who share a common cultural heritage, language, religion, and a history of greatness in learning and military prowess. Pan-Arabs among these millions of Arabs see themselves as having been artificially divided into twenty-one states by Western colonial powers after World War I and hence believe that the current borders have no real relevance. Furthermore, these existing national boundaries have led to an inequitable distribution of wealth. According to the Pan-Arab view, some national leaders, such as those in Saudi Arabia, the United Arab Emirates, and Kuwait, have cooperated with the West to exploit the Arab people and to prevent their banding together to reclaim their rightful place in world affairs. These Arab sheiks pump as much oil as the West desires, depriving the Arab peoples of what is rightfully theirs. As a result, a fortunate few are relatively wealthy while others live in poverty. The per capita income of the United Arab Emirates is $16,000 and that of Kuwait and Saudi Arabia is $13,000. In contrast, Egypt's per capita income is $625, Jordan's $1,750, Syria's $1,650, and Iraq's $1,950.

The Pan-Arab solution has several elements. First is a strong Arab leader who will unite all Arabs and drive out foreign influence—including the Israelis. Second is the use of oil revenues for the benefit of all Arabs in order to restore greatness to the Arab nation by improving its military strength, its cultural achievements, and its educational, scientific, and cultural base. To reach this goal, Pan-Arab Nationalism calls for higher oil prices—to increase the revenue available to the Arab people—and the use of oil as a political weapon—refusing to sell oil at any price to nations that will not cooperate with these goals.

Prior to Desert Storm, Pres. Saddam Hussein was portrayed by some as the leading candidate for the role of Arab leader, since he possessed the largest armed force in the region. Others viewed Pres. Hafez al-Assad of Syria and Pres. Hosni Mubarek of Egypt as equally qualified. Just as Saddam Hussein is the leader of the Iraqi Baath Party, which embraces the political goals of Pan-Arab Nationalism, so Hafez al-Assad is the head of the Syrian Baath Party. Hafez al-Assad's willingness to join the Coalition opposed to Iraq was not, therefore, based upon philosophical differences. Rather, it seems to have been the result of personal jealousy over Pan-Arab leadership and resentment over past slights. In 1970, for example, Syrian troops had entered Jordan to assist the PLO in fighting Jordan's King Hussein. Despite Hafez al-Assad's plea to Saddam Hussein to use his 12,000 troops in Jordan to assist the Syrian forces, the president had refused, thus laying part of the groundwork for Syria's opposition to the Iraqi invasion of Kuwait decades later.

Pres. Hosni Mubarek of Egypt also saw himself as the natural Pan-Arab leader. A direct philosophical descendant of Gamel Abdul Nasser, who led Egypt against the British, French, and Israelis in the Suez Canal War in 1956, Mubarek could lay claim to Arab leadership through this opposition to the French and British, the colonial powers who arbitrarily divided the region. Moreover, Egypt, with its population of some 55 million is the largest Arab nation in the world.

Despite this deep-seated rivalry for leadership in the Arab world, a Coalition made up of Western (and hence detested colonial powers) and Arab nations joined together to defeat another Arab nation. Napoleon once said that if he must fight, he hoped it would be against a coalition, but in this case Lord Palmerston's dictum seems to have been more to the point: nations have no permanent friends, only permanent interests.

Access to oil at a reasonable price also played an important role in forging this wartime Coalition. Two-thirds of the world's proven oil reserves are found in the Persian Gulf region. The United States imports roughly 30 percent of the oil it consumes from the area, and Western Europe imports 70 percent from there. While the Organization of the Petroleum Exporting Countries (OPEC) plays an important role in setting oil production levels and prices, to allow any one nation to control these vast oil reserves could be intolerable both to the other OPEC nations and to the industrialized nations of the world, whose lifeblood is petroleum. The United States, for instance, uses 65 percent of its petroleum for transportation, 24 percent for industrial products, 7 percent for heating, and 4 percent for the generation of electricity. While Americans may be rightly accused of wasting oil in their transportation uses, their choices of where to live and work have been largely predicated upon inexpensive transportation. These patterns cannot be changed quickly, and the development of alternate sources of energy will take decades. Plentiful and inexpensive oil is, in the meantime, essential.

Before Desert Storm, Iraq possessed about 10 percent of these proven reserves and Kuwait another 8 percent. Iraq's annexation of Kuwait meant that almost one-fifth of these reserves were controlled by Saddam Hussein, too large a portion for the world to accept. Furthermore, the world could not count upon his being content with this percentage. The vast reserves of Saudi Arabia and the other sheikdoms along the Persian Gulf could well have been the next target for acquisition if Iraq were permitted to annex Kuwait.

That there were ample incentives for Saddam Hussein to continue to seize and hold additional oil is clear. Over 90 percent of Iraq's income came from oil sales, and Iraq was saddled with massive foreign debts resulting from the purchases of military arms and hardware and from the eight-year war against Iran, which totaled close to $40 billion, $4 billion of which was owed to Kuwait. The primary way, therefore, for Iraq to pay these debts would be to control more and more oil and to drive up the prices — and of course, canceling the separate existence of Kuwait canceled that portion of the debt. Before Iraq invaded Kuwait, oil had been selling for $18 per barrel, and Iraq had persuaded OPEC to raise the price to $21 per barrel at a meeting held on 26 July 1990. On 1 August, Saddam Hussein demanded an increase to $25 per barrel. When this request was denied, Iraq withdrew and the talks broke down. The stage was then set for Iraq, with the fourth largest army in the world, to view war, as Clausewitz had suggested, as but an extension of diplomacy.

One last factor was a catalyst for Desert Storm. The apparent end of the Cold War, symbolized by the reunification of Germany and the crumbling of the Iron Curtain, seemed to offer the world the chance to resolve international differences through peaceful means in what Pres. George Bush identified with the label New World Order. The Iraqi invasion of Kuwait could be seen as dashing these expectations.

Haunting President Bush and the other leaders of the Western world, according to their public statements, was the memory of the prelude to World War II. Adolf Hitler had been permitted by a compliant world to commit one act of aggression after another, aggression that eventually led to war. In violation of the Versailles Treaty, which had ended the First World War, Hitler had sent troops into the Ruhr. Next he was permitted to annex the Sudetenland in Czechoslovakia and then Austria. His move into Poland finally proved to be too much for the British and the French, and World War II with its millions of dead ensued. Similarly, Italy's invasion of Abyssinia went unchallenged other than by futile words — calls for peace from the League of Nations. Since many member nations of the North Atlantic Treaty Organization (NATO) argued that the NATO charter prohibited military actions outside the North Atlantic area, NATO could not be used as a vehicle to oppose Iraq in this instance of naked aggression. However, such NATO nations as the United Kingdom and France did send armed forces to join the Coalition under the UN's auspices.

When Iraq invaded Kuwait early on August 2, a convergence of interests created near unanimity in condemning this act. Jealous leaders in the Arab world temporarily at least set aside their ambitions, to join in opposing Saddam Hussein. Muslims around the globe suspended religious differences to fight another Muslim nation. Western European nations, believing that world peace was closer to hand than ever before during the hope-filled days of the diminishing Cold War, saw this aggression as a threat to what President Bush had called a New World Order and moved to respond with UN support. The Coalition against Iraq began to form.

2 Pre–Desert Shield

26 June–1 August 1990

The genesis of Desert Storm goes far back into the history of the Middle East, but the more immediate antecedents can be traced to Iraq's need to increase the price of oil on the world market so that it could meet its foreign debt.

In theory, oil prices have been determined by oil production quotas agreed upon by the member nations of the OPEC cartel. In practice, however, many of the individual members of OPEC have disregarded these quotas to serve their own national interests. Typical of the disputes that have arisen over the quotas was a warning by Pres. Saddam Hussein on 26 June 1990 to Kuwait and the United Arab Emirates that they must stop production in excess of their prescribed quotas so that the price of oil on the world market could rise from $14 to $25 per barrel. At an OPEC meeting in Jiddah, Saudi Arabia, on 10 July, Kuwait and the United Arab Emirates agreed to abide by their production quotas, and Saudi Arabia agreed to reduce its production. Iran, still technically at war with Iraq, proposed that oil prices should be set at $25 per barrel, a proposal that was accepted by Iraq and the other OPEC members.

While this agreement should have brought peace to the region, on 15 July Saddam Hussein increased the pressure on Kuwait by surfacing its dispute over oil production from the Rumalia oil field, which stretches across the Iraq-Kuwait border. Iraq and Kuwait had agreed to share the oil from this most productive field, but Iraq now claimed that Kuwait was pumping more than its agreed-upon share. The Iraqi president chose to voice his complaint in a letter from his foreign minister, Teriq Azziz to Secretary General Chedli Klibi of the Arab League. In this letter, Iraq accused Kuwait not only of stealing Iraqi oil but also of attempting to reduce Iraq's oil income.

Two days later, on 17 July, Saddam Hussein in a speech to

the Iraqi nation threatened to take military action if Kuwait and the United Arab Emirates continued to violate their production quotas. The president, invoking the tenets of Pan-Arab Nationalism, complained that the low level of oil prices was costing Iraq $14 billion annually and was the result of United States policy. In response to this threat, the Kuwaiti cabinet met to discuss the Iraqi demand for $2.4 billion in compensation for oil Iraq alleged had been stolen by Kuwait from the Rumalia oil field. At the same time, Kuwait put its military on alert and called for an emergency meeting of the Gulf Coast Cooperation Council, the oil-producing states along the Persian Gulf coast: Kuwait, Saudi Arabia, Bahrain, Qatar, the United Arab Emirates, and Oman.

By this time, the Central Intelligence Agency reported that Iraq had moved approximately 30,000 troops to the Iraq-Kuwait border, and Pres. Hosni Mubarek went to Baghdad to attempt to resolve what appeared to be a crisis. President Mubarek apparently believed that the tensions had been reduced and said that he had received assurances from Saddam Hussein that he would not take military action against Kuwait.

On 24 July, the United States deployed six combat ships to the Persian Gulf to participate in joint maneuvers with the United Arab Emirates, and the State Department said that although the United States had no defense treaties with Kuwait, it was still committed to maintaining the security of the nations in the region. On the next day, 25 July, American ambassador April Glaspie met with Saddam Hussein. While the accounts of this meeting vary, the United States believed that the Iraqi president had given assurances that he would not use force against Kuwait.

On 26 July, OPEC met in Geneva, and Kuwait agreed to reduce its oil production so that the price of oil could rise to $21 per barrel. Despite this apparent resolution of the Iraq-Kuwait dispute, Iraq moved another 30,000 troops to the border, and on 30 July, the CIA reported that Iraq had 100,000 troops with tanks on the border. On the following day, 31 July, Iraq and Kuwait met in Jiddah, Saudi Arabia, in another attempt to resolve their problem. By now, Iraq was demanding $10 billion in compensation, and complaining that Kuwait was not bargaining in good faith, Iraq walked out of the meeting.

On 1 August, the Iraqi ambassador in Washington was called

in to be warned that Iraq must settle its disputes peacefully, and the stage was set for the Iraqi invasion of Kuwait.

From Saddam Hussein's point of view, the invasion and annexation of Kuwait as Iraq's 19th Province must have appeared expedient. Deeply in debt as a result of his drive to create the most powerful armed forces in the Middle East and his eight-year war with Iran, Saddam Hussein was desperately seeking to increase Iraq's income. From his stated perspective, OPEC was bowing to Western pressures to keep oil prices low, and since income from oil sales was almost Iraq's entire source of funds, he had to do something to raise oil prices. In addition, he claimed to be convinced that Kuwait was illegally pumping more than its share of oil from the Rumalia oil field, thereby depriving Iraq of rightful income. Furthermore, since the existing boundary between Iraq and Kuwait was one imposed upon Iraq by the old colonial powers, in his view it was not binding. The Arab world should be able to resolve such a dispute internally without outside interference, he claimed. In sum, seizing Kuwait would restore to Iraq what was rightfully its own—including whatever assets Kuwait possessed, such as the gold in its banks—and simultaneously enable Iraq to eliminate a $4 billion debt owed to Kuwait.

From the point of view of both the Western powers and the other Arab nations in the Middle East, except Yemen, the Iraqi leader's claims were invalid. Whatever disputes Iraq had with Kuwait must be settled by diplomacy and not force. Moreover, the United Nations existed to resolve disputes between nations peacefully, and it was to the United Nations that President Bush turned when Iraq seized Kuwait. If Iraq, our former ally in our disputes with Iran, elected to violate the UN charter, then the permanent interests of the United States in that region would replace earlier national friendships. If Iraq persisted in its aggression, then the world would indeed turn to war as an extension of diplomacy.

3 Desert Shield

2 August 1990–16 January 1991

2 Aug 90   At 0200 2 August, Iraq invaded Kuwait. By the end of the day, for all practical purposes Iraq had accomplished its mission, and as a sign of its success, Iraq installed a provisional government replacing the existing Kuwaiti regime. Reaction was swift in coming. The United States froze Kuwaiti and Iraqi assets and imposed a trade embargo on Iraq. This step was intended first to prevent Iraq from profiting from transferring ownership of Kuwaiti assets to Iraq and second to punish Iraq economically for its aggression. Iraq, in retaliation, suspended all debt payments to the United States. In response to President George Bush's initiative, by a vote of 14-0 (with Yemen not participating) the United Nations Security Council passed Resolution 660, which condemned the invasion and called upon Iraq to withdraw all its troops from Kuwait. While this resolution was similar to the condemnation by the League of Nations of the Italian invasion of Abyssinia before World War II, it differed in being but the first of many resolutions, including the critical one that authorized the use of force to compel withdrawal.

3 Aug 90   As Iraq began to move its troops to the Kuwait–Saudi Arabia border, the Arab nations agreed to have a meeting to discuss possible actions. The United States and the Soviet Union issued a joint statement condemning the Iraqi invasion, and the Soviet Union, which had been a major arms supplier to Iraq, froze all arms shipments to Iraq. That the Soviet Union would issue a joint statement with the United States was especially significant in that it indicated that Iraq could not play one nation against the other as might have occurred only months before. Furthermore, it suggested that the Soviet Union would not use its veto in the UN Security Council to thwart resolutions designed to aid Kuwait. Italy, the United Kingdom, Germany, Belgium, Holland, and Luxembourg froze Kuwaiti assets, as the United States had done. This action by these European nations foretold the worldwide support of actions intended to curb Iraq and punish its aggression. President Bush directed Secretary of Defense Dick Cheney to go to Saudi Arabia to discuss the situation and announced the following national objectives:

1. The immediate, unconditional, and complete Iraqi withdrawal from Kuwait,
2. The restoration of Kuwait's legitimate government,
3. The protection of United States citizens in the region, and
4. The stability and security of nations in the Persian Gulf region.

This statement of objectives so soon after the invasion established the national goals of the United States in the region, and these objectives formed the basis for subsequent UN resolutions. As events unfolded in the following weeks, the word "unconditional" would play a major role in ensuring that the status quo existing before the war was achieved.

4 Aug 90   Facing the possibility of an invasion by Iraq, Saudi Arabia began to mobilize its forces. French and British warships began to move to the Persian Gulf, a movement that may have been seen by Saddam Hussein as the normal, relatively routine reaction of major powers when their citizens could be threatened by an outbreak of hostilities. Meanwhile, the European Community (EC) announced broad sanctions against Iraq, including prohibition of oil and arms transactions. This action by the EC, the supranational organization of twelve major Western European states (Belgium, Denmark, France, Germany, Greece, Ireland, Italy, Luxembourg, The Netherlands, Portugal, Spain, and the United Kingdom), should have sent warning signals to Iraq. Not only were these sanctions a potential blow to Iraq's economy and war machine, but they were also steps taken by an organization two of whose members, the United Kingdom and France, along with the Soviet Union and the United States, have veto powers in the UN Security Council. Thus it was probable that if the UN Security Council chose to pass further resolutions contrary to Iraqi interests, only China had the power to block them, and with the easing of relations between China and the Soviet Union, Iraq could not count on a Chinese veto.

5 Aug 90   The Arab summit meeting called for on 3 August was canceled. Given the diversity of the Arab national interests, the cancellation of their summit meeting was hardly surprising, since the governments required more time to prepare their positions. Secretary of Defense Cheney was discussing access for United States forces in Saudi Arabia, and the outcome of the secretary's meeting with the Saudi Arabian government was critical. Unless Saudi Arabia agreed to allow foreign troops on its soil and to permit the use of its ports and bases, it would be virtually impossible for the United States and other members of the budding Coalition to mass sufficient forces and equipment to affect Iraq's seizure of Kuwait.

6 Aug 90   By a vote of 13-0 (with China and Yemen abstaining), the United Nations Security Council passed Resolution 661, which prohibited trade and financial transactions with Iraq and called upon all nations to protect Kuwaiti assets. Resolution 661 placed Iraq in an untenable position. With all trade embargoed, Iraq would lose all its income from the rest of the world. No nation can long survive under these conditions, much less a nation whose income is almost completely derived from the sale of oil on world markets. Significantly, China abstained from the vote of this resolution when it had the right to veto the embargo. Thus, all five superpowers—the United States, the Soviet Union, the United Kingdom, France, and China—had stood together to thwart Iraq's invasion of Kuwait.

   In support of this resolution, the United States proposed a multinational force, including the Soviet Union, to enforce the trade sanctions if required. As urged by Secretary of Defense Cheney, the Saudi Arabian government requested United States troops on its soil to help protect the country from an Iraqi attack, and the Carrier Battle Group *Independence* arrived in the Gulf of Oman. The arrival of an aircraft battle group—normally consisting of an aircraft carrier and supporting surface warships such as cruisers, destroyers, frigates, and other smaller vessels—ensured that even without ground troops present, some support could be given to Saudi Arabia if Iraq attacked across the border.

At the same time, the Emir of Kuwait offered to talk with Iraq about territorial exchanges if Iraq would withdraw from Kuwait. This Kuwaiti offer to discuss territorial differences, summarily dismissed by Saddam Hussein, reflected the remnant of hope that Arab nations acting without outside interference could solve what was, after all, a dispute between Arab neighbors.

Iraq began to move Westerners in Kuwait to Iraq, a movement that appeared to be an attempt to use these people as some form of hostage.

7 Aug 90   Turkey closed its pipelines to the shipment of Iraqi oil across Turkish territory to the Mediterranean Sea and concurrently authorized the movement of United States combat aircraft to Turkish air bases. Cutting off the flow of Iraqi oil through Turkish pipelines was significant for many reasons. If Iraq could continue sending oil through these pipelines, it could avoid attempting to ship Iraqi oil by tanker through waters now patrolled by Coalition warships and could thereby possibly escape the oil embargo imposed by the UN and still get Iraqi oil to market. Furthermore, this Turkish action indicated the strength of the Turkish commitment to stopping Iraq since a significant portion of Turkish income came from the movement of oil through the pipelines on its territory. Permitting U.S. aircraft to use Turkish bases put northern Iraq in jeopardy if war should come. Thus, Iraq was now faced with possible aerial attacks from both Turkey in the north and Saudi Arabia in the south.

Secretary of Defense Cheney obtained permission for the aircraft carrier U.S.S. *Saratoga* to transit the Suez Canal, thus also committing Egypt to an anti-Iraq policy.

8 Aug 90   Iraq announced that Kuwait was formally annexed to the state of Iraq, to become its 19th Province. This action went even beyond the previous formation of a provisional Kuwaiti government and flaunted defiance of the United Nations. In response to the Saudi Arabian invitation to send troops to help defend that nation, President Bush announced that the United States was sending ground forces, probably numbering about 50,000, to Saudi Arabia. Simultaneously, the 82nd Airborne Division received its deployment orders to Saudi Arabia. The 82nd Airborne, along with the 101st Air Assault Division, is

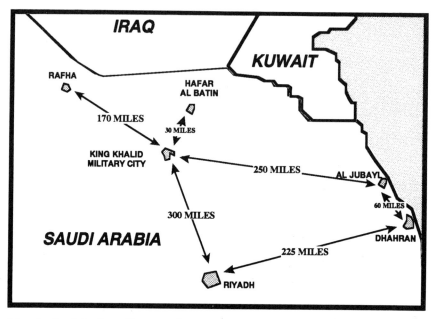

MAP 1. Straight-line distances between major Saudi Arabian cities involved in Operation Desert Storm. Source: *Army Focus* (June 1991): 19.

part of the XVIII Airborne Corps, that portion of the Army intended for immediate deployment when the situation called for armed intervention to protect our national interests.

This troop deployment was codenamed Operation Desert Shield by the Department of Defense. The use of a code name for military operations is a common and long-established practice. The invasion of the European continent during World War II, for instance, was called Overlord, and the more recent operations in Panama were given the name Just Cause.

9 Aug 90   As Iraq sent 50,000 more troops to the Kuwait–Saudi Arabia border, the first elements of the 82nd Airborne Division began landing in Saudi Arabia within thirty-one hours of the initial alert, and the 24th Mechanized Division received its orders to deploy to Saudi Arabia. Even before the first brigade of the 82nd Airborne was on the ground, United States Air Force F-15 combat aircraft from the 1st Tactical Fighter Wing were in Saudi Arabia ready to fly patrols. These were followed by more fighter aircraft, bringing the total to five squadrons, and a contingent of AWACS (Airborne Warning and Control), radar-equipped aircraft capable of tracking airborne aircraft and directing the flights of the hundreds of Coalition aircraft that were soon to fill the sky. Thus only seven days after Iraq invaded Kuwait, the first American troops and planes were landing in Saudi Arabia in consonance with the stated objectives of the United States. While denying he was subject to the Congress's War Powers Resolution (a resolution which since its passage by Congress all presidents have refused to accept on the grounds that it violates the constitutional rights of the president), President Bush sent a letter to the Congress informing that body of his actions.

In continuation of its illegal treatment of foreigners in that country, Saddam Hussein sealed its borders—now both Iraq and what Iraq called its 19th Province, Kuwait.

Although a meeting in Cairo of Arab leaders failed to materialize, Secretary of State James Baker met with members of the Turkish government to coordinate activities and to discuss Turkey's possible roles in Desert Shield.

The UN Security Council unanimously passed Resolution 662, which declared Iraq's annexation of Kuwait null and void. Significantly, even Yemen, which had abstained from the two previous resolutions, voted with the rest of the members of the Security Council, as did Cuba, which had abstained from voting on Resolution 661 imposing trade embargoes.

10 Aug 90   What turned out to be possibly one of the more significant events transpired on 10 August, when the Arab League voted 12-9 to send Arab troops to Saudi Arabia. One of the major questions hanging over the scene had been whether Arab nations would send troops alongside Western nations' forces for possible combat against the Arabs in Iraq. Egypt had already shown that it would at least cooperate when it authorized the passage of a U.S. warship through the Suez Canal, but the placing of ground troops from other Arab nations in Saudi Arabia was an even more significant act. In response, Saddam Hussein declared a Holy War in what turned out to be a vain attempt to make religion rather than economics the basis of hostile operations.

In defiance of UN Resolution 662, Iraq continued to maintain the position that Kuwait was now an integral part of Iraq by ordering foreign governments to close their embassies in Kuwait on the pretext that since Kuwait was no longer a separate state but only a province of Iraq, no embassies were appropriate in Kuwait. While the invasion of Kuwait had basically affected only the Kuwaitis, this order to close embassies, along with the illegal treatment of foreign nationals in Iraq and Kuwait, was a concrete step that affected governments around the world and helped harden their animosity toward Iraq.

Meanwhile back in the United States, the first of the United States' fast sealift transports (specially designed naval ships used to move heavy military equipment at high speeds across long distances), the F.S.S. *Capella*, arrived in Savannah, Georgia, to load the 24th Mechanized Division for its movement to Saudi Arabia. (It would leave Savannah loaded with 24th Division equipment on 13 August.)

11 Aug 90   In a rapid response to the Arab League's decision to authorize troops of member nations to go to Saudi Arabia, the first contingent of Egyptian troops began to arrive in Saudi Arabia. While the arrival of these troops was critical in demonstrating Arab support, in terms of combat effectiveness their presence was less significant. The state of training and the quality of their equipment at that time was less than that of the Iraqi forces they might face.

12 Aug 90   The chances of armed conflict grew when President Bush ordered U.S. naval vessels to stop any Iraqi oil exports as well as ships hauling cargoes embargoed by UN Resolution 661. This decision to act was a unilateral one, since as yet the United Nations had not passed a resolution authorizing the use of armed force to carry out the provisions of Resolution 661.

The oft-stated position of Pan-Arab nationalists was that Israel was illegally occupying such territories as the Golan Heights and the West Bank. Thus when Saddam Hussein proposed on 12 August that *all* occupations in the Middle East end simultaneously, he was attempting to link his annexation of Kuwait with what he must surely have known to be a condition that neither Israel nor the United States would accept. Moreover, the Iraqi president's offer put him in the garb of the Pan-Arab leader he had so long sought in the region and cloaked his aggression with conditions that might appeal to Palestinians throughout the Middle East.

14 Aug 90   Iraq is bordered by Turkey, Syria, Jordan, Saudi Arabia, and Iran. Although there was little doubt that Turkey, Syria, Saudi Arabia, and Iran (still at war with Iraq) would abide by the UN's embargo, there were some questions about Jordan. The population of that small nation, sandwiched between Israel, Syria, and Iraq, contained a significant number of Palestinians who saw in Saddam Hussein a champion of Palestinian rights. King Hussein's hold on his country was at times tenuous at best, and he had survived several attempted coups during his reign. With the borders of Turkey, Syria, Saudi Arabia, and Iran closed to Iraqi trade, the only possible route open to Iraq was from or through Jordan via Aqaba, Jordan's port to the Red Sea. While King Hussein had long been one of the United States' closest allies in the Middle East, it was clear that he was under great pressure from Iraq and his Palestinian population to permit trade with Iraq to continue. As a countermeasure, therefore, and in the face of an upcoming visit by King Hussein to the United States, President Bush threatened to blockade Aqaba under the UN's trade embargo.

15 Aug 90   Technically, Iraq was still at war with Iran at this time although few if any hostilities were underway. Iraq and Iran had been unable to agree on peace terms, but now, without warning, Iraq agreed to the last offer Iran had made. The primary elements were Iraq's withdrawal from all territory it had seized during this eight-year war and the exchange of all prisoners of war. Under normal circumstances, this move would have been tantamount to accepting defeat at the hands of the Iranians, but Saddam Hussein was obviously seeking some semblance of peace with Iran in order to free his troops tied down on the Iranian border for action in Kuwait if that became necessary.

By now U.S. aircraft had begun arriving in Saudi Arabia, warships were patrolling the Persian Gulf, and ground forces were in place. The United States through diplomatic channels warned Iraq to keep their aircraft and ships clear of U.S. forces and reiterated that close encounters in a situation such as this could lead to bloodshed.

16 Aug 90   On 12 August, President Bush had given orders to naval vessels to enforce the UN trade embargo. Now to carry out these orders the Navy established zones in which Iraqi ships would be intercepted. Such an action was intended to make it even more clear to Saddam Hussein that Bush was determined to make aggression unviable.

King Hussein had met with President Bush at Kennebunkport, and Bush announced that King Hussein had agreed to abide by the UN trade embargo. Thus, if King Hussein kept his word, the last possible trade avenue was closed to Iraq.

Saddam Hussein, in his turn, attempted to bring more pressure to bear on the United States and the United Kingdom, his two most vocal opponents. He ordered all Americans and British citizens to assemble at two hotels in Kuwait. While most complied, some went into hiding with Kuwaiti friends or attempted to escape to Saudi Arabia. Furthermore, Iraq began detaining all foreign nationals in both Iraq and Kuwait and reminded the world that these foreigners would, as would Iraqis and Kuwaitis, suffer from any food shortages brought on by the UN embargo. As a further threat, Saddam Hussein declared that foreigners would be used as shields around key installations to safeguard them from attacks.

17 Aug 90   One of the criticisms of the United States' conduct of the war in Vietnam has been that the military buildup of combat forces was too gradual. That is, additional combat troops were added in small increments over long periods of time. Apparently to avoid a repeat of this pattern if war actually came to the Persian Gulf region, the U.S. military, with the consent of the president, activated the Civil Reserve Air Fleet just two weeks after Iraq invaded Kuwait. Under the provisions of this program, a number of aircraft used in the daily business of American airlines could be called to service in the Air Force if their use was required. Thirty-eight airliners, such as an American Airlines DC-10 normally used on a route between Hawaii and the mainland, were called upon to supplement the Air Force's Military Airlift Command to speed the movement of men and materiel to Saudi Arabia.

18 Aug 90   In reaction to the Iraqi detention of foreign nationals and the threats to use them as human shields, the UN Security Council unanimously passed Resolution 664, which demanded the immediate release of all foreign nationals in Iraq and Kuwait and the recision of the Iraqi order to close embassies in Kuwait. Cuba and Yemen, which had previously abstained from one or more of the anti-Iraq Security Council resolutions, voted for this resolution apparently because violations of international law set undesirable precedents rather than because of any opposition to Iraq's seizure of Kuwait.

The first shots of Desert Shield were fired by U.S. naval vessels across the bows of Iraqi tankers attempting to run the UN blockade. The warning shots turned back the tankers, and no further firing occurred.

With the loss of Iraqi and Kuwaiti oil from the world markets and the prospect of settlement dim, oil prices had jumped to about $28 per barrel. One means of holding down these prices was for OPEC members to increase production, and Saudi Arabia called for an emergency meeting of OPEC to change the existing production quotas. It further announced that it could increase its own production by two million barrels per day if other OPEC nations could not or would not.

19 Aug 90   Perhaps reacting to UN Resolution 664 calling for the release of all foreigners in Iraq and Kuwait or perhaps attempting to drive a wedge in the united front opposing Iraq, Iraq offered to release all foreign nationals if the United States would withdraw all its forces from the region. By this time, some 5,000 Egyptian troops had arrived in Saudi Arabia as well as 1,000 Moroccan troops, these latter reinforcing the impression that Muslim troops were coming to oppose Iraq.

20 Aug 90   The situation did not improve for Iraq when the United Arab Emirates granted the Coalition forces access to bases in that small country on the Persian Gulf. On the other hand, an Iraqi tanker had passed through the U.S. naval blockade headed for Yemen. When Yemen announced that it would not permit this tanker to dock and unload its oil, the UN Security Council deferred action on a proposed resolution to uphold the UN embargo with force.

Iraq carried through on its threat to place foreigners as shields at critical installations, and President Bush strongly denounced these actions, saying that he would hold Iraq responsible for any harm that might come to them. Continuing the buildup of U.S. forces, a squadron of F-117 stealth fighters was sent to Saudi Arabia.

With oil prices only marginally higher, OPEC refused the Saudi call for an emergency session, and Saudi Arabia announced that it would unilaterally increase its production by two million barrels per day.

21 Aug 90   Iraq attempted to end the crisis by offering negotiations, but President Bush, bolstered by American polls that strongly supported his Gulf policies, refused, reaffirming that the Iraqi withdrawal from Kuwait had to be unconditional. At the same time, Iraq responded to the American demand that Iraqi forces stay clear of U.S. forces by warning the United States to keep a safe distance from Iraqi forces. The noose around Iraq tightened further when the Western European Union (WEU) announced its decision to increase its naval presence in the region and to coordinate the operations of its warships there. This organization of Western European nations (Belgium, France, Germany, Italy, Luxembourg, The Netherlands, and the United Kingdom), while less influential than NATO, did provide a forum for integrated military security actions outside the geographic constraints of NATO.

22 Aug 90   By now, it seemed that only Iraq among the nations involved did not recognize that the United States would not deviate from the firm stand President Bush had proclaimed in his statement of U.S. national objectives. This was further emphasized by Bush's announcement that 40,000 reserves would be called to active duty. The Saudi government announced that it would provide fuel for the U.S. forces in that country, thereby reducing the logistics strain that would continue to increase as more and more U.S. forces were sent to Saudi Arabia.

Even within Iraq, many appeared to fear the developing situation. So many non-Iraqi Arabs were attempting to flee the country into Jordan that Jordan closed its border with Iraq. It had become impossible to provide adequate food, water, and shelter to the many thousands of refugees who were seeking safety outside Iraq.

23 Aug 90   On the eve of the Iraqi ultimatum's deadline for closing foreign embassies in Kuwait, Saddam Hussein staged a televised interview with hostage families—including little children—in an apparent attempt to frighten off the nations opposing his aggression. World reaction of rage and scorn indicated that he had miscalculated. If he had thought to arouse the response received by the captors of American hostages held by Iran when they seized the U.S. embassy years before, he had thought wrong.

24 Aug 90   Although some nations elected to accede to Iraq's demand to close their embassies, several, including the United States, did not. Iraqi troops surrounded these embassies; although they did not cross into these grounds traditionally safe from unauthorized entry, it was clear that Saddam Hussein was attempting to use diplomatic personnel as higher-level hostages. Furthermore, Iraq prevented U.S. diplomats in Baghdad from leaving the country. These clumsy attempts to frighten Iraq's opponents, far from inducing a change in the world's attitude toward Iraq, merely strengthened resistance.

25 Aug 90   In reaction to these Iraqi efforts to loosen the pressures, the UN Security Council passed Resolution 665 by a vote of 13-0 with Cuba and Yemen again abstaining. This resolution called upon all UN member nations to abide by the previous UN resolution imposing a trade embargo. Cargoes on Iraqi vessels were to be inspected to verify that they did not contain contraband.

26 Aug 90   As Spain sent three ships to the Gulf to add to those already there, the Soviet Union announced that it would not use force to ensure compliance with the UN resolutions. The Soviet Union had long been a major supplier of arms to Iraq and still had technical advisors in country. Now the Soviet Union was apparently reluctant to take any more steps that might hamper a close relationship with Iraq after the crisis was settled. The Soviets would vote with the other major power members of the Security Council, but they would not take concrete actions, such as the use of armed force, to jeopardize their post-crisis status in the Middle East.

Like the rest of the world, the secretary general of the United Nations, Javier Perez de Cuellar, hoped that the crisis could be settled short of war. He announced that he would meet with Iraqi foreign minister Tariq Azziz to begin talks aimed at resolving the crisis.

27 Aug 90   The day of 27 August held mixed news for the world. OPEC, by a 10-1 vote, agreed to increases in oil production, and oil prices dropped $4 per barrel. Reportedly, Iraq directed its shipping not to resist the inspections called for by UN Resolution 665, an order that reduced the risk of incident. This good news was balanced, however, by the expulsion of two-thirds of the Iraqi mission to the United States in Washington, D.C. This sort of action, the forced reduction of personnel assigned to a nation's mission, is a normal display of diplomatic maneuvering intended to convey displeasure — short of the complete rupture of diplomatic relations — at conduct considered inimical to good relations.

The first shipload of the 24th Mechanized Division's equipment reached Saudi Arabia after its trip across the Atlantic from Savannah, Georgia.

28 Aug 90   Some rays of hope still remained. Saddam Hussein modified his hostage policies to permit women and children to leave Iraq. The Bush administration emphasized that its goal was the withdrawal of Iraq from Kuwait without any violence and not the overthrow of Saddam Hussein. This moderate position was reinforced by Egyptian President Mubarek's statement that if Iraq would leave Kuwait, the Arab nations would ask all foreign troops to leave the area.

Although details of troop movements were clouded with secrecy, estimates by military spokesmen reported in the national press put the Iraqi strength in Kuwait at more than 250,000 troops with 1,500 tanks. U.S. strength was put at 50,000 ground forces, 70 ships, and 300 aircraft.

29 Aug 90   The month of August drew to a close more quietly than it began, with one exception. In Syria, troops killed pro-Iraqi demonstrators who had taken to the streets in support of Saddam Hussein. On the other hand, although thousands of troops armed for war faced each other across the Saudi Arabia–Kuwait border, no shots had yet been fired in anger. On the diplomatic front, President Bush and his officials were working publicly and privately to rally virtually almost all the world in opposition to Iraq. There were indications that Saddam Hussein had miscalculated the reactions of his fellow Arab nations to his seizure of Kuwait. Instead of joining him in opposition to the Western nations whom he attempted to cast as "colonial powers," the Arab world with the exception of Yemen was siding with the United States. Moreover, his attempt to use as hostages American and European nationals caught in Kuwait and Iraq appeared to have backfired. Other OPEC nations were increasing oil production to offset the embargo on Iraqi and Kuwaiti oil. Still, Saddam Hussein remained adamant in his holding of Kuwait, even to the extent of annexing that nation as the 19th Province of Iraq and renaming Kuwait City al-Kadhima. The only glimmer of hope to a peaceful resolution of the situation was a plan for talks between the UN secretary general and Saddam Hussein.

On the military front, the remainder of the 82nd Airborne Division reached Saudi Arabia.

4 Sep 90   September began with mixed signals. The United States indicated that it was prepared to stay over a long term in the region and that a new security organization or structure might well be required. Saudi Arabia began to mobilize its population in response to the threats to its security. By now, 3,000 Syrian troops were in Saudi Arabia along with 2,000 Moroccans and 2,000 Kuwaiti troops who had fled after the invasion.

The refugee situation had become even more desperate as thousands more were attempting to leave Iraq, many leaving behind all their belongings other than what they could carry with them. The Soviet Union, still straddling the fence between condemning Iraq in the United Nations and trying to preserve its presence in the Middle East, again called for an international conference on all Middle East issues.

5 Sep 90   Not surprisingly, the United States' response to this Soviet proposal was lukewarm at best. The U.S. position was still that the Iraqi invasion of Kuwait was absolutely unwarranted aggression and was an issue separate from all other Middle East problems and its solution should, therefore, be treated separately. Any Middle East conference would undoubtedly include the Arab-Israeli problem, which could only create more difficulties in holding together the fragile Coalition now opposed to Iraq. Exacerbating the situation was Saddam Hussein's renewed call for a jihad (a Holy War) with specific targets being King Fahd of Saudi Arabia and President Mubarek of Egypt.

6 Sep 90   To counter this threat, the Saudi government offered funds to cover the operating costs of the U.S. forces in Saudi Arabia, now reported by Secretary of Defense Cheney at 100,000, and to provide financial assistance to Arab nations within the anti-Iraq coalition. Iraqi Foreign Minister Tariq Azziz, who had been in Moscow attempting to ease the universal condemnation of Iraq, left these talks without success.

10 Sep 90   Following a meeting on the previous day in Helsinki, Finland, between President Bush and Pres. Mikhael Gorbachev, administration officials indicated that the United States had suggested that the Soviet Union take a greater role in resolving Middle East problems. This invitation reversed the long-standing U.S. position of minimizing Soviet participation in that region's affairs. The statement issued jointly by the United States and the Soviet Union following their Helsinki meeting pledged cooperation in denying the Iraqi annexation of Kuwait but acknowledged that there were still differences in the U.S. and Soviet positions.

Iraq made two attempts to ease its increasingly difficult situation. On the one hand, Iran and Iraq announced the resumption of diplomatic relations, marking the complete end of their long and bloody war. The immediate concern of the Coalition was, of course, that this resumption of normal relations between Iran and Iraq would open the long common border to trade, thereby circumventing the UN trade embargo. The other attempt was an Iraqi offer of free oil to developing nations, an offer that might induce these countries to further trade. Fortunately for the Coalition, neither of these attempts bore fruit.

11 Sep 90   With public opinion polls continuing to show support for President Bush's position in the crisis, the president decided to address the Congress on his actions. He reaffirmed his belief that Iraq would fail in its aggression and restated his concept of a new world order in the wake of the relaxation of tensions in Europe. He reiterated his belief that the suppression of this Iraqi aggression was more than an isolated incident, portraying it rather as a matter of principle for international relations.

Iraq released its version of the meeting Saddam Hussein and April Glaspie had held on 25 July. According to Iraq, the ambassador had indicated that the United States had no opinion on the dispute between Iraq and Kuwait over their border problems.

12 Sep 90   In a follow-up to the U.S. offer of a greater role for the Soviet Union in the Middle East, Israel announced that it too would welcome such a step. Over the long term, this development probably overshadowed the immediate crisis at hand since it could change considerably the players in any future conference on the long-festering Arab-Israeli problem.

13 Sep 90   The United Nations continued to apply world pressure against Iraq with passage of Security Council Resolution 666, again with a 13-0 vote with Yemen and Cuba abstaining. This resolution once more required Iraq to provide for the safety of foreign nationals under its control and expanded upon the specific items of food and medical supplies exempt from the general embargo.

Support for the Coalition continued with the announcement by Syria that it would send 10,000 more troops and 300 tanks to help defend Saudi Arabia against any Iraqi attack. Japan pledged an additional $1 billion dollars in aid, bringing its total pledge to $4 billion. Japan explained that it could not send troops to the region because the Japanese Constitution prohibited any military actions besides defense of the homeland.

One of the fears that faced the worldwide Coalition arrayed against Iraq was that Iraq would instigate terrorist attacks against its foes. Saddam Hussein had long harbored some of the more radical terrorist groups, and the United States now warned Iraq that it would not tolerate such activities.

To counter Saddam Hussein's call for a Holy War, a meeting of conservative Muslim clerics convened in Mecca and condemned Iraq for its aggression against Kuwait, calling it an unwarranted violation of Muslim principles.

14 Sep 90   On 10 August, Iraq had given notice that all foreign embassies in Kuwait must be closed by 24 August. While some nations had accepted this order, some had not, and Iraqi troops had surrounded the embassies and official ambassadorial residences. Now in defiance of UN Resolution 664, which called upon Iraq to rescind the order, Iraqi troops entered the Belgian Embassy and the residences of the French and Canadian ambassadors to Kuwait.

The United Kingdom, which from the outset of the crisis had concurred with the United States' position, announced that it would send 6,000 troops and 300 tanks to Saudi Arabia. These troops were nicknamed the "Desert Rats" after the British troops who had served in North Africa during the Second World War in the famous campaigns against German Field Marshal Edwin Rommel.

15 Sep 90   France swiftly followed the British commitment of troops with an announcement that 4,000 French troops would be sent to join the Coalition. These would join the U.S. forces, which were reported to number 150,000 with 420 combat aircraft and 250 support aircraft. France also expelled twenty-four Iraqi attachés in retaliation for the Iraqi intrusion into the French ambassadorial residence the day before. In addition, it called for the extension of the embargo to include air traffic.

Germany, for reasons similar to Japan's, was unwilling to send troops into the Gulf region. Instead, like Japan, it pledged financial aid—in this instance $2 billion. The Soviet Union again attempted to play the part of broker, offering to lodge

Iraq's complaints through diplomatic channels once Iraq withdrew from Kuwait.

16 Sep 90   Six weeks after the Iraqi invasion of Kuwait, the conflict was still a "war of words." Saddam Hussein had been using the television as a propaganda device, as in the case of the 23 August television broadcast of his meeting with hostage families. In an attempt to counter the influence of such broadcasts, the United States persuaded Iraq to televise a speech by President Bush to the Iraqi people. In his speech, the president reviewed the positions of the United Nations on Iraq's actions, emphasizing that the crisis was not a dispute between Iraq and the United States (as depicted continually by Saddam Hussein) and that the United States had no quarrel with the Iraqi people, only with their government's actions.

Arab support of the Coalition continued with the announcement that Egypt would send a mechanized division of some 15,000 men to Saudi Arabia, and the situation along the Jordan-Iraq border seemed to be easing somewhat, with fewer refugees leaving Iraq.

The world community had been stung by the Iraqi violation of diplomatic norms in its actions against diplomatic facilities in Kuwait. The UN Security Council unanimously adopted Resolution 667 which condemned Iraq for these diplomatic violations. This was the seventh resolution condemning Iraq, none of which seemed to have modified Iraqi behavior. The next day, the European Community took concrete steps to indicate its disapproval by expelling the Iraqi military attachés to all twelve member nations.

18 Sep 90   By now, the Pentagon estimated that Iraq had moved 365,000 troops into Kuwait region with 2,800 tanks, 1,800 other armored vehicles, and 1,450 artillery pieces. U.S. forces were placed at something more than 150,000. The Netherlands announced that it would send a squadron of F-16s to Turkey, where they would operate from NATO bases, and Argentina announced that it would send armed forces—two warships—to the Gulf.

19 Sep 90   The next day in retaliation against the UN sanctions, Iraq seized all assets of nations that were complying with the UN sanctions against Iraq. In a related financial matter, Jordan asked the world for economic assistance, fearing its economy would collapse under the weight of the loss of income from the trade embargo and its assistance to the thousands of refugees who had flooded into Jordan from Iraq.

20 Sep 90   Jordan was indeed in dire straits. In addition to its dependence upon trade with Iraq, a significant portion of its Palestinian population was strongly supporting Saddam Hussein and his actions against the oil-rich Kuwait. King Hussein, threatened economically and politically, suggested negotiations with Iraq. As it had since the beginning of the crisis, the United States came out against any negotiations, reiterating its requirement of unconditional withdrawal from Kuwait. In support, Saudi Arabia cut off oil shipments to Jordan.

23 Sep 90   In a radio broadcast Saddam Hussein threatened to attack Saudi oil fields and Israel if the embargoes strangled Iraq.

24 Sep 90   In response to the new Iraqi threats, the UN Security Council unanimously passed Resolution 669, which stated that only a special sanctions committee could authorize the shipment of food and other aid materials to either Iraq or Kuwait. Simultaneously, rumors spread that some food was reaching Iraq from Iran in the wake of the resumption of normal relations between these two states.

Up to now, the primary condemnation by the United Nations had come from the fifteen-member Security Council in which the five superpowers—China, France, the United Kingdom, the Soviet Union, and the United States—had veto power. On 24 September, the UN General Assembly convened, and that body, in which every member nation had a vote and none the veto power, also condemned Iraq. Thus, the international community represented by the full United Nations, instead of only the smaller Security Council, had ruled against the Iraqi aggression.

The international community, however, still hoped that diplomatic pressure would resolve the crisis before armed force became necessary. In this vein, Pres. François Mitterrand of France suggested that even an Iraqi commitment to withdraw, not necessarily an actual withdrawal, might be sufficient to lead to negotiations for resolving the crisis. This French action was consistent with France's long pursuit of an independent approach to diplomacy.

25 Sep 90   The United Nations, however, continued to apply diplomatic pressure; the Security Council passed Resolution 670 by a vote of 14-1, with Cuba this time casting an opposing vote instead of abstaining. This resolution closed the last loophole of the trade embargo that was being violated by air shipments from nations sympathetic to Iraq.

Meanwhile at the UN, Soviet Foreign Minister Eduard Shevardnadze warned that war might be imminent if Iraq did not withdraw from Iraq. Syria's Pres. Hafez al-Assad completed a four-day visit to Iran with a joint statement with the Iranian president declaring opposition toward Iraq coupled with opposition to any foreign presence in the Gulf region after the crisis ended.

The Pentagon raised its estimate of Iraqi forces in the Kuwaiti area to 430,000 and revealed that between 500 and 1,000 Soviet advisors remained in Iraq. At the same time, it announced that the aircraft carrier U.S.S. *Independence* would enter the Gulf.

30 Sep 90   September ended as it had begun, on a mixed note. On 27 September, the United Kingdom and Iran had resumed diplomatic relations, a welcomed event deemed likely to keep Iran from supporting Iraq against the Coalition in which the United Kingdom had an active voice. The United States Navy had reported that because only fourteen of forty-one ships in its Ready Reserve Fleet were available for use in the crisis, the United States had to lease foreign vessels to move troops, equipment, and supplies to Saudi Arabia. Iraq was threatening terrorist attacks by openly claiming connections with the more radical Palestinian terrorist groups, and Saudi Prince Sultan declared that Saudi Arabia would never permit Israel to help defend Saudi Arabia. Saddam Hussein, apparently hoping to drive a wedge between Coalition members, announced that he would consider President Mitterrand's proposal for ending the Gulf crisis. In keeping with his attempt to link his Iraqi actions against Kuwait with such matters as the Israeli-Arab dispute and the general Middle East antipathy to any Western presence in the region, Saddam Hussein linked a resolution of the crisis with the creation of a Palestinian state and the withdrawal of all Western forces from the Middle East.

1 Oct 90   President Bush addressed the United Nations and characteristically spoke of a new future to be derived from the present, involving such issues as improvements in the Iraq-Kuwait relationship, in Gulf security, and even in the Arab-Israeli problem. Casting a shadow on this future was the pragmatic announcement by the Israeli government that in anticipation of Iraqi chemical attacks on Israel, the government would begin issuing gas masks to its civilian population.

2 Oct 90   President Mitterrand visited the 4,000 French troops that had arrived in Saudi Arabia, joining the 200,000 U.S. troops with their 54 ships, including the recently arrived U.S.S. *Independence*, now in the Gulf region. U.S. strength was now about one-half that of the Iraqi forces estimated to be in the area.

3 Oct 90   Saddam Hussein visited Kuwait and made a defiant speech to the troops.

7 through   The next week was a tumultuous one. On 7 October the Is-
14 Oct 90   raeli government began its promised issue of gas masks to the civilian population. The next day, Israeli police killed nineteen Palestinians in riots near the Temple Mount. Both Syrian and Egyptian officials stated that their forces would fight only in defense of Saudi Arabia but would not participate in an attack on Iraq. On 9 October the United States, in a marked departure from previous policy towards Israel, proposed a UN Security Council resolution condemning Israel for the excessive use of force in the killing of the nineteen Palestinians. The situation was not eased by Saddam Hussein's claim that Iraq possessed missiles that could strike Israel from within Iraq or by the PLO's demands for an even harsher condemnation of Israel. On 12 October, the UN Security Council censured Israel for the violence of 8 October, and two days later, Israel announced that it would not accept the UN mission to Israel ordered by the Security Council.

16 Oct 90   The Iraqis, apparently still testing the word "unconditional" in the mandate for their withdrawal, gave hints that they would agree to withdraw; but they hedged this offer with such terms as possession of the Kuwaiti islands at the head of the Persian Gulf (which would give them better access to the Gulf). The United States promptly rejected this gesture. Kuwaiti citizens reported another series of Iraqi atrocities in their country. This followed a Kuwaiti resistance statement of 4 October that they were reducing their opposition to the Iraqis because of reprisals against civilians and gave additional credibility to a report issued the day before by Amnesty International of Iraqi atrocities against Kuwaitis.

17 Oct 90   With oil prices now hovering around $40 per barrel, Iraq offered to sell oil at $21 per barrel, in an obvious attempt to break the UN trade embargo. Oil prices fell to about $37 when President Gorbachev met with Secretary of Defense Cheney and reaffirmed previous Soviet commitments to require the Iraqi withdrawal from Kuwait. As the British Desert Rats (the 7th Armored Brigade) began to arrive in Saudi Arabia, members of Congress indicated to Secretary of State James Baker that the Bush administration should seek congressional authorization before the president made any major move against Iraq.

The Coalition, put together with such difficulty, was still fragile at this time. Despite the Soviet statement on 18 October that Saddam Hussein should not be rewarded for his actions if he withdrew from Kuwait and the affirmative votes the Soviet Union had cast in support of the U.S. positions on all the UN Security Council resolutions opposed to the Iraqi invasion, the Soviet Union had played up to now a somewhat ambiguous role brokering what seemed to be a conditional withdrawal from Kuwait. In addition, it had constantly refused to send troops into the region or to support the use of force in the naval blockade. Furthermore, if the Coalition were to be successful, it must have in its ranks Arab nations firmly opposed to the Iraqi aggression. Iraq had worked at every opportunity to exploit any event in Israel that might cause Arab defections from the Coalition. Barely underneath the surface lay Pan-Arab Nationalism with its roots in the suspicion of the former colonial powers England and France, its hatred of the state of Israel (whose staunch ally the United States had long been), and the jealousy of the poorer Arab countries toward such oil-rich nations as Kuwait, Saudi Arabia, and the other Gulf Coast states. To a degree never before possible, an informed world held its breath as events unfolded in the waning days of October.

The ministerial council of the Arab League met and condemned Israel for its killing of the Palestinians, but it refused the PLO proposal to condemn the United States for its aid to Israel. Antiwar marches by several thousand protesters were held on 20 October in cities across the United States. On 21 October a Palestinian in Israel knifed three Israelis in revenge for the 8 October killings of Palestinians, and Israel blamed the United States for this, arguing that its condemnation of Israel had incited the retaliation. Comments made the next day by Saudi Prince Sultan were interpreted in some quarters to mean that after an Iraqi withdrawal, some territorial concessions might be possible. This possible weakening of the Saudi position sent shock waves throughout the Coalition.

23 Oct 90   President Bush's immediate response completely eliminated any such compromise, and he hinted that more U.S. troops would be sent to the Gulf to add to the Pentagon's list of 210,000 including more than 100,000 Army troops and 45,000 Marines, of whom 1,000 were on board ships in the Gulf. On the other hand, only one of the two promised Egyptian armored divisions had arrived, and the Syrian armored division promised by Pres. Hafez al-Assad was not yet on the ground. Iraq, attempting to play one Coalition member against the others, announced that French nationals were free to leave Iraq. Israel increased the tensions by closing its borders to Palestinians. The American response the next day was to join in the unanimous vote by the UN Security Council condemning Israel for not permitting the UN mission to enter Israel. On 25 October, Secretary of Defense Cheney confirmed that more U.S. troops were to be sent to the Gulf, and the Soviets reported that a member of the Presidential Council, Yevgeny Primakov, sent by President Gorbachev to the Gulf region on 3 October, believed that the Iraqis were not ready to withdraw from Kuwait. Two days later, Primakov went to Baghdad, and Gorbachev hinted at a possible solution short of war. The next day, Israel reopened its borders to Palestinians and the tensions were relieved one notch.

29 Oct 90   The UN Security Council again addressed the crisis by passing Resolution 674, which demanded that Iraq cease mistreating Kuwaitis and foreign nationals left in the area under Iraqi control. Further, it stated that under international law, Iraq could be held liable for damages resulting from its actions. This resolution passed 13-0 with Cuba and Yemen again abstaining. Soviet President Gorbachev, once more playing the peacemaker, urged that the Arab nations use their initiative to reach some sort of solution to the Iraq-Kuwait crisis. On the following day, President Bush sought to allay fears in the United States by telling the Congress that he did not believe war was imminent. By the end of the month, only 4,000 Syrian troops were in Saudi Arabia.

1 Nov 90   November began on a hopeful note, but as the days passed, tensions slowly increased, fired by the debate both within the United States and abroad over the use of force to compel Iraq to leave Kuwait. Even though both Iraq and the Coalition increased their military forces facing each other across the Saudi Arabia–Kuwait border, propaganda and diplomacy rather than tanks and planes were still the primary weapons used to attempt to resolve the crisis.

At his 1 November press conference, President Bush denied that this was a war about oil and reiterated that even though it was a fight about "naked aggression," he still sought a peaceful solution. Gen. Norman Schwarzkopf, the commander of all U.S. forces in the Gulf region, said that the U.S. goal was not the ruin of Iraq. The next day, this conciliatory theme continued when Iraq freed three French soldiers who had wandered into Iraq on a patrol. The emphasis on a war over oil was further diminished when it was reported that the increase in Saudi oil production, along with that of other oil-producing countries, had matched the loss of Iraqi and Kuwaiti production. On 4 November, the long-promised Syrian armored division began to arrive in Saudi Arabia, bolstering the Arab input to the Coalition. Anti-American demonstrations in Iran were poorly attended, easing the fear that the civilian government in Iran would have to lean toward support of Iraq.

On the military side of events, the Pentagon announced that it would call up Reserve combat units to supplement the call-up of support units previously. In addition, the Congress extended the call-up time to 360 days. A nagging problem of coordination was overcome on 5 November when the U.S. and Saudi governments reached an agreement on the conduct of war should it come. It was concluded that both governments must agree on the commencement of hostilities and that if war came, the United States could operate outside Saudi Arabia. This agreement was critical since the presence of U.S. forces in Saudi Arabia had been initially only to help defend Saudi Arabia against an Iraqi attack. The president's position was strengthened by the release of an opinion poll indicating that a majority of Americans supported military actions if the boycott failed.

On 6 November China answered a question that had hung over the planners, when it announced that it would not block a UN resolution authorizing the use of force. Until now, China had voted with the other veto-holding superpowers in the Security Council, and these four — France, the Soviet Union, the United Kingdom, and the United States — had shown surprising unanimity in the major steps taken by the United Nations in condemning Iraq. Nonetheless, questions remained in diplomats' minds whether China would remain with them when it came to armed force instead of words.

7 Nov 90   If the first day of November had begun with encouraging words, by the end of the first week public statements had become bellicose. Soviet Foreign Minister Shevardnadze said he could envision a situation where force would be required. The Bush administration argued that a UN Security Council resolution to authorize the use of force was essential since, as Secretary of State Baker said, the credibility of the UN was at risk. Prime Minister Margaret Thatcher of the United Kingdom was even more blunt. She said that if Saddam Hussein did not leave Kuwait soon, the Coalition would drive him out. The Israelis reminded the world of their policy of retaliation when attacked, even hinting that they might use nuclear weapons if subjected to chemical attack, and called for joint Israeli-U.S. planning for possible war. Saddam Hussein continued his divisive strategy by releasing hostages in small groups to visiting leaders from different Coalition nations.

8 Nov 90   On 8 November President Bush ordered new and larger deployment of forces to the Gulf so that the Coalition could have the capability to wage offensive war if that became necessary. The first increment of American forces to reach Saudi Arabia had been scarcely more than a trip wire if Iraq had attacked across the Saudi border. These early units—including the 82nd Airborne Division, the 101st Air Assault Division, and the 5th Special Forces Group— were well-trained and well-equipped, but without the support of heavy armored units, they could have done little more than force the heavily armored Iraqi forces to spill American blood, an event that would have catapulted the United States into full scale war. The addition of such units as the 24th Mechanized Division, the 1st Cavalry Division, and an assortment of infantry, armored, artillery, and aviation brigades had done little more, it was thought at the time, than provide a credible defense force, which could have delayed but not stopped an Iraqi assault. Even the more than 400 Air Force combat aircraft, four aircraft carrier battle groups, one battleship, and 45,000 Marines backed up by the French, British, and other Coalition air and ground forces did not seem enough to do more than save Saudi Arabia from conquest. The Pentagon believed that only the addition of heavy armored and mechanized divisions and more aircraft would permit the Coalition to engage the Iraqi forces of 500,000 ground forces, 4,000 tanks, and thousands of artillery pieces backed up by 500 combat aircraft and drive them back out of Kuwait.

10 Nov 90   Secretary of State Baker returned from a long trip taking the pulse of the Coalition, having visited Saudi Arabia, Egypt, Turkey, the Soviet Union, and China, to report that the Coalition seemed to be in good health but that there seemed to be no urgent desire to have a UN resolution permitting the use of force. Perhaps keying on this apparent lack of urgency, on 11 November some members of the Democratic Party took issue with the president's decision to make such a massive deployment of forces to the Gulf, arguing that he had not sufficiently explained this need to the American people. The voices of the American Catholic bishops were also heard, in their plea that the use of force in the crisis be limited. At the same time, King Hassan of Morocco, a nation which had sent troops to support Saudi Arabia, called for yet another Arab summit meeting. The next day, Iraq demanded that any such meeting deal not only with the present crisis but also with the long-standing Arab-Israeli problem.

13 Nov 90   The political debate over President Bush's handling of the crisis continued with a demand by some members of Congress that he call a special session of Congress to discuss the situation. In an announcement that was to bear significant fruit some months later, the Marines made known that they would conduct amphibious exercises beginning the next day only ten miles from the Kuwaiti border. On 14 November, President Bush, without calling a special session of Congress, tried to calm the situation by saying that he had not yet resolved to use force and that the buildup of forces only made the use of force possible and credible. In the same vein of avoiding political confrontations, the Saudi government said that an Arab summit would be useless unless Iraq had withdrawn from Kuwait. In addition to the deployment of active-duty forces, Secretary of Defense Cheney authorized the call-up of 72,500 additional Reserves.

15 Nov 90   Mid-month brought a flurry of diplomatic activity. Both Egypt and Syria joined the Saudis in rejecting any call for an Arab summit before Saddam Hussein was thwarted. Secretary of State Baker was in Europe holding discussions on the possible UN resolution on the use of force while President Bush said that he would not permit a Vietnam War–style "long, drawn-out agony." Egyptian President Mubarek said that he had asked President Bush not to attack Iraq for at least three months. Both Protestant and Catholic organizations in the United States took positions opposing a Gulf war. The president of the body of Catholic bishops said that an attack on Iraq might not be defined as a "just" war. The National Council of Churches announced its opposition to the Bush administration's Gulf policy, although the next day the Council of Jewish Foundations supported firmness in opposing Iraq. Meanwhile, Saddam Hussein promised to release all hostages if the United States would promise in turn not to attack.

16 Nov 90   There was some evidence that support for Saddam Hussein was eroding. Those Palestinians who had looked to him as their champion appeared to be becoming concerned over the Iraqi brutality being reported, and the African members of the Security Council appeared to be supporting the attempts by the United States to have the Security Council pass a resolution authorizing the use of force against Iraq.

18 Nov 90   Even with these signs of progress, the vote on this desired resolution did not get closer. Saddam Hussein kept playing his hostage card by, on the one hand, continuing the flights carrying some hostages out of Iraq while, on the other, holding others as bargaining chips. The U.S. Embassy in Baghdad reported that 104 Americans were being held at strategic locations as human shields. The Soviets continued to be cool to a use-of-force resolution, and Chancellor Helmut Kohl of Germany expressed the desire for negotiations to prevent war.

19 Nov 90   U.S. forces in the Gulf region reached 230,000, and Iraq announced that it would call up reserves and send 250,000 more troops to Kuwait. At a meeting of the Conference of Security and Cooperation in Europe (CSCE) Prime Minister Thatcher took the position that if Iraq did not withdraw, the use of military force would become necessary. The meeting of CSCE apparently did not bring forth a consensus on the force issue; President Bush meeting with President Gorbachev could not reach an agreement with the Soviet Union.

20 Nov 90   The next day, in the wake of Chancellor Kohl's call for negotiations, Iraq announced that it would release all German hostages. The stated purpose was more general, to show other nations that their independence would be rewarded, but it was clear that Iraq's leader was still trying to break apart the Coalition against him before it could agree on the use of force. Within the United States, divisiveness appeared in earnest. Forty-five Democrats in the House of Representatives sought an injunction in U.S. District Court to bar President Bush from initiating hostilities without first obtaining congressional approval.

21 Nov 90   As had Iraqi President Saddam Hussein and French President Mitterrand, President Bush went to visit the troops in the field, where he again reiterated the national objectives he had announced in early August when Iraq launched its invasion. The Bush administration eased some trade restraints on Turkey as a reward for the Turkish support of the U.S. position. In addition to taking a heavy financial loss by cutting off the flow of Iraqi oil through pipelines across Turkey, the Turkish government had opened its air bases to U.S. combat aircraft and moved almost 100,000 troops to the Turkish-Iraqi border. These Turkish troops required Iraq to keep numerous Iraqi forces in that northern region, preventing them from being deployed in southern Iraq or in Kuwait.

Soviet President Gorbachev, seeking to exercise Soviet influence in the Middle East, called publicly for a meeting of the full United Nations as soon as possible to discuss the Gulf crisis and related issues.

22 Nov 90   In a series of decisions, the Department of Defense took actions typical of an armed force preparing itself for hostilities. The armed services were authorized to curtail leaves, transfers, and retirements, and at once, the Army announced a suspension on separations from the service. On the day that Prime Minister Thatcher resigned, the United Kingdom announced it would send 14,000 more troops and more aircraft to the Gulf region, moves which would bring the total number of British forces there to 30,000. On the same day, PLO Chairman Yassar Arafat, not surprisingly, expressed his views that the Kuwait-Iraq crisis was linked to the broader Palestinian problem.

23 Nov 90   In an unprecedented move, President Bush met in Geneva with Syrian president Hafez al-Assad to discuss the crisis. Prior to the Gulf crisis, the relations between the United States and Syria had been far from cordial. Among other complaints, the United States looked upon Syria as a nation harboring terrorists, and Syria's antipathy for Israel did not help smooth the way to better relations. Now, Syria had responded to President Bush's initiatives in the Gulf crisis not just with diplomacy but also with troops in the field. From a major Arab power in the Middle East, this sort of support was critical, and despite criticism from Israel, President Bush rewarded Pres. Hafez al-Assad with a summit meeting.

26 Nov 90   Following a visit to Yemen by Secretary of State Baker to consult with its government, Yemeni president Ali Abdullah Saleh announced that a UN resolution authorizing the use of force was inadvisable. He suggested instead that the United States send an emissary to Iraq. Iraq in its turn freed all Swedish hostages, causing the Soviet Union to demand for the first time that Soviet citizens in Iraq be released. The Iraqi position had been that some Soviet technicians could not leave until they had fulfilled the terms of their employment contracts. Muddying the waters as world leaders tried to assess the situation came the statement by Egyptian President Mubarek that despite all the preparations by the United States for possible war, Mubarek believed that Saddam Hussein thought President Bush was only bluffing.

27 Nov 90   As if to echo President Mubarek, Iraq announced that even if the United Nations should authorize the use of force against it, Iraq would never yield to pressure. With an estimated 430,000 troops in the Kuwait region supported by thousands of armored vehicles, tanks, and artillery pieces and backed up by several hundred combat aircraft, Saddam Hussein clearly felt that the world would believe him.

With the UN Security Council set to meet on 29 November, the maneuvering picked up both in the United States and abroad. The PLO urged that the United Nations act on the West Bank Palestinian problem before voting on the use of force against Iraq. The U.S. Senate Armed Services Committee opened hearings on the Gulf crisis with the Democratic members urging a cautious approach.

28 Nov 90   As the UN vote to authorize the use of force approached, King Fahd of Saudi Arabia ruled out as pointless any negotiations with Iraq. The Saudi government also agreed to lend the economically hard-pressed Soviets $1 billion, clearly in response to the Soviet support of Saudi Arabia against the Iraqi threat.

On the eve of this momentous vote, the UN Security Council passed yet another resolution, Number 677, by a vote of 13-0 with Cuba and Yemen abstaining, condemning Iraq for its attempts to alter the demographic records of Kuwait. Iraq was seizing Kuwaitis and taking them to Iraq, while moving Iraqis into Kuwait and destroying the census records. The clear intent was to bolster Iraq's claims that Kuwait was an integral part of the state of Iraq and to ensure an Iraqi majority in the event of a plebiscite to establish the national identity of the population in that region.

In the Senate Armed Services Committee's hearings, two former chairmen of the Joint Chiefs of Staff, Adm. William Crowe and Air Force Gen. David Jones, recommended that the world wait for the United Nations' sanctions to bring Iraq around. Henry Kissinger, on the other hand, warned that a prolonged stay of Coalition forces in the region could damage Saudi domestic affairs. Saudi women, seeing the way women were treated in the Coalition's armed forces, were already demanding changes such as the right to drive automobiles.

29 Nov 90   For the first time in modern history, an international peacekeeping body voted to authorize the use of force to stop what was characterized as naked aggression. The League of Nations had only condemned Italy when it invaded Abyssinia before World War II. The UN had endorsed after the fact President Truman's sending of troops to South Korea after the North Koreans had invaded. Now the die was cast determining Iraq's future when the UN Security Council passed Resolution 678. The vote had twelve nations voting for the resolution, Cuba and Yemen voting against it, and China abstaining. The resolution permitted members of the United Nations to use "all means necessary" to enforce the previous UN resolutions concerning Iraq if Iraq did not withdraw from Kuwait by 15 January 1991. This gave the world six more weeks to solve this problem, during which time it was improbable that war would break out. Saddam Hussein, clearly as hostile as ever, announced that he was ready for war if it should come. So mixed did the domestic response remain that some congressional leaders advised President Bush against calling a special session of Congress lest the Congress would not endorse the use of force as the United Nations had done.

30 Nov 90   On the last day of this tumultuous month, President Bush with the authority of the United Nations behind him offered an olive branch to Saddam Hussein. He proposed sending Secretary of State Baker to Baghdad to meet with Saddam Hussein. In return, he invited Iraqi Foreign Minister Azziz to Washington to meet with him.

1 Dec 90   Hopes that diplomatic talks might still bring a solution to the Gulf crisis were buoyed by Iraq's acceptance of President Bush's offer of direct talks with Iraq. The Iraqi acceptance was clouded by its continued insistence that the Palestinian problems be tied to any agreement on Kuwait, but at least the offer had not been rejected out of hand. A comment by a Soviet aide that the aftermath of the Soviet experience in Afghanistan would keep the Soviet Union out of a Gulf war was interpreted in different ways. That the Soviets would not themselves engage in combat could be seen as a factor militating against any fighting by the Coalition. On the other hand, it did not appear to suggest a Soviet veto of military actions taken by others in the Coalition.

2 Dec 90   Secretary of State Baker sought to reassure Iraq by saying that the United States would not attack if Iraq withdrew from Kuwait and released all the hostages. Iraq's response was to test fire two SCUD missiles inside Iraqi territory. This test firing of SCUDs, medium-range ballistic missiles, at this critical time was particularly unsettling since what could be described as peace talks were virtually in the negotiation phase.

Two versions of the SCUD existed. One type had a range of about 200 miles, carried a 1,000-pound warhead, and was quite accurate. The other type sacrificed warhead weight for both range and accuracy. It could fire only about a 500-pound warhead, but the range was extended to approximately 400 miles. The accuracy dropped from a margin of hundreds of feet to an area about one-third of a mile around its intended target. Purportedly, both types of SCUDs could be armed with a conventional high-explosive warhead or, more ominously, nuclear or chemical warheads. Whether Iraq had a nuclear capability was hotly debated, but Iraq's use of chemical warfare against both its own Kurdish citizens and Iranian soldiers was well documented. It was not known if Iraq could construct a chemical warhead for the SCUD, but its 400-mile range gave Iraq the ability to fire SCUD missiles into Israel, and if it could arm them with chemical warheads, this was frightening indeed. Such attacks might have little military significance, but they would be a form of psychological warfare similar to that used by Hitler against England when he launched the "buzz bombs" against civilian targets during World War II.

Aggravating the problem was the fact that the SCUD missile launchers were highly mobile and easy to conceal. These launchers were a type of large truck similar in size and mobility to the eighteen-wheel semitrailer so common on American highways. Furthermore, it took only a couple of hours to position a launcher and send its missile on the way to its target. If war did come, therefore, it would be extraordinarily difficult to eliminate this threat to Israeli and Coalition targets.

The threat against Israel was the one that haunted Coalition planners. The world was well aware of the Israeli policy of retaliation against attacks on its territory and people. The Israeli government had already warned that it would not sit idly by if Iraq launched attacks with weapons of mass destruction—nuclear or chemical—against it. Hence, these test firings did little to reassure those who hoped for a peaceful settlement.

3 Dec 90   Appearing before the Senate Armed Services Committee, Army General Colin Powell, chairman of the Joint Chiefs of Staff, disputed the previous testimony on 28 November by the two former chairmen of the Joint Chiefs, Admiral Crowe and General Jones, who had said that they believed it would be prudent to await the effects of the UN sanctions before launching any attack. General Powell warned against waiting indefinitely for sanctions to persuade Iraq to withdraw. He further indicated that he did not believe air action alone could bring about the defeat of Iraqi forces if war did come. With U.S. forces in the Gulf region now placed by Secretary of Defense Cheney at 240,000 and the estimate of Iraqi forces in that region at 450,000, the limit of the Reserve call-up was raised to 188,000 with some 93,000 now on active duty. New Zealand joined the Coalition by announcing its decision to send two C-130 transport aircraft to the Gulf. In the meantime, the Soviet Union announced that Iraq had decided to release 1,000 Soviet hostages.

4 Dec 90   One of the most significant troop movements, not in terms of size but in the pre-crisis location of the troops, occurred when the 2nd Armored Cavalry Regiment left Europe for the Gulf.

During all previous military crises after World War II, the United States had been loathe to transfer troops from Western Europe to the point of danger. During the Korean War, even when the U.S. forces were in grave danger of being overrun by the North Korean army and later when the intervention of the Chinese army sent the U.S. forces reeling in defeat, U.S. forces were not moved in any major way from Europe to the Far East. At this early stage of the Cold War, the United States had feared that the Korean War was only a diversion intended to draw U.S. forces from Western Europe to the Far East and hence weaken the deterrence of any Soviet attack on NATO. Instead, the United States had moved units from the United States to Korea, instituted the draft, and called up Reserves and Guard units to bolster the forces in Korea. In fact, the strength of U.S. forces in Europe was not only maintained but increased as the Korean War progressed.

During the conflict in Vietnam, similar practices were followed. The United States did not draw down its forces committed to NATO to meet the apparently ever-increasing need for more troop strength to fight the North Vietnamese army and the Viet Cong. Although the Reserve Component was not mobilized, the draft was again reinstituted to meet the demand for more troops after units from the United States had been sent to Vietnam.

Now, however, the tensions of the Cold War appeared to be lessening, and the United States could contemplate reducing its forces facing the Soviet and Warsaw Pact forces. The transfer of even such a relatively small unit as the 2nd Armored Cavalry Regiment from Germany to the Gulf region, therefore, was the first concrete reduction in force in Western Europe, a historic event.

The Turkish government, which already had provided considerable support to the Coalition by opening its air bases to Coalition combat aircraft and moving almost 100,000 troops up to the Iraqi border, announced that it was considering sending troops to the Gulf region.

The diplomatic front sent out mixed signals on the prospects of peace. Saddam Hussein met with the political leaders who had given him at least partial support: Jordan's King Hussein, PLO leader Arafat, and the vice-president of Yemen. All of these leaders applauded the proposed talks between Iraq and the United States. On the other hand, the Iraqi handling of the Soviet hostages was confusing. The Soviet Union had historically been one of Iraq's best friends through its role as a major arms supplier and source of technicians and advisors of all sorts. But as the crisis developed, these Soviet citizens were given no more favorable treatment than those of other nations, and they too had been refused permission to leave Iraq. Despite the announcement the day before by Soviet officials that 1,000 of their people had been given permission to leave, Iraq now added a condition, stipulating that all Soviets could leave, but only if Iraq was compensated by the Soviet government for the uncompleted portions of the contracts between the two governments.

Back in the United States, the political path for President Bush was equally rocky. Democrats in the House kept insisting that congressional approval was constitutionally required before the president could order offensive military action against Iraq. Meanwhile, Bush, who was on a Latin American tour, was saying that he did not believe sanctions alone would be sufficient to make Saddam Hussein order the withdrawal of Iraqi forces from Kuwait.

5 Dec 90   In Argentina, President Bush continued to express his pessimism regarding the efficacy of the UN resolutions, adding that he had seen no evidence they were convincing Saddam Hussein to bow to world opinion. In response to calls for some face-saving way out for the Iraqis, Bush insisted that compliance was more than a face-saving matter. It was still a clear-cut matter of aggression being punished. At hearings being conducted by the Senate Foreign Relations Committee, Secretary of State Baker echoed the president's views on the ineffectiveness of the UN sanctions. Democratic members of the Committee responded with the view that the Bush administration was hurrying the United States into a war. In House hearings being held by the Armed Services Committee, the director of the Central Intelligence Agency, William Webster, estimated that it would take nine more months for the sanctions to have serious effects on the Iraqi economy. Even then, he argued, there could be no guarantee that these sanctions would persuade Iraq to comply with the UN resolutions.

To add to the pressure on Iraq, the most hawkish Israeli government in recent times said that the United States should not ignore the Iraqi threat. The Israelis went so far as to imply that they might act if the United States did not.

Iraq finally, after days of shifting positions, formally announced that it had agreed to the talks proposed by President Bush. The European Community also formally proposed that additional talks be held after the bilateral ones between Iraq and the United States. Reports circulated that the United States would support a United Nations resolution calling for an international conference on the Middle East.

7 Dec 90   Predicting the next move of Saddam Hussein had proved difficult through this crisis period, as he radically altered his positions almost from day to day. Barely three days after it had announced that the Soviet Union would, in effect, have to buy
back its hostage citizens, Iraq announced that all hostages
would be released. In keeping with his previous hard-line policy, President Bush insisted that the Coalition had to maintain the pressure on Iraq. But the next day the United States
said that after all U.S. citizens had left, it would close the embassy in Kuwait.

From the beginning of Iraq's demand that foreign embassies
in Kuwait be closed, the United States had refused to comply
with this order. From the point of view of the United States,
to do so would have suggested concurrence with the Iraqi claim
that Kuwait was no longer an independent state to which diplomatic representation was warranted. The U.S. embassy had
been kept under a virtual state of siege for weeks while the
American ambassador and a reduced staff had defiantly stayed
in place. Now that all Americans would have left the country,
there was no practical reason for the embassy to remain open,
and the symbolic reason did not alone justify the danger to
the individuals. The release of the hostages gave the United
States a reason to bring its ambassador home without significant loss of face.

Apparently in reaction to the rumors and calls for an international conference on the Middle East, Jordan's King Hussein
lent his support to the holding of Middle East talks by saying
that he was positive Iraq would not leave Kuwait unless there
was a solution to the Palestinian problem. This position, unfortunately, implied that an Iraqi withdrawal could only follow
talks. The Israeli prime minister, Yitzhak Shamir, dashed cold
water on all the hopes of an international conference when
he announced that Israel would not participate in any such
meeting. The positions of neither King Hussein nor Prime
Minister Shamir helped the relations of their countries with
the United States, but in many ways, neither man had much
choice.

King Hussein was in a most difficult spot. Jordan had long
been seen by the United States as one of its closest friends
and allies in the Arab world. King Hussein's position towards
the state of Israel in the recent past had been, for that region,

relatively moderate, and the king had enjoyed U.S. support in
both military and economic aid. Now he was in serious difficulties. Jordan depended heavily upon such Arab neighbors as
Saudi Arabia for oil, and because of an apparent pro-Iraq position, this had been cut off. Jordan's economy was closely tied
to trade with Iraq, and compliance with the UN trade embargoes and sanctions had crippled that. Exacerbating this economic problem was the massive influx of refugees from Iraq,
many with only the clothes on their backs and what they could
carry, who required massive assistance just to survive. On top
of all these problems was that of the large number of Palestinians in the Jordanian population. They had long been vehemently, and often violently, opposed to Israel and they were
now equally vehemently in support of Saddam Hussein because of his espousal of the Palestinian cause. Thus King Hussein had to tread a very fine line just to retain his crown, and
perhaps even his life, in this turbulent area and to manage to
have some reasonable position in the post-crisis Middle East
no matter how the crisis was resolved.

Similarly, Prime Minister Shamir governed by the slimmest
of parliamentary majorities. For years, the United States had
seen Israel as the only democratic state in the Middle East and
had been one of Israel's few friends; U.S. military and economic
aid were essential to Israel's survival. The United States had
indeed almost blindly supported every Israeli foreign policy
position toward the Arab states. Israel had always feared an
international conference on the Palestinian problem, prefer-
ring bilateral talks instead; the United States had concurred.
Moreover, the United States had attempted to keep the Soviet
Union from any position of prominence in Israeli affairs.

Now there appeared to be a shift in U.S. support for Israel
by the Bush administration induced by the complexities of the
Gulf crisis. For virtually the first time, the United States had
joined in UN condemnation of Israeli actions towards Palestinians. Now it appeared that the United States was throwing
its support toward an international conference on the Palestinian problem, placing the Israeli preference for bilateral talks
at risk. In addition, it seemed that, to ensure Soviet support
of the U.S. goals in this crisis, the United States was opening
the door to Soviet participation in the solution of the Arab-
Israeli problem.

Prime Minister Shamir appeared to hold a trump card, however. The anti-Iraq coalition had to have significant Arab participation if the crisis were to be seen as a world condemnation of Iraqi aggression instead of only a dispute between Iraq and the United States, supported by the Western colonial powers that were seen by many Arabs as the root of all the problems in the Middle East. Iraq was doing everything in its power to cast the United States in the role of a regional bully who put support of the hated Israelis above all else and to minimize the role of the United Nations in the crisis. A major fear of the United States was that Iraq could provoke Israel into some hostile military action against Iraq, or any other Arab state, which would shatter the Coalition. Should that occur, war could break out between Israel and, for instance, Syria. If Israel called upon the United States for military assistance, the current Iraq-Kuwait crisis could fade into insignificance.

A glance at the map of the region is sufficient to show the magnitude of the problem. By now, most of the military forces that could be called upon to come to the aid of Israel were located in Saudi Arabia facing Iraq with an army said to be the fourth largest in the world poised on the Kuwait–Saudi Arabia border. To withdraw U.S forces to aid and defend Israel—if that were even possible—could jeopardize the U.S. forces in the region. As a result, the United States itself was virtually held hostage to Israeli intentions. The only saving grace was Israel's knowledge that the ultimate outcome of any Arab-Israeli conflict could not be predicted with any certainty. Every word and deed by every government was placed under a diplomatic microscope and dissected for every possible implication.

8 Dec 90   Jordan's King Hussein, undoubtedly recognizing that his previous call for a solution of the Palestinian problem could not be achieved before the UN's deadline of 15 January 1991, modified his position to ask for an international conference to be held simultaneously with an Iraqi withdrawal. The bilateral talks between the United States and Iraq proposed by President Bush were bogged down by a dispute over the dates of these talks. Iraq was holding out for a mid-January date for the last talk, but the United States, with an eye on 15 January, wanted it to be earlier. Clearly, the United States was worried that Iraq would drag out these talks well past the deadline to buy more time, hoping that the longer the crisis lasted, the higher the possibility that internal disputes within the Coalition would weaken its resolve. President Bush's firm stand was bolstered by a major U.S. public opinion poll, which indicated that almost two-thirds of Americans supported war if that were the only way to drive Iraq from Kuwait.

A small group of the estimated 750 Americans still in Kuwait left the country, along with 2,000 more Westerners and Japanese still held in Kuwait and Iraq. By 11 December, it appeared that all hostages who wanted to leave had done so, and their departure coupled with the closing of the U.S. embassy made it easier, in President Bush's words, for war to come.

9 Dec 90   As the United States asked Turkey to deploy more forces on the Iraq-Turkey border, a presence which would pin down more Iraqi divisions along that northern border and deny their use in the south, Secretary of State Baker indicated that as the United States added more combat aircraft, the Coalition forces in the Gulf region would approach 550,000 to oppose the estimated 500,000 Iraqi troops.

Oil experts said that world oil production had matched world consumption despite the loss of production of Iraqi and Kuwaiti oil and that oil stocks were at or near normal levels. Balancing that good news was the forecast that oil production was close to its maximum capability.

11 Dec 90   While France announced that its present 6,000 troops in the Gulf would be raised to 10,000, Soviet Foreign Minister Shevardnadze made two important statements. In one, confirming a hint by an aide on December 1, he stated that there would be no Soviet troop commitment to the Coalition. This was not too surprising in view of the internal economic problems facing the Soviet Union and the post-Afghanistan reaction similar to that of the post-Vietnam feelings in the United States. In the second statement, he proposed a chemical- and nuclear-free zone in the Middle East, a proposal toward which Secretary of State Baker appeared sympathetic. If the report of this reaction on Baker's part was accurate, it signaled a shift in U.S. policy. It was widely believed that Israel had achieved a nuclear capability, and a nuclear-free zone in the Middle East if adopted would deny Israel the right to use those weapons to defend itself against the larger opposing Arab forces. It would also indicate a further change in U.S. policy towards Israel in particular and the Middle East in general.

Israeli Prime Minister Shamir said that he had been heartened by conversations with President Bush. According to Shamir, the president had allayed Israeli concerns that the United States would seek an agreement on the Gulf crisis that would be contrary to Israeli interests. On the Arab side of diplomacy, Algeria's president Chadli Bendjedid initiated yet another attempt to bring the Saudis and the Iraqis together to resolve the crisis.

12 Dec 90   In a move that puzzled Coalition members intently studying every Iraqi gesture, Saddam Hussein replaced his minister of defense with Maj. Gen. Saadi Tuma Abbas, who brought with him a fine combat commander's reputation from the Iran-Iraq war. The president had made a habit of replacing senior military figures without warning in what before had seemed insurance against their becoming a threat to him. International observers wondered whether this change was in the same vein, a chastising of a minister who had not achieved the success the president expected and demanded, or a preparation for going from the defensive to the offensive. The days passed without clues to his motivation.

The OPEC ministers agreed to a suspension of the production quotas with concurrent authorization to increase production. Although some analysts disputed the previous estimate that recent production had met world needs, the price of oil dropped to $25.35 per barrel, the lowest price since the previous August.

13 Dec 90   A chapter in history closed when the U.S. embassy staff left Kuwait, and the Bush administration accused Iraq of stalling tactics on setting dates for Iraqi-U.S. talks, which more and more seemed to offer the last real chance for averting war. On another diplomatic front, Algerian President Bendjedid was in Iran attempting to set the stage for the long-sought regional solution to this international crisis.

Meanwhile on the domestic political front, in a victory for the executive branch, the U.S. District Court rejected the injunction sought by forty-five House Democrats which would have prevented the president's initiating hostilities without congressional approval.

14 Dec 90   Neither President Bush nor President Bendjedid scored diplomatic successes in their attempts to get talks underway. Saddam Hussein apparently was absolutely unyielding to the Algerian president's pleas for some Iraqi concessions that would have enabled Saudi-Iraqi talks to take place. President Bush, after suspending the proposed Washington visit of Iraqi Foreign Minister Azziz unless Saddam Hussein received Secretary of State Baker on 3 January 1991, was rebuffed by Iraq. The Iraqi government cancelled Azziz's visit entirely, saying that only Iraq could set the dates of Secretary of State Baker's visit to Iraq. In President Bush's view, unless Baker met Saddam Hussein no later than 3 January, there would be insufficient time for any real talks before the UN's 15 January deadline.

In a House Armed Services Committee hearing, General Powell said that regardless of the 15 January date, it could be mid-February before U.S. Forces were ready and capable of going fully on the offensive against the Iraqi forces.

16 Dec 90   Israel took a drastic step when it ordered the deportation of four Palestinians from Israel and received a harsh reaction from the United States. The day before, Palestinians had murdered three Jews in Jaffa, and reportedly 500 Palestinians had been arrested as a result. The Bush administration was clearly concerned that these sorts of Israeli government actions would unsettle the Coalition and interfere with efforts at curbing Iraq.

17 Dec 90   After saying that he still hoped the Iraqi-U.S. talks could come about despite the Iraqi cancellation of the Azziz visit, Secretary of State Baker warned the NATO ministers to anticipate some sort of Iraqi gesture, even a partial withdrawal, just before 15 January. The NATO ministers threw down the gauntlet by saying that only a complete withdrawal could avert hostilities.

Iraq seemed to remain obdurate, even tweaking the nose of former allies, by apparently forbidding the departure of 2,300 Soviet technical advisors even after having said that all hostages could leave Iraq and Kuwait. At the same time, Iraq asked the European Community to conduct talks with Foreign Minister Azziz in the wake of the delayed, or cancelled, trip by Azziz to Washington. The next day, the Community sent back a response almost as harsh as the NATO ministers' message to Iraq. The EC ministers declined to see Foreign Minister Azziz until after he had talked with President Bush.

Three weeks before, Egyptian President Mubarek had said that he believed Saddam Hussein thought President Bush was only bluffing about waging war against Iraq. The American president apparently took this warning to heart and made a series of statements that were intended to convey to Saddam Hussein his seriousness in contemplating the use of force after the 15 January deadline had passed. In the same vein, the United Kingdom, as if anticipating that hostilities would start on 15 January, warned its nationals to leave the Gulf region before that date.

With U.S. armed strength in the Gulf region reaching 260,000, the Army took the initial steps to recall a limited number of retirees, primarily medical personnel such as doctors and nurses. This and the other announcements of the day indicated that war was becoming more than a remote possibility although the Bush administration had not given up all hope.

19 Dec 90   French President Mitterrand similarly cast a pall over the situation when he announced that Iraq must withdraw completely from Kuwaiti territory. Thus France, which had so often hewed to an independent path, seemed to throw in with the United States, the United Nations, NATO, and the European Community.

In Saudi Arabia, Army Lt. Gen. Calvin Waller, the deputy commander of the Central Command (CENTCOM) — the U.S. headquarters directing all operations in the Gulf Region — echoed General Powell's assessment of U.S. capability in testimony before the House Armed Services Committee on 14 December, when he said that not all the U.S. units would be ready for combat until some time after 1 February 1991. Notwithstanding the fact that Secretary of Defense Cheney had said much the same thing a few days before, Lt. Gen. Waller's comment created a major furor. In point of fact, the major reinforcements called for by President Bush on 8 November were still streaming into Saudi Arabia. Lt. Gen. Waller's statement appeared to some to offer further grounds for delaying the outbreak of hostilities. Turkey seemed to have its doubts too and called upon NATO to send additional air strength to shore up Turkish defenses.

20 Dec 90   Not surprisingly, the Department of Defense immediately responded to Lt. Gen. Waller's statement by assuring the world that the U.S. forces in the Gulf would be ready, if called upon, by the 15 January deadline. Still, although the Bush administration said there was only a dim hope that Saddam Hussein would meet with Secretary of State Baker, no decision to attack had yet been made. At a press conference President Bush asserted his total certainty that if war came, Iraq would be roundly defeated.

In response to Israel's deportation of four Palestinians on 15 December, the UN Security Council unanimously passed Resolution 681, which denounced these Israeli deportations and called for the UN Security Council to monitor the West Bank. The resolution even spoke of Jerusalem as occupied territory. A separate Security Council statement mentioned a possible international peace conference.

The Israeli government was appalled. To call Jerusalem "occupied territory" was unthinkable. To denounce the deportation represented, they argued, unwarranted intrusion into Israel's internal affairs. To call for UN monitoring of the West Bank was unacceptable.

Another shocking development was Soviet Foreign Minister Shevardnadze's unexpected resignation from his government post. Shevardnadze had become close friends with Secretary of State Baker over the years. Moreover, the reason he gave for his action, the threat of Soviet dictatorship, was seen by many as perhaps adversely affecting all Soviet-U.S. relations. When a thousand Soviet citizens refused to leave Iraq to spend a winter in the Soviet Union, further doubt was cast on the state of the Soviet economy and other domestic problems.

21 Dec 90   Saddam Hussein announced flatly that he would not withdraw from Kuwait by the 15 January deadline. The reaction of Britain's new prime minister, John Major, was both conciliatory and blunt. Major said that if the Iraqis elected to withdraw, they would not be attacked. On the other hand, he restated the possibility that force might be necessary to accomplish the UN goal of complete withdrawal. Secretary of Defense Cheney agreed and added that if war came, no restrictions would be placed on the military. He was implying that the kind of restrictions placed upon the armed forces during the Vietnam War— prohibitions of certain types of targets, safe havens for enemy forces, and the like—would not apply in this case. Two days later as he concluded a tour of the units in the Gulf, Cheney made the pessimistic comment that time was running out before force might have to be used.

Meanwhile back in Washington, the speaker of the House of Representatives, Tom Foley, assessed the political situation in the Congress and came to the conclusion that the president could win a vote on a resolution authorizing the use of force but the vote in favor would not be substantial.

24 Dec 90   In the war of nerves, Saddam Hussein went on the offensive by declaring that Israel would be the first target if war broke out. He had used every opportunity to fracture the Coalition by setting Arab against Arab, Muslim against Christian. This explicit threat raised the specter of an Iraqi attack against Israel that would provoke such an Israeli response that the Arab members of the Coalition would subordinate their quarrel with Iraq to the older anti-Israel feud.

On the diplomatic front, Iraq recalled its ambassadors to the Coalition nations for consultations, raising speculation that some change in Iraqi policy was in the making.

25 Dec 90   On Christmas Day, Pope John Paul II in his annual message called for a peaceful resolution to the Gulf crisis. The secular leaders of the Gulf Coast Council closed their meeting on a pessimistic note stating that only Iraq's withdrawal from Kuwait could avert war.

26 Dec 90   With the U.S. presence in the Gulf now standing at 300,000 —180,000 Army, 50,000 Marines, 35,000 Air Force, and 35,000 Navy—all nonessential American personnel and their dependents were ordered to leave Jordan and Sudan. Sudan had sided with Iraq during the crisis, and there had been reports of an Iraqi military presence there.

Israel sent mixed signals in response to the Iraqi threat to attack Israel if war began. Prime Minister Shamir promised serious retaliation for any such unwarranted assaults, but other government officials said that Israel would not make any preemptive strikes.

27 Dec 90   There had been newspaper reports on Christmas Eve that Secretary of Defense Cheney and Chairman of the Joint Chiefs

General Powell believed that U.S. forces would not be ready for war by 15 January. President Bush took pains to quash these rumors, as preparations for war continued. The Air Force began for the first time to call up Reservists for service in combat units instead of merely in support roles. Overall, with 57,000 more members of the Reserve Component (the Guard and the Reserves) now called to active duty, nearly 25 percent of the men and women in the Gulf were from the Reserve or the Guard.

Iraq returned its ambassadors to their posts; they had been recalled to Baghdad from Coalition capitals for consultations on 24 December. Hope tentatively sprang up in the wake of an announcement that Iraq was now ready for productive talks. One hundred members of the U.S. House of Representatives called upon President Bush to wait for the UN's economic sanctions to work before initiating hostilities.

Tensions increased, however, when Jordan conducted large-scale military maneuvers. Israel promptly responded by placing its forces on full alert, but it did not call up its reserves to active duty.

28 Dec 90   Two U.S. aircraft carriers, the U.S.S. *Roosevelt* and the U.S.S. *America,* set sail for the Gulf, while 16,000 U.S. troops sailed from ports along the East Coast. The press reported that by the middle of December there had been naval intercepts of shipping during which 500 ships had been boarded and 24 required to turn back.

As a reward for Egypt's steadfast support of the U.S. goals, President Bush directed that Egypt did not need to repay the remaining $1 billion of its total $6.7 billion debt for military assistance.

29 Dec 90   The Coalition added another member when Poland sent two ships and medical personnel to the Gulf. In response to a Turkish request for combat aircraft support to counter the Iraqi threat, which increased as Iraq increased its forces on its northern border, Germany announced that it was contemplating sending aircraft to Turkish bases.

Iraq and the Soviet Union announced that the dispute over the termination of the contracts of some 2,500 Soviet technicians still in Iraq had been resolved, but reports still circulated that 1,000 of them had elected to stay in country.

30 Dec 90   In these last days of December, there was a flurry of diplomatic activity. Japan offered to renew its economic aid to Iraq if that nation would pull back within its borders. The European Community announced that it would meet on 2 January 1991 to consider a proposal independent of those of other organizations and states which would persuade Iraq to withdraw from Kuwait. Saddam Hussein, still hoping to divide the Coalition along religious lines, called for an Islamic meeting a week later to discuss a Holy War if the Coalition attacked Iraq. Still, the next day Iraq announced that it would entertain a new U.S. offer of meeting dates, and the Bush administration replied that a meeting could come when Secretary of State Baker visited the Gulf in the first week in January.

While Saddam Hussein threatened what he described as Muslim guerrilla attacks, which some feared would mean worldwide terrorism, fifteen separate Iraqi groups opposing their president announced that they had united to become a more effective opposition force. The year 1990 had begun with high hopes, as tensions in Europe were decreasing and with them the threat of a major war in Western Europe. The year ended with tension and fear that war might instead break out in the Middle East — and the volatility of the region along with Iraqi threats to expand the bounds of any hostilities meant that there were no clear limits to the violence if it did begin.

1 Jan 91   As 1991 opened, the only glimmer of hope was that UN Security Council Resolution 678 did not *require* the use of force to compel Iraq to withdraw from Kuwait and abide by all the previous resolutions which had addressed the crisis. Rather it only *authorized* force — or in its diplomatic terms, "all means necessary." If President Saddam Hussein would only recognize that the Coalition arrayed against him was remaining a cohesive body firmly united in the belief that Iraqi aggression was an unacceptable threat to the world, one that overrode national rivalries and the immediate solution of the longstanding Palestinian problem, then war might not come. This glimmer, however, seemed to dim in the light of warlike words and actions in the region.

The Iraqi attitude seemed intransigent: Iraq and Iraq alone could have Kuwait, or Kuwait would be destroyed. Jordan deployed 80,000 troops in defensive positions along its border with Israel and announced that it would be prepared to withstand assaults by either Iraq or Israel. Iran announced that it too would begin military maneuvers along the Iraqi border in the near future. On the more positive side, despite an announcement by Egypt's President Mubarek that Iraq faced a bloody war if it did not leave Kuwait, Libya said that Syria, Egypt, Libya, and an unnamed fourth country would convene a summit meeting on the crisis.

2 Jan 91   As a major amphibious Marine force sailed from the Philippines and NATO announced that in response to the request of Turkey, one of its members, fighter aircraft from Germany, Belgium, and Italy would fly to Turkish bases, the United States announced that facing the 510,000 Iraqi troops were 325,000 U.S. forces. The United Kingdom also said that its 4th Armored Brigade had left to join the 7th already training in Saudi Arabia.

In a somewhat conciliatory statement, PLO Chairman Arafat said that he thought Iraq might evacuate Kuwait, but only if there were a strong tie to a solution of the Palestinian problem. In a somewhat similar tone, the Bush administration seemed to hold out the hope that the dispute over meeting dates with Iraq could be resolved.

3 Jan 91   Following an announcement by the Department of Defense that 580,000 Coalition forces faced 530,000 Iraqis in what was being called the Kuwait Theater of Operations (basically southern Iraq, Kuwait, and the Persian Gulf), President Bush proposed that Secretary of State Baker meet Foreign Minister Azziz in Geneva on 7, 8, or 9 January, perilously close to the 15 January deadline, but still an offer of the olive branch of peace. President Mitterrand tried yet again to use France's good offices where others had failed. This attempt made foregoing the use of force conditional on an Iraqi withdrawal coupled with an "understanding"—a softer diplomatic word than "promise" —that an international conference on regional problems would follow.

In further diplomatic moves abroad, Syria, Egypt, Libya, and Sudan (the unnamed nation in Libya's proposal of New Year's Day) met in Cairo but apparently failed to find any new approach to resolving the crisis. On a more somber note, the United Kingdom expelled seven Iraqi diplomats for "unacceptable conduct." In the United States, in the political arena, the

Congress convened, and its first order of business was to decide when to conduct a debate on the crisis.

4 Jan 91   Congress agreed to open the debate on 10 January. Iraq accepted the date of 9 January for the meeting of Secretary of State Baker and Foreign Minister Azziz in Geneva, although the president said that Baker would not go on to the meeting in Iraq as originally proposed. The European Community accepted the proposal advanced by President Mitterrand and invited Azziz to meet with them on 10 January, immediately following his meeting with Baker.

Throughout the formation of the Coalition, the matter of offensive operations on the part of individual nations had been a point on which there had been some question. Both Egypt and Syria had said earlier that they would engage only in combat that protected Saudi Arabia from an Iraqi attack. Now the foreign ministers of Iran and Turkey said they had agreed that neither would attack Iraq. While these were not defections from the Coalition's primary goal of preventing Iraq from enjoying the fruits of its aggression, they could diminish the size of the force which would go into Iraq if war came.

5 Jan 91   In a radio address, once more President Bush restated the threat that had faced Iraq since the passage of UN Security Council 678: withdraw unconditionally and immediately or face the consequences of war. There could be no misunderstanding the words; but despite this, Iraq rejected the European Community's offer of talks based on the Mitterrand proposal of a withdrawal linked with an international conference.

6 Jan 91   Along with Iraq's tacit rejection of President Mitterrand's suggestion, the United States rejected it explicitly because it unacceptably allowed conditions to be linked to a withdrawal. Saddam Hussein warned his people to expect a long, bloody war to safeguard Iraq and to free Palestine. Five airlines, facing what seemed to be an increase in the threat of war that might include Israel and the consequent rise in insurance premiums, cancelled flights to Israel, as Pan American had done three days before.

Weeks before, Henry Kissinger had warned that a prolonged stay by Western forces in Saudi Arabia could have adverse effects on the domestic affairs of that nation. Saudi King Fahd now took the occasion of a public statement to deny that the Western presence was presenting problems, but he added that he expected that once the crisis was resolved all foreign troops would be withdrawn quickly from Saudi Arabia.

Congressional leaders speculated that the Congress would support the use of force but not by a large majority. Whereas before the Bush administration had worried that it might lose such a vote, in the face of this welcome assessment, it now deemed congressional action desirable.

7 Jan 91   The first week of the new year ended with reports both good and bad. On the positive side was a report that Saddam Hussein had told a French reporter that if he received assurances Iraq would not be attacked, he was prepared to make some concession, albeit unhappily. On the ominous side, the United Nations took Iraqi threats of attacks on Israel seriously and advised all nonessential staff members to leave Israel.

A major U.S. opinion poll indicated that almost two-thirds of Americans favored the use of force if that is what it took to achieve the nation's goals. This percentage was little changed from that reported some weeks earlier.

In a sequence typical of times of great international tension, the defection of six Iraqi helicopters to Saudi Arabia was reported by the United States, immediately denied by Iraq, and the next day also denied by Saudi officials.

8 Jan 91   With a week to go before the 15 January UN deadline, President Bush formally asked the Congress to authorize the use of force to compel Iraq to withdraw from Kuwait. The chair of the House Armed Services Committee, Les Aspin, a most well informed and influential member of Congress, speculated in a prepared statement that if war came it would begin with an air war followed by a ground assault, with a swift Iraqi defeat and relatively low Coalition casualties.

Facing the prospects of Iraqi-inspired terrorism, the U.S. military in Germany increased security measures. In other steps to enhance their national security, the Iraqis and the Iranians agreed to keep their troops one-half mile away from their border. The United States and Spain seized a Soviet cargo vessel headed for Jordan with a cargo of military spare parts.

Saudi Arabia was reported to hold the position that it would support attacks on Iraq, particularly its chemical and nuclear capabilities, but did not want to see the nation of Iraq cut up.

9 Jan 91   On 9 January, as agreed, Secretary of State Baker and Foreign Minister Azziz met in Geneva; no progress resulted. Azziz, in a diplomatic maneuver, refused to accept a letter from President Bush, but he did agree to permit U.S. Embassy officials to leave Iraq on 12 January. Only a faint ray of hope remained, and UN Secretary General Perez de Cuellar seized it, with a visit to Baghdad on 12 January.

Iraq once again warned that it would attack Israel if, but only if, war came. Egyptian President Mubarek sent a warning to Israel: stay clear of this conflict or Egyptian policy could change.

French President Mitterrand said that war would come if Iraq did not withdraw, and if war came, France would play its part. Pakistan sent 5,000 more troops to the Gulf to bring its strength to 10,000. Secretary of Defense Cheney announced that he would ask that Reserve tours of active duty due to expire in February be extended. The Central Command said that the VII Corps (the 1st Infantry Division, the 1st Armored Division, and the 3rd Armored Division) would not be fully deployed in the Kuwait Theater of Operations by 15 January. As thousands more refugees attempted to flee Iraq across the Jordanian border, Jordan in desperation announced it had closed this land exit.

10 Jan 91   To ensure that no avenue to peace was blocked, Secretary of State Baker said that the United States would not preclude a possible European Community proposal to hold an international conference after Iraq withdrew from Kuwait. Reportedly, the United States would even let France, Algeria, and the United Nations take the lead in arranging some sort of peace agreement at this late date.

As the House of Representatives and the Senate began their debate on the authorization to use force, the United States ordered all but essential staff and all dependents to leave the American embassy in Yemen. All remaining Western embassy personnel began to leave Iraq, and Israel warned its people to be ready for war. With terrorism in mind, the Justice Department directed that all people holding Iraqi or Kuwaiti passports entering the United States be photographed and finger-printed.

Despite published opinion polls that showed up to two-thirds of Americans supporting war if it came, the *New York Times* reported that all major American religious denominations opposed a war on moral grounds and that nine labor unions similarly were in opposition.

11 Jan 91   American citizens were advised to leave Israel as Saddam Hussein continued to fan the flames of war with provocative public statements. Meanwhile, both houses of Congress continued their debate, and Saudi officials said they would agree to war if the use of force became necessary.

The foreign ministers of the European Community communicated with the UN's secretary general that they would urge an international conference if Iraq would leave Kuwait. The EC proposal contained five major points, including a UN-monitored withdrawal of Iraqi troops and the withdrawal of all foreign forces, with no attack, and a neutral peace-keeping force for the region.

12 Jan 91   As Secretary General Perez de Cuellar met with Saddam Hussein, the United States closed its embassy in Baghdad and expelled all but four Iraqi diplomats from the United States.

In a move that brought great relief to the Coalition members, Israel reiterated that it would not launch preemptive strikes on Iraq. Further, it would absorb any first attack by Iraq before retaliating. Egypt changed its former position that it would not engage in any attack on Iraq, but Syria still withheld its agreement to participate.

The Congress, in a close vote in the Senate but with a larger majority in the House, voted to authorize the use of force to carry out the resolutions of the UN Security Council. From a legal standpoint, nothing now stood in the way of an attack on Kuwait if Iraq did not change its position and withdraw.

13 Jan 91   Secretary General Perez de Cuellar had no more luck than other diplomats in his talks with Saddam Hussein and reported to the world his lack of progress toward peace. Even as Arab nations made a last desperate appeal to Iraq to avoid bloodshed, Secretary of State Baker said that he had reached agreements with all the members of the Coalition that there was no need for any more consultations before an attack.

Jordan responded to these increased tensions by raising the level of its military alert and by moving troops to its border with Israel. The United States called on Israel to permit the United States to respond to any Iraqi attack on Israel. Rejecting this plea and appearing to reverse earlier assurances, Israel again said it would retaliate if attacked.

14 Jan 91   On the eve of the UN deadline, Secretary General Perez de Cuellar, after his abortive meeting with Saddam Hussein, met with French President Mitterrand and after this meeting said there was no hope left that a peaceful solution could be achieved. In response, the French proposed that the secretary general agree in advance to an international conference if Iraq would withdraw, a proposal promptly rejected by the United States as a conditional withdrawal contrary to the UN resolution. The president of the European Community, agreeing with the UN Secretary General, told President Bush that the EC had given up on peace efforts.

As antiwar demonstrations continued in Europe and the United States, the United States tightened its antiterrorism security measures. PLO Chairman Arafat sent a message to Iraq that he and the PLO were standing shoulder to shoulder with the Iraqis. Arafat's deputy Abu Iyad was assassinated, sparking rumors that it had been done by the Abu Nidal group which was being sheltered by Iraq and sowing some confusion in the PLO ranks.

15 Jan 91   UN Security Council Resolution 678 said that Iraq had to withdraw from Kuwait by 15 January, but 15 January came and went without war.

Other members of the Security Council rejected the latest French proposal as just a form of appeasement, and Perez de Cuellar, back in New York, again called upon Saddam Hussein to withdraw from Kuwait. If he did, Perez de Cuellar said, there would be no attack on Iraq and the Palestinians would get a complete hearing. Egypt's President Mubarek took to the television to plead with Iraq's president to change his mind before it was too late. Saudi Arabia's King Fahd warned of the consequences of war.

Iraq closed its border with Turkey, and Turkey said that it would not be a part of an attack on Iraq. Jordan's King Hussein told his country that war was coming, but he assured his citizens that he would keep Jordan out of the conflict. The chief of staff of the Israeli Air Force increased the pressure on Jordan, however. He warned that if there should be an air war between Israel and Iraq and Israeli aircraft were not permitted to overfly Jordan, the Jordanian Air Force faced certain destruction.

16 Jan 91   The French National Assembly, like the United States Congress, approved the use of force and placed French forces under U.S. control if war came. Greece approved the use of its military bases and ports for the logistical support of U.S. forces.

On these supportive notes, Desert Shield—although the world did not yet know it—came to an end. In the United States and elsewhere serious attempts had been made to prevent war. Try as he might, Saddam Hussein had not yet been able to drive wedges between Coalition members by convincing his fellow Arabs that either their disputes with Israel or the festering Palestinian problem was more important than curbing his driving ambition. One miscalculation after another had been heaped into a mound that pointed inexorably to war.

Top: A-10 Thunderbolt; *bottom:* B-52G

Top: C-5A Galaxy; *bottom:* C-130 Hercules

Top: E-3A AWACS (Airborne Warning and Control); *bottom:* F-4 Phantom

Top: F-15 Eagles flying with a B-52G Stratofortress; *bottom:* F-111E

F-16 Fighting Falcon

Top: F-117 Stealth Fighter; *bottom:* KC-10 Extender refueling an F-15 Eagle

Top: AH-60 Black Hawk modified for aeromedical evacuation; *bottom:* AH-64 Apache helicopter

Top: DH-58D Kiowa Warrior scout helicopter; *bottom:* Patriot Surface-to-Air Missile Launcher

Top: High Mobility Multipurpose Wheeled Vehicle (HMMWV); *bottom:* MAIA "Abrams" Main Battle Tank

M-2 "Bradley" Infantry Fighting Vehicle

Top: M-109 155mm Self-Propelled Howitzer; *bottom:* M-113 Armored Personnel Carrier

U.S.S. *Kennedy*

4 Desert Storm

17 January–28 February 1991

17 Jan 91 President Bush waited two days after the UN deadline for Iraqi withdrawal from Kuwait before ordering the Coalition to begin action against Iraqi forces. The winds of Desert Storm began howling across Iraq at 0230 hours Baghdad time. As the chair of the House Armed Services Committee, Les Aspin, had so accurately predicted weeks before, Desert Storm began with air warfare, not a ground assault.

The Coalition was facing an estimated 500,000 men armed with 4,230 tanks, 2,870 armored personnel carriers, 3,110 artillery pieces (some of which could outshoot the Coalition's by five miles), 160 helicopters, and 809 support aircraft. With fewer than 600,000 men and women, far under the conventional 3:1 ratio of attackers to defenders, the Coalition could not afford to begin ground combat until air power had cleared the way. Before Desert Storm was over, the Air Force would fly more than 65,000 sorties (one sortie is one aircraft flying on one mission) against the enemy.

The air war began with strikes by Air Force F-117 stealth fighter-bombers, Navy Tomahawk cruise missiles, and Army Apache helicopters. In the broadest sense, the first set of targets included everything that Iraq could use to command and control its armed forces, its air power, its air-defense system, fixed SCUD launchers, and chemical and nuclear sites. If these targets were eliminated, Coalition air forces would be able to fly virtually unchallenged over both Iraq and Kuwait. The enemy's war-making capabilities would be destroyed, its ground forces isolated from their supplies, and the ability of these forces to resist a ground attack severely impaired.

Complete tactical surprise was achieved. During Desert Shield, Coalition aircraft had flown numerous missions directly at Iraq before turning back to avoid violating Iraqi air space. Iraqi aircraft had scrambled; and more important, the Iraqi air-defense commanders had turned on their radars to track these approaching aircraft. These defensive reactions had enabled the Coalition to plot enemy reactions to approaching air strikes and to record enemy radar transmissions so that they could be jammed when war did come. When the Iraqis deduced what the Coalition was doing, they adopted the practice of keeping their radars turned off. Thus when the initial Coalition air strikes began during the hours of darkness on D-Day, 17 January, Coalition planes were able to approach Iraq undetected.

The radar-evading stealth technology built into the F-117 added to the surprise. This fighter-bomber was able to get to its targets virtually before it was picked up by any working radars and drop its precision-delivery weapons with deadly accuracy. In fact, the first bomb dropped during the war was by an F-117 on an enemy air-defense control center. According to Air Force reports, on many occasions the Iraqis did not react to an F-117 raid until after the first bombs had been delivered on their targets. Before the war was over, F-117s had dropped over 2,000 tons of munitions in almost 1,300 sorties.

Even as the F-117s were at work, the Navy was launching Tomahawk cruise missiles from a battleship in the Persian Gulf. This lethal weapon could be fired at a range of up to 400 miles to cruise at about 500 miles per hour at an altitude of 500 feet and deliver its warhead within a radius of 30 yards of its intended target. This combination of low-altitude flight and relatively high speed made the Tomahawk extremely difficult to shoot down even when the Iraqi air defenses came into action.

The Army played its part too in these early hours of Desert Storm. Its Apache attack helicopters took out Iraqi ground air-defense radars. In comparison with jet fighter-bombers and cruise missiles, the Apache is relatively slow, with a speed of about 165 miles per hour, but its armament makes it a deadly weapon. With its capability to navigate at night, it can approach a target at close to ground-level altitude and bring its Hellfire missile (which homes in on a laser spot that can be aimed by ground observers), its Hydra 70 (2.75-inch) rockets, and its 30mm chain gun to bear on targets with incredible accuracy. The chain gun, an updated version of the Gatling gun, fires multiple barrels in rotation to increase the rate of fire of its bullets. This contrasts with the conventional machine gun, which uses one barrel for firing all its rounds; the chain gun's bullets are almost four times as large as the conventional machine gun's.

As this first day of combat wore on, Turkey reversed its previous position and opened its air bases for use in attacks on Iraq and also announced that Turkish troops could enter Iraq if that became necessary. Iran threatened to join in too if Iraq provoked that action. Not surprisingly, Jordan and the PLO condemned the Coalition attack, although a chorus of approval came from other nations and opinion polls revealed that 75 percent of Americans approved the decision to commence hostilities. The U.S. Senate, after barely agreeing to the use of force some days before, passed a resolution praising the president and the troops in the field.

18 Jan 91   During the first twenty-four hours of the air war, the Coalition flew about 2,000 sorties and dropped 2,500 tons of bombs, some from air strikes from Incirlik, Turkey. By the end of the day, the Coalition had lost 8 aircraft. F-15Cs and F-15Ds, of which there were 120 deployed in the region, provided air cover in the first of over 5,900 sorties. Every Iraqi fixed-wing aircraft shot down in air-to-air combat was accounted for by these aircraft. F-15Es—and 48 of these multipurpose fighters were in the region—sought out SCUD missiles and launchers and used their laser systems to attack other hard targets, such as command and control facilities and airfields. By the end of Desert Storm, these aircraft had flown more than 2,200 sorties with the loss in combat of only 2 aircraft.

F-111s and F-16s shared in the destruction of the enemy's capabilities. In the course of the combat, during daylight and darkness 84 F-111s flew more than 4,000 sorties, and the 249 F-16s flew over three times that many, for a total of 13,500. These and the other Coalition aircraft were protected at their work by 18 EF-111s and 48 F-4Gs, which during the war flew 900 and 2,500 sorties respectively. The EF-111s were capable of jamming enemy radar, thus eliminating the ability of the Iraqi air defenses to find and attack aircraft coming in on a strike. The F-4Gs were equipped with High Speed Anti-Radiation (HARM) missiles and so consistently destroyed enemy radars that the Iraqis were reluctant to leave theirs on or even turn them on. When the Iraqis, for example, fired one of the surface-to-air missiles (SAMs), they would turn off the guiding radar while the SAM was in flight, thus depriving this weapon of its ability to track its intended target. Even on this first day, B-52 bombers began to attack Iraqi ground troops with what were called "dumb bombs" in contrast to the precision-guided "smart bombs." These heavy bombers, even though they were up to thirty years old, were extremely effective against such area targets as airfields and troop areas since they had been continuously modified and upgraded over the years. On 18 January they flew the first of 1,624 missions and dropped the first of 25,700 tons of munitions.

The precision-guided munitions with which such aircraft as the A-10, F-15E, F-16, F-111, and F-117 were equipped matched the effectiveness of the aircraft that delivered them. These weapons were far superior to those used in Vietnam decades before. About 7,400 tons of these munitions were delivered on targets during the course of Desert Storm. GBU-12s, 500-pound laser-guided bombs, were dropped by F-111s against Iraqi armored vehicles such as tanks. F-111s also dropped GBU-15s, 2,000-pound electro-optical-guided glide bombs, on the oil-field manifolds, which the Iraqis had opened to allow oil to flow into the Persian Gulf. GBU-24s, 2,000-pound laser-guided bombs, were used by F-111s and F-15Es on such targets as chemical, biological, and nuclear storage areas, bridges, aircraft shelters, and other strategic targets. F-117s used GBU-27s, laser-guided 2,000-pound bombs, on such pinpoint targets as hardened aircraft shelters, bunkers, and targets in built-up areas. The air-to-ground Maverick (AGM-65), a television-guided missile, was launched by F-16s and A-10s against armored vehicles such as tanks and armored personnel carriers. In aerial combat, two air-to-air missiles proved to function superbly. The Sparrow (AIM-7), a radar-guided missile, accounted for twenty-two fixed-wing aircraft and three helicopters. The Sidewinder (AIM-9), a heat-seeking missile, brought down eight aircraft.

What Coalition leaders had dreaded occurred this day. Iraq fired SCUDs against Israel and Saudi Arabia early in the morning. A U.S. Patriot ground-to-air missile unit brought down one of the missiles fired on Saudi Arabia, but no such defensive system was in place in Israel. The United States promptly promised an all-out effort to destroy both the SCUDs themselves and their fixed and mobile launchers. In addition, the

United States said it would send Patriot missiles to Israel in hopes of averting the promised, and feared, Israeli retaliation.

Leaders around the world quickly joined in a chorus of condemnation of this Iraqi attack, and Western leaders in the Coalition must have heaved a sigh of relief when Egypt said that under the circumstances it would tolerate some Israeli response and Syria signaled that it too would not object. It appeared for now at least that a threat to the Coalition's cohesion might be escaped.

As President Bush and others warned against euphoria in the wake of the early success of the Coalition's air war and the Coalition cautioned that it did not yet control the skies, the president signed an executive order that would permit the retention of reserves beyond 180 days and authorize the call up of 1 million more men and women if they were needed.

As had the Senate, the House of Representatives passed a laudatory resolution of support for the conflict. An opinion poll revealed that more than two-thirds of Americans disapproved of American antiwar protests and more than four-fifths supported Desert Storm. There were anti-American protests in a few countries abroad, and the Jordanian parliament called the United States a "great Satan."

19 Jan 91   The air war continued unabated, with a loss of ten Coalition aircraft to date (six of which were U.S. planes). The Iraqi SCUD attacks on Israel also continued, with three SCUDs landing in Israel before dawn. In order to provide some defense against these air-to-ground missiles, the United States deployed two Patriot missile batteries to Israel. Previously, as part of the U.S. military aid to Israel, the United States had offered the Patriot to Israel, but this offer had been declined by the Israelis because they were developing their own antimissile system. Meanwhile, aerial reconnaissance was conducted at an even more intense level to attempt to locate SCUD launchers both fixed and mobile.

As preparation for the expected ground war, the Coalition air attacks were expanded to Iraqi troop concentrations, especially the Republican Guard. These ground units were the elite of the Iraqi army—the best-trained and best-equipped— and were traditionally loyal to Saddam Hussein himself, a sort of palace guard. During the early stages of the eight-year Iran-Iraq war, they had seen service in combat, but as the war dragged on, they had been withdrawn from frontline duties. Despite their superior training and equipment, they had therefore seen less combat than the lesser trained and more poorly equipped troops in the positions along the Kuwait–Saudi Arabia border. Even so, the Republican Guard units were seen as the primary threat to a Coalition ground assault.

There had been very little contact between Coalition and Iraqi ground forces other than the capture of nine Kuwaiti oil platforms in the Gulf, captures which produced twelve Iraqi prisoners of war (POW). Iraq claimed that Coalition air raids had killed seventy civilians and that both civilians and religious shrines were deliberately being made targets of air strikes.

Diplomatic attempts to bring about a cease-fire continued, with feelers from Algeria, India, and the Soviet Union. Iran, which had indicated earlier that it would remain neutral in the struggle, reaffirmed this position with a vote in parliament.

20 Jan 91   Some 7,000 sorties had been flown over Iraq with a loss of 15 Coalition aircraft to date, including 9 U.S. aircraft. Iraq claimed to have shot down 154 Coalition aircraft and marched blindfolded POWs through the streets of Baghdad. Later Iraqi television would show seven captured pilots, six U.S. pilots and one from the United Kingdom. By now, Iraqi nuclear and chemical facilities had received heavy damage, as had the air-defense system. Iraq continued to fire SCUDs into Saudi Arabia, aiming 10 at Riyadh and Dhahran. U.S. Patriot missiles fired against these incoming missiles prevented their striking any significant ground targets. The Patriot missiles being launched by the 11th and 69th Air Defense Artillery Brigades were originally designed for action against enemy aircraft, but they had been modified to provide some capability against ballistic missiles such as the SCUD.

Saddam Hussein alleged that the full might of Iraqi power had not yet been used against the Coalition and called again for a Holy War against Coalition targets wherever they might be found, an implied threat that terrorism might still be a means to the end.

With Iraq unable to conduct any aerial reconnaissance to detect the movement of Coalition troops, XVIII Airborne and VII Corps troops began to move forward to assembly areas to ready themselves for a ground assault if it came to that.

21 Jan 91   With bad weather slowing down the sortie rate—to 1,100 for the day, with a total so far in the war of 8,100—and hampering the assessment of the air campaign, there was some dispute within the military chain of command as to the effectiveness of Coalition strikes against the Iraqi air force and air-defense system. Secretary of Defense Cheney indicated that the Coalition had achieved air superiority, but the battlefield commander, General Schwarzkopf, said that was yet to come. Perhaps the general was influenced by the fact that while Coalition air shot down two Iraqi aircraft, it lost three of its own planes and rescued only one pilot. U.S. Patriots brought down two SCUDs fired at Riyadh and Dhahran before they could do serious damage, and Israel announced that it would coordinate any retaliatory measures with the United States.

Iraq announced that it would use Coalition POWs as human shields, much as it had used hostages before they were released, even though the International Red Cross said that this would be a violation of the Geneva Convention. Iraq's only partially veiled threats of terrorism caused many Coalition nations to increase their security measures against worldwide terrorism, and several expelled Iraqi diplomats in the belief that Iraqi diplomatic personnel were engaged at least in the planning stage. Although Iraq rejected a Soviet peace feeler, Egypt continued to call for some sort of peace plan keyed to an Iraqi withdrawal.

The Iraqi SCUD attacks on Israel created difficulties for NATO. Furthermore, the question of what would be the NATO response to missile attacks on Turkey had arisen since this nation is a member of NATO. With the prospect of such attacks more remote than on Israel, no consensus of an appropriate NATO response had been reached.

22 Jan 91   With a slight improvement in the weather, the Coalition flew 1,900 more sorties with a loss of one aircraft from the United Kingdom. Iraqi television interviewed two more captured airmen in an apparent attempt to influence those Arabs who had only Iraqi television as a source of information. A Soviet general officer, perhaps stung by the failure of the Iraqi air defenses designed and largely equipped with Soviet equipment, alleged that 90 percent of the U.S. air attacks were missing their targets. Iraq claimed that in the first six days of the air war, 41

Iraqi civilians had been killed and 191 more wounded. While such a claim was clearly meant to suggest the Coalition was cruelly targeting innocent civilians, it unintentionally proved the opposite. Had such actually been the case, the thousands of Coalition sorties with the tons of ordnance fired onto targets would have made the civilian casualty toll run into the thousands instead of low hundreds.

The Iraqi version of the air war was limited to SCUD attacks, again on Riyadh, Dhahran, and now on Tel Aviv. U.S. Patriot missiles were unable to shoot down the SCUDs fired at Tel Aviv, and 70 Israelis became casualties. Neither Egypt nor Syria lent any kind of support to these Iraqi attacks, so the Coalition's bonds were strengthened against the patent Iraqi attempts to fracture it. With this lack of success, Iraq loosed another arrow from its bow.

Iraq took aim not just at one nation but at the world when its president ordered the destruction of Kuwaiti oil wells. Such an act not only deprived the world of oil that could never be replaced but also filled the sky with plumes of smoke from burning wells, polluting the air of the region and perhaps ultimately the world. This wanton destruction had only a minor effect on Coalition air strikes and was judged by many to be gratuitous destructiveness if not childish vindictiveness. Perhaps inspired by Iraqi rhetoric, Turkish terrorists set off three bombs at a U.S. installation in Turkey, but the results were inconsequential in the total war effort.

Reports from Baghdad indicated that the Coalition's efforts to cripple Iraq's war-making abilities were having serious effects on the civilian population in that city. Fuel supplies were said to be low, and the bombing of electric power facilities outside the city was affecting civilian utilities as well. Perez de Cuellar again called on Saddam Hussein to withdraw his occupation troops from Kuwait.

23 Jan 91   Iraq continued its SCUD attacks on Israel and Saudi Arabia and again achieved more psychological than military effects, partially as a result of the Patriot batteries in those two countries. Israel continued also to withhold any retaliatory actions thanks in part to the strength of the Israeli government in power. This government, led by Yitzhak Shamir, represented the "hawk" faction of Israeli politics. Hence, its rejection of retaliation was not seen as "dovish," as it might have been with a different government, but rather as a sign of real strength. Then too, the United States, long Israel's major supporter in the region, was using every persuasive measure to keep Israel from unleashing its forces on Arab nations.

As Iraq reported 60 more civilian casualties from air attacks, Secretary of Defense Cheney and General Powell said that the Coalition was extending its air efforts to isolating the Iraqi frontline forces and destroying their ability to fight. These two officials joined President Bush in warning that all might not continue as well as it had gone so far. As in all wars, reverses could occur, and, they said, no one could tell what Saddam Hussein would do next. The greatest dread was that Iraq did in fact have a chemical warfare capability and might use it as it had in the past.

The war was having adverse effects elsewhere. There were reports that Egyptian public opinion was being influenced by Iraqi propaganda, and the fear of Iraqi-inspired terrorism was decreasing air travel within the United States and abroad. On the positive side, however, Germany announced that it was sending millions of dollars to Israel in emergency humanitarian aid.

Within Iraq, domestic supplies of gasoline were curtailed as a result of Coalition air strikes on supplies and on production and distribution facilities. On the ground in Kuwait, there were minor skirmishes between Iraqi and U.S. forces as both sides began probing operations.

24 Jan 91   Coalition aircraft logged 2,000 more sorties with the loss of one U.S. F-16. Balancing this loss was the kill of two Iraqi combat aircraft by a Saudi Arabian Air Force F-15 guided to its combat by a U.S. AWACS orbiting over Saudi Arabia. Despite the extremely large expenditures of bombs and missiles, the United States said that it did not anticipate any significant shortages developing in these essential munitions. As U.S. force levels reached 475,000 in theater, with an expectation of their growing to 500,000, ground combat was limited to the capture of a small Kuwaiti island that had been occupied by Iraq. In the Gulf, U.S. Marines practiced an amphibious landing. This exercise helped convince Iraq that such a landing could take place when ground combat began in earnest and helped pin a significant portion of their ground forces in positions to defend the Kuwaiti coast.

The president of Yemen, one of the very few countries still siding with Iraq, declared that the United States was attempting to go beyond military objectives and destroy the nation of Iraq. Whether for fear of this, to escape the war, or to escape President Saddam Hussein himself, so many Iraqis were attempting to flee their country that Iraq closed its border with Jordan.

Even as the air war continued to grind Iraq down, attempts to seek a solution went on. The Maghreb states—Morocco, Algeria, and Tunisia— approached the UN Security Council in a failed attempt to seek a cease-fire to permit an Iraqi withdrawal from Kuwait to begin. The United States responded that there was absolutely no evidence that Saddam Hussein had any intentions of withdrawing.

25 Jan 91   With more than 2,000 additional sorties, the Coalition now bolstered by Qatari F-1 Mirage aircraft had flown more than 17,500 sorties in these first ten days of Desert Storm. With fewer strategic targets left in Iraq, the strike list was broadened to include supply dumps, artillery pieces, and such critical transportation targets as roads and bridges. Almost at the head of the list, however, were SCUDs and their fixed and mobile launchers. Targeting the SCUDs was essential because Iraq continued to fire the ground-to-ground ballistic missiles into both Saudi Arabia and Israel, where despite the defenses put up by U.S. Patriot missiles, some civilian casualties were being taken.

Iraq and its allies were still not powerless. Iraq began to pour millions of gallons of oil into the Gulf, although it claimed that these spills were unintentional and the result of Coalition air raids. The flow of oil was endangering the ecology of the Gulf waters. From the military point of view, the danger was even more immediate. There was the possibility that the oil could hinder the operation of warships and the amphibious fleet as well as close down the operations of the Saudi desalinization plants along the coast. These plants, which converted seawater to potable water, could become fouled by oil and be forced to shut down. Since they provided a very significant portion of the water needed by both the civilian sector and the military forces, such a development could prove very costly.

26 Jan 91   Oil continued to flow into the Gulf as Coalition aircraft kept up their strikes on Iraq, although weather reduced the sorties to about 1,000 for the day. A surprising development came to light with the news that around two dozen Iraqi aircraft had fled to Iran. Whether these flights came under orders from the Iraqi high command or were the result of Iraqi pilots' seizing the initiative was not known, but it did appear to confirm the fact that the precision-guided munitions were being highly effective. The hardened bunkers built by Iraq to safeguard their aircraft from attack were providing inadequate protection from aerial attack. Preserving combat aircraft could be achieved only by dispersing them to civilian locations immune from Coalition air strikes or by getting them out of the country to neighboring Iran.

The SCUD war continued too, even as Coalition aircraft searched without total success for SCUD launchers. However, Patriot missiles intercepted most of those fired, whether into Saudi Arabia or Israel, and Israel continued to exercise restraint. Muslim support for Saddam Hussein appeared to be moderate also at this stage in the war; many Muslims had opposed him before the war began and even those who had not seemed by and large to feel that Iraq was not justified in firing missiles that killed civilians.

Not everyone agreed with the U.S. and Coalition actions. Soviet Foreign Minister Alexander Bessmertnykh warned the United States not to destroy Iraq with its bombing raids, and antiwar activists in both Washington and Bonn turned out in large numbers to protest the bombing. Opinion polls in both the United States and Germany indicated that these marchers were in the minority; they showed that three-quarters of Germans and Americans alike approved of the policy of the United States in waging war against Iraq.

27 Jan 91   Despite the Iraqi president's attempt through wildly exaggerated claims of civilian casualties to mobilize antiwar support to end the bombing that was destroying his warmaking abilities, General Schwarzkopf assured the world that Coalition pilots were taking extreme pains to avoid killing civilians. Even official Iraqi numbers of casualties confirmed Schwarzkopf's statement. The flight of still more Iraqi aircraft, bringing the total now to thirty-nine, to safe haven in Iran indicated that

Coalition pilots were in fact highly accurate when Iraqi aircraft were the intended targets. Not only had Coalition pilots been overwhelmingly successful in air-to-air combat, but also they were destroying almost at will Iraqi planes on the ground —even when they were located in supposedly bombproof underground shelters. Apparently, Iraqi pilots recognized that their only chance for survival lay in fleeing to Iran. The Iranian government said it would confiscate the planes. The Coalition's success in shooting down planes that did attempt aerial combat was shown when two U.S. F-15s shot down four Iraqi MiG-23s. More evidence of Air Force skill was demonstrated when F-111s, delivering precision munitions, destroyed the manifolds the Iraqis had opened to let oil stream by the millions of gallons into the Gulf. The consequent reduction in oil flow markedly reduced the danger to the Saudi desalinization plants down the Gulf coast. When his strategy of using oil to foul the Saudi plants seemed to have failed, Saddam Hussein once again threatened to use unconventional weapons, presumably poisonous gas, against the Israeli civilian population.

This threat and one the previous day by George Habash, leader of the Popular Front for the Liberation of Palestine (PLFP), to attack U.S. installations abroad caused European and Asian governments to increase their anti-terrorism measures. In an apparent effort to sway world opinion, Iraq opened its Jordanian border, which it had closed on 24 January, but it made leaving more difficult for its citizens by requiring exit visas available only in Baghdad.

The United States showed its determination to carry the war to a successful conclusion when Secretary of Defense Cheney said that a ground assault on Iraq had always been assumed, even though Marine intelligence reported that Iraq had sowed 500,000 mines across its frontline positions.

28 Jan 91   An additional 2,000 sorties brought the Coalition total to more than 24,000, with a loss of one more U.S. aircraft, a Marine Harrier jet. By now, more than 80 Iraqi aircraft had survived destruction by fleeing to neutral Iran. Although some observers felt that Iran might release these aircraft to fly against Coalition targets, Secretary of State Baker said that the United States believed Iran would not violate its neutrality.

Iraq alleged that Coalition air attacks had killed 324 civil-

ians, wounded more than 400, and hit such non-military targets as religious shrines. Iraq also said that some of the U.S.
pilots it claimed to be using as human shields had been
wounded in Coalition air attacks and announced once again
that if Iraq began to suffer inordinately high casualties, it would
retaliate with unconventional weapons. There were reports
of possible terrorist attacks in such widely separated spots as
Greece, Lebanon, and the Philippines, and Baghdad Radio
blared that Egyptian President Mubarek would soon be assassinated.

Turkey was reported to have now 120,000 troops massed on
its border with Iraq, and experts in cleaning up oil spills began to arrive in Saudi Arabia to assess the effects of Iraq's release of Kuwaiti oil into the Gulf.

29 Jan 91   Desert Storm continued unabated in the air to ensure that Iraq's
strategic targets were destroyed, that the expected battlefield
in Kuwait was isolated from all movement of troops, equipment, and supplies, and that the ability of the troops deployed
in the area to resist a ground assault was minimized. Flying
now virtually without fear of enemy action, Coalition aircraft
took to the air with 2,600 more sorties. Now more than 90
Iraqi aircraft had sought safety in Iran, and the Iranian government gave its assurances that these aircraft would stay put
until the end of hostilities. These Iraqi losses were clearly Iranian gains, since Iraqi aircraft in Iran could no longer threaten
Iran as they had during the eight-year struggle with Iraq.

Tensions increased significantly when Israel shelled the
Rashidiyyah Refugee Camp in Lebanon in retaliation for
rockets launched from Lebanon that had struck what Israel
called a security zone in southern Lebanon. While the exchange was relatively minor, the war situation made any
Israeli-Arab hostilities more ominous.

In the political arena, France's minister of defense was forced
out of office in the wake of his open opposition to the outbreak of hostilities against Iraq. Next a joint statement issued
by the United States and the Soviet Union caused considerable reaction. In what was seen at the time as a radical departure from previous U.S. positions, the statement said that an
unequivocal commitment by Iraq to withdraw from Kuwait
could bring an end to the fighting. Further, the statement went
on to say that the United States and the Soviet Union would

work significantly to achieve a comprehensive settlement of
Middle Eastern problems after the war. The perceived change
in U.S. policy was its acceptance of a "commitment" to withdraw instead of an actual pull-out. In addition, this would have
been the first official U.S. agreement to seek a broader Middle
East settlement.

30 Jan 91   The immediate reaction of the White House was a form of
disclaimer indicating that the wording of the joint statement
was misleading and that interpreting it as a change of policy
was simply incorrect. The Soviet Union, on the other hand,
in an attempt to keep up its position as a friend of the Arabs,
made much of the language that spoke of the joint effort to
resolve the Palestinian question.

The firing of rockets and artillery in southern Lebanon continued sporadically. PLO Chairman Arafat disavowed any responsibility for ordering a rocket attack. A Turkish security
official was assassinated in an apparent terrorist attack. In response to the earlier Turkish appeal for support, the Netherlands announced that it would send Hawk missiles to Turkey.
The Hawk missile is intended to provide medium-range air
defense and would help guard Turkish installations against any
Iraqi air strikes. Chancellor Kohl of Germany attempted to
rally political support for Desert Storm by saying that Germany would face up to its responsibilities even if they were
not entirely to its liking.

The air war was temporarily eclipsed by two ground actions
on the southern Kuwait–Saudi Arabia border. In one action,
the Iraqis sent a tank battalion into Kuwait in a "reconnaissance in force." This is a probing attack intended only to gather
information about the enemy with a subsequent return to the
original position. The Coalition's reaction was so violent that
the Iraqis had to send in another tank battalion to extricate
the first. In other action, closer to the Gulf coast, the Iraqis
made another reconnaissance in force and occupied a deserted
village named Khafji. The U.S. Marines lost twelve killed in
action, and the media, since it finally had a place name to
use in news stories promptly dubbed this action the Battle of
Khafji. The Iraqi media, in its turn and since the Iraqi forces
were still in Khafji, bragged that this attack had been planned
by Saddam Hussein himself.

31 Jan 91   In an immediate response to the Iraqi raid, Saudi troops supported by U.S. Marines easily recaptured Khafji. Iraq paid an awful price for its moment of media glory with a loss of 41 tanks and more than 500 POWs. The thrill of this Coalition victory was dimmed somewhat by the announcement that a U.S. female soldier had been captured by the Iraqis.

As rockets still fell in what seemed to be a PLO-Israeli skirmish, Israel said that it would oppose an international conference as proposed in the joint United States–Soviet statement. The U.S. State Department announced that seventy incidents of terrorism had taken place since the beginning of the war, and representatives of France, Algeria, Yemen, and Iraq met in Iran in yet another attempt to work out some peace plan.

In the air war, some 2,600 Coalition sorties were flown, some by B-52s flying out of Spain. The Air Force announced that additional B-52s would soon begin operating from the United Kingdom to bomb Iraqi targets. These heavy bombers would be refueled in flight by Air Force tanker aircraft, as were the hundreds of Coalition fighters and fighter-bombers operating from Saudi Arabia and U.S. Navy aircraft carriers. In all, the Air Force deployed 256 KC-135s and 46 KC-10s (the military version of the civilian airliner DC-10). During Desert Shield, these aerial tankers had refueled 14,588 aircraft of all types with 68,200,000 gallons of fuel. During Desert Storm, 45,955 aircraft would receive 110,200,000 gallons from them. Among the primary targets of the air strikes now were the thousands of Iraqi troops and vehicles of all types attempting to get to Kuwait, some of which were trapped in a fifteen-mile-long convoy halted by the destruction of a key bridge.

Thus the first month of 1991, and the fifteenth day of Desert Storm, ended on a note of military success. In the air war, the Coalition had absolute command of the skies. Those Iraqi aircraft which had escaped destruction were fleeing to Iran. Strategic targets in Iraq were being systematically destroyed, and the isolation of the expected battlefield had begun even as the annihilation of Iraqi ground forces got underway. The Coalition had stayed cohesive, even though Iraq had indiscriminately rained SCUD missiles on Israeli civilians.

Iraq showed no signs of giving up its occupation of Kuwait, and diplomats around the world continued to seek some sort of peace plan that would bring an end to the war. They were no more effective on this diplomatic front than the Iraqi military was on the war front, but obviously hope still lingered on.

1 Feb 91   The first day of February saw 2,500 more Coalition sorties flown against all manner of targets. France granted permission for the overflight of U.S. bombers, this time B-52s, taking off from English airfields, a permission it had not granted five years earlier when the United States had bombed Libya in response to Libyan support of terrorism. There were reports that several Tomahawk cruise missiles had fallen on civilian areas in Baghdad. In a press briefing, field commanders issued assurances that these missiles had been aimed at military targets and had probably been knocked off course by Iraqi ground anti-aircraft fire. Perhaps in response to the inaccurate strikes, Iraq branded captured air crews as war criminals instead of POWs as the Geneva Convention dictated, thereby depriving these airmen of such internationally recognized safeguards as inspections by the Red Cross to ensure humane treatment and adequate food and shelter. As "war criminals," they could be treated however Iraq decided.

Coalition forces saw some good luck added to their own skill in pursuing the combat. Southerly winds pushed the oil slick created by the Iraqi release of oil into the Persian Gulf away from the Saudi desalinization plants, thus relieving one more Coalition worry.

Jordan came under verbal attack by the United States when the Department of State accused Jordan of violating the UN's embargoes by buying Iraqi oil. Such a purchase was probably not only a covering of Jordanian bets for the environment but also almost a necessity since Saudi Arabia had cut off its sales of oil to Jordan.

2 Feb 91   Another 2,600 sorties were added to the Coalition total, unfortunately with the loss of two U.S. aircraft. The overnight attacks destroyed the remnants of the Iraqi navy. Some Iraqi SCUD launchers continued to evade detection, and two SCUDs landed on the West Bank while one was shot down by a Patriot near Riyadh.

Some in the United States had wondered about a reestablishment of the draft, but the Department of Defense announced that one was neither wanted nor needed. A military draft takes months from the initial call-up to the arrival of troops in the field, and the military argued that the combination of the Active Component and the Reserve Component as presently existing could meet the needs of Desert Storm without additional drafted troops.

The Iranian government, this time speaking to the Iraqi deputy prime minister, reiterated the Iranian position that Iraqi aircraft which had fled to Iran would stay there until the end of the war and called once again for an Iraqi withdrawal from Kuwait.

3 Feb 91   The air war, in 2,500 more sorties, struck a variety of targets ranging from strategic targets to SCUD launchers to aircraft on the ground to Iraqi troops. Central Command increased its accounting of Iraqi aircraft destroyed in hardened bunkers by 68, and Iraqi supply trucks suffered heavy losses as destroyed bridges forced them to line up on highways. By now, in only eighteen days, the rain of bombs on Coalition targets was estimated to have exceeded the total tonnage dropped in World War II. The Coalition suffered its losses, although from mechanical failures, not enemy fire, with the loss of one B-52 and two helicopters. SCUDs continued to be fired into Israel and Saudi Arabia where, even after being struck by a Patriot, one fell, injuring twenty-nine civilians.

On the ground, all the units of XVIII Airborne and VII Corps, except those elements of the 3rd Armored Division which had not yet arrived from Germany, completed their move to forward assembly areas undetected by Iraqi intelligence. This movement of some 65,000 vehicles went on twenty-four hours a day, with a vehicle passing through traffic control checkpoints every fifteen seconds.

Air strikes, no matter how necessary and well planned and executed, invariably go astray in the confusion of war. Such was the case in Desert Storm, as the United States reported that some few of the casualties suffered by U.S. forces came at the hands of friendly aircraft. It appeared that in the close contact between U.S. and Iraqi forces, a U.S. vehicle had been mistaken for an Iraqi armored vehicle and been taken under fire.

The Department of Defense announced that it would not release the number of enemy casualties, the infamous "body count" of the war in Vietnam. The rationale for this policy was that the number of casualties was an inaccurate and often erroneous means of judging the success or failure of an operation, while giving the enemy intelligence information it might not have the means to acquire otherwise. Even the count of Iraqi POWs was reported only in round numbers, and these figures were reported now to be over 800.

In the festering duel between Israel and Palestinian militia, the Lebanese army was reported to be deploying in southern Lebanon to control the militia actions. The Lebanese government also reported that it had arrested Walid Khalid, the senior advisor to the notorious terrorist Abu Nidal.

4 Feb 91   The PLO, apparently yielding to this Lebanese pressure, said that it would no longer fire rockets into Israel from southern Lebanon, but an incident in the United States itself was at first feared to be the work of terrorists. Two bombs were discovered near two large chemical storage tanks in Norfolk, Virginia, not far from military installations there. A subsequent investigation revealed that the bombs were planted in a criminal act, not a terrorist move, but until that was determined, the episode heightened tension.

Coalition sorties, with 2,700 more in the last twenty-four hours, reached a total of 44,000. Unable to bring any effective air defense to bear on the Coalition aircraft and cruise missiles, Iraq began to move military equipment into civilian areas, knowing that the Coalition's policy was to withhold an air strike if significant civilian casualties would result. Traffic on the main highway connecting Iraq and Jordan did contain a mixture of civilian and military vehicles, and some Jordanian truck drivers were reportedly killed as Coalition aircraft went after legitimate military targets, bringing a denunciation from UN Secretary General Perez de Cuellar. For the first time, Syrian troops engaged in a brief exchange of fire with Iraqi forces on the ground. Sudan, reportedly ready to harbor Iraqi armed forces, drew an Egyptian warning to cease and desist or risk being attacked. The European Community called for joint EC-U.S. attempts to solve Middle East problems after the shooting stopped.

Meanwhile, Israeli sources estimated that 10 percent of Iraq's heavy weapons—tanks, armored vehicles, and artillery—and 20 percent of its air force had been destroyed. U.S. sources, however, indicated the losses were probably lower. The 16-inch

guns of the U.S.S. *Missouri* firing on Iraqi positions undoubtedly did inflict significant losses with their almost unbelievable accuracy.

5 Feb 91   The targets of the day's 2,000 sorties included Republican
Guard units and key bridges, with the results that by now one-
third of these critical links in Iraq's transportation net had been
destroyed. Twenty more Iraqi aircraft were flown to Iran to escape the pinpoint attacks of Coalition aircraft, bringing the
total to 120 in this safe haven. Reports indicated that 80 percent of Iraqi oil refineries had been destroyed, and the Iraqi
government was forced to halt the sale of all fuels — cooking
gas, gasoline, and fuel oil — to civilians.

President Bush sent Secretary of Defense Cheney and chairman of the joint chiefs General Powell to the Gulf to assess
the situation there and report back to him. The president confirmed the views of the Department of Defense regarding a
possible draft and flatly stated that no draft would be needed
even though he thought that air power alone could not bring
an end to the fighting.

Two events occurred that increased the tension levels. One
was a Radio Baghdad broadcast of coded messages which many
feared were orders for terrorist attacks worldwide. The other
was the Israeli air force's attacks on Palestinian areas in Lebanon; these were to continue into the next day. This latter tension was eased somewhat, however, when Israel relaxed the
curfew that had been in effect on the West Bank since Desert
Storm began.

6 Feb 91   In the air, two U.S. F-15s brought down four Iraqi jets attempting to escape to Iran. In the air-ground effort, the French commander of troops in the Gulf region estimated that the Republican Guards were now only 70 percent effective. General
Powell in his turn estimated that at least one Guards division
was down to 50 percent effectiveness and reported that 600
Iraqi tanks had been destroyed in the Kuwait Theater of Operations. With the arrival from Germany of the last elements
of the 3rd Armored Division, VII Corps was at full strength
and the build-up of the U.S. forces in the Coalition was virtually complete.

Iraq announced that it was breaking off diplomatic relations
with several major members of the Coalition: Egypt, France,

Italy, Saudi Arabia, the United Kingdom, and the United States. Jordan's King Hussein, obviously feeling the pressure of domestic politics, made a speech criticizing the West as being the opponents of all Muslims and charged the West with wanting to assert control over the region. The main thrust of his address moved him closer than ever to being in support of Iraq.

7 Feb 91   The U.S. State Department engaged in a little diplomatic war by responding to King Hussein's speech with the comment that U.S. aid to Jordan would come under review. In the United States, twenty-one members of the House of Representatives sent around a letter calling upon the president not to increase the scope of the war. The current troubles between the PLO and Israel continued as Israeli commandos conducted a raid on a PLO base in southern Lebanon.

As Iraq continued to move military equipment into the safety of civilian communities to protect it from Coalition air attacks, Coalition aircraft took to the air with 2,600 more sorties. Iran reported that five Iraqi air planes had crashed in a vain attempt to flee into Iran. Targeting was increasingly shifting to Iraqi ground forces to reduce their combat capability before a ground assault began. Naval gunfire was brought to bear again, this time when the battleship U.S.S. *Wisconsin* unlimbered its weapons for the first time on shore targets.

8 Feb 91   Keeping track of the war situation was akin to watching a three-ring circus. There were the action in Israel, the air war over Iraq and Kuwait, and diplomatic exchanges all around the world. In Israel, three Arab terrorists who crossed over from Jordan to attack an Israeli bus lost their lives in the attempt. A SCUD was fired toward Riyadh but destroyed in flight by a U.S. Patriot. Thirteen more Iraqi jets took flight and successfully reached Iran, to bring the total there to 147. The air war went on with 2,500 sorties primarily against bridges — to isolate Iraqi forces in the field — and against these troops and their heavy equipment. These assaults were clearly effective: more than 900 Iraqis fleeing the air bombardment had become POWs of the Saudis. These Iraqi deserters alleged that Iraq had formed units whose duties were to kill or capture any who tried to escape into Coalition hands. Although the diplomats seemed to be taking a break from their labors, Secretary of Defense Cheney and General Powell arrived in Saudi Arabia to make their assessment of the situation and of the more than 500,000 U.S. troops in the theater.

9 Feb 91   With 2,400 more sorties added to the count, the Coalition total was now over 57,000. Central Command reported to Cheney and Powell the results of air strikes against Iraqi ground forces to date: 750 tanks destroyed out of an estimated total of 4,000; 650 artillery pieces out of 3,200 total; and 600 armored personnel carriers of the 4,000 that had started the war. Measured against this success of the air war, a SCUD had landed in Israel the previous night injuring twenty-six, despite having been hit by a Patriot from the unit now stationed in Israel. In a move in the psychological war, the leader of the Jordanian Islamic Jihad (Holy War), Sheik Tamimi, announced that he had put out a death warrant on Egypt's president Hosni Mubarek. In response, Syria issued a call to kill Saddam Hussein.

Soviet President Gorbachev stated that the Coalition's air attacks had approached the point of exceeding the mandate of the United Nations. He called upon Saddam Hussein to be realistic in his assessment of the future. Iraq, as it had threatened, broke diplomatic relations with the United States. Iran, which had sent its recent enemy sixteen tons of medicines under the supervision of the Red Cross, announced that it had received a peace feeler from Iraq.

10 Feb 91   Iran announced that the latest peace initiative had fallen flat, and the Iraqi president took to the air waves to appeal to his people to keep up their resolve. Coalition intelligence reported that now, thanks to the air attacks on communications lines, it took twenty-four hours for Iraqi commanders to get orders to the frontline units. As 2,800 more sorties were undertaken, more and more isolating the coming battlefield and softening up the troops, it was reported that U.S. senior commanders wanted to continue the bombing before other actions were taken.

11 Feb 91   President Bush announced his agreement with the plan to continue air bombardment even as the Coalition added 2,600 more sorties to the count. In the face of Iraqi claims that civilians were being targeted along with military objectives, Coalition commanders reiterated that every attempt was being made to minimize civilian casualties.

The Iraqi government announced that it had reduced the draft age to seventeen as Soviet envoy Yevgeny Primakov, who was a member of the Soviet Presidential Council and who had previously visited Iraq on 3 October 1990, reached Baghdad. Perhaps coincidentally, Iraq denied that it had called for a cease-fire, saying that only an Iraqi victory could bring about a cessation of hostilities. Iranian president Hashemi Rafsanjani criticized both sides in the conflict for acting unjustly but re-affirmed his nation's neutrality.

In a welcome turn of events, it was reported that Syria and Israel were unofficially working jointly to decrease the PLO's power in southern Lebanon. Around the world, however, the power of terrorists was reflected in the approximately one hundred incidents since the war began. As terrorism from the skies—the SCUDs—was countered by Patriots in Saudi Arabia and Israel, Israel's minister of defense, Moshe Ahrens, discussed the effects of the SCUD attacks on Israel with President Bush and asked the United States to provide Israel with the IFF (Identify Friend or Foe) aircraft identification codes being used by U.S. aircraft. With these codes, Israel could identify U.S. aircraft, but without them, friendly aircraft could be mistaken for Iraqi combat planes. Since knowledge of these codes might encourage Israeli retaliatory air strikes against Iraq, the United States had not before and did not now share that information with Israel.

Support for the Coalition came from an unexpected source. Three hundred Afghan Mujaheddin freedom fighters joined the other members of the Coalition in Saudi Arabia. Although the numbers were small and realistically the aid they could provide was negligible, the symbolism of this cooperation against Iraq was important.

12 Feb 91   In the diplomatic ring, Saddam Hussein practiced the old device of "divide and conquer" when he told envoy Yevgeny Primakov that he was ready "to extend cooperation" in attempts to stop the war after just days before saying that he would fight until Iraq won. Syria showed a remarkable spirit of cooperation with beleaguered Jordan by reportedly agreeing to supply one-fourth of Jordan's oil requirements.

As the Coalition air forces struck hard at strategic targets in the Baghdad area, fifty oil wells were set ablaze in Kuwait. The U.S. Marines and Navy worked with Saudi troops to bombard a major Iraqi troop concentration in Kuwait. That this operation and other attacks on Iraqi forces were being successful was indicated by Iraqi deserters' reports of 20,000 Iraqi military deaths.

13 Feb 91   Soviet Councillor Primakov went back to Moscow reporting that he had seen signs of hope for negotiations to end the war. Coalition members of the UN Security Council prevented an open discussion of the war, which they feared would have provided too many opportunities for propaganda speeches by Iraqi supporters. They did, however, agree to hold closed sessions beginning on 14 February.

Flying 2,800 more sorties, Coalition aircraft destroyed four transports and a helicopter, but one U.S. strike created a major international stir. A precision-guided munition struck what the U.S. forces identified as a purely military target, a command and communications center in Baghdad. Iraq quickly claimed that it was instead a civilian bomb shelter and alleged that more than 400 civilians had died in this attack. The Bush administration just as promptly denied this claim, and Secretary of Defense Cheney suggested that Iraq was quite deliberately putting civilians where they could be killed in strikes on military targets. Lt. Gen. Thomas Kelly, the director of operations for the Joint Chiefs of Staff who had been serving as the Department of Defense briefer in Washington, said that between 50 and 100 Iraqi combat aircraft had been moved into civilian areas to protect them from air attacks, precisely because the Iraqis knew the Coalition was avoiding civilian targets.

14 Feb 91   As Iraq claimed that it had removed 288 bodies from the alleged civilian bomb shelter with more still inside, the United States produced evidence that the structure had in fact been a military target. This dispute did not stop the Coalition's air war. By now, the United States estimated that nearly one-third of the Iraqi armored capability in the region had been destroyed, with U.S. air losses reportedly one-fourth of those experienced in the Vietnamese conflict.

As the UN Security Council began its meetings behind

closed doors, Iraq condemned Secretary General Perez de Cuellar for incompetent and criminal conduct in being unable to prevent the conflict. UNICEF and the World Health Organization announced that they would send $600 million in emergency supplies to assist Iraqi mothers and children who were suffering from the air attacks. The Soviet government, still attempting to use its pre-war influence in the region, said it was hopeful that negotiations could bring an end to the war.

15 Feb 91   In what the Soviet government called an important first step, Iraq offered to pull out of Kuwait, but with so many conditions attached that the Coalition rejected the offer out of hand. Even as these sorts of discussions were going on, thoughts about a postwar environment were being discussed. The foreign ministers of the Arab nations in the Coalition met in Cairo to talk about military and economic conditions they hoped to realize; and Israel's Prime Minister Shamir voiced his government's view that Saddam Hussein could not be allowed to stay in power.

Coalition aircraft flew 2,600 more sorties, and new weapons were introduced in the air campaign. One was the 10,000-pound BLU-82 bomb known from its lethalness as the "Daisy Cutter." This extremely powerful bomb was designed to be used against surface targets and simply eliminated all structures within its target area. The other weapon new both to the theater and to warfare was the fuel-air bomb. This weapon released an explosive vapor into the air, which exploded to produce a tremendous over-pressure that crushed structures below it. Given the right circumstances, the fuel-air mixture could penetrate a building or bunker and produce an explosion within the structure to match the pressure from outside.

Iraq launched another SCUD toward Saudi Arabia, and President Bush announced that of the 42 launched, 41 had been intercepted.

16 Feb 91   In the diplomatic arena, the Soviet Union agreed with the Coalition that the Iraqi peace offer was too conditional to be a way to end the war but still maintained that it was at least a starting point. The Arab foreign ministers meeting in Cairo announced proposals for a wide range of postwar security and economic agreements, which included an Arab force to maintain the peace and ensure the security of all nations in the region.

In the military arena, the Coalition lost two A-10 jet aircraft in the 2,600 sorties flown on this date. Balancing that loss was the estimate that by now the Iraqis had lost 1,400 tanks, 1,200 artillery pieces, and 800 armored personnel carriers. Some of these losses had come through the efforts of the A-10s. These aircraft proved to be invaluable tank killers during the war although they were also used against SCUD launchers and Iraqi air-defense installations. Before Desert Storm came to an end, the 144 A-10s in the theater had flown close to 8,100 sorties; two of their "kills" had been the only ones scored with airborne guns rather than rockets during the war. With 523,000 U.S. military personnel in the region, there were reports that the U.S. ground forces were in position for a ground assault whenever it should be ordered.

17 Feb 91   A new flurry of diplomacy began when Iraqi Foreign Minister Azziz arrived in Moscow to discuss ways to end the war. The United States, without committing itself to any agreement, said that it would welcome any unconditional withdrawal the Soviet Union could work out with Iraq. In this connection and displaying a flexibility previously missing, the Iraqi ambassador to the United Nations indicated that the Iraqi conditions for any withdrawal were not so much firm demands as preliminary points to be explored. On the other hand, even as the United Nations announced that emergency supplies had reached Baghdad, the International Red Cross said that Iraq had denied it the right to visit Coalition POWs inside Iraq. India, reacting to domestic pressures, said that U.S. military aircraft could not be refueled at Indian bases.

On the military fronts, two more SCUDs landed harmlessly in Israel, missing their target of an Israeli nuclear facility at Demona. There were reverses in the Coalition air war, though. The United States lost two killed in action and six wounded in action as a result of a misdirected air strike, and the United Kingdom showed film of one of their bombs, which the Iraqis claimed killed 130 civilians, missing its intended military target of a bridge abutment. In ground action, the 1st Infantry Division artillery conducted a heavy attack on Iraqi frontline positions, and Coalition ground troops conducted seven skirmishes. In the Gulf, there were reports of 31 U.S. amphibious ships poised for a landing.

18 Feb 91   Iraqi Foreign Minister Azziz returned to Baghdad from Moscow reportedly carrying with him a proposal from President Gorbachev to President Saddam Hussein for an immediate and unconditional withdrawal from Kuwait as mandated by the UN Security Council resolution but with added provisos for guarantees of Iraq's territorial integrity, the lifting of mandated sanctions, and negotiations on regional problems after the withdrawal, and no requirement for a replacement of Iraq's leader. The Israeli government, however, vowed an assault against Iraq if Iraq retained the capability of launching missile attacks or pursuing nuclear, biological, or chemical warfare. In other Israeli actions, the government lifted the curfew which it had imposed on 2 August on the occupied territories. The Lebanese government demanded that Israel evacuate the security zone now that the Lebanese army had moved into southern Lebanon.

In the Persian Gulf, two U.S. warships struck mines, reportedly taking only slight damage. Coalition ground forces were reported to be ready to go on order. In the air war, Coalition aircraft flew 2,600 sorties but lost one F-16. These air attacks were increasingly against Iraqi troops in the field and their supporting logistical elements.

19 Feb 91   Another 2,800 Coalition sorties pounded targets in Iraq and Kuwait, resulting in the loss of one A-10. The U.S.S. *Princeton*, one of the vessels that had struck an Iraqi mine, was pulled back from combat duty to permit repair of mine damage. General Schwarzkopf announced that on the tactical level Iraqi tanks were being destroyed at the rate of close to 100 per day. On the strategic level, he said, in keeping with the Coalition intent to cripple the Iraqi capability to wage war but not destroy the nation, only Iraq's oil refineries were being destroyed and not their production capability. Similarly, the UN Security Council authorized the Red Cross to send water purification equipment to Iraq to relieve civilian suffering. The Chinese government, although it had not voted against any of the UN Security Council anti-Iraq resolutions, indicated that it was skeptical of U.S. intentions in the Gulf region. Czechoslovakia, however, was sure enough of the Coalition goals to send a 200-man chemical decontamination outfit to join the Coalition.

President Bush, speaking for the Coalition, kept up the pressure on Iraq by saying that the latest Soviet peace plan did not measure up to what he required to bring about a cease-fire.

20 Feb 91   Iraqi Foreign Minister Azziz again shuttled back to Moscow with the Iraqi response to this last Soviet peace proposal. President Bush issued what many viewed as an ultimatum: Iraq must withdraw within four days, release all POWs, and disclose the location of all Iraqi mines — allegedly numbering in the hundred of thousands.

As Coalition sorties added 2,600 more to the massive air war, U.S. forces in limited ground actions captured close to 500 POWs and destroyed a considerable number of tanks and artillery pieces. In other areas, it was estimated that four Iraqi Republican Guard mechanized divisions had been reduced to 50 percent combat effectiveness by Coalition air strikes. The size of the oil spill was now estimated to be considerably smaller than first thought, 1.5 million barrels rather than 11 million; but the cleanup was running into bureaucratic problems.

21 Feb 91   Saddam Hussein responded to President Bush's message to President Gorbachev with defiance. The Soviet government, still trying for a peaceful solution, said that Iraq had accepted a peace plan tied into a truce and other conditions, but President Bush, along with the other Coalition members, immediately expressed reservations. Later the Bush administration rejected it altogether.

The United States now estimated that 2,100 Iraqi tanks had been destroyed, about half of the estimated total in the area, and U.S. and British artillery took Iraqis under heavy fire as Coalition forces for the first time conducted ground reconnaissances across the border. SCUDs continued to be fired into Saudi Arabia, and Patriots continued to intercept them, as Iraqi mobile launchers continued to elude the hunt for them by every Coalition asset available.

22 Feb 91   President Gorbachev announced a peace plan, accepted for Iraq by Foreign Minister Azziz, which would begin a withdrawal in one day to be completed within three weeks, coupled with

the cancellation of all the UN Security Council resolutions. President Bush, with the support of the Coalition members, responded at noon by giving Iraq twenty-four hours to begin an unconditional withdrawal to be completed in one week. The UN Security Council endorsed neither plan.

President Bush denounced what he called an Iraqi scorched earth policy in Kuwait, and as minor but sharp fighting broke out along the borders, the Coalition used incendiary devices to ignite oil in the trenches Iraq had dug along the front lines. This preempted Iraq's ability to ignite this oil to stop ground assaults against their lines.

24 Feb 91   Thirty-eight days into Operation Desert Storm, Iraq flatly rejected President Bush's twenty-four-hour ultimatum, and President Bush authorized the commander of Central Command, General Schwarzkopf, to commence ground operations. President Gorbachev made a last desperate plea to delay; and at the United Nations, the Soviet Union suggested—but without sufficient authority to bring about a delay—that Iraq had accepted President Bush's criteria. Even as the United States accused Iraq of systematically executing Kuwaitis and there were reports of three hundred oil wells ignited by Iraq, Iraq stated that it had the establishment of a democratic government in Kuwait as its goal.

The air war shifted in earnest to attacks on Iraqi frontline positions, with 2,900 sorties devoted primarily to those targets. In continued defiance, Iraq fired one more SCUD into Israel.

24 through   In what proved to be the shortest and most successful ground
27 Feb 91   campaign in U.S. history, at 0400 hours the Coalition ground forces moved across the borders of both Kuwait and Iraq, encountering scant opposition, and with relatively few Coalition casualties took more than 10,000 Iraqi POWs in the first twenty-four hours.

Desert Storm was a military masterpiece in both planning and execution and at both the strategic and tactical levels. Once any political government has decided that military means must be employed to achieve national objectives, the military's objectives are twofold: to destroy the enemy's ability to fight and to crush the enemy's will to fight.

In Desert Shield and Desert Storm, the Coalition's overall objectives were basically as stated in UN Security resolutions;

once the military option was taken, the military objective was to defeat the Iraqi armed forces to cause their complete, unconditional withdrawal from Kuwait. During Desert Shield, the Coalition had gathered sufficient strength in the Kuwait Theater of Operations to enable it to fight effectively if and when the time came. Among the most difficult accomplishments of the Bush administration was keeping the Coalition intact despite every effort made by the Iraqi government to arouse latent Arab-Israeli tensions and shatter the allies along Arab-Western lines during Desert Shield and keeping the Coalition together when it became time for Arabs to fire upon Arabs.

As the ground war began, Iraq had what military analysts believed was the fourth largest army in the world, ranking only behind that of the Soviet Union, China, and the United States. Although its navy was only negligible, its roughly 500,000-man ground forces, many of whom were battle-hardened veterans of the eight-year Iran-Iraq war, were equipped with some of the most powerful and sophisticated tanks and artillery pieces in the world. Its air force contained top-of-the-line fighter bombers: French Mirage jets and Soviet MiG-29s. Its air-defense system was equally potent, with radars, surface-to-air missiles, and anti-aircraft guns. This formidable force would have to be shattered if the Coalition, which numbered between 600,000 and 700,000 troops total, were to eject the Iraqi forces from Kuwait.

The first phase of the Coalition's drive to destroy the enemy's will and ability to fight had begun with the establishment of air supremacy over both Iraq and Kuwait. Not only would this accomplishment permit Coalition aircraft to attack strategic and tactical targets with minimum losses but also it would permit Coalition ground forces to move and operate with impunity from enemy air strikes. In addition, such air capability would deny the enemy the ability to observe the Coalition ground forces as they moved from defensive to assault positions and maneuvered during the attack phase. The second phase of the air war concentrated on interdicting the battlefield. That is, the air objectives were (1) to cut all means of communication between Iraqi headquarters and the troops in the field so that the commanders could not direct the operations of their forces in any reasonable and timely fashion, (2) to isolate the front lines and the troops in the Kuwait Theater of Operations from resupply of food, water, and munitions,

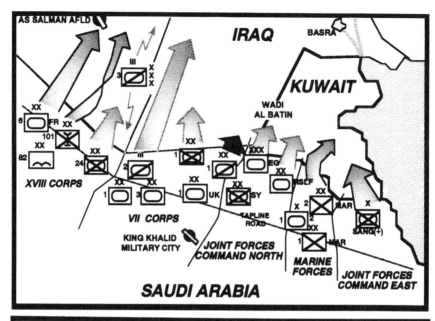

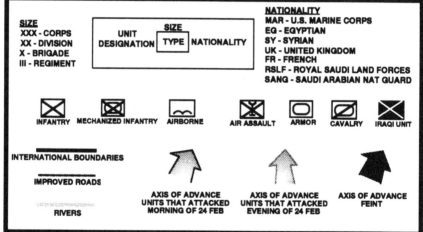

MAP 2. Initial Coalition attacks, 24 February. Source: *Army Focus* (June 1991): 23.

and (3) to destroy as many troops in the field as possible, as much of their supplies in the immediate area as possible, and the frontline defensive fortifications along the Saudi Arabia–Kuwait border and the Gulf coast.

When these aerial missions had been accomplished, the ground forces began their assaults supported by close air support. All in all, 65,000 sorties had accomplished the air objectives.

The build-up of ground forces began with the arrival of the first elements of the 82nd Airborne Division and continued almost without respite until just days before the ground assault began. Major U.S. units included another air assault division, mechanized infantry divisions and brigades, armored cavalry regiments, tank divisions, and artillery brigades. They were joined by Saudi Arabian divisions, Egyptian and Syrian divisions, and major elements from France and the United Kingdom. To support these combat units were thousands of support troops on the ground and a naval armada of surface ships and aircraft carriers.

During Desert Shield, the period of 3 August 1990–16 January 1991, the preponderance of Coalition ground forces were located south of the Saudi Arabia–Kuwait border where resupply could more easily be achieved from Gulf ports and facilities. Beginning on 17 January, when the air war of Desert Storm started, and continuing until 23 February, Coalition air supremacy allowed major troop movements to begin undetected, spreading westward to jump-off positions along the Saudi Arabia–Iraq border. During the same period, well-publicized maneuvers of Marines on board amphibious ships were conducted in the Gulf to pin the Iraqis in positions along the Kuwaiti coast.

During Desert Shield, the bulk of Iraq's 500,000 men, except for the Republican Guard, were dug in along the Kuwaiti coastline to guard against an anticipated amphibious assault and along the Saudi Arabia–Kuwait border. Most of these Iraqi troops were veterans of the eight-year war with Iran, and although they were battle-hardened, they were not as well equipped or well trained as the Republican Guard tank and mechanized divisions occupying reserve positions astride the Iraq-Kuwait border. The frontline troops were established in a cordon defense, multiple lines of dug-in positions fronted by mine fields, anti-tank ditches and fortifications, and deep trenches filled with oil to be ignited when the Coalition attacked. Although these were formidable defenses, they were not a defense in depth which would guard against major penetrations of armor and infantry. The Republican Guards, on the other hand, were well back from this front ready to move to threatened points when attacks came.

During the first phases of Desert Storm, Coalition air forces took a heavy toll of both the Republican Guards and the front-line troops. By the time General Schwarzkopf gave the order for the Coalition ground troops to move across the borders, the Iraqi troops had lost much of their ability and will to fight. Thousands of soldiers had been killed; much of their armor and artillery had been destroyed; their oil-filled ditches had been ignited before the troops had to cross them; their anti-tank defenses had been badly battered; their mine fields had been damaged by air and artillery strikes; and their supplies had been reduced to what they had on hand with them. Furthermore, their reconnaissance had been restricted to what they could see from their battered bunkers.

Just as the initial air campaign of Desert Storm had been planned and executed following the latest doctrine and tactics of combat, so too was the ground phase. The doctrine was that of the "AirLand Battle" laid out in the U.S. Army's field manual FM 100-5 *Operations;* the tactics were the tried and true, fire and maneuver approach of land warfare updated with modern equipment.

The principles of this battle doctrine are relatively simple. Success depends upon coordination of force both at the point of attack and in the enemy's rear, rapid decision making, and deep attacks. The assault forces avoid enemy strong points or soften them up at the point of attack and by rapid movement and aggressive actions maintain the initiative, creating a fluid situation that destroys any coherent enemy defense.

The primary tactical maneuvers followed in this battle plan are the envelopment and the penetration of enemy positions, and both rely upon the principle of mass — having more forces than the enemy can bring to bear at the critical point *and* at the critical time.

The envelopment can be described as comparable to football's end run. The attacking force's axis of advance is around the enemy's flank, the end of his prepared defensive positions, to avoid having to assault these positions and to get into the enemy's rear area as quickly as possible. By executing this maneuver, the attacker forces the enemy's troops to fight where they are least prepared to resist, disrupts their ability to command and control their forces, and cuts off their frontline units from reinforcement and resupply.

The difficulties for the defender are obvious, but the attacking army has problems too. It must move assault units from in front of the enemy to the jump-off point on the flank, and this movement must be undetected or the offensive army may itself be attacked while moving and least able to resist. When it is attacking the enemy's rear, its own flanks are open and vulnerable to counterattack. Hence, the attacker must have a screening force to conceal the main attack and to prevent surprise assaults. Finally, the attacking army's supply lines, its logistical tail, are stretched as the assault elements move around the enemy's flank.

A penetration, on the other hand, is a direct assault on the enemy's frontline positions, much like football's off tackle play. The attacking army either finds a soft spot in the enemy's lines or brings so much destructive force to bear on the point of attack that a penetration can be achieved without disruptive losses to its own numbers. The offensive army masses its assault forces so that it has overwhelming superiority as it attacks, and success is achieved when the army breaks through the enemy's front and exploits this success in the enemy's rear while attacking on both sides of the breach in the lines. As with the penetration, once in the enemy's rear, the attacker can bring chaos, but again the attacker faces difficulties as well. Should the enemy be able to resist this direct assault on its front line, the attacker is extremely vulnerable to counterattack because it is out in the open. Even if the attacked army is unable to resist the initial assault, it may still be able to close the gap after the attacker has passed through, thereby cutting off the attacking elements.

If the attacker can mount a penetration and an envelopment simultaneously, the troops being attacked obviously are in deeper trouble than with either tactic alone. Their forces are pinned down at both points resisting the attacks, and they cannot move forces from one area to the other to reinforce. In World War II, Gen. George Patton used these tactics and described the action in graphic terms as "Hold 'em by the nose and kick 'em in the pants."

The tactical plan of attack adopted by General Schwarzkopf was just this dual approach. His plan had two major thrusts: an envelopment through Iraq of the Iraqi right flank simultaneous with penetrations of the Iraqi front lines in Kuwait. The objective of the enveloping force was the Republican Guard concentrated on the Iraq-Kuwait border; the objective of the penetration was Kuwait City and the road junction just to its west. The intent was to cut off the Iraqi forces in Kuwait, force them to surrender, and destroy those units which would not yield.

The troop movements of Coalition forces across the Iraqi front to a point opposite the border with Iraq went undetected by the Iraqi forces, as did the massing of units on the Kuwait border. Moreover, both attacks jumped off with the advantage of an essential military principle: clear military objectives.

The 5th Special Forces moved into Iraq prior to the ground assault, and during the hours of darkness of 24 February, on the western flank of the envelopment, the French Daguet Division (6th Light Armored Division) and the 2nd Brigade of the U.S. 82nd Airborne Division moved out to screen the attack. The U.S. 101st Air Assault Division moved in ahead of the VII Corps to establish a logistical base deep inside Iraq. This base would be used later by the 101st Division to conduct operations to seize important terrain on the Euphrates River and to block Highway 8 to prevent movement of Iraqi forces from Baghdad to reinforce its units in Kuwait.

At the same time, the 1st and 2nd Marine divisions, the "Tiger Brigade" of the 2nd Armored Division, and the Saudi Arabian National Guard initiated their attack north into Kuwait. To their west, in the center of the Coalition lines, the 1st Cavalry Division conducted a feint to conceal from the Iraqis the location of the main attack, which was to be conducted by VII Corps.

The assaults of the XVIII Corps units were so successful in getting behind the Iraqi lines that the main attack by VII Corps was moved forward fourteen hours. The 24th Division and the 3rd Armored Cavalry Regiment attacked deep into Iraq screened by the Daguet Division and the 101st. The 1st Infantry Division launched its attack through the vaunted Iraqi defensive line and in eight hours during the night of 24–25 February established twenty-four lanes through these gaps and secured the Corps's right flank. To the west of the 1st Infantry Division, the 2nd Armored Cavalry Regiment led the attack of the 1st and 3rd Armored divisions around the western end of the Iraqis' fixed defenses. In between the 1st Cavalry Division and the Marine divisions, the troops from Syria and Egypt pressed another secondary attack alongside the Royal Saudi Land Forces to hold in place the Iraqi forces to their front to ensure that they could not thwart the attacks on the east and west. All the while, Coalition aircraft flew cover and attacked any Iraqi units that tried to resist.

Farther to the southeast, the penetration was an assault by the 1st and 2nd Marine divisions supported by Army brigades and the Saudi armored division, with the axis of attack pointed toward Kuwait City and the main road junction west of the city which controlled the escape route of all the Iraqi troops between Kuwait City and the Saudi Arabia–Kuwait border. The points of attack had been pounded by air and artillery bombardments to destroy the fixed positions through which the Marines and Saudis had to pass. Although many of the mines laid in front of the Iraqi lines had been destroyed by this attack and many of the defensive works had been eliminated as well, combat engineers still had to perform the perilous tasks of clearing lanes through the remaining mines while tanks equipped with plows shoved aside others. Armored bulldozers too cleared a gap in the earthworks to allow Coalition tanks and armored personnel carriers to roll into the enemy's rear. Shortly after the penetration had begun, the Egyptian and Syrian forces just to the west started a secondary or supporting attack to ensure that Iraqi forces were pinned in place and unable to move to attempt to thwart the Marine, Army, and Saudi assault. Meanwhile, the other Marine units threatened an amphibious landing along the coast, thereby forcing the Iraqi units along the coast to remain in their positions and preventing them from serving as reinforcements.

Even as the Coalition forces moved out on the attack, the Soviet Union kept up its criticism with the comments that another twenty-four to forty-eight hours' delay could have resolved the issues surrounding an Iraqi withdrawal. The Bush administration reiterated the Coalition objectives of driving Iraq from Kuwait, declaring that while the overthrow of Saddam Hussein would be desirable, it was not a Coalition objective. The Israeli government praised the start of the ground action and simultaneously, as a security provision, reimposed the curfew on the occupied territories.

The success by sunset on 26 February of the Coalition's ground assaults was phenomenal. The penetration by the U.S. Marines and Army and the Saudis reached the outskirts of Kuwait City, and the Marines and the Army's 1st "Tiger" Brigade of the 2nd Armored Division engaged the Iraqis in a sharp tank battle near the Kuwait airport. The penetration rolled on between seventy-five and ninety miles into Iraq. XVII Corps had effectively cut off the Iraqi forces in Kuwait and southeastern Iraq from resupply and reinforcement. The Daguet Division had established an effective screen along the west flank. The 101st Division and elements of the 24th Division had cut Highway 8, and the remainder of the 24th Division had reached the Euphrates River. Now the 24th Division and the 3rd Armored Cavalry Regiment turned east to attack the Republican Guard. VII Corps had penetrated far enough into southeastern Iraq to fix in place the Republican Guard units there to prevent their movement. In all of this, the Coalition lost 9 killed in action and 41 wounded in action, while 4 aircraft were downed. The enemy's losses, on the other hand, were severe. By now more than 25,000 Iraqi POWs had been taken, and 270 tanks put out of action.

Diplomacy had not taken a break during these first hours of ground combat. UN Secretary General Perez de Cuellar gave his opinion that the fighting within Iraq did not exceed the UN mandate of all necessary force since the entry into Iraq had become necessary to free Kuwait. During the afternoon (New York time), the Soviet Union presented a plan for an Iraqi withdrawal, and later, at about 1730 hours (5:30 P.M.), the Iraqi government announced that in accordance with this Soviet move, Iraqi forces had been ordered to begin withdrawing. At 2000 hours (8:00 P.M.), the White House responded that only a public statement by Saddam Hussein himself, in which he announced an unconditional withdrawal and the acceptance of all the pertinent UN Security Council resolutions, would bring a cease-fire. Since Iraqi actions in the past had been less than trustworthy, President Bush said, he would require more than a radio announcement purporting to come from the Iraqi government before he would jeopardize the lives of Coalition men and women by holding fire. Later that evening, the UN

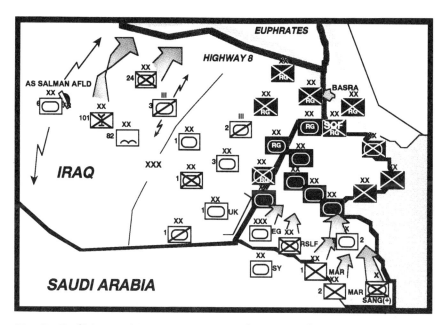

MAP 3. Coalition positions at sunset, 26 February. For legend to map, see Map 2. Source: *Army Focus* (June 1991): 24.

Security Council met to consider the events of the previous hours but adjourned without taking any actions.

That night the joy over the successes of the Coalition forces with such light casualties was crushed by the news that an Iraqi SCUD missile had hit a U.S. barracks in Dhahran, killing 28 and wounding 100 men and women. A Patriot missile had been fired to intercept this incoming SCUD, and it was not yet clear if the intercept had totally failed or had only partially destroyed the SCUD before it hit. This was to be the greatest number of U.S. casualties from any single action in Desert Storm.

At 0320 hours (New York time), Saddam Hussein announced that the withdrawal of Iraqi forces from Kuwait would begin that day, but he made no statement about the other UN Security Council resolutions. The Soviet government said that a cease-fire should begin at once but also that Iraq must accept all of the UN Security Council resolutions that applied to the crisis. The Iraqi ambassador to the United Nations, however, told the Security Council that Iraq would at this time agree only to a withdrawal. President Bush then at 0945 hours called Saddam Hussein's statement outrageous and said that the war would go on. He called simultaneously for the Iraqi troops to surrender.

The 24th Division and the 3rd Armored Cavalry Regiment continued their attack toward Basra and the coast. To their south, the 1st Cavalry Division pressed forward to prevent an attempt by Iraqi forces to flee north. Just to the south, the 1st and 3rd Armored divisions attacked side by side to destroy the Republican Guard divisions now pinned in an ever-shrinking perimeter. The 1st Infantry Division passed through the 2nd Armored Cavalry Regiment in an attack to the east.

These attacks continued throughout 27 February as fighting continued in the vicinity of Kuwait City. The total of U.S. casualties stood at 4 killed in action and 21 wounded, excluding those who had been casualties in the SCUD attack at Dhahran.

The Iraqi casualties were massive. Throughout the Kuwait Theater of Operations, the Iraqi ground forces were in a rout as those who would not surrender were being wiped out. Twenty-one Iraqi divisions were reported to be unable to fight effectively, as 2,085 tanks and 1,005 artillery pieces had been taken out. The destruction of Iraq's will to fight was indicated

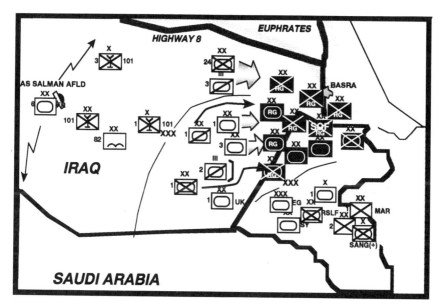

MAP 4. Coalition night attack, 26–27 February. For legend to map, see Map 2. Source: *Army Focus* (June 1991): 25.

by the Iraqi POW count, which soared above 30,000. In revenge for their ongoing defeat, Iraq set ablaze more than six hundred oil wells and destroyed Kuwaiti refineries. There were also numerous reports that as the Iraqi forces retreated, they took with them thousands of Kuwaiti hostages.

At 1030 hours (New York time), Foreign Minister Azziz said in a letter to the United Nations that Iraq would accept those Security Council resolutions which pertained to Kuwaiti sovereignty (662) and the liability for damages under international law (674) after a cease-fire and the end of mandated embargoes. In the middle of the afternoon, the Security Council rejected this letter with its conditions and restated the demand that Iraq accept all twelve resolutions.

The allies entered Kuwait City amid jubilant crowds, and General Schwarzkopf briefed the media and the world on Desert Storm. More than 110,000 sorties had been flown by Coalition aircraft, and on the ground, he estimated, 29 Iraqi divisions had been effectively destroyed, along with 3,700 tanks. There were so many Iraqi POWs that it was impossible to maintain an accurate count. As of the time of his briefing, U.S. ground casualties totaled 29 killed in action (79 dead in all), 213 wounded in action, and 44 missing in action. One last action was reported in Desert Storm, in which VII Corps and the 24th Division mauled a Republican Guard tank unit.

At 2100 hours (9:00 P.M.) President Bush announced that Kuwait was now free, after the complete defeat of Iraq. The president's terms to Saddam Hussein included the release of all POWs and Kuwaiti hostages, the revelation of all Iraqi mine fields, and compliance with all the UN Security Council resolutions on Iraq. He said that military commanders on both sides should meet to make the necessary arrangements for an orderly end to the war.

At 2300 hours (11:00 P.M.), Iraq informed the United Nations that it had accepted the Security Council resolutions.

28 Feb 91   At 0800 hours Gulf time, the Desert Storm was over, as the Coalition forces suspended combat operations. The Iraqi government started the process of meetings between the commanders to arrange a permanent cease-fire. There were by now an estimated 80,000 Iraqi POWs, and the number of Iraqi dead was unknown. The estimates of those killed ranged from a conservative 25,000–50,000 to a perhaps exaggerated 85,000–

100,000. As the counting went on, the estimates of tanks destroyed in combat reached 4,000. Forty-two Iraqi divisions had been rendered combat ineffective, captured, or simply destroyed; and only about 15,000–20,000 troops remained in anything like a combat unit. In order to ensure that Iraq could not reconstitute an effective military threat against its neighbors in the region, Coalition troops began to destroy all remaining captured and abandoned military equipment.

If the success of the combat operations seemed incredible, the logistics effort required to sustain this combat was equally astounding. More than 5.7 million metric tons of cargo, including more than 100,000 vehicles, were moved to the Kuwait Theater of Operations on more than 500 ships. In more than 14,000 flights, 473,000 men and women and 489,000 tons of supplies were moved by air. More than 17,000 rockets were fired from the Multiple Launch Rocket System (MLRS), and artillery pieces fired more than 44,000 rounds. Some 94 million meals were prepared, and 1 billion gallons of fuel were pumped as the vehicles of Desert Shield and Desert Storm drove over 35 million miles. And all of this was accomplished at the end of a supply line that stretched 8,700 miles from the United States to the Gulf.

5 The End and the Aftermath

The week following the official cessation of hostilities proved the truth of the old adage that it is easier to declare a cease-fire than to stop the fighting. Because of the chaos inside Iraq, the meeting of the military commanders was postponed a day. An Iraqi busload of soldiers fired on U.S. forces, and in the return fire, the bus was destroyed. Troops from the 82nd Airborne Division took 1,000 POWs when a captured battalion commander ordered his troops to surrender. Two U.S. soldiers were killed by an unmarked Iraqi mine, bringing the total U.S. killed to 89, with total Coalition killed at 148.

As the United States reopened its embassy in Kuwait on 1 March, a still arrogant Iraqi Foreign Minister Azziz demanded that U.S. forces withdraw from Iraqi territory.

On 2 March, a retreating Iraqi armored unit, apparently unaware that the war was over, attacked U.S. troops and in the process lost 500 armored vehicles either destroyed or captured. The United States suffered no casualties in this engagement, but there were 2 more U.S. personnel killed by mines. The International Red Cross, after discussions with the Iraqi government, said that Iraq was prepared to return Coalition POWs in exchange for Iraqi POWs.

Just two days after the ending of hostilities, the United States said that its troops would start returning to the United States within days, and at 2200 hours (10:00 P.M.) in New York, the UN Security Council adopted Resolution 686 by a vote of 11-1 with three abstentions. Cuba was the sole dissenting vote, while China, India, and Yemen abstained. This resolution demanded that Iraq stop all hostile actions, return all POWs and hostages, rescind its annexation of Kuwait, accept liability for war damages, return all seized Kuwaiti property, and disclose the location of all mine fields.

The next day, 3 March, General Schwarzkopf met with his Iraqi counterpart to lay out the precise military terms of the cease-fire. He told the Iraqis where Coalition troops would be located within Iraq, and the Iraqis agreed to start returning Coalition POWs and provide the location of mine fields.

As agreed, on 4 March the Iraqis began the release of allied POWs, with the release of 10 in exchange for 300 Iraqi POWs. The next day, 35 more POWs, of whom 15 were American, were released. Iraq said that these were the last they had under their control, and the Coalition accepted this as fact since the circumstances under which the remaining unaccounted-for missing in action were lost indicated that they were probably killed in action. For reasons that are not entirely clear, 2 more U.S. POWs actually were in Iraqi custody and were released to the Red Cross on 8 March.

On 6 March President Bush spoke to the Congress to declare that the war was over and announce that the troops would begin coming home. The first planeloads began to arrive in the United States on 8 March.

The crisis in the Gulf had begun on 2 August 1990, and the hostilities ended on 6 March 1991. The aftermath in the region confirmed the truism that it is far easier to win the war than to win the peace. Saddam Hussein's aggression was but another chapter in the book of war that has been written since history began in the Middle East. To believe that peace could come to the region with the military defeat of Saddam Hussein is to misread the history of the Middle East.

On the other hand, there was a military defeat of the fourth largest army on earth by a coalition of nations determined that aggression would not go unpunished. On 3 August 1990, immediately after Iraq invaded Kuwait, President Bush had announced four national goals: (1) the unconditional withdrawal of Iraq from Kuwait, (2) the restoration of the legitimate government of Kuwait, (3) the safety of U.S. citizens in the region, and (4) the stability and security of nations in the region. On 3 March 1991, Iraq had accepted UN Security Council Resolution 686, the resolution which dictated to Iraq the terms of its defeat. In effect, the military victory of the Coalition forces, made up largely of U.S. components, achieved three of these four objectives completely and achieved the fourth in part. With its armed forces so thoroughly defeated, Iraq itself no longer posed an immediate military threat to its neighbors in the Middle East. Thus for a time at least, military force had eliminated one threat to the security of the Middle Eastern nations. The stability of the region, however, must wait for diplomatic forces to solve such seemingly intractable problems as the dispute between Israel and the Arab nations surrounding it.

That the Coalition won an astounding military victory with incredibly few casualties is without question. Of Iraq's 545,000 troops in the Kuwait Theater of Operations, between 25,000 and 100,000 are believed to have lost their lives. Of Iraq's 44 army divisions, 42 were rendered combat ineffective. By the end of the hostilities, estimated losses of Iraqi equipment were as follows: 4,000 out of 4,230 tanks; 2,140 out of 3,110 artillery pieces; 1,856 out of 2,870 armored personnel carriers; 7 out of 160 helicopters; and 240 out of approximately 800 aircraft. In contrast, the Coalition lost 4 of 3,360 tanks, 1 of 3,633 artillery pieces, 9 of 4,050 armored personnel carriers, 17 of 1,959 helicopters, and 44 of 2,600 aircraft. Coalition combat casualties of all types numbered less than 500 of a total of approximately 737,000.

For military strategists and tacticians, war planners and politicians, the smashing success of the Coalition will have demonstrated many things. First is that coalitions can succeed, whatever Napoleon believed in praying that if he must fight let it be against a coalition. One key to this coalition's success was the establishment early on of a single commander, in this case Gen. Norman Schwarzkopf, who had the authority to command and control all elements of the force — air, ground, and sea forces — from every nation in the organization. Without such authority, coordination is reduced to cooperation, and national and service rivalries override the common cause.

Second is the certain knowledge that air superiority is absolutely essential. The complete domination of the skies over Iraq and Kuwait by the Coalition air forces eliminated a powerful Iraqi air force equipped with top-of-the-line combat aircraft, reduced a coordinated air-defense system to ineffectiveness, took away the ability to detect the movement of Coalition ground forces thereby enabling the Coalition to achieve tactical surprise, isolated the battlefield so that resupply and reinforcement were impossible, and ultimately destroyed the Iraqi ability and will to fight and to use its sophisticated equipment and massive number of troops.

Third is the knowledge that funds spent on research and development in peacetime pay off in combat. The advancements in munitions and equipment in the last two decades allowed the Coalition to fight a 21st-century war against a 20th-century force. Whether it was laser-guided artillery shells or bombs, radar- or television-directed munitions, heat-seeking missiles or night vision devices, the Coalition forces were able to destroy with pinpoint accuracy hardened bunkers or moving tanks both on the battlefield and in heavily populated areas with minimum civilian loss of life.

Finally, leadership and training are critical. On the fluid battle field of the desert, unit commanders reacted spontaneously to changing situations. Individual soldiers used every capability of their equipment in the most arduous circumstances. Units such as the 24th Mechanized Infantry Division moved their personnel, equipment, and hundreds of tons of supplies across hundreds of miles to reach the jump-off point in time to execute the mission. There was no time to train these men and women to fight over terrain heretofore unknown to most of them, but their peacetime training stood them in good stead.

Despite the seeming ease with which the Coalition defeated Iraq, Iraq was no paper tiger. From the very beginning, Saddam Hussein seemed to have made a series of miscalculations. Although no one has claimed to read his mind, his actions and public statements speak loudly about these assumptions. First, he erred in believing that Saudi Arabia would stand idly by when the annexation of Kuwait endangered its own national security. Next, he made the mistake of believing that the other Arab nations in the region would see the condemnation of his actions by the United States and other Western nations as the reactions of the old colonial powers with whom they would never join forces. Furthermore, he overestimated the Muslim religious bonds by thinking that Muslims and Christians could not be united into a coalition against another predominantly Muslim state. Similarly, he miscalculated when he thought that he could goad Israel into a retaliatory strike by firing SCUDs into Israel, attacks which he believed would rupture the Coalition along Arab-Western lines. He made the serious error of believing that the United Nations would never authorize the use of force against him. Finally, he believed that the sheer size of his armed forces could withstand the Coalition's multinational forces. All in all, he failed to recognize that he would not be seen by the nations of the Middle East as the Pan-Arab leader, the one man who could lead the Arab world to its long-awaited place in the sun.

In contrast, the leadership displayed by President Bush on the national and international level was highly successful. American public opinion polls heavily supported him throughout the period, and crucial votes came from the Congress at key moments. The president's administration put together—and kept together—a coalition of diverse nations to act in a common cause that overrode the historic tensions between Christians, Muslims, and Jews and that overcame the heritage of animosity between Arabs and the former colonial powers.

On the larger scale, one fact stands out above all others. Unlike the United Nations' ancestor, the League of Nations—and for the first time in its own history—the United Nations took action when faced with aggression. It condemned the aggression as soon as it occurred; it warned of punishment if this aggression did not stop; it authorized the use of force to bring it to an end; and it dictated the peace terms at the end of war. Had the League of Nations behaved in this fashion, the blood bath of the Second World War might have been averted, and perhaps in the future, the United Nations will again rise up when called upon to act.

Appendix A
Components of the U.S. Forces

Maintaining the armed forces of the United States to provide for its security is a function of the perceived threat and the nation's financial resources that can be devoted to its defense. The elements of the threat are its source, size, capabilities, and the location of hostilities. The United States, under what is termed the Total Force Policy, maintains two components of its armed forces: the Active Component and the Reserve Component. The Active Component consists of the land, sea, and air units and vessels on active duty around the world. The Reserve Component comprises the reserve units and individuals and the national guard. The division between the Active Component and the Reserve is determined by what is deemed essential to have ready at once to meet the threat and that which can be called to active duty only when required to supplement the Active forces. In general, the Active Component is smaller than the Reserve because maintaining active elements is far more expensive than maintaining the Reserve.

After World War II, the major threat to the security of the United States was seen to be a surprise attack on NATO by the Soviet Union and its Warsaw Pact allies in Europe. The other significant threat was believed to be in the Pacific area. Given that view, the Active Component was constructed around the types of forces needed to counter these threats. Other forces that would be necessary to supplement the Active Component were maintained in the Reserve Component. Typical of these were the support units needed to sustain a larger force for extended periods of time and specialists whose skills would be essential in war but who were too costly to be kept on active duty at other times.

When Desert Shield began, it was clear that the Active Component needed to be rounded out with numerous elements and individuals from the Reserves and from National Guard units to meet the peculiar needs of combat in a desert environment and to support the combat forces that would be assembled there to counter the huge Iraqi war capability. Hence, thousands of individual reservists, several complete reserve units, and some guard units were called to active duty. Some served outside the Kuwait Theater of Operations to replace active-duty personnel and units sent to the Gulf and some were sent into the Kuwait Theater.

The Reserve Component performed with exemplary skill and commitment. With few exceptions, those Reserve units and individuals called to serve required only minimum preparation and training to ready them for active duty. It is no exaggeration to say that without the Reserve Component, Desert Storm could not have achieved its successes with such rapidity and with so few casualties.

Appendix B
Coalition Nations

The armed force of the Coalition that defeated Iraq totaled 737,000 men and women in ground units, aboard 190 vessels, and flying or maintaining 1,800 aircraft. While the United States provided the bulk of the Coalition forces—with 532,000 troops, 120 ships, and more than 1,700 aircraft—thirty-four other nations provided personnel and equipment in action or in support of Desert Storm. The roll of countries that supported the efforts of the United Nations is listed below:

Afghanistan	Morocco
Argentina	The Netherlands
Australia	Niger
Bahrain	Norway
Bangladesh	New Zealand
Belgium	Oman
Canada	Pakistan
Czechoslovakia	Poland
Denmark	Portugal
Egypt	Qatar
France	Saudi Arabia
Germany	Senegal
Greece	Spain
Hungary	Syria
Honduras	Turkey
Italy	The United Arab Emirates
Kuwait	The United Kingdom

At War in the Gulf was composed into type on a Compugraphic digital phototypesetter in nine and one-half point Trump Medieval with two and one-half points of spacing between the lines. Trump Outline was selected for display. The book was designed by Jim Billingsley, typeset by Metricomp, Inc., printed offset and bound by Hart Graphics, Inc. The paper on which the book is printed bears acid-free characteristics for an effective life of at least three hundred years.

TEXAS A&M UNIVERSITY PRESS : COLLEGE STATION